MONOGRAPHS OF THE HEBREW UNION COLLEGE • NO. I

AN ANALYSIS OF
VATICAN 30

AN ANALYSIS OF
VATICAN 30

by

Lewis M. Barth

HEBREW UNION COLLEGE-JEWISH INSTITUTE OF RELIGION
CINCINNATI, NEW YORK, LOS ANGELES, JERUSALEM
1973

SBN 0-87820-400-8

LIBRARY OF CONGRESS CATALOG CARD NUMBER: 72-8353
MANUFACTURED IN THE UNITED STATES OF AMERICA

Published on the
GEORGE ZEPIN
Memorial Publication Fund

CONTENTS

INTRODUCTION

With *An Analysis of Vatican 30,* the Hebrew Union College-Jewish Institute of Religion inaugurates a new monograph series. On occasion, the students and faculty of the College-Institute will produce works of scientific caliber richly deserving publication, but unlikely to be commercially profitable. The purpose, therefore, of the "Monographs of the Hebrew Union College" is to offer scholars the opportunity to present their findings to the academic world, albeit the circle of readers for each specific publication may be limited.

The Nazi Holocaust took the lives of many scholars and completely disrupted the work of the "Science of Judaism" which had been at home in Germany ever since the early nineteenth-century career of Leopold Zunz. It is imperative that "pure science," detailed critical studies in the field of Jewish history, literature, rabbinics, and the classics, be encouraged everywhere through adequate publication. American Jewry, now the largest in the world, is certainly conscious of this imperative and has already begun to address itself to this task. This country contains scholars, excellent libraries, and—we hope—imaginative philanthropists willing to further this cause so that future generations may be enabled to build on the historic-critical investigations of our own day.

To this purpose, the new series is dedicated. It is the profound and pious hope of the Faculty Publications Committee that the series will meet with a favorable reception in the world of scholarship.

Jacob R. Marcus, Chairman

ACKNOWLEDGEMENTS

The help and encouragement of the Hebrew Union College Faculty have made this study possible. I am grateful to the Committee on Graduate Study for granting me fellowships to study at the University of Chicago, the Hebrew University in Jerusalem, and the Hebrew Union College in Cincinnati. I wish to express appreciation for the National Defense Education Act Fellowships which enabled me to continue my studies at H.U.C. In addition, I am grateful to the late President Nelson Glueck, President Alfred Gottschalk, and Dean Kenneth Roseman for the opportunity to teach at the College while completing this thesis.

I would like to extend my thanks to those who were helpful in the thesis preparation. Mr. Herbert Zafren and his staff aided in every way and made available for me the great resources of the College Library. Many faculty members have offered their knowledge and advice, and I have learned from them all. Particularly, I want to thank my advisors, Drs. Eugene Mihaly, Ben Zion Wacholder, Ellis Rivkin, and Isaac Jerusalmi. I am especially grateful to Dr. Mihaly who first opened the field of Midrash for me when I was a rabbinic student. He has given generously of his time and of his penetrating insight into the literature of the rabbis. His guidance and friendship have seen me through the graduate program at the College and the long and sometimes frustrating preparation of this thesis. Dr. Wacholder has served as co-referee; his sound judgement has guided me ever since I was his student at the California school. Dr. Mihaly and Dr. Wacholder have read the manuscript and made many valuable criticisms and suggestions. I wish to thank the typists for the great care they took in preparing the manuscript: Mrs. Alisa Charash and Mrs. Karen Harb. This thesis could not have been completed without the constant help of my wife Nancy who has encouraged me from the beginning. "What is mine and thine is hers."

Lewis M. Barth

ABBREVIATIONS AND SYMBOLS

The first citation of books and articles in the footnotes will contain the complete bibliographical reference. Thereafter, only an abbreviated reference, indicated below, will be used. Standard abbreviations for well known journals and periodicals are employed throughout.

Albeck, Introduction	Chanoch Albeck, Einleitung und Register zum Bereschit Rabba. Berlin, 1931-1936. Included in Midrash Bereshit Rabba, ed. J. Theodor and Ch. Albeck. Vol.III. Second printing. Jerusalem, 1965.
Albeck, Registers	See Albeck, Introduction.
Aruch	Aruch Completum, ed. Alexander Kohut. 8 vols. Vienna, 1878.
Assemani	Stephanus Evodius Assemanus and Joseph Simonius Assemanus, Bibliothecae Apostolicae Vaticanae, Partis Primae, Tomus Primus, Codices Ebraicos et Samaritanos. Rome, 1756; reprinted Paris, 1926.
Cassuto	Humbertus Cassuto, Bibliothecae Apostolicae Vaticanae (Codices Vaticani Hebraici). Vatican. 1956.

XIII

Epstein, _Mavo_	J. N. Epstein, _Mavo L'Nusah Ha-mishna_. Jerusalem, 1965.
Ginzberg, _A Commentary_	Louis Ginzberg, _A Commentary on the Palestinian Talmud_. 4 vols. New York, 1941-1961.
Goitein	S. D. Goitein, _A Mediterranean Society_. Berkeley and Los Angeles, 1967.
_G. V._	Leopold Zunz, _Die gottesdienstlichen Vorträge der Juden_. Berlin, 1832. Translated into Hebrew by Chanoch Albeck, _Hadrashot B'yisrael_. Jerusalem, 1947
Hadrashot	See _G. V._
_H U C A_	_Hebrew Union College Annual_
Jastrow	Marcus Jastrow, _A Dictionary_. Reprinted New York, 1950.
_J Q R_	_Jewish Quarterly Review_
Kutscher,"Lešon Hazal"	Ezekiel Kutscher, "Lešon Hazal," _Henoch Yalon Jubilee Volume_, ed. Saul Lieberman. Jerusalem, 1963.
Kutscher, "Studies"	Ezekiel Kutscher, "Studies in Galilean Aramaic," _Tarbiz_ XXI-XXIII (1949-1952). Cited by consecutive pagination in the offprint, Jerusalem, 1952.

Levy	Jacob Levy, _Neuhebraisches und Chaldaisches Worterbuch_. 4 vols. Leipzig, 1889.
Lieberman, _Tosephta_	_The Tosephta_, ed. Saul Lieberman. 3 vols. New York, 1955-1967.
Lutski	_Sifre or Torat Kohanim_, ed. Louis Finkelstein. With an introduction by Finkelstein and Moses Lutski. New York, 1956.
Maas	Paul Maas, _Textual Criticism_. Oxford, 1958.
Margulies, "Fragments"	_Midrash Wayyikra Rabba_, ed. Mordecai Margulies. Part V. Jerusalem, 1960. Fragments of Leviticus Rabba from the Cairo Geniza, pp. 1-86.
Margulies, _Introduction_	_Midrash Wayyikra Rabba_, ed. Mordecai Margulies. Part V. Jerusalem, 1960. Pp. IX-XL.
MGWJ	_Monatsschrift für Geschichte und Wissenschaft des Judentums_.
Palestinian Syriac Texts	_Palestinian Syriac Texts_, ed. Agnes Smith Lewis and Margret Dunlop Gibson. London, 1900.
REJ	_Revue des Etudes Juives_.

Rosenthal   A.S.Rosenthal,"Lešonot Soferim,"_Yuval Shay_,A Jubilee Vol-
ume dedicated to S.Y.Agnon,ed.
B.Kurzweil. Ramat Gan, 1959.

Rosenthal, An Aramaic Handbook   An Aramaic Handbook, ed. Franz
Rosenthal. 2 vols. Wiesbaden,
1967.

Rosenthal, Muslim Scholarship   Franz Rosenthal, The Techniques and Approaches of Muslim
Scholarship. Rome, 1947.

Sifre or Torat Kohanim   Sifre or Torat Kohanim, ed.
Louis Finkelstein. New York,
1956.

Payne Smith   J. Payne Smith, A Compendious
Syriac Dictionary.Oxford,1903.

Sokoloff   Michael Sokoloff,"The Hebrew
of Bereshit Rabba According
to Ms.Vat.Ebr.30," Lešonenu,
XXXIII,No.1 (October,1968)
25-42; Nos.2-3 (January-April,
1969) 135-149.Cited by consecutive pagination.

T.A.   Midrasch Bereschit Rabba, ed.
Judah Theodor and Chanoch
Albeck. Berlin, 1903-1929.
Second printing: Midrash
Bereshit Rabba. 3 vols.,with
Introduction and Registers by
Ch. Albeck. Jerusalem, 1965.
All citations refer to the
second printing.

Theodor, "Drei unbekannte Paraschas"	Judah Theodor, "Drei unbek- annte Paraschas aus Bereschit Rabba," _Festschrift zum siebzigsten Geburtstage Jakob Guttmanns_. Leipzig, 1915.
_Y.F._	_Yerushalmi Fragments_, ed. Louis Ginzberg. New York, 1909.

Regarding citations from Vat. 30, each folio of Vat. 30 is numbered in the upper left hand corner of the _recto_ side, that is, the side to be read first. The _verso_ side is never numbered. When referring to the _recto_ side, an abbreviation of folio (f.) will precede the number appearing on the page of the manuscript. For the _verso_, this abbreviation (f.) and the number of the page will be followed by a lower case "v." Examples: this word will be found on f. 3 and f. 4v. Wherever possible, line numbers are included with the reference to Vat. 30 and also to _T.A._

CHAPTER I

A REVIEW OF THE SECONDARY LITERATURE ON VAT. 30

The first recorded mention of Vat. 30 is found in
the catalogue of Hebrew and Samaritan manuscripts in the
Vatican Library, compiled by the Assemani Brothers and
published in Rome in 1756. The manuscript is labeled

מדרש על ספר בראשית MEDRASC AL SEPHER BERESCITH,
Expositio allegorica in Librum Genesis," and dated in
the thirteenth century.[1] Apparently the Assemani Brothers
did not know that this codex contained the midrash Bereshit
Rabba; had they known, we may assume that they would have
identified it properly, as they did in the case of another
codex of this midrash, Vat. 60.[2] This error is probably
responsible for the relative neglect of Vat. 30 until the
close of the last century. It is certainly the source of
Leopold Zunz's incorrect reference to Vat. 30 in his pioneer
study of the Jewish sermon, Die gottesdienstlichen Vorträge
der Juden. Zunz includes a " מדרש על בראשית

---

[1]Stephanus Evodius Assemanus and Joseph Simonius
Assemanus, Bibliothecae Apostolicae Vaticanae (Rome, MDCCLVI,
reprinted Paris, 1926), Partis Primae, Tomus Primus, Codices
Ebraicos et Samaritanos, p. 23.

[2]Vat. 60 is identified as " בראשית רבה BERESCITH
RABBA Glossa Magna" (Assemani, p. 46).

1

(Cod. Vatic. 30)" in a list of anonymous midrashic works from the thirteenth through fifteenth centuries.[3] He must have relied on the Assemani description without actually seeing the original.[4]

Vat. 30 was correctly identified in the last decade of the nineteenth century by Dr. Abraham (Adolf) Berliner. Berliner, a scholar who wrote extensively on Italian Jewry, personally examined collections of Hebrew manuscripts in Italian libraries. He recognized that codex Vat. 30 contained the text of Bereshit Rabba and thought that it also contained a dated copy of Torat Kohanim from A.D. 1073; he took this as the date of the Bereshit Rabba text as well. Berliner communicated his information to Judah Theodor, who was then preparing the ground work of a scientific edition of Bereshit Rabba. In 1893, Theodor acknowledged Berliner's contribution in an article describing all the manuscript material to be used in the projected edition.[5] He also accepted Berliner's dating. Much later Theodor

---

[3] Leopold Zunz, Die gottesdienstlichen Vorträge der Juden (Berlin, 1832), p. 306, note A; Hebrew translation by Ch. Albeck, Hadrashot B'yisrael (Jerusalem, 1947), p. 448, note 2.

[4] The fact that Zunz presented a detailed reconstruction of the last chapters of Bereshit Rabba in G. V. also indicates that he never actually saw Vat. 30. Had he seen it he would have realized that it contains the "original" last chapters, as Theodor was to prove later. See note 12 below. For Zunz's reconstruction see G. V., p. 254ff. and notes; Hadrashot, pp. 123-124 and notes.

[5] J. Theodor, "Der Midrasch Bereschit Rabba," MGWJ, XXXVII (1893), 170, note 4.

discovered that the text of <u>Torat Kohanim</u> belonged to another codex, Vat. 31, and could shed no light on the date
of Vat. 30.[6]

The next stage in the development of scholarly
interest in Vat. 30 is directly related to the scientific
edition of Bereshit Rabba, begun by Theodor and completed
after his death by Chanoch Albeck.[7] Theodor chose for
the basis of his edition, the London manuscript, Add. 27169.
In the article previously mentioned, Theodor justified
the choice of the London manuscript from among the eight
or nine others available to him. He argued that the London
manuscript represented the earliest extant form of Bereshit

---

[6]J. Theodor, "Drei unbekannte Paraschas aus Bereschit
Rabba," <u>Festschrift zum siebzigsten Geburtstage Jakob
Guttmanns</u> (Leipzig, 1915), p. 148, note 1. On Vat. 31,
see Assemani, pp. 23-24; and Humbertus Cassuto,
<u>Bybliothecae Apostolicae Vaticanae</u> (Vatican, 1956),
Codices Vaticani Hebraici, pp. 38ff.

[7]<u>Midrasch Bereschit Rabba</u>, ed. J. Theodor and Ch.
Albeck (Berlin, 1903-1929); Ch. Albeck, <u>Einleitung und
Register zum Bereschit Rabba</u> (Berlin, 1931-1936). This
scientific edition was published in fascicles by Theodor,
and after his death in 1923, by Albeck. The fascicles
appeared in 1903, 1904, 1906, 1908, 1909, 1912, 1913, 1914,
1916, 1921, 1926, 1927, 1928 and 1929. Chapters 1-64 were
prepared by Theodor alone; Chapters 65-86 were primarily
the work of Theodor supplemented by some additional notes
by Albeck; Chapters 87 to the end are entirely Albeck's
work. Both the text of the midrash with apparatus and
commentary and Albeck's <u>Introduction</u> have been reprinted and
bound together in three volumes by Wahrmann Books (Jerusalem,
1965). I have used the Wahrmann "second printing" for this
paper. On the details of Albeck's contribution to the
latter part of the edition, see Albeck's comment <u>El HaKoré</u>,
appearing on an unnumbered page preceding <u>T.A.</u>, Vol. II,
p. 479.

Rabba, and that it was similar to the Palestinian Talmud in style, diction and spelling. In addition, the London manuscript agreed in over three hundred cases with readings from the _Aruch_, thereby testifying to the antiquity of the manuscript and its importance.[8]

In 1903, ten years after Theodor had published the background material on the London manuscript, the first fascicle of his edition of Bereshit Rabba appeared. It contained the text of Bereshit Rabba according to the London manuscript with variant readings from eight other manuscripts, medieval compendia, lexicons and unpublished commentaries.[9] In addition, Theodor prepared his own

---

[8]All the factors regarding the choice of the London manuscript are found in Theodor's article, "Der Midrasch Bereschit Rabba," _MGWJ_, XXXVII (1893), pp. 169-173, 206-213, 452-458; XXXVIII (1894), pp. 9-26, 436-440; XXXIX (1895), pp. 106-110, 241-247, 289-295, 337-343, 385-390, 433-441, 481-491. Specifically, he comments on the London manuscript: "Was die HS. noch bedeutsamer macht, ihr einen besondern Character verleiht und gewiss auch die wichtigsten Momente zur Beurtheilung ihres Alters wie der treuen Wiedergabe ihrer Quelle darbietet -- ist, dass in ihr der Midrasch, der ja anerkanntermassen eine palästinensische Agada und dem jer. Talmud so nah verwandt ist, auch in formaler Beziehung, durch Diction und Orthographie das Gepräge des j.T. erhält, viel mehr als die Ausgaben und andere HSS. es erkennen lassen" (_MGWJ_, XXXVII, 173). The fact that the London manuscript agrees with the _Aruch_ in so many instances suggests that the manuscript was written previous to the eleventh century. Evidence for dating the London manuscript before the year 1000 A.D. is found in the article just quoted, p. 172, note 6; in _T.A._, p. 780, end of note 1; and in Albeck, _Introduction_, p. 105.

[9]For a survey of the manuscript material, see Theodor, "Der Midrasch Bereschit Rabba," _MGWJ_, XXXVII (1893), 169 - 173, and Albeck, _Introduction_, pp. 104-138. For the other literature, see the previous note .

commentary, the _Minhat Yehudah_, in which he deals with textual problems and refers to the contemporary scientific
literature in the fields of semitics, patristics, archeology
and geography. The commentary also includes extensive
citations from parallels to the passages under discussion.[10]
Both text and commentary were greeted with acclaim when
they first appeared, and upon completion of the entire work
one reviewer wrote: "Die Ausgabe des Bereschit Rabba gilt
mit Recht als Ehrensache der Judischen Wissenschaft."[11]

In 1915, after the appearance of a number of fascicles,
Theodor published an article, "Drei unbekannte Paraschas
aus Bereschit Rabba," containing the text of Chapters 95-97
from Vat. 30.[12] Zunz and others had already argued that
the concluding chapters of Bereshit Rabba in the printed
editions contained material which was not original to this
midrash.[13] In Chapters 95-97 of Vat. 30, Theodor justi-
fiably claimed to have found the original Bereshit Rabba
text: "Die drei Paraschas in V [Vat. 30] zeigen in ihrer

---

[10] For a partial list of the extensive literature
Theodor utilized, see the Bibliographical Note.

[11] Bernhard Heller, "Theodor-Albecks Bereschit Rabba,"
MGWJ, LXXI (1927), 471. For a complete review of _T.A._, see
Heller's remarks on pp. 466-472 of the same article and in
his concluding review "Der Abschluss von Theodor-Albecks
Bereschit Rabba," _MGWJ_, LXXVIII (1934), 609-615. When the
first fascicle of the edition appeared in 1903, it was re-
viewed by Wilhelm Bacher, _Revue des Etudes Juives_, XLVI
(1903), 301-310.

[12] Theodor, "Drei unbekannte Paraschas," _Festschrift zum
siebzigsten Geburtstage Jacob Guttmans_ (Leipzig, 1915).

[13] See note 4 above and especially Albeck, _Introduction_, p. 103.

Anlage und Ausfuhrung das Gepräge des echten Bereschit Rabba."[14] These three chapters represent the exegetical style which is typical of Bereshit Rabba and contain verse by verse interpretations of Genesis 46,28-48,14. Consequently, Chapters 95-97 of Vat. 30 stand in sharp, formal contrast to much of the material found in the printed editions of these chapters, most of which has its source in the Tanchuma and represents the homiletical midrashic style.[15]

In addition to these literary and formal features, Theodor described some of the scribal characteristics of Vat. 30 more fully than he had done in his first article on the manuscript material of Bereshit Rabba. He stated that the manuscript was written in German square script, and that in language and orthography it was similar to the Palestinian Talmud and the London manuscript.[16] Eventually Theodor came to realize that Vat. 30 as a whole, and not merely its last few chapters, represented an original version of Bereshit Rabba. In a note to Chapter 75 dealing with late additions to the text, Theodor wrote: "The Vatican manuscript has a special excellence in that it neither added nor diminished nor changed; and this superior

---

[14]Theodor, "Drei unbekannte Paraschas," p. 150.

[15]Ibid., pp. 149-150.

[16]Ibid., p. 148, note 1; pp. 150-151, p. 155.

manuscript was certainly copied from a very old copy which
was the original version of Bereshit Rabba."[17]

Building on the foundations established by Theodor,
Chanoch Albeck utilized Vat. 30 as the cornerstone of his
research into the manuscript tradition of Bereshit Rabba.
Vat. 30 was the measure by which all the manuscript material
and printed editions of this midrash were to be judged.
"Bereshit Rabba, as it is in most of the manuscripts and
printed editions, contains different additions which were
added already at an early time and also later by the scribes
and the printers. But the preferred manuscript is the manuscript which is in the Vatican library in Rome (Vat. 30),
according to which we can clearly distinguish the additions
which are found in the rest of the manuscripts and in the
printed editions, and also what the scribes deleted from
the original Bereshit Rabba, because it [Vat. 30] contains
in the main the original Bereshit Rabba without additions
or deletions."[18] In his Introduction, Albeck lists the

---

[17]T.A., p. 885, end of note 3. This comment is found
in the commentary to Ch. 75, published after Theodor's
death by Albeck in 1927. I think it is fair to say that
Theodor did not initially appreciate the value of Vat. 30.
This may have been related to the fact that he possessed
a very poor handwritten copy of the first 53 chapters upon
which he based his judgement. He did receive photographs
of the manuscript from the middle of Ch. 53 to the end.
See Albeck, Introduction, p. 107.

[18]Albeck, Introduction, p. 103. Pp. 107-108 of the
Introduction contain Albeck's brief description of Vat. 30
and further remarks on the importance of its readings.

numerous additions, primarily from the Tanchuma, which have entered the received text of Bereshit Rabba.[19] In addition, he is able to show that a manuscript similar to Vat. 30 served as one of the sources for the first edition of the Midrash Rabba (Constantinople, 1512), in which Bereshit Rabba appears.[20] Albeck sums up the results of his research in a brief statement describing the primary position of Vat. 30 in the manuscript tradition of this midrash: "The copy of the Rome manuscript [Vat. 30] is the most superior copy and not very different at all from the original Bereshit Rabba."[21]

In recent years Vaṭ. 30 has again become the object of significant scholarly interest. Umberto Cassuto, while preparing a catalogue of Hebrew manuscripts in the Vatican

---

[19]Albeck, Introduction, pp. 103-104.

[20]Albeck, Introduction, pp. 117ff. contains a description of the first edition and a list of additions in this edition which are not found in any of the extant manuscripts On p. 128 Albeck sums up his evidence which indicates that "in front of the printers was a manuscript like Vat. 30 and another manuscript from the other manuscript types." Albeck (loc. cit.) also brings ample evidence to show that the Venice edition of 1545, with significant exceptions, was based on the Constantinople edition. It was from the Venice edition that all later printed texts of Bereshit Rabba are descended (p. 132). Consequently, the present printed editions must be viewed as descendents of a text partly based on a manuscript like Vat. 30. For a minimum list of printed editions of Midrash Rabba, see I. A. BenJacob, Ozar Ha Sepharim (Wilna, 1880), pp. 301-302, numbers 620-642, and M. Steinschneider, Catalogues Librorum Hebraeorum in Bibliotheca Bodleiana (Berlin, 1931), Section I, pp. 589-593, numbers 3753-3775.

[21]Albeck, Introduction, p. 137.

library, was the first to work directly with Vat. 30 and to describe it in detail. He noted, for example, the size and number of pages (folios), the extant and missing folios, the number of groups of bound pages (fascicles), and the names of the owners of the manuscript.[22] Cassuto's most significant contributions to the study of Vat. 30 are his hypothesis that more than one scribe worked on the text and his observation that a particular form of punctuation was used in certain sections. "Three copyists, as it appears, wrote the codex in oriental square character -- the first ff. 2-9v, 146-end; the second ff. 10-81; the third ff. 81v-145v. . . . The end of each paragraph (except in ff. 10-81) is indicated by the sign $\emptyset$." Cassuto also observes that "individual fascicles are provided with guards (custodibus) with ornaments being added as much as possible with a pen."[23]

Cassuto's observations were followed by extensive linguistic study of Vat. 30. Ezekiel Kutscher argued that Vat. 30 is a primary source of the Galilean dialect of Amamaic. He used this manuscript as a basis for his "Studies in Galilean Aramaic," and published selected passages from it in the recent collection, An Aramaic Handbook, edited

---

[22]Cassuto, pp. 36-38. These details will be presented in the section on the description of the manuscript.

[23]Ibid., p. 37. The significance of the number of scribes working on Vat. 30 and the ornamentation of the guards will be treated in the section on the Scribes of Vat. 30.

by Franz Rosenthal.[24] Kutscher became convinced of the
linguistic purity of Vat. 30, and lamented that Theodor
did not use it, rather than the London manuscript, as the
main text of the scientific edition of Bereshit Rabba.[25]
In comparing Vat. 30 with the citations taken from it in
Theodor's variant readings, Kutscher discovered significant
omissions and inaccuracies in the apparatus.[26] Consequently,
he points out that it is nearly impossible to achieve an
adequate appreciation of the linguistic details of Vat. 30
from the scientific edition. Working from a microfilm copy
of the manuscript, Kutscher proceeds to describe the phonetic

---

[24]Ezekiel Kutscher, "Studies in Galilean Aramaic,"
Tarbiz, XXI (1949-50), 192-205; XXII (1950-51), 53-63,
185-192; XXIII (1952), 36-60. This article will be cited
here according to the consecutive pagination found in the
offprint. An Aramaic Handbook, ed. Franz Rosenthal
(Wiesbaden, 1967); sections on Palestinian Aramaic prepared
by Kutscher, Vol. I/1, pp. 59-67.

[25]Kutscher, "Studies," 7. After quoting Albeck on
the value of readings from Vat. 30, he writes:
לפיכך יש להצטער, כי הוא לא הודפס בתורת פנים של ההוצאה
המדעית – אע"פ שלקה בחסר – ע"י ומתחיל במצוה זו, הוא
טהעאדאר...המנוח, כי אם "נגנז" בחילופי נוסחאות....

[26]Kutscher,"Studies," 8, note 4. Dr. Kutscher points
out a number of significant omissions and errors in the
citation of Vat. 30 in Theodor's variants which are taken
from Aramaic passages. In working through the manuscript
myself, I began to note all the errors found in the
variant readings for Vat. 30 with the thought of publishing
a list of corrections. However, the errors are so numerous that it would be simpler to produce a facsimile edition
of the entire manuscript. Chapter VI of this paper contains
the text of four chapters from Vat. 30 which may be compared
with Theodor's variants for a clearer picture of the
problems involved.

and grammatical features of the Galilean Aramaic dialect.
He compares the examples of this dialect from Vat. 30 with
parallel linguistic evidence from the Palestinian Talmud
and Targumim, and with Samaritan and Christian Syriac
texts.[27] The results of his research are summed up in the
statement that: "Vat. 30 is a faithful source for the
recognition of the Aramaic language of Palestine."[28]

A. S. Rosenthal accepts the judgements of Albeck and
Kutscher regarding the midrashic and linguistic significance
of Vat. 30.[29] His own contribution to the study of the
manuscript is an examination of the terms or formulas used
by the scribes to abbreviate midrashic passages and to refer
the reader to a more complete version of the text. These
terms had already been listed by Albeck in his Introduction,
with no detailed explanation of their significance.[30]
Following Kutscher's analysis, Rosenthal argues that the
Aramaic form of these terms and their varied style suggests
that Aramaic was the mother tongue of the scribes. The
terms thus represent contemporary Aramaic usage because the
scribes themselves abbreviated passages in the process of

---

[27]Kutscher, "Studies," pp.10ff.

[28]Ibid., p. 10.

[29]A. S. Rosenthal, "Lešonot Soferim," in Yuval Shay,
A Jubilee Volume dedicated to S. Y. Agnon, ed. B. Kurzweil
(Ramat Gan, 1959), p. 293.

[30]Albeck, Introduction, p. 108.

copying the manuscript.[31] This hypothesis would explain
why the terms used for abbreviation, whose purpose is to
refer the reader to a complete text of the passage, are
terse, difficult to comprehend, and communicate imperfectly.
Rosenthal examines the linguistic composition of these
scribal formulas and their referential functions; in
addition, he offers a series of examples which indicate the
importance of scribal terminology in unravelling the problems of textual transmissions.[32]

The latest scholarly investigation of this manuscript
is a linguistic study, "The Hebrew of Bereshit Rabba According to Vat. 30," by Michael Sokoloff.[33] Sokoloff has chal-
lenged Kutscher's view that Vat. 30 as a whole is a faithful
source for Galilean Aramaic.[34] Using Cassuto's hypothesis
that three scribes wrote the manuscript, Sokoloff shows
that a large section, written by the second scribe represents

---

[31]Rosenthal, p. 294.

[32]Ibid., pp. 307ff.

[33]Michael Sokoloff, "The Hebrew of Bereshit Rabba
According to Ms. Vat. Ebr. 30," Lešonenu, XXXIII, No. 1
(Oct. 1968), 25-42. Hereafter cited by the offprint
pagination. After completing my own analysis of Vat. 30,
I became aware of Mr. Sokoloff's article. Where possible
I have cited him in the notes to the following sections.
Mr. Sokoloff has in part confirmed the results of my own
research, and I am indebted to him. However, there
remain some significant areas in which I disagree with
his position regarding the composition of the manuscript.
These areas will become evident in the presentation of my
comments on Vat. 30.

[34]Ibid., pp. 12ff.

12

a text strongly influenced by the spelling of the Babylonian
Talmud, while the rest contains well attested Palestinian
linguistic features.[35] Sokoloff further argues that it is
unlikely that a scribe would completely revise the material
he is copying; consequently, Vat. 30 must represent two
different exemplars, one containing the Palestinian format,
the other the Babylonian.[36] In a promised continuation of
his article, Sokoloff will present a linguistic analysis
of the Hebrew of Vat. 30.

Some general conclusions emerge from the often detailed
discussions of Vat. 30 in the scholarly literature. This
manuscript contains a text of Bereshit Rabba closely related
to the earliest form of this midrash. A comparison of Vat.
30 with the other manuscripts and printed editions of
Bereshit Rabba supports this conclusion. Vat. 30 does not
contain late additions to the text which can be identified
by their homiletic rather than exegetical form and which have
their source primarily in the Tanchuma. Linguistic features
also reinforce the view that Vat. 30 represents an early
version of Bereshit Rabba. Some, if not all, of its Aramaic
passages are similar phonetically and orthographically to
the Palestinian Talmud and to other Palestinian texts.
Since the time of Theodor a consensus has emerged among

---

[35]Ibid., pp. 16ff.

[36]Ibid., p. 15.

scholars that the manuscript was written in oriental square script. There is no agreement regarding the provenance or precise date of Vat. 30.

CHAPTER II

DESCRIPTION OF THE MANUSCRIPT[1]

Vat. 30 is damaged at the beginning and the first pages (folios) have been lost. Consequently no identification of the title of the work remains in the text. The manuscript clearly contains the midrash generally known as Bereshit Rabba.[2] It is found in the Vatican collection of Hebrew manuscripts, and was formerly in the Palatine library. The upper margin of f.2 contains the price of the codex, זהובים 'ב, and the name of one owner, Samuel, the son of Eliezer; in the upper margin of f.3 it is possible to make out the name of another owner, Meshullam, של משלם...שי '[3]

The manuscript is parchment, about 215 x 147 mm., except for f.140 which probably is a repaired page and is about 212 x 147 mm.[4] In its present state the manuscript

---

[1]Many of the details in this section are taken from Cassuto's description of Vat. 30. Because he worked with the manuscript directly, he was able to see numerous details which do not appear clearly on my Xerox copy.

[2]For a history of the manuscript and the process by which it became properly identified, see my summary in Chapter I. On the name, Bereshit Rabba, see Albeck, Introduction, p. 93-94.

[3]These details are barely visible on my copy.

[4]Additional support for the view that this folio has been repaired is that it contains text material written in a hand that appears nowhere else in the manuscript and which seems to cover a text which has faded or been erased.

contains 192 folios numbered in Arabic numerals at the upper
left corner from 2 through 193. Because the manuscript
begins with f.2, it may be assumed that one folio preceding
f.2 was in existence when the manuscript was numbered, and
that it was later lost.[5] Each page is lined and the number
of lines varies from 22 to 26:

```
ff.   2 -   9v ...................... 25 lines
ff.  10 - 145v ...................... 26 lines
ff. 146 - 153v .................22 or 23 lines
ff. 154 - 193  ................24 or 25 lines
```

According to Cassuto there were originally twenty-
four separate groups of bound pages (fascicles) of which
the manuscript was composed. The first, fourth, fifth and
last six fascicles contain four folded sheets (quaternion),
the rest contain five folded sheets (quinternion).[6] Since
nearly ten chapters (end of Ch. 6 - beginning of Ch. 17)
are lacking between ff. 9v and 10, that is between the end
of the first and the beginning of the present second
fascicle, we may assume that two original fascicles containing this material have fallen out. Each fascicle concludes
with the first word of the next fascicle specially placed in
the lower margin of the verso side of the last folio (guard);
this practice served as an aid for collating the various

---

[5]Unlike the traditional Jewish system of pagination
in which the first folio is numbered א, the Vatican
manuscripts in general are numbered from 1 on, in Arabic
numerals. This can be readily seen by leafing through
Cassuto's Catalogue.

[6]Cassuto, p. 37.

fascicles. I have found twenty-one such guards.[7] Since
f. 193v contains the guard דרבי, it appears that another
fascicle was to follow it, and has been lost.[8] If there
were two fascicles between the present first two and another at the end of the manuscript, then Cassuto's count
of twenty-four is correct.

The fascicles are numbered in Latin letters in the
lower margin of the last page of each, in reverse order,
beginning with the last fascicle first.[9] The folios of
the seventh fascicle were first numbered upside down and
incorrectly, and then properly numbered. In the margins,
chapter numbers are found in Hebrew letters corresponding
to the present chapter division of the Book of Genesis;
they were added by a later hand which Cassuto has also
found in codexes 23 and 24.[10]

---

[7]The guards are found on ff. 9v, 19v, 29v, 37v, 45v,
55v, 65v, 75v, 85v, 95v, 105v, 115v, 125v, 135v, 145v, 153v,
161v, 169v, 177v, 185v, 193v.

[8]The word in the guard on f. 193v, דרבי, matches
what follows in the Constantinople edition, 'דר, and in
the Venice edition, דרבי.

[9]These letters cannot be clearly seen on my copy.

[10]For example, in the margin of 57v, opposite the
chapter number, is found the number 15 in Hebrew characters
(טו). Chapter 44 of Bereshit Rabba begins here with a
comment on Gen. 15,1. These biblical chapter numbers were
added by a later hand. Vat. 30 contains no indication of
the division of the Torah into parashyot according to the
present annual cycle.

17

The Vat. 30 text of Bereshit Rabba is incomplete at
the beginning and end and lacks a number of passages in the
body of the midrash. The following material is found in
Vat. 30 with the corresponding page numbers from the Theodor-
Albeck edition:

<pre>
        Vat. 30   T.A.

    ff. 2 - 9v .... pp. 23,11 - 50,2
    ff. 10 - 19,2 .... pp. 151,7 - 200,7
    ff. 19,4 - 132v,15 .... pp. 229,5 - 884,2
    ff. 132v,16 - 133,2 .... pp. 892,6 - 894,2
    ff. 133,3 - 166v,20 .... pp. 896,5 - 1118
    ff. 166,21 - 173,9 .... pp. 1126,3 - 1161,4
    ff. 173,10 - 175v,7 .... pp. 1171,3 - 1185
    ff. 175v,8 - 193 .... pp. 1231 - 1276,11
    ff. 193v .... pp. 1283,8 - 1285,5
</pre>

There are various reasons that much of the material
found in T.A. is lacking in Vat. 30: manuscript damage,
scribal error, defects and additions in the manuscripts
(exemplars) from which the scribes copies. The following
material is not found in Vat. 30:

1. T.A., pp. 1 - 23,11, Chapters 1 - 3,7, because
    of missing folios at the beginning of the manu-
    script.[11]

2. T.A., pp. 50,2 - 151,7, end of Chapter 6 through
    the beginning of Chapter 17, because two fascicles
    have been lost.[12]

---

[11]See the beginning of this chapter and T.A., p. 25,
note to Chapter 4. Actually, f.2 of Vat. 30 begins with
the text found in T.A., p. 23,11, but this page is very
difficult to read.

[12]See the beginning of this chapter.

3. T.A., pp. 200,8 - 229,4, Chapters 21,5 through 23, probably because of a fault in the exemplar.[13]

4. T.A., pp. 1285,5 - 1296, Chapter 100, last half of paragraph 2 to the end, because the last fascicle was lost.[14]

The following later additions are not found in Vat. 30:

1. T.A., pp. 884,2 - 892,5; Chapter 75,8 - 11.

2. T.A., pp. 894,6 - 896,4; Chapter 75,12 - 13.

3. T.A., pp. 1118,4 - 1126,2; Chapter 91,5 - 6.

4. T.A., pp. 1161,5 - 1171,3; Chapter 93,7 - 11.

5. T.A., pp. 1185,12 - 1230; Chapters 95 - 97 of the other versions.

6. T.A., pp. 1276,12 - 1283,7; Chapter 99,5 - 12 Lišnā Ahārinā.[15]

The version of Bereshit Rabba in Vat. 30 is divided

---

[13]This is Cassuto's view. In addition, Cassuto wrote that Theodor traced the origin of the defect to a lost folio. I could not find Cassuto's source for this view ascribed to Theodor; the latter merely remarks and laments the loss of the material. See T.A., p. 200, note 7. In any case, Cassuto was probably right that the exemplar is faulty because f. 19 line 2 contains a large space which has been filled in partially by a later hand, and line 3 contains the opening words from Chapter 24. These words are repeated immediately at the beginning of that chapter in line 5 of the manuscript.

[14]See the beginning of this chapter.

[15]For a discussion of each of these later additions, see T.A., pp. 884, note 3; 1118, note 4; 1161, note 5; 1185, note 11; 1276, note to Lišnā Ahārinā. Also, Albeck, Introduction, pp. 103f.

into 101 chapters;[16] each chapter opens with the word פרשתה,
פרשתא or an abbreviation thereof, followed by the number
of the chapter. Chapters 54 – 59 are misnumbered כד – כט;
this is due to the slight, but common error (in the exemplar
or by the scribe?) in which the <u>nun</u> and the <u>kaph</u> are
confused.[17]

In ff. 26 – 29, covering Chapters 28 – 31 in <u>T.A.</u>,
there is great confusion in the sequence of the text. The
proper order and continuity corresponding to the <u>T.A.</u>
pagination is as follows:

1. Proper order ends Vat. 30, f. 26,15 ....
.... <u>T.A.</u>, p. 268.

2. Text continues on f. 28,1 to 29v,21 ....
.... <u>T.A.</u>, p. 269,4 – 278,1.[18]

3. Text returns to f. 26,16 to 27v ....
.... <u>T.A.</u>, p. 278,3 – 286,10.[19]

4. Proper order begins again, f. 29, end of line 21..
.... <u>T.A.</u>, p. 287,1.

---

[16]For the number of chapters in the other manuscripts
and printed versions see Albeck, <u>Introduction</u>, pp. 96-102.

[17]Other examples of the confusion of <u>kaph</u> and <u>nun</u> in
Vat. 30 are:

1. f. 81v, בעלת כור, = <u>T.A.</u>, p. 572,3-4, בעלת נוד.
2. f. 82v, שעדייך היה כבודו קיים, = <u>T.A.</u>,p. 578,2,
שעדיין היה נכדו קיים.

[18]<u>T.A.</u>, p. 269,1-3, is lacking in Vat. 30.

[19]<u>T.A.</u>, p. 278, end of line 1 to the beginning of
line 3, is also missing in Vat. 30.

Theodor has shown that this confusion occurred in the manuscript of Bereshit Rabba used by the _Aruch_, which testifies to the antiquity of Vat. 30 or the exemplar from which it was copied.[20]

Two other matters noted by Albeck in the description of Vat. 30 found in his _Introduction_ need to be mentioned here, but will be fully treated later. In Vat. 30 numerous passages are abbreviated, and in most cases reference is made to where they are found elsewhere in Bereshit Rabba or in other rabbinic works.[21] These abbreviations have a particular pattern and will be dealt with in the section on the composition of Vat. 30. Albeck also lists "additions" found only in Vat. 30 and in the printed editions or in Midrash Haggadol, but not in the other manuscripts of Bereshit Rabba.[22] Since these "additions" fall under the category of textual transmission and the relation of Vat. 30 to other manuscripts, they will be treated in Chapter V.

Marginal notes also appear in Vat. 30. They include interpretations of difficult words based on the _Aruch_,

---

[20] _T.A._, p. 268, note to Chapter 29 and Theodor, _MGWJ_, XXXVIII, 486, note 1.

[21] Albeck, _Introduction_, p. 108. See Chapter I, and notes 29-32 for A. S. Rosenthal's discussion of the scribal notations used in these passages.

[22] Albeck, _Introduction_, p. 108. New manuscript material indicates that some of the passages considered by Albeck to be additions to the basic text of Bereshit Rabba are actually well attested original readings.

alternate readings of particular words, corrections, and
additions to the text from later versions.[23] Most of the
notes are the product of one hand although at least two
other annotators can be detected. In one case, f. 121v,
it appears as if the scribe writing the text added in the
margin material which he inadvertently omitted and then
enclosed his "note" in a decoration. As mentioned above,
some of the guards are also decorated.

---

[23]The following cases are only a small sample of the
many marginal notations found in Vat. 30.

1. Some examples of interpretations based on the
    <u>Aruch</u> which are found in the margins of Vat. 30.

    a) On f. 117, to the word תרכוס, the marginal
        note פי׳ בערוך ארגז. See the <u>Aruch Completum</u>,
        ed. Alexander Kohut, VIII, (Vienna, 1878),
        p. 279, תרכוס, and <u>T.A.</u>, p. 786-787, note 7.
        The original reading was probably תרנוס; for
        the typical confusion of <u>nun</u> and <u>kaph</u>, see
        note 15 above.

    b) On f. 132v to אוגדמי, the marginal note,
        פ"ע רשות להיות מוכס. See the <u>Aruch</u>, I, p. 29,
        אגרמי, and <u>T.A.</u>, p. 894, note 1. The spell-
        ing of this word in Vat. 30 with a <u>daleth</u>
        instead of a <u>resh</u> is supported by Vat. 60.

2. Some examples of alternate readings:

    a) On f. 3 to אפרכס, in the margins, נ"א ארפכס.
        See <u>T.A.</u>, p. 27, note and variants to line 5.

    b) On f. 5v to מטרין, in the margin, נ"א מיסטורין.
        See <u>T.A.</u>, p. 34 note and variants to line 6.
        Vat. 30 is incorrectly cited in the variant
        readings where the marginal note is quoted
        rather than the body of the manuscript.

    c) On f. 132v to the word שבועתי, in the margin,
        נ"א שבא עתו. See <u>T.A.</u>, p. 882, note and

variants to line 1. The reading שבועתי is
supported by Vat. 60.

d) On f. 168v to שאבה, in the margin, נ"א שעוה.
See <u>T.A.</u>, p. 1136,1 and variants, and Kutscher,
"Studies," 10.

3. Some examples of corrections found in the margins:

   a) On f. 7 to the last two words of the saying,
   ליט ביזה דהכן .. יונק, is found in the margin דהדין יניק. See <u>T.A.</u>, p. 39, notes and
   variants to line 2.

   b) On f. 17, the words יש בו הנייה are added in
   the margin; a circle in the body of the text
   indicates that these words were deleted by
   mistake. See <u>T.A.</u>, p. 192,5.

   c) Similarly, on f. 18, the words שהן באין בעור
   are added in the margin; a circle in the body
   of the text indicates that they were deleted
   by mistake. See <u>T.A.</u>, p. 197,3 and variants.

4. An example of additions to Vat. 30 found only in
   later manuscripts: on f. 170, in the margin, the
   words שנ׳ ולקדקד נזיר אחיו and שנפרש מאחיו,
   which occur only in the Paris and Munich manuscripts. See <u>T.A.</u>, p. 1143, variants to lines
   5 and 6, and note to line 5.

CHAPTER III

THE SCRIBES OF VAT. 30

Features Common to all Scribes Working
on the Manuscript

Before dealing with the question of the number of
scribes working on Vat. 30 and the differences between them,
a few words are in order regarding features common to the
manuscript as a whole. Whatever the number of scribes, all
of them wrote in "oriental square script."[1] This script
was common to the Near East and is remarkably similar to
later Ashkenazic square script. The similarity is probably
the reason for Theodor's conjecture that Vat. 30 was
written in "alte deutsche Quadraschrift."[2]

Considerable study has been devoted to "oriental
square script," but because it was in use for many centuries
and throughout the entire Mediterranean area, the few dated
manuscripts offer little aid in establishing precisely the

---

[1]Albeck, Introduction, p. 7; Cassuto, p. 37.

[2]Theodor, "Drei unbekannte Paraschas," 149, note 1.
A good example of Ashkenazic square script is contained
in the Erfurt ms. of the Tosephta. See Tosephta, Zeraim,
ed. Saul Lieberman (New York, 1955), Introduction, p. 9.

age or provenance of Vat. 30.[3] However, Vat. 30 does contain some vocalized words which might suggest a clue to origin. A word with supralinear pointing, קְלֵיל, is found on f. 109v. The vowels appear to belong to the scribe who wrote this folio. This vocalization resembles that found in the facsimile edition of Vat. 66, published by Dr. Finkelstein; it could indicate Babylonian origin. On the other hand, the section of the manuscript in which the word is found contains some of the best readings of Palestinian Aramaic. Of course, it is not inconceivable that a Palestinian document of such importance as Bereshit Rabba would find its way to Babylonia and be reproduced there. Another

---

[3]For example, see the comments of Moses Lutski on the scribal features of Vat. 66, Sifra or Torat Kohanim, published in facsimile edition with a Hebrew introduction by Louis Finkelstein (New York, 1956), Introduction, pp. 70-77. Lutski lists manuscripts of biblical texts from the tenth through twelfth centuries of which facsimiles have been published. However, it is difficult to compare our own manuscript with them because scribal techniques were more formalized in regard to Biblical material than with midrashic texts. This fact is also mentioned by Lutski (p. 72); nevertheless, using criteria from the Biblical manuscripts, he dates Vat. 66 in the tenth century. Cassuto had dated it in the seventh (see Cassuto, pp. 95-99).

Other manuscripts and Geniza fragments with paleographical features similar to Vat. 30 have also been assigned to the tenth and eleventh centuries, but their dating also rests on little convincing evidence. See the palimpsests from the Cairo Geniza published in Palestinian Syriac Texts, ed. Agnes Smith Lewis and Margret Dunlop Gibson (London, 1900), Plate II, Fragment II and Plate III, Fragment III. All that can be said is that the eleventh century is not an improbable date for the origin of Vat. 30.

possibility, however, is that the manuscript was produced in an area inhabited by Palestinians, but where scribes trained in the Babylonian Talmud and vocalization also might have resided. As far as I can tell, it is impossible to determine the precise geographical origin of Vat. 30; as I will later argue, however, Egypt is not an unlikely location.[4]

All of the scribes of Vat. 30 were professionals. This is evident from the layout of each page, the rather uniform adherence to margins, the orderly pattern of punctuation, and the neatness of the text. As previously mentioned, each folio is lined; right and left hand margin lines are also impressed into the parchment. Letters are written from the line downward and this adds to the impression of precision and neatness on the part of each scribe.

The same type of writing instrument was used throughout the manuscript, a _calamus_, a pen made from a hollow reed. Such pens were common to the Near East during the Middle Ages.[5] Because the type of writing instrument was

---

[4]See my comments at the conclusion of Chapter IV.

[5]Lieberman, _Tosephta_, Introduction, p. 10; Lutski, in the introduction to _Sifra or Torat Kohanim_, p. 74. For the use of the _calamus_ by Muslim scholars, see Franz Rosenthal, _The Techniques and Approaches of Muslim Scholarship_ (Rome, 1947), p. 13: "The calamus should not be very tough, since this would impare its writing speed, nor should it be too soft, since this would cause it to wear away too quickly . . . if you want your handwriting to improve, lengthen the part of the calamus which is cut away to shape the pen (_jilfah_) and make it thick, and nib the point obliquely and to the right."

the same, the shape of the letters and the form of the lines
are also similar. For example, in all cases in Vat. 30, the
base of the _ayin_ consists of a curving down-stroke in which
the line becomes progressively thicker toward the left end.[6]

In spite of similarities of script, scribal training
and pen, important differences exist between parts of the
manuscript. These differences can be traced to the peculiarities of the individual scribes and to the exemplars
from which they copied.

The Number of Scribes in Vat. 30

Cassuto was the first to realize that more than one
scribe wrote Vat. 30. He suggested that there were three
who worked on different sections of the manuscript.[7]
However, he did not go into any detail or produce evidence
to support this assertion. Because Cassuto had first-hand
contact with the manuscript, his view must be given serious
consideration. Nevertheless, my own examination of the
Xerox copy in my possession has led me to a different conclusion regarding the number of scribes and the sections
each wrote.

---

[6] See Chart I.

[7] Cassuto, p. 37.

The test I have applied consists of two parts: a comparison of individual letters and groups of words from representative folios, and a comparison of other scribal characteristics.[8] The results of this test are presented here and the details will follow in the next section. It seems to me that there are at least four and possibly six main scribes in Vat. 30.

1. Scribe A, ff. 2-9v.

2. Scribe B, ff. 10-81v, line 6 על שכמה.

3. Scribe C, ff. 81v, line 6 ואת הילד -140v.

4. Scribe D, ff. 141-145v; plus the following:

        f. 107v, line 13 to the end of the page.

        f. 121v, line 1, last word to line 7

          and line 14, third word to line 17.

        f. 128v, line 5 to the end of the page.

Two other hands are involved in the manuscript which are similar to Scribe A, but not identical to him.

5. Scribe A2, ff. 146-185v.

6. Scribe A3, ff. 186 to the end of the manuscript.

Distinguishing Features Peculiar to
Each Scribe or Group of Scribes

Paleographical distinctions.--This section treats those paleographical features which are common to some

---

[8]For a detailed treatment of similar features in the Dead Sea Scrolls, see Malachi Martin, S. J., _The Scribal Character of the Dead Sea Scrolls_ (Louvain, 1958), especially his chapter dealing with methodology.

scribes and distinguish them from others. It is based on
an analysis of certain letters, words, and groups of words
as well as on other external phenomena such as margins,
indentations, spacing and punctuation, and fascicle ornamentation. The description of letters and other details
presented here is related to Chart I, which contains a
typical alphabet of each scribe, and to Chart II, which
represents selections from each scribe's work brought
together for purposes of comparison.[9]

Alef

A3	A2	D	C	B	A
א	א	א	א	א	א

All the scribes except B construct this letter
usually in three strokes: a vertical left line, a slanting center line, and a right arm. The center line touches
the left line slightly below the top of the left line. The
scribes can be distinguished from one another by the position of the foot of the left line and by the construction
and position of the right arm. In A and C, the foot is
found extending leftward from the base of the left line;

---

[9]It is important to note at the outset that scribes
are not consistent in their writing; there is considerable
variation in the many appearances of a particular letter
or word written by the same man. This variation is taken
into account in the present discussion. The material
presented here does not claim to be exhaustive; it is
hoped that the sampling will provide sufficient evidence
for the differentiation of scribes in Vat. 30.

in D and A2, to the left, right, or directly under it; in
A3, the foot either extends leftward or appears as a tri-
angle. The right arm in A, A2, and A3 looks like a tilted
square; it is attached by a thin line from its lower corner
to the middle of the center line; in C, the square is
attached from the middle of its left side to the center line,
and not from the lower corner; in D, the right arm may
appear merely as a straight or slightly curved line or even
as a teardrop, and is attached anywhere on the lower half
of the center line.

   The alef in B is quite different in that it is made
in two strokes. The pen is not lifted at the top of the
broad center line, and the vertical left line continues
from there. In addition, the left line has a foot which
appears as a square placed to the right of this line.

Gimel

A3		A2		D		C		B		A

   The gimel is very similar in A, C, A2, and A3. It
begins with a pronounced square head, slightly tilted, from
which the vertical line descends. The foot is attached to
the lower half of the vertical line and extends down and
to the left. However, it does not descend any lower than
the vertical line, but continues leftward so that the
following letter often is suspended above or touching it.

30

In the abbreviation, ׳ננו, the bottom of the second <u>waw</u>
touches the left tip of the foot. In B, the head of the
<u>gimel</u> is less pronounced and the foot begins lower on the
vertical line than in the other scribes. The <u>gimel</u> in D
often has no head at all and the foot may begin anywhere
from the middle to the base of the vertical line. The left
tip of the foot is almost always connected to the following
letter (ligature); in addition, the length of the foot varies
considerably. If the following letter is a <u>waw</u>, the foot
of the <u>gimel</u> may touch its base or continue beyond it.

Pe

A3	A2	D	C	B	A

Scribes A, C, A2, and A3 make this letter in the same
manner. They begin with the center arm, then usually continue to the roof without lifting the pen, making a rounded
top left corner. However, A occasionally lifts the pen
after the arm is made, so that the roof begins with a second
stroke, and the top left corner has a point. C makes this
second stroke more often than A, and A3 always has it. In
these four scribes the base of the <u>pe</u> tilts down and extends
to the left far beyond the left edge of the roof. In B, the
<u>pe</u> is very compact. The top left corner is never rounded
and has a point on the top. The roof curves slightly downward in the middle. The upper right corner is square.

31

The base remains horizontal rather than tilting downward,
and extends only minutely beyond the left edge of the roof.
In D, the pe is almost triangular; it has a short roof and
the back slants downward to the right. The base is horizontal.

Qoph

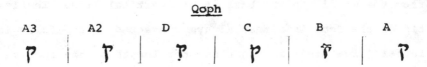

| A3 | A2 | D | C | B | A |

In A, the roof is horizontal with a slight upward
point at the left tip. The vertical line begins to the
right of this point and usually touches the roof. In B,
the qoph is made with the same basic strokes as in A, but
all the lines are thicker and the roof is slightly curved
in the center. C, A2, and A3 are similar to A except that
in C the roof is quite curved at the center. The roof is
also very curved in D, and the bottom of the vertical line
in this scribe sometimes swings to the left.

Sin

| A3 | A2 | D | C | B | A |

In all scribes the sin is composed of three lines.
In A, C, A2 and A3, the right arm curves into a horizontal
or slightly tilted base. The left arm, which looks like
a waw, is attached to the left tip of the base. It sometimes extends slightly below the base so that a small point

32

appears. The middle arm joins the left arm just above the
left corner, near the base. In B, the slanted base and
the left arm form almost a "V." The middle arm is usually
attached to the corner or the base, but never to the left
arm. In addition, the middle arm looks like a _yod_. The
sin in D is generally like A's except that the base can be
round, horizontal or slanting. The middle arm is very
mobile and sometimes is attached high on the left arm so
that the letter appears like a Rǝshi _sin_.

From the brief description of these sample letters,
it should be clear that there is no radical difference in
the basic writing habits of the various scribes.[10] However, certain characteristics do emerge which suggest a
grouping of the scribes into the following divisions:

1. A, C, A2, and A3.

2. B.

c. D.

The first group shares so many similar traits that one may

---

[10]Examples could be brought from other letters as well,
especially _bet_, _daleth_, _he_, _waw_, _kaph_ and final _pe_. When
letters are taken out of their context on a page, it is often
difficult to point out characteristic details. After having
worked with a Xerox copy of the manuscript for over a year
and repeatedly compared its sections, minor differences
among the scribes are very obvious to me. This is particularly true in the case of the "group," A, C, A2, and A3,
where the differentiation often rests on the total impression
of a page. Nevertheless, precise description of differences
is often impossible. However, even Cassuto, who worked with
the manuscript itself, was able to differentiate between
what he considered to be the work of one scribe, ff. 146-193v,
and the work of another, ff. 81v-145v; and it is in these
folios that a distinction is so hard to make.

assume that all its members are from the same scribal family.[11] This "group" is quite different from B, and in certain ways different from D.

The letters of the "group" convey an impression of squareness and spaciousness.[12] Sometimes letters in the same word touch one another, but there is no ligature and the letters are usually well spearated.[13] The writing of Scribe B appears to be rounder, shorter and more cramped than that of the "group," and his letters often touch one another. This impression may be due to the relatively thicker lines produced by B's pen and to the fact that he puts more words on a page than the other scribes.[14] The handwriting of D is peculiar in that it seems careless, as if the scribe were in a hurry. Ligature is very prominent and the _ayin_ with an extremely long base is

---

[11]From the appearance of their work, the shape of their letters, and the layout of the page, it seems that the background and training of these scribes was the same and that they worked under single guidance. Permit me a personal note: my mother and her five sisters attended the same school in New York City early in this century. Their handwriting is practically indistinguishable to me. In those days penmanship was of much greater importance than today.

[12]For this section consult Chart II. In these two characteristics, squareness and spaciousness, the work of the "group" is closer to the appearance of a biblical scroll than the other scribes. See Lutski, pp. 72-73, and the facsimiles of the biblical texts he mentions.

[13]The occurence of letters touching one another is more common in C than in A, A2, and A3.

[14]Note on Chart II that his left margin extends out far beyond the other scribes.

34

characteristic.[15] A special trait in D is the fact that the bottom of the vertical lines in the daleth, qoph, final nun and final sadhe swings slightly to the left.[16] In the "group" the base of the letters bet, qimel, teth, final mem, nun, ayin, pe, sin and taw usually slants downward to the left; in B and D the base of these letters is horizontal and occasionally curved.

In addition to the shape of the letters, there are other external features peculiar to each of the scribes which reinforce the primary differentiation suggested above. The first of these features is the appearance of the right and left hand margins on each page. Throughout the manuscript, the right hand margin is almost perfectly straight. However, indentation does occur, and its use reveals patterns which are characteristic of individual scribes or a scribal group.

With some significant differences between them, scribes A, C, A2, A3, and also D are similar in their frequent use of indentation. This indentation is merely a form of spacing and has nothing to do with "paragraphs." In the exemplar, if a midrashic passage or a biblical verse is

---

[15]In Chart II, the second line belonging to D contains the word, עלין, in which the base of the ayin extends under the lamed and yod and touches the kaph.

[16]This is the result of D's tendency to join one letter to the next. Even though these particular letters cannot be joined, they swing in the direction of the next letter.

35

concluded near the left margin of a line, and a space exists
after this passage or verse, the space is indicated in the
copy by indenting the next line. Spacing appears frequently
to set off biblical verses, interpretations, parables,
stories, and other blocks of material. It may also appear
because of a defect in the exemplar, but in most instances
this is not the case. Consequently, the high frequency of
indentation in this "group" is the result of the frequent
spaces in the exemplar.[17]

In contrasting the "group" with B in the use of indentation, the most significant factor is spacing. A glance
at the overall appearance of B's work reveals that he did
not use spacing to any great extent. Where spacing does
occur within a line in B, it serves to set off a new Torah
verse or an independent block of material, such as a mashal
or ma'aseh. Otherwise it represents a defect in the exemplar,
possibly a mistake which was deleted in the manuscript
tradition, leaving a space. In this case B often puts a
series of dots in the space to indicate that a new passage

---

[17]There are significant differences between the scribes
mentioned in the "group." Scribes A and D do not indent for
Torah verses which begin a chapter; A2 sometimes does indent
in such a case, and C and A3 almost always do. In addition,
Scribe A does not often indent for any biblical verses which
occur within the body of a chapter while the other scribes
usually do, for both Torah verses and proem texts. All the
members of the "group" indent for interpretations, parables
and tales. A special characteristic of Scribe C is that he
indents when passages in the exemplar are defective.

does not begin at its termination.[18] B does not indent
often; when he does it is rarely for the purpose of indicating spacing within a line in his exemplar.[19]

Indentation and spacing are the first indications we
have that Scribe B worked in a manner quite different from
Scribes A, C, A2, A3, and D.[20]

Left hand margins also reveal typical patterns. Two
devices are used by the scribes in order to conclude a line
as close to the left margin as possible: lengthened letters
and special signs. Scribes A, C, A2, and A3 lengthened
these letters at the end of a line: _alef_, _bet_, _he_, _lamed_,
final _mem_, _samekh_, _resh_ and _taw_. Occasionally A and A3
will go beyond their left margin up to three letters to
complete a word. If a line is short, they fill in the
remaining space with a series of dots ending at the margin
with a mark that looks like a small _alef_ (א) or like an
English "X." Scribes C and A3 go beyond their left margin
very often, sometimes up to four and five letters. They

---

[18]For example, ff. 15, 17, 18, 18v.

[19]Compared to the "group," B seldom indents. Indentation is found in B occasionally at the beginning of a chapter
and before a Torah verse in the body of a chapter if the
preceding passage ends in the previous line. In one case,
f. 14v, the "b" part of a verse is indented because it is
specially commented upon. An occasional proem verse is
indented and spaces may be left at the beginning of a line
where the exemplar is faulty.

[20]Again, from what has been said, it should be stressed
that an indented line does not begin a new "paragraph" in
the modern sense of the term.

do not fill a space at the end of a line, but place an <u>alef</u>-like mark after the space, at the margin (C ℵ, A2 ℵ). In addition, on ff. 178v–179 and 184v–185, Scribe A2 uses a wavy line to fill the space to the margin (〰〰).

Scribe D also lengthens many of the same letters that the above group does. Often the length of these letters is quite extreme, taking up the equivalent space of a four or five letter word. If a line is short, D leaves the remaining space empty or places within it a series of checks followed by a sign which looks like an anchor (ℤ ⌄⌄⌄⌄), or merely places this "anchor" at the margin. On the basis of this sign and D's characteristic hand, it is possible to isolate the passages he has written which appear in the block of material prepared by Scribe C.

In Scribe B, the following letters are lengthened at the end of a line: <u>alef</u>, <u>bet</u>, <u>daleth</u>, <u>he</u>, <u>het</u>, <u>kaph</u>, final <u>kaph</u>, <u>lamed</u>, final <u>mem</u>, <u>samekh</u>, <u>qoph</u>, <u>resh</u>, and <u>taw</u>. This scribe carefully seeks to preserve his left margin and rarely goes two letters beyond it to complete a word. If a line is short, he fills it in with a series of dots or ends it with an "X," but rarely uses both together.

In regard to left hand margins, A, C, A2, A3 and D again emerge as a group with characteristics quite different from Scribe B.

Punctuation marks are also used in a characteristic way by each of the scribes. As Cassuto pointed out, the

38

sign ⊙ is used throughout the manuscript except in ff. 10-81, that is, by all scribes except B. Scribe B employs a dot for the functions served by our comma, semi-colon, period and quotation mark, placing it near the upper left corner of a concluding word. In rare cases a circle does appear in B; however, it is for correction purposes and not for punctuation.[21] I have found only one case in B where a circle is used for punctuation, and it comes at the conclusion of a passage which appears to have been rewritten.[22]

The dot is also used as a punctuation mark by the other scribes; however, among these scribes the most conspicuous sign is the dotted circle ⊙. Cassuto's view was that this sign marked the end of paragraphs in the manuscript, yet we have seen that the concept of "paragraph" has no meaning in our text.[23] The sign is used rather consistently by Scribes A, C, A2, A3, and D. Its primary function seems to have been to separate the comment on one biblical verse from the next verse and its comment.[24]

---

[21]ff. 17, 18, 20v.

[22]f. 39v.

[23]See note 20.

[24]The dotted circle is employed by <u>hadith</u> scholars in the Muslim world for the same purpose. Franz Rosenthal, <u>Muslim Scholarship</u>, p. 16, quotes a passage from the Muʿid fî adab al-mufîd wa-l-mustafîd, by ʿAbd al-Bâsit b. Mûsû al-ʿAlmawî (15th century), in which this author summarizes centuries-old scribal traditions: "A circle or a thick (point made with the) calamus should be used to separate the various stories or traditions (which occur in a manuscript). A complete lack of punctuation would make a manuscript difficult

Some peculiarities do appear among the scribes as they employ this sign. In the material written by D, the dotted circle appears infrequently. At the beginning of Scribe A2's work, ff. 146-154f, the sign is found in abundance but is confusing in its use, as if the scribe thought it best to insert the dotted circle wherever a space was

---

to understand. For purposes of punctuation a circle is preferable to any other sign and has been used by most hadith scholars. It looks like this: ⊙."

In Vat. 30, this sign has a number of other functions which seem to be consistent throughout the manuscript. The dotted circle ⊙ also appears:

1. at the end of some chapters (ff. 2v, 7, 83v, 85, 90)

2. at the beginning of some chapters after the citation of the chapter number (ff. 2v, 4v, 82v)

3. between blocks of text which are connected in subject matter and are really parts of an extended comment on a particular verse (ff. 3, 4, 5, 5v, 8v, 9, 93v, 100, 101v, 111 top, 117, 118v-121, 131). In these cases the use of the dotted circle is often confusing because the sign separates material which belongs together.

4. after the Torah verse at the beginning of a chapter in order to separate it from the proem verse which follows (ff. 83v, 93, 96v, 106, 123, 131v, 140v, 147, 148, 163, 191)

5. occasionally in the middle of a long biblical verse which concludes a passage, so that the "b" part of the verse appears incorrectly as the proem text of the next passage (f. 84v). This may be considered a mistake and certainly leads to confusion for the reader.

6. sometimes before various parts of the same verse when there are separate comments on each of those parts (ff. 106v-107, 113-113v)

7. sometimes merely to indicate the margin at the end of a line (ff. 101v, 110v, 114v, 115).

found.[25] Thus, Scribe A2 seems to have least understood the proper functions of the dotted circle.

A remarkable piece of evidence suggests that the dotted circle or a similar punctuation mark was part of the manuscript tradition of Bereshit Rabba underlying Vat. 30. A palimpsest from the Cairo Geniza containing a passage from Bereshit Rabba has been published which is similar in almost every detail to material copied by Scribe C in Vat. 30.[26] The passage contained in the palimpsest will be discussed later; it is sufficient to note here that the sign "O," a circle without the dot in the middle, occurs three times in the fragment, twice in the same place that a dotted circle is found in Vat. 30, and a third time at the end of a chapter, where it might occur in our manuscript but in this case does not.[27] The absence of either the circle or dotted circle from Scribe B is of great significance in indicating that the practice of scribe B was not merely different from A, C, A2, A3, and D; it was different from the tradition represented in the exemplar from which these scribes copied.

---

[25]For example, on f. 148, it appears immediately after a proem verse and before the interpretation of that verse. On ff. 149, 153, and 154ff. it appears in the middle of passages and biblical verses.

[26]The palimpsest is found in Palestinian Syriac Texts, Plate III, Fragment III; the passage contained in the palimpsest corresponds to Vat. 30, ff. 88 bottom-88v; T.A., pp. 608,12 - 613,5. I am grateful to Dr. Mihaly for referring me to this passage.

[27]See note 24, example 1.

One final feature in Vat. 30 sheds light on the differences between the men who wrote this manuscript: the
ornaments which are added to the guards found at the end
of the fascicles. These ornaments are found only in the
material written by A, C, A2, and A3; they do not appear
in either B or D.[28] The common ornamentation is another
indication that these scribes were members of the same
family and received a similar training. The lack of the
ornament in D may suggest that the material he wrote was
added after the completion of the rest of the manuscript.
Some support for this view is given in the fact that the
bulk of his work appears at the end of a fascicle and
looks hurried and careless.

The external evidence drawn from the appearance of
the alphabets, the margins, indentations and spacing,
punctuation and ornamentation suggests a clear division in
the manuscript. Scribes A, C, A2, and A3 seem to have oper-
ated in the same way. Scribe D is often associated with
this group, especially regarding characteristics influenced
by the exemplar. In each of the areas covered, Scribe B's
work contains characteristics unlike those of the other
scribes.

---

[28]Ornaments appear on ff. 9v, 85v, 95v, 105v, 115v,
125v, 135v, 153v, 161v, 177v, 185v, 193v; they do not appear
on ff. 19v, 29v, 37v, 45v, 55v, 65v, 75v, or 145v.

Thus far only external evidence has been offered to show the distinction between the scribes. A survey of internal textual and linguistic phenomena will now be made to see if this distinction can be supported by evidence which significantly affects the understanding of the midrash itself.

Linguistic and technical distinctions.--Internal evidence sheds further light on the characteristics of the individual scribes. The examples presented here are drawn from the spelling of selected nouns, pronouns, prepositions, particles and verb forms. Features which distinguish the scribes are also found in the frequency of certain technical terms and abbreviations, the methods of citing biblical verses, and characteristic spelling of the names of certain sages. No attempt is made here to present a grammar of the Hebrew or Aramaic portions of the manuscript or to provide a complete description of its linguistic features.[29]

---

[29] The grammatical and linguistic features of the Aramaic portions of Vat. 30 have been fully treated by Kutscher in his "Studies." Sokoloff promises a study of the Hebrew characteristics of the manuscript in the forthcoming section of his article. For general studies of Rabbinic Hebrew based primarily on the Mishna, see Hanoch Yalon, Introduction to the Vocalization of the Mishna (Jerusalem 1964); M. H. Segel, A Grammar of Mishnaic Hebrew Oxford, 1927); Ezekiel Kutscher, "Lešon Hazal," Henoch Yalon Jubilee Volume, ed. Saul Lieberman and others (Jerusalem, 1963), pp. 246-280; and Abba ben David, Biblical Hebrew and Mishnaic Hebrew (Tel Aviv, 1967).

The examples have been chosen because they reveal patterns
which are typical of the scribes who wrote them.[30]

A. <u>Characteristic spelling</u>.

1. אדן - אדם

Scholars have singled out the spelling אדן
(man), with a <u>nun</u>, as one of the outstanding
features of the Palestinian Talmud.[31] Albeck
and Kutscher noted the appearance of this
spelling in Vat. 30; however, neither
commented on its frequency or distribution.[32]
The spelling אדן occurs nine times in Vat. 30

---

[30]As will become apparent, these examples are
also significant because of their relationship to
forms found in the Palestinian Talmud. At this
point in our presentation, they are listed merely
to show the varying practices of the scribes of
Vat. 30.

[31]Saul Lieberman, <u>Ha-y'rusalmi Ki-fshuto</u>
(Jerusalem, 1935), Introduction, p. 22. For the
spelling אדן in early Mishna manuscripts see H. L.
Ginzberg, "Zu den Dialecten des Talmudisch-Hebraischen,"
<u>MGWJ</u>, LXXVII (1933), 421; and in the same volume,
Henoch Yelon, "Nachtrag zur palastinischen Aussprache
des Schluss -m wie <u>n</u>," 429; J. N. Epstein, <u>Mavo</u>
<u>L'nusah Ha-mishna</u> (Jerusalem, 1965), pp. 1230-<u>1231</u>;
H. Rosenberg, "Un Fragment de Mishna au British
Museum," <u>REJ</u>, LIII (1907), 214.

[32]Albeck, <u>Introduction</u>, p. 107; Kutscher, "Studies,"
12. The spelling אדן also appears in the London
manuscript; see Albeck, <u>Introduction</u>, p. 105.

and only within the sections written by
Scribes A and C.[33]

2. The _alef_ or _he_ as the Aramaic definite article
    and in other characteristic functions.

    In Vat. 30, _alef_ and _he_ are used in Aramaic
    passages as the definite article and as a
    mater lectiones for â.[34]   Kutscher has already
    noted that the two letters are not equally
    distributed throughtout the manuscript.   "In
    Vat. 30 at the beginning, _he_ and _alef_ are
    mixed (although extended Aramaic texts do not
    appear there), but from the middle onward,
    the _he_ prevails and the _alef_ appears only as

---

[33]The spelling appears on:

    f. 3v, line 19......T.A., 29,2
    f. 4,16.............T.A., 30,10
    f. 6,10.............T.A., 36,1
    f. 6v,6.............T.A., 37,3 variant to אחד מהם
    f. 83v,26...........T.A., 585,3
    f. 89v,21...........T.A., 617,9
    f. 92,15............T.A., 635,1 variant to יש לך
    f. 95v,6............T.A., 652,7
    f. 105,11...........T.A., 706,4

Sokoloff's list of the occurences of אדן should be
corrected to include T.A., 617,9.

[34]The _he_ definite article is also characteristic of
the Palestinian Talmud.   See Louis Ginzberg, A Commentary
on the Palestinian Talmud (New York, 1941), Vol. I, Hebrew
Introduction, pp. 39-40.

a barely recognizable minority."[35] Differences in the frequency and distribution of
the _he_ and _alef_ do exist, although not quite
as Kutscher describes them. These differences
can be traced to the work of the various
scribes.

Although Scribe A has an insufficient
number of Aramaic passages from which to form
conclusive judgement, his preference seems to
be for the _alef_.[36] In the rest of the manuscript there is an abundance of Aramaic
material which indicates a significant difference in the use of these two letters by Scribe
B and by the "group" C, D, A2, and A3. In thir-
teen lengthy Aramaic passages in B, the _alef_
almost always serves as the definite article,
while the _he_ is rarely found.[37] Further, in
Scribe B, there are over ninety shorter Aramaic
passages, folk sayings and interpretations, in
which the ratio of the _alef_ to _he_ is 2:1.[38]

---

[35]Kutscher, "Studies," 10. For the use of _he_ in the
London manuscript see Theodor, MGWJ, XXXVII, 208, note 2;
Albeck, Introduction, p. 105.

[36]See the Aramaic Appendix, Longer Passages of Scribe A.

[37]See the Aramaic Appendix, Longer Passages of Scribe B,
especially numbers 4, 7, 11, 12.

[38]See the Aramaic Appendix, Shorter Passages of Scribe B.

The _alef_ also appears throughout B in the
spelling of common pronouns, adverbs and
verbs: נסבא, חמא, אתא, הכא, אנא.

With some significant variations between
them, the Scribes C, D, A2, and A3 appear to
be almost the reverse of B. On the average
they use the _he_ twice as often as the _alef_.
In long passages C employs the _he_ more than
A2; but in the shorter passages, of which
there are over one hundred, the preference of
all the members of this group is for the _he_
over the _alef_ at the ratio 2:1.[39] The pre-
dominance of the _he_ extends to the spelling
of the common pronouns, adverbs and verbs:
אנה, הכה, אתה, בעה. It should be added that
these same ratios exist in the appearance of
the _alef_ and _he_ for the sound ā at the end
of foreign words and place names: B prefers
alef, the "group" prefers _he_.[40]

---

[39]See the Aramaic Appendix, Longer Passages of Scribes
C and A2 and Shorter Passages of C, A2, and A3.

[40]For example, the following list of nations appears in
B: אפריקי וגרמניא ומדא ומקדוניא איסוגיא איסונא חירס,
f. 41v,14, _T.A._, 343,4. However, in the other scribes the
following examples occur:

1. מוסופוטמיה, f. 93,12, _T.A._, 640,2. Contrast this
   with B's מיסופוטמיא, f. 29v,14; _T.A._, 227,3 and
   variants and f. 57v,19, _T.A._, 426,4.

47

3. The preposition, ל, with the third masc.sing.
suffix spelled לה or ליה.

There are significant differences among
the scribes in the spelling of the Aramaic
preposition ל with the third masc. sing.
suffix. This word occurs throughout the manuscript, in Aramaic passages and in Hebrew
sections as part of the Aramaic phrase אמר ליה/
לה. Scribe A uses the plene form three times
more often than the defective one.[41] In Scribe
B, the defective form occurs only five times
out of one hundred thirty-six appearances of
the word; the ratio of ליה to לה is 26:1.[42]

---

2. אנטוכיה, f. 105v,13, T.A., 710,5 and variant.
   Compare with B's אנטוכיא, f. 13v,6, T.A., 172,9.

3. אספנייה, f. 6v,20, T.A., 38,2 and f. 191v,19,
   T.A., 1271,11. Compare with B's אספניא, f. 61v,6,
   T.A., 446,3.

In spite of these examples, there is a clear tendency
among the scribes of the "group" to "correct" the he to
alef. This tendency can be seen especially in foreign words
and place names which appear more than once in the same
passage. For Example:

1. פרדיסא, פורדיסה, f. 113,10,14, T.A., 761,3 and 762,2.

2. קפדוקיה, קפדוקייא, קפאדוקייא, קפאדוקיה, f. 116v,14,19,
   T.A., 785,1,2,5.

[41]There are only eight occurences of ל with the third
masculine singular suffix in A; six are spelled ליה and two לה.

[42]For example, see the Aramaic Appendix, Longer Passages of Scribe B, number 11, where the spelling throughout
is ליה with one exception in line 7.

However, in the "group," C, D, A2, and A3, the situation is quite different; in over two hundred fifty cases, the form לה is more common than ליה by a ratio of 9:4.[43]

4. _Plene_ and defective spelling of words with the vowels ê and î: אֵין – אֵן, הֵין – הֵן, בֵּין – בֵּן, אֵין – אֵן.

In Vat. 30 these "little" words with the vowels ê and î are spelled both _plene_ and defective. In Scribe B, the defective spelling of אֵן and בֵן does not occur; the forms הדין and הדן appear about equally.[44] In Scribes C, D, A2, and A3, the defective spelling of all these words is very common.[45]

---

[43]See the Aramaic Appendix, Longer Passages of C, especially numbers 1 through 5; the Longer Passage of C and D; and the Longer Passages of A2, numbers 1 and 4.

[44]Some examples of דין and הדין in Scribe B are:

f. 32v,11...........T.A., 302,1
f. 32v,14...........T.A., 302,4 variant to להון
f. 32v,16...........T.A., 302,5 variant to לתרויהו
f. 44,25............T.A. 357,6 variant to קרון, not noted by Theodor.
f. 45,21............T.A., 363,3

Some examples of דן and הדן in B are:

f. 33v,16...........T.A., 307,1 variant to מהו
f. 36v,10...........T.A., 319,5 variant to דידך, not noted by Theodor.
f. 45,20,21.........T.A., 363,2,3
f. 49v,23...........T.A., 385,5,6 variants to ההן ... וההן.

[45]Note the examples in the Aramaic Appendix: Longer Passages from C, number 1; Longer Passage of C and D; Longer Passages from A2, number 2.

5. אמתי and אמתיי.

This word is always spelled אמתי with one

yod, by B.[46] In the "group," in at least

sixteen cases it is written אמתיי or איתייי,

and in only four cases is it spelled אמתי/

איתיי.[47]

---

[46]In T.A., the variants from Vat. 30 to this word are
rarely noted. The spelling אמתי occurs in Scribe B on:

f. 27v,20..............T.A., 286,4
f. 34,9................T.A., 309,6
f. 35v,24..............T.A., 316,9
f. 36v,24..............T.A., 320,10
f. 37v,6...............T.A., 321,5
f. 57,5................T.A., 423,2
f. 59v,22..............T.A., 435,6
f. 63v,10..............T.A., 456,8
f. 67,14...............T.A., 477,2

Two alternate spellings of this word are "exceptions
which prove the rule"; the word מאימת occurs on f. 37,3,
T.A., 321,2 as a variant to מאמתי; in a marginal gloss,
f. 38,3, in another hand, the spelling איתיי appears,
T.A., 326,1.

[47]The spellings אמתיי and איתיי are found on:

f. 2v,2.............T.A., 24,12
f. 3,3.............T.A., 26,9
f. 89,18...........T.A., 614,6
f. 91v,9...........T.A., 631,4
f. 99,23...........T.A., 674,11
f. 107v,13.........T.A., 723,6, see variants to איתיי,
                   כלבי
f. 111,13..........T.A., 747,2
f. 116,11..........T.A., 781,4 variant to מתי
f. 122v,9..........T.A., 817,3
f. 131v,21.........T.A., 878,3
f. 138v,24.........T.A., 935,1
f. 139,5...........T.A., 936,1
f. 164v,15.........T.A., 1098,3
f. 181v,21.........T.A., 1242,26
f. 182v,8..........T.A., 1244,9
f. 187v,15.........T.A., 1260,2 variant to רבנן אמרי

50

6. ‏כאילו – כילו‎.

The form ‏כילו‎ for ‏כאילו‎ never occurs in B; in C and A2 it is found at least seven times.[48]

7. ‏אתיבון – התיבון‎.

The third person plural perfect _hafel_ of ‏תוב‎ is spelled with an _alef_ in B, with only one exception; in C, D, A2 it is always spelled with a _he_.[49]

The four exceptions are:

f. 91v,8...........T.A., 631,4
f. 104v,5..........T.A., 702,2
f. 107v,7..........T.A., 723,2 variant to ‏יום המיתה‎.
f. 152,2...........T.A., 1020,1

[48]The spelling ‏כילו‎ appears on:

f. 87v,22,23,25....T.A., 605,5,6,7
f. 137v,8..........T.A., 926,4
f. 148v,17.........T.A., 1004,4
f. 156v,21.........T.A., 1047,4
f. 180,3...........T.A., 1239,7

[49]The occurences of ‏אתיבון‎ in B are:

f. 22,7............T.A, 246,6
f. 28v,3...........T.A., 271,6
f. 28v,26..........T.A., 273,6 variant to ‏מתיבין‎
f. 36,15,18........T.A, 318,2,4,6
f. 44,24...........T.A., 357,5
f. 45,8............T.A., 361,3
f. 53v,18,24,26....T.A., 405,3,7,9 variants to ‏מתיבין‎
f. 54,4,5..........T.A., 406,1,2 variants to ‏מתיבין‎
f. 54,7,8..........T.A., 406,3,5 variants to ‏והא כת/, והכח/‎
f. 54,10...........T.A., 407,1 variant to ‏והא כתי/‎
f. 54,18...........T.A., 407,5 variant to ‏מתיבין והא כת/‎
f. 62,15...........T.A., 449,9
f. 73v,18..........T.A., 518,5
f. 75,6............T.A., 528,8
f. 76,8............T.A., 535,3
f. 76v,6...........T.A., 538,5 variant to ‏והכת/‎
f. 77,19...........T.A., 543,6

8. Forms of the verb אמר with the <u>alef</u> quiescent.

All scribes in Vat. 30 use regularly

declined forms of אמר retaining the <u>alef</u>. How-

ever, the following forms of אמר with the <u>alef</u>

quiescent are very common in the "group," A,C,

D, A2, and A3: תומר, תימר, חמר, דמר (דאמר),

נימר, תימרינה, איתמר, אתמר, ומר (ואמר).[50]

In Scribe B, the form דמר appears once, and

the other forms with <u>alef</u> quiescent are

totally absent.[51]

B. <u>Technical terminology and abbreviations.</u>

1. על אחת כמה וכמה – על אחת כמה ואחת כמה.

A standard conclusion to the קל וחומר

syllogism is the phrase על אחת כמה וכמה which

The only exception in B is התיבון f. 12,3, <u>T.A.</u>,
165,5. In Scribes C, D,and A2 the spelling התיבון appears on:

f. 94v,5...........<u>T.A.</u>, 646,9 variant to אתיבון והכת′
f. 115,24..........<u>T.A.</u>, 777,2 variant to והא כת′
f. 121v,6..........<u>T.A.</u>, 812,7 variant to אתיבון
f. 126v,9..........<u>T.A.</u>, 845,1 variant to אתיבון
f. 157v,18.........<u>T.A.</u>, 1053,5

[50]The forms דמר and חמר occur over thirty times each in
the "group," the other forms less frequently. A few examples
of the less common forms with the alternate reading found in
the London manuscript:

f. 81v,12,13 ולהלך איתמר ... הכה איתמר,   <u>T.A.</u>, 571,3
    הכא את אמ′ ... ולהלך אמ′
f. 83v,18 נימר, <u>T.A.</u>, 584,2 נאמר
f. 187,11   ולהלך אתמר ... הכה אתמר, <u>T.A.</u>, 1258,3
    הכא הוא אומר ... ולהלך הוא אומר
f. 188v,3 ותימרינה <u>T.A.</u>, 1262,5

[51]In B, דמר appears on f. 65v,11, <u>T.A.</u>, 468,5 דאמר.

occurs throughout our manuscript. However, a
variation of this phrase, על אחת כמה ואחת כמה,
is also found in Scribes A, C, D, and A2.[52]
This variation never appears in Scribe B.

2. וגו.

In rabbinic literature, a common sign of
abbreviation of a biblical verse or rabbinic
passage is וגו (an abbreviation of וגומר).
In the section written by Scribe B, covering
seventy-one folios, this abbreviation occurs
only fourteen times. In the material written
by Scribes A, C, D, A2, and A3, covering one
hundred twenty-two folios, וגו is found over
nine hundred times.

3. כולי, כול - גרש - גרש, גרשה.

For the abridgement of larger midrashic
passages, Scribes A, C, D, A2, and A3 generally

---

[52]This variation is found on:

f. 3,25................T.A., 28,1
f. 4,9.................T.A., 30,6
f. 7v,18...............T.A., 42,5
f. 8,21................T.A., 44,1
f. 119,10..............T.A., 799,2
f. 121v,19.............T.A., 812,10
f. 142,18-19...........T.A., 959,7. Here the vari-
    ation appears as על אחת ואחת כ; the word כמה
    was left out by mistake at the end of a line.
f. 144v,20.............T.A., 978,5-6. The variation
    appears here as ואחת כמ', in an abbreviated form.
f. 160v,19.............T.A., 1071, 3 variant to כל שכן.

use the term גרשה or גרש, follwed by a reference to the location of a complete form of the
passage. In B, these terms are never found;
instead, this scribe uses כול/כולי.[53]

4. הדה היא.

    There are many formulas in Bereshit Rabba
which introduce a biblical verse used as a
proof text. The formula הדה היא appears
throughout Vat. 30. In Scribes A, C, D, A2,
and A3 it is never abbreviated; in addition,
the first word, הדה, is usually spelled with
a **he** and not an **alef**. In Scribe B, the
phrase is often abbreviated, but there is no
consistency in the method of abbreviation.
It appears as: הד׳ הי׳, ה׳ה׳, הד׳ היא, הד׳ ה׳,
הדה ה׳, and occasionally in the full form
הדה/הדא היא.

5. היך מה דאת אמר – הכמה דתמר.

    Another introductory formula for a biblical
verse found in Scribes A, C, D, A2, and A3 is

---

[53]See Albeck's list of abridged passages in Vat. 30,
Introduction, p. 108, for all the references. It should
also be noted that Scribe B uses כול twice for the abbreviation of biblical verses:

> f. 25v,5...............T.A., 265,6
> f. 31,12...............T.A., 293,4

    For a full discussion of the meaning and function of
גרש, see Rosenthal, pp. 294ff.

הכמה דתמר or its abbreviated form הכ׳ דת.[54]
Neither of these is used in B; instead, this
scribe employs a formula which is parallel in
meaning: היך מה דאת אמר or its abridged forms,
היך דאת אמר and היך מ׳ ד׳ אמר.[55] Only in a
few cases does the phrase כמה דאת אמר/אמ׳
occur in B.[56]

6. דבר אחר.

Scribes A, C, D, A2, and A3 always use the
abbreviation ד׳א׳ for the formula which intro-
duces another interpretation of the passage
under discussion. Scribe B abbreviates this
formula דב׳ אח׳.

7. פרש׳ – פרשתא – פרשתה.

Scribe A writes out fully the Aramaic word
for chapter, using a _he_ for the definite article. Except for one case, B writes the word
fully and spells it with an _alef_. Scribes C
and A2 usually abbreviate it פרש׳; where the
word is spelled out, no preference is discern-
ible in the use of _alef_ or _he_. Scribes D and

---

[54]For example, see f. 118v, _T.A._, 795-797, where this
formula occurs five times.

[55]This formula occurs for example, on f. 57, _T.A._,
442-424, six times.

[56]For example on f. 81,10, _T.A._, 567,5 variant to
היך דאת אמ׳, not noted by Theodor.

A3 do not contain sufficient examples for a
judgement of their practice to be made.

8. The citation of biblical verses.

As noted above, Scribes A, C, D, A2, and
A3 frequently use וגו when abbreviating a
biblical verse, while B does not. This is not
the only difference between the "group" and B
in citing the Bible. The members of the
"group" tend to cite smaller parts of a verse,
and do not abbreviate any words they cite.
For example: המקרה במים עליותיו וגו.[57]
When they do abbreviate a word, it is usually
the last one in the phrase cited: באשר דבר
מלך שלט׳ וגו.[58] Scribe B quotes much more of
a verse and abbreviates many of the words,
merely giving the first or second letter:
ומפרי העץ אשר בתוך הגן אמ׳ אים לא תא׳ ממ׳ ול׳
חג׳ בו פן תמות.[59]

C. **Characteristic spelling of the names of certain
sages.**

Characteristic spelling of the names of certain
sages is presented here in two columns, one for

---

[57] f. 2v,12, <u>T.A.</u>, 25,4 (Ps. 104,3).

[58] f. 84,6, <u>T.A.</u>, 586,8 (Ecc. 8,4).

[59] f. 13,26, <u>T.A.</u>, 172,4 (Gen. 3,3).

Scribes A, C , D, A2, A3	Scribe B
ר׳ יינ יי, ר׳ יינ י, ר׳ ינ יי	ר׳ ינ יי, ר׳ ינאי
ר׳ יוסי	ר׳ יוסי, ר׳ יוסה
ר׳ יוסי בן חלפתא	ר׳ יוסי ביר חלפתה
ר׳ יוסי בר חלפתה	
ר׳ אלעזר בש׳ ר יוסי בן זימרה	ר׳ לעזר בשם ר׳ יוסי בר זימרה
ר׳ יוסי בן חנינה/חנינא	ר׳ יוסי בן חנינה
ר׳ יוסי בר חנינה/חנינא	
ר׳ יהודה, ר׳ יודה, ר׳ יודה	ר׳ יהודה, ר׳ יודן
ר׳ יהודה בר אלעיי	ר׳ יהודה בירבי אלעאי
ר׳ יודה בירבי אלעאי	
ר׳ יודה בר אלעאי	
ר׳ יודה ביר אלעיי	
ר׳ יהודה בר סימון	ר׳ יהודה ביר סימון
ר׳ יודה בר סימון	ר׳ יודה ביר סימון
ר׳ יודן בר סימון	ר׳ יודה בר סימון
ר׳ אליעזר בנו שלר׳ יוסי הגלילי	ר׳ ליעזר בנו שלר׳ יוסי הגלילי

---

[60]This list represents the most common spelling of names by the various scribes. In some cases it is exclusively the way the name is spelled and in all cases exceptions are so rare as to be insignificant. This list was formed using the names found in Albeck's Register as a guide.

Scribes A, C, D, A2, A3		Scribe B

ר׳ אליעזר . . . . ר׳ ליעזר

ר׳ אלעזר . . . . ר׳ לעזר

ר׳ אלעזר בר שמעון . . . . ר׳ לעזר ביר שמעון

ר׳ אלעזר בן עזריה . . . . ר׳ לעזר בן עזריה

ר׳ חונא, ר׳ הונא . . . . ר׳ חונא, ר׳ חונה

ריש לקיש . . . . ר׳ שמעון בן לקיש

ר׳ פנחס . . . . ר׳ פינחס

רבנן . . . . **ff. 10v-23** רבנן

רבנן, רבנין **ff. 23v-27**

רבנין **ff. 36v-80v**

This list reveals a number of significant patterns. The spelling ביר is used often by the "group," but never by B. The name Yose is often found with a _he_, יוסה in the "group," but never in B.[61] For the sound $\bar{a}$ appearing at the end of a name, the "group" prefers _he_, while in B the

---

[61] For example:

f. 4....................T.A., 30,8
f. 116v................T.A., 785,4
f. 88v.................T.A., 612,1

he and alef are mixed.[62] For the name Yehudah the

"group" uses יהודה and יודה but never יודן, which

is often found in B along with the other names.[63]

In the "group" the alef in the names Elazar and

Eliezar is almost always quiescent, לעזר, ליעזר;

however, in B the alef is usually found, אלעזר,

אליעזר.[64] The het is usually retained by the

"group" in the spelling of חונה, חונא; in B the het

and he appear equally, הונא, חונא. Finally, the

name Simon ben Lakish is never abbreviated by the

"group"; in B it is almost always abbreviated

ריש לקיש.[65]

---

[62]For example, B writes חלפתא, f. 42v, T.A., 349,8; but
the "group" writes חלפתה in all but one case.

f. 4.....................T.A.,	30,3
f. 6.....................T.A.,	36,8
f. 101v..................T.A.,	688,1
f. 115v..................T.A.,	777,4
f. 155...................T.A.,	1038,4
f. 187v..................T.A.,	1259,6

The exception is found in C, חלפתא, 116v, T.A., 784,6.

[63]In Scribe B, the name יודן for יהודה appears on:

f. 16v...................T.A.,	188,2
f. 19v...................T.A.,	234,4
f. 22v...................T.A.,	249,1

[64]This covers all sages with the name Eliezar and
Elazar found in Albeck's Register. In the "group," the name
of the biblical character, Eliezar, is spelled with an alef.

[65]The full name, Simon ben Lakish, appears four times
in B compared to nearly thirty occurences of Resh Lakish. In
the "group," Resh Lakish is found once, f. 141, T.A., 951,3,
where it is added by a later hand in a space containing an
erasure.

Summary and Implications

Which sections of Vat. 30 represent the original spell-ing of Bereshit Rabba?--From the foregoing analysis it appears that Vat. 30 was produced by six scribes whom we have designated A, B, C, D, A2, and A3. In noting the shapes of letters, the layout of the pages and the use of punctuation marks, we have seen that Scribes A, C, A2, and A3 share many common features which distinguish them from Scribe B. Spelling habits, the use of certain technical terminology, and the spelling of names adds support to this division among the scribes. Scribe D has some indi-vidual peculiarities but also much in common with the other members of the "group."[66] This "group," taken as a whole is significantly different in a number of outstanding features from Scribe B.

Most striking about the evidence drawn from our manu-script is the appearance of two seemingly different spelling traditions. Is it possible to discover which of these two traditions is closer to the earliest form of Bereshit Rabba? In order to answer this question, we have to deal briefly with a problem external to Vat. 30: the relation of Bereshit Rabba to the Palestinian Talmud.

---

[66]A curious trait of D is that he frequently writes the name Jacob, יעקוב with a _waw_; while the other scribes in Vat. 30 all have יעקב. See f. 128v,9,13,15,18,21,22, _T.A._, 858-861; f. 142v,13, _T.A._, 963,2; f. 143,6, _T.A._, 965,5.

Scholars have long been in agreement that Bereshit
Rabba is a Palestinian midrash.[67] Disagreement exists however, concerning the nature of the relationship between
Bereshit Rabba and the Palestinian Talmud, since both works
contain similar and sometimes identical material. Zunz,
Frankel and I. H. Weiss argue that Bereshit Rabba used the
Palestinian Talmud directly as a source; Lerner, L. Ginzberg,
and later Albeck, Epstein, and Margulies reject this view
and posit as the source for Bereshit Rabba either an earlier
form of the Palestinian Talmud than our present version or
else lost collections of Agadah.[68] In spite of these differences regarding the literary relationship of the two works,
most scholars have agreed that Bereshit Rabba and the
Palestinian Talmud contain the same Palestinian forms of

---

[67]The most recent summary of the characteristics of all
Palestinian midrashim, including Bereshit Rabba, can be found
in Mordecai Margulies, Midrash Wayyikra Rabba (Jerusalem,
1960), V, Introduction, pp. XIV and XXVII-XXXI.

[68]Zunz, G.V., p. 175; Hadrashot, p. 77. Z. Frankel,
Introductio in Talmud Hierosolymitanum (Breslau, 1870),
pp. 51b-53. I. H. Weiss, Dor Dor We-Dorshaw (New York and
Berlin, 1924), Vol. III, pp. 252-255. M. Lerner, Anlage und
Quellen des Bereshit Rabba (Berlin, 1882), pp. 78-95.
L. Ginzberg, A Commentary, IV (appeared in 1961, arranged and
edited posthumously by David Halivni), p. 150. J. N.Epstein,
Introduction to Amoraitic Literature (Jerusalem, 1962),
pp. 287-290. I am grateful to Dr. Mihaly for referring me
to the comments of Ginzberg and Epstein. For a summary of
the debate, see Albeck, Introduction, pp. 66-84, and more
recently Margulies, Introduction, pp. XVII-XXII. The most
recent contribution has been a thorough but limited study by
Rabbi Edward A. Goldman, Parallel Texts in the Palestinian
Talmud to Genesis Rabba, (Chapters I-V), unpublished Rabbinic
thesis, Hebrew Union College, 1969.

Hebrew and Aramaic.[69] In fact, this similarity of language

has been a prime consideration in determining the pedigree

of manuscripts of Bereshit Rabba: if the language of a

manuscript is close to that found in the Palestinian Talmud,

then the manuscript is more likely to be closer to the

earliest form of Bereshit Rabba.[70] By utilizing the

criterion of language it should become clear whether the

"group" or B is closer to the Palestinian Talmud and thus

to the earliest form of our midrash.

Unfortunately, the printed editions of the Palestinian

Talmud cannot be used for such a comparison. In the course

of transmission, European scribes and printers, intention-

ally or through ignorance, imposed upon the text of the

Palestinian Talmud vocabulary and spelling derived from the

---

[69]Zunz, G.V., p. 176, Hadrashot, p. 77; Herman L.
Strack, Introduction to the Talmud and Midrash, (New York,
1959), p. 217; Albeck, Introduction, p. 96; Margulies,
Introduction, pp. XIV and XXVII-XXXI. Only Theodor seems to
call into question the linguistic similarities of Bereshit
Rabba and the Palestinian Talmud. "Die Ansicht in den G.V.
S. 176,dass B. r. auch in Bezug auf die Sprache . . .'dur-
chaus mit der jerusalemischen Gemara übereinstimmt,' ist nicht
zutreffend. Das Verhältnis zwischen dem Hebräischen und
Aramäischen in j.T. bedarf noch der Feststellung." Theodor,
"Drei unbekannte Paraschas," p. 150, note 2.

[70]The numerous linguistic similarities between the
the London manuscript and the Palestinian Talmud were a prime
factor in Theodor's choice of that manuscript for the basis
of his scientific edition. See Theodor, MGWJ, XXXVII (1893),
206-210 and especially, 208, note 4. However, see also my
previous note, number 69.

more widely known Babylonian Talmud.[71] Only the Geniza
fragments published by Louis Ginzberg and others seem to
preserve the original language and characteristic spelling
of the Palestinian Talmud.[72] Consequently, we may compare
the language of the "group" and Scribe B to the Geniza
fragments with confidence.[73]

The "group" and the Geniza fragments of Berachot share
many of the same distinguishing characteristics: the use of
the circle as a punctuation mark,[74] the spelling אדן [75] and
כילו [76] the preference for the he as the Aramaic definite
article and as a mater lectiones for â,[77] the spelling
ביר,[78] the names יוסה, לעזר, ליעזר,[79] the forms of אמר

---

[71]Louis Ginzberg, A Commentary, Hebrew Introduction,
pp. 39-40.

[72]Yerushalmi Fragments, ed. Louis Ginzberg (New York,
1909). Dr. Kutscher has argued convincingly that these fragments could not have been altered by European scribes and
that they represent most faithfully the original Hebrew and
Aramaic of the Palestinian Academies. "Studies," 2. Other
Geniza fragments of the Palestinian Talmud which have been
published are mentioned by Kutscher (ibid., note 2).

[73]Sokoloff has used the same procedure except that he
has chosen for comparison the Geniza fragments published by
D. S.Levinger in the Alexander Marx Jubilee Volume (New York,
1950), Hebrew Section, pp. 237-286.

[74]Y.F., pp. 2:15, 16, 23, 25; 3:1, 5; 9:25.

[75]Y.F., p. 5:17, 18.

[76]Y.F., p. 3:9.

[77]Y.F., pp. 1:6,11,26,27,28; 2:6,9,12; 3:23; 9:1,9, etc.

[78]Y.F., pp. 1:19,27; 8:15, and others.

[79]Y.F., pp. 1:5,19,27; 3:7; 6:2,3,9,15.

with the _alef_ quiescent: דמר and ותמר,[80] and the unique

ending of the _kal v^ehomer_ כמה כמה ואחת על אחת.[81] The

language and terminology of the "group" and of the

Palestinian Talmud fragments are the same.

Further, these same characteristics also occur in

Geniza palimpsests containing selections from Bereshit Rabba.

For example, in a fragment of an extract of Bereshit Rabba

published by Charles Taylor, we find: אן, הדן, ותמר, אמתיי,

על אחת כמה ואחת כמה, ר יודה ביר אלעיי, ר שמעון בן לקיש,

ר יוסה ביר חלפתה;[82] and in the Lewis-Gibson palimpsests:

רבנן, ביר, ר יוסה בן חנינה, אן, ותמר, Θ, וגו, גרשה, הכ',

דחמר, ר יודה ביר סימון.[83]

The sections of Vat. 30 written by the "group" repre-

sent a form of Bereshit Rabba closest in language and spell-

ing characteristics to the earliest form of the Palestinian

Talmud. These same characteristics have been shown to be

the outstanding signs of Palestinian Aramaic and Hebrew by

Kutscher and others.[84] At least in these external linguistic

---

[80]Y.F., pp. 1:19,26; 3:19,20,21; 9:5; 10:29.

[81]Y.F., p. 4:25,26.

[82]Cairo Geniza Palimpsests, ed. Charles Taylor (Cambridge, 1900), p. 93 and Plate XI.

[83]Palestine Syriac Texts, Plate II, Fragment II and
Plate III, Fragment III.

[84]Kutscher, "Studies," passim, and his comments in
"L'shon Hazal," p. 250. For the use of לעזר and ליעזר in the
Kaufmann Codex of the Mishna and in Palestinian inscriptions
as well as Josephus and the New Testament, see Kutscher,
"L'shon Hazal," pp. 255-256 and Sokoloff, 15-16.

aspects, the "group" (ff. 2-9; 81v,6-193v) appears to
represent the extant form nearest to the original text of
Bereshit Rabba.

CHAPTER IV

THE CRUCIAL QUESTION

Was Vat. 30 copied from more than one exemplar?--The
crucial question must now be raised regarding the composition of Vat. 30: how can we account for the differences between the "group" and Scribe B? Are the distinctive
features noted in the previous section due to habits of the
scribes, or do they reflect differences in the exemplars
from which the various scribes copied?[1] As pointed
out in the review of secondary literature on Vat. 30,
Michael Sokoloff opts for the second possibility. He
writes:[2]

אין להעלות על הדעת שכל כי"ו הועתק מאותו מקור, אלא אם כן
נניח שסופר 2 [=B] או סופר 1 ו- 3 [=the "group"] עשו
ריביזיה שלמה ומכוונת בכתיב. מסתבר יותר שכי"ו שלפנינו
הועתק משני כי"י, דהיינו 1) החלקים שכתבו 1-3; 2) החלקים
שכתב 2.

---

[1]Malechi Martin has a detailed description of scribal
activity in The Scribal Character of the Dead Sea
Scrolls, p. 6. He indicates three primary ways scribes
work: (1) the scribe may "copy his text by eye having beside him the exemplar to be transcribed,"
(2) "he may transcribe his text from dictation," or
(3) "he may transcribe his text from memory." The
assumption in this paper is that the scribes of
Vat. 30 used primarily the first method.

[2]Sokoloff, p. 15.

At first glance this observation seems correct. It
appears unreasonable to think that a scribe would completely
and consistently revise spelling characteristics and
technical terminology while copying a manuscript. Further,
it could be argued that since scribal excellence consists
of copying as accurately as possible, the decisive
factor in determining the spelling of words or the
use of formula must be the exemplar. The decision
of the individual scribe is inconsequential. The
argument might conclude: Scribe B's exemplar had to
be different from the one used by the "group"; the
man B could not be responsible.

It should be pointed out that if such a hypothesis
were confirmed, the position of Vat. 30 in the
development of the text of Bereshit Rabba would have to
be reappraised. Since, on this view, Vat. 30
represents two different spelling traditions, it must also
reflect two separate textual traditions of the
midrash. By implication, those sections copied by the
"group" would contain a significantly better - or
at least more original - text of Bereshit Rabba than
that copied by B. A new pedigree of Bereshit Rabba
manuscripts would have to be constructed in such a
way as to indicate the separate relationship of the
two different parts of Vat. 30 to the original Bereshit
Rabba.

However, this line of reasoning which suggests that Vat. 30 was copied from two different manuscripts is not entirely convincing. Clearly some human being had to be responsible for the special characteristics which distinguish B from the "group": either B himself, the unknown scribe who wrote the exemplar which B copied, or yet an earlier unknown scribe or scribes from whom the exemplar used by B was ultimately derived. To put it another way: since the original spelling of Bereshit Rabba is most clearly represented by the "group," some scribe - either B or his predecessors - must have made a revision while copying a manuscript of this midrash. The probability that the revision was made by B's predecessors is no greater than if it were done by B himself.

Evidence exists which supports the view that Scribe B was responsible for the revision. In the preceding section it was shown that the folios written by B were influenced by the spelling of the Babylonian Talmud. However, judging from all the available evidence, the extent of this influence was restricted. B shows a preference for the *alef* as the Aramaic definite article and spells a number of common words and proper nouns as they are found in the Bavli. On the other hand, he retains many well attested Palestinian characteristics also found in the "group." The clearest example is provided by the spelling of the proper names ציפורין, יוחיי, ינגיי which have not been altered to conform to Babylonian practice, ינאי, יוחאי, ציפורי.[3] As for the technical terminology, the phrase מה דאת אמר היך is not found in the Babylonian Talmud, to my knowledge.[4]

Actually, many words whose spelling is typically Palestinian are to be found in the section of Vat. 30 written by B. The following examples are taken from the list prepared by Sokoloff; the consonental and vocalic changes considered to reflect the Palestinian dialect are based on J. N. Epstein's description of Palestinian spelling found in early Mishna manuscripts.[5]

---

[3]For ציפורי/ציפורין see Kutscher's remarks, "L'šon Hazal," p. 258.

[4]In the Geniza material of Lev. Rabba collected by Margulies, the form כמה דאת אמר is very common. See Margulies, "Fragments of Wayyikra Rabba," in Midrash Wayyikra Rabba, V, p. 13, lines 15, 17, 23. In B this form is found on:

f. 61,20...............T.A., 447,13 variant
f. 62,7................T.A., 449,1 variant
f. 66v,10..............T.A., 474,5 variant
f. 69,7................T.A., 489,5 variant

[5]Sokoloff,pp.6ff;Epstein, Mavo, pp. 1120-1234.

		T.A.	Vat. 30
		p. 178	ב-ו גיועה קומתו
		p. 287	ר׳ חייה בר ווה
		p. 486	נווטי
אפופלסמון	p. 311	p. 257	ב-פ אפובלסמון
		p. 261	ד-ז לוז שיזרה
		p. 161	כ-ק תכשיטין
נתכרכמו	p. 306	p. 185	נתקרקם
		p. 440	דוכסין
		p. 361	ל-ר בור סיף, בול סיף
לידים (C)	p. 795	p. 396	רירם
		p. 236	מ-נ לשם מרדות
		p. 159	ש-ס להתבסם
		p. 450	לסיחתן
		p. 426	סוטמים
		p. 158	א-ע ונתכארה בפניו, נתאכרתי בעיניו
		p. 461	קימאה
		p. 372	ה-י מתהי
		p. 482	שרי

In addition, the spelling of the diphthong ai̯, יי‗, noted
by Sokoloff, is found prominently throughout Scribe B.[6]
From this list it is clear that the section written by B
reflects to a large measure the linguistic phenomena

---

[6]Sokoloff, p. 10.

typical of the Palestinian dialect.[7] Conversely, in the
"group" and in the Geniza fragments of the Palestinian
Talmud and Leviticus Rabba, the alef as the Aramaic definite
article occurs frequently.[8] In this particular detail, B
is merely carrying out with greater consistency a tendency
already prevalent in the linguistically "purer" Palestinian
documents. B's language is certainly not far removed from
the dialect found in the rest of the manuscript.

The hypothesis that B is responsible for revising
his exemplar is also supported by a comparison of similar
passages within Vat. 30. It is well known to students of
rabbinic literature that a single passage of halachic or
aggadic content may be repeated in quite unrelated contexts
or in conjunction with different Biblical verses.[9] Albeck
has catalogued the outstanding reasons for such repetitions
occurring within Bereshit Rabba.[10] For our present

---

[7]Every example cited by Sokoloff, pp. 6-11, which
refers to T.A., pp. 151,7-570,2, belongs to Scribe B. Except
for the cases previously noted, typically Palestinian dialect and spelling phenomena are equally distributed throughout the manuscript. Babylonian influence however, is found
only in B; see Kutscher, "Studies," 20, and the examples
added by Sokoloff, 18, Number 3.

[8]Y.F., p. 9, lines 15 and 17: יומא; Margulies,
"Fragments," especially the Aramaic passages on pp. 82-83,
where the alef is quite prominent; Vat. 30, in the Aramaic
Appendix, Longer Passages of Scribe A, Number 1, and many
places throughout the Longer Passages of C, D, and A2.

[9]Albeck, Untersuchungen uber die hal. Midraschim
(Berlin, 1927), pp. 26ff.

[10]Albeck, Introduction, pp. 1-11.

71

discussion, a sampling (Appendix II) has been made of passages repeated more than once in Bereshit Rabba and found in Vat. 30 in sections written by both B and the "group."[11] These passages have been compared to see if they reflect significantly different textual traditions or if they are different primarily in regard to scribal characteristics.

From the fifteen passages surveyed, the following general conclusion emerges: with two exceptions to be discussed below, no differences exist which are of sufficient magnitude to suggest that the passages were based on differing textual traditions. Most important, all specific differences can be accounted for by individual scribal characteristics, common scribal errors, or by variations which are transmitted in all manuscripts of Bereshit Rabba.[12]

---

[11] The sample passages are found in Appendix II, and are accompanied by a tabulation of differences.

[12] A few examples may be mentioned here. In Sample I (Scribe A, ff. 4v-5, T.A., 32,1-11; Scribe B, f. 24v, T.A., 260,2-12), the differences in scribal characteristics are representative of the basic differences between Scribe B and the "group." Other distinctions may be noticed. The exclamation אתמהא, which occurs three times in A is completely absent in B. This conforms generally to B's practice of eliminating superfluous words and expressions. In addition, B tends to use shorter forms of words and expressions without, of course, changing the meaning of a passage:

	B	A
	בס	בהם
	בה	בתוכה
ומרד		ומרד בו

A good example of a variation transmitted in all of the manuscripts of Bereshit Rabba is found in Sample II

Sample Number 8 is an exception which proves the rule. It

is a proem which appears twice in B and once in C, in each

case with a slight variation in the text.[13] A comparison

with other manuscripts indicates that numerous versions of

this proem existed. Other manuscripts also contain signi-

ficant internal variations of the proem; and in the case

of Vat. 60 the differences are considerably more pronounced

than in Vat. 30.[14] Sample Number 15 is similar in that the

concluding mashal reflects at least two separate textual

traditions in all manuscripts.[15] Conversely, passages

(Scribe B, ff. 12v-13, T.A., 168,5-169,1; Scribe A2, f. 154,
T.A., 1031, 6-1032, 3). The Serpent, after seeing Adam and
Eve copulating, desires to have a sexual experience too. A
variation of possible significance has to do with the object
of the Serpent's desire:

B: ונתאוה להן   A2: נתאוה לה

The reading in B is of interest because it suggests the
Serpent was interested in Adam as well as Eve. However, such
a reading must be rejected on two counts. Rabbinic tradition
gives no other indication of a homosexual tendency in the
Serpent. More important, Vat. 30 and the other manuscripts
of Bereshit Rabba offer numerous examples of the haphazard
interchange of the singular and plural of this pronoun. Regarding the particular passage, the same variation occurs in
nearly all the other manuscripts with the difference that
they read the singular לה in the first citation of the passage and להן in the later repetition. See T.A. and variants.

[13]Sample VIII; Scribe B, f. 30v, T.A., 290, 1-8; Scribe
B, f. 35, T.A., 314, 5-11; Scribe C, f. 84, 585, 8-586,7.

[14]See the variants in T.A. to the passages mentioned in
the previous note. The passage as it appears in Vat. 60 is
found appended to Sample VIII of Appendix II.

[15]Sample XV, Scribe B, ff. 77-77v, T.A., 544, 5-547,2;
Scribe C, ff. 129-129v, T.A., 864,1-865,4. See the variants
in T.A.

repeated only within B often contain differences which are at least as striking as those found in B and the "group";[16] this suggests that an individual scribe may be quite inconsistent in his copying or that an exemplar may contain much diversity. In sum: based on identical passages occurring in B and the "group," it is clear that differences may be ascribed primarily to scribal characteristics. There is no reason for assuming that these reflect the exemplar rather than B himself.

A third argument for the view that B is responsible for revising his exemplar comes from the composition of Vat. 30. It is difficult to explain how the work of B and the "group" could exist side by side, unless a single underlying manuscript is assumed. In the production of Vat. 30, B, who represents a later spelling system, did his work before C, who has the typically Palestinian characteristics. Scribe B stops copying near the end of line 6 on f. 81v; Scribe C completes this line and continues on with the following folios. To assume that B possessed an exemplar reflecting the later system and that another scribe, C, used a manuscript representing the original system, is unreasonable. The scribe and his style are different, the exemplar is the same.

External evidence also supports this view. A manuscript containing the distinctive Palestinian characteristics

---

[16]Three such passages found only in B are attached to Appendix II.

found in the "group" must have once existed for the entire text of Bereshit Rabba, including those portions copied by B. Fragments of Bereshit Rabba found in the Cairo Geniza offer undeniable proof for this assertion. Two of the fragments, previously mentioned, appear in _Palestinian Syriac Texts_, edited by Lewis and Gibson; they are described in Sections XI and XII of the introduction to that volume. The first of the two, Plate II, Fragment II, contains material from Bereshit Rabba, Chapters I and II, T.A., 16, 4-22,4; a section lacking in Vat. 30. This fragment is considerably damaged and difficult to decipher from the photograph. The second fragment, Plate III, Fragment III, is much better preserved. It contains material from the conclusion of Chapter 56 and the beginning of Chapter 57; T.A., 608,12-613,5; in Vat. 30, this section was written by Scribe C, ff. 88 bottom to 88v. A transcription of both plates is found in Appendix III. Variants from Vat. 30 are provided for Plate III; a glance at these variants will reveal that Plate III and Vat. 30 are almost identical.[17]

These two fragments then, represent the kind of exemplar from which the "group" copied. Is there any evidence of the existence of such an exemplar for the sections of Bereshit Rabba which were written by B? A third Geniza fragment is referred to in Theodor's variants on pp. 309-314,

---

[17]For a precise list of Palestinian characteristics of these plates, see the preceding section, p. 64.

and indicated by the letter ז. This fragment covers a passage found in Scribe B; however, it conforms to the usage of the "group," of the Palestinian Talmud, and of the Geniza material just mentioned. In the following examples, one may compare readings from the Geniza fragment cited by Theodor with the text as found in Scribe B:

Variant to:	Geniza Fragment	Scribe B
310,7	ר׳ שמעון בן לקיש	ריש לקיש
310,11	ר׳ יוסה בן חנינה	ר׳ יוסי בר חנינא
312,1	דמר	lacking
312,1	ר׳ יוסה בן חנינה	ר׳ יוסי בר חנינא
313,10	אמ׳ לה	אמ׳ לו
313,10	ר׳ אליעזר ... ר׳ ליעזר	ר׳ אליעזר ... ר׳ אליעזר
314,4	צדיקייה	צדיקייא
315,5	החכמה תעוז לחכם וגו	החכמה תעוז לחכם

Adding this fragment to the two previously mentioned, it is clear that a manuscript of the entire Bereshit Rabba once existed which contained the language and spelling characteristics found in the "group." On the other hand, no evidence exists of a complete manuscript of Bereshit Rabba which has precisely the characteristics found in B. The exemplar underlying all of Vat. 30 contained the Palestinian features. Someone must have altered it in those sections copied by B, and the responsibility seems to lie with B himself.

A plausible explanation of the composite character of Vat. 30 is that it was written in a "scribal factory"

dominated by a single family of scribes.[18] Parts of the
text to be copied were distributed among the scribes and
the finished product was collated by fascicle.[19] The
assumption of a scribal family would help to explain why
four of the sections - those written by A, C, A2, A3 - are
so similar in script and scribal characteristics. Scribe B,
unrelated to the "group," received a portion to copy and
simply revised it in line with spelling practices and
scribal techniques acquired in a different school. Pressing
the "family" image, it appears that Scribe D is a "cousin"
to the "group" and served to complete unfinished passages or
lacunae in the text. This would explain his activity at
the end of a fascicle (ff. 141-145v) and within the section
written by Scribe C (on ff. 107v, 112v, and 128v).

One final point: this hypothesis on the composition
of Vat. 30 implies that the manuscript was copied in one

---

[18]The Cairo Geniza offers ample evidence that members
of the same family were often engaged in the scribal
profession and worked together. See S. D. Goitein,
A Mediterranean Society (Berkeley and Los Angeles, 1967),
Vol I, p. 79.

[19]Rosenthal, Muslim Scholarship, p. 2., remarks that
the origin of the "Western institution of the pecia, ie, the
custom of copying manuscripts in various sections," was the
lack of well trained people who could quickly and accurately
copy manuscripts. He further suggests that in the East this
institution did not develop because of the large number of
well trained scribes, and that rarely was a work parcelled
to more than one copyist. From the evidence collected by
Goitein, it appears that in Jewish circles some collaboration
did occur between scribes in Egypt in the tenth and eleventh
centuries. See note 23 below.

location. Does the manuscript offer enough evidence to
permit us to infer what place that might be? Further, is
the precise origin of the manuscript of great consequence?
As mentioned above, scholars have laid the blame for the
"Babylonianization" of the text of the Palestinian Talmud
upon European scribes who were familiar with the language
of the Babylonian Talmud.[20] Since this process of
"Babylonianization" is also to be found in the text of
Bereshit Rabba, it is possible that Scribe B was a
European.[21] In a masterful work on Jewish communities of
the Arab world, S. D. Goitein has suggested that Egypt became the home of numerous European scribes in the tenth and
eleventh centuries.[22] These scribes worked in close co-
operation with Egyptian scribes of Palestinian ancestry.
Goitein writes: "Thus we may assume that the presence of
scribes from Europe in Egypt was conducive of a fusion of

---

[20]Note the comment by Ginzberg, A Commentary, Hebrew
Introduction, p. 40:

... שהסופרים בארצות איירופא נגררו אחר הכתיב הבבלי שהחליף
ה' בא', אולם בכתבי היד שנכתבו בארצות המזרח לא נתעקרה הה'
ונשארה במקומה.

[21]Similarly, it may be argued that the "group" was
composed of Palestinians who were familiar with the Galilean
dialect and well versed in the Palestinian Talmud.

[22]Goitein, p. 51. On the general question of European
scribes in Egypt, Goitein writes: "A little puzzling is
the frequent presence of Rūm scribes in Egypt throughout
the centuries. Perhaps the reason for this was that the
Egyptian Jews themselves preferred to choose more lucrative
occupations."

styles, which we are able indeed to observe in the Geniza."[23]
Such a fusion of styles is also strikingly exemplified in
Vat. 30; and this fact is more significant than the precise
origin of the manuscript.[24]

Our manuscript is the result of a joint effort of men
with diverse backgrounds and training. It is unique in
containing the original spelling and terminology of Bereshit
Rabba and an early example of the transformation of the
text into a more common linguistic form. In regard to the
latter, responsibility for the spelling changes may be
traced to an individual human being. Scribe B represents

---

[23]Goitein, loc. cit. The full quote is instructive:
"In the Geniza records we see that craftsmen, for various
reasons, at least traveled widely, which cannot have been
without influence on the technique of work and the style
of products. To quote an example from the craft of copyist;
in a letter in a hand of exquisite beauty sent from a little
town in Egypt to Old Cairo, the writer asks the addressee
to have a scribe from Rum living there copy out two squires
and two leaves in order to complete a volume for a customer,
which he himself had been unable to do while in the
capital. It seems highly unlikely that a man who betrayed
such style even in an everyday letter should have
entrusted the completion of a codex written by him to a
fellow copyist whose hand differed very much from his
own. Thus we may assume that the presence of scribes from
Europe in Egypt was conducive to a fusion of styles,
which we are able indeed to observe in the Geniza. The
writer of our letter, as may be gleaned from other details
mentioned in it, seems to have been a Palestinian."

[24]While an airtight case cannot be made for the
provenance of the manuscript, the evidence presented by
Goitein supports the view that Egypt is a likely place of
origin. In any case, the process of transition of
the text of Bereshit Rabba from the original linguistic format to the "common" format of the present
editions is clearly evident in Vat. 30.

79

a broad trend in scribal activity to "modernize" the text being copied, and to bring it in line with the document which became the standard of language and law for most Jews in the Middle Ages, the Babylonian Talmud. Since, however, Scribe B is still so close to the "original," the unity of the textual tradition underlying Vat. 30 is not a matter for significant debate. Clearly there is need for further clarification of particular language details of the manuscript; however, the basic evaluation of the linguistic and midrashic importance of Vat. 30 as a whole by Theodor, Albeck, and Kutscher remains unchallenged.[25]

---

[25]Just as this section was completed, the continuation of Sokoloff's article reached me. His presentation is restricted to linguistic details and does not deal further with the composition of the manuscript. See Lešonenu, Vol. XXXIII, Number 2-3, January - April, 1969, pp. 135-149 (pp. 19-33 of offprint.) A third installment is promised. In an article just published, Dr. Kutscher gives the clearest statement of his view on the linguistic changes in Palestinian texts: He states that scribes and printers "systematically corrected the language of the texts . . . in order to bring them closer to Biblical Hebrew and to the Aramaic of Targum Onkelos and the Babylonian Talmud." Yehezkel Kutscher, "Articulation of the vowels u, i in Galilean Aramaic and Mishnaic Hebrew transcriptions of Biblical Hebrew," Benjamin De Vries Memorial Volume, ed. E. Z. Melamed (Jerusalem, 1968) p. 229; and see note 42 there. In light of what has been said, Vat. 30 becomes a prime witness for the "systematic" changes executed by the scribes.

CHAPTER V

THE RELATIONSHIP OF VAT. 30 TO
THE OTHER EARLY WITNESSES

General Considerations

In discussing basic notions of textual criticism,
Paul Maas writes, "The business of textual criticism is to
produce a text as close as possible to the original."[1] The
task of reconstructing "a text as close as possible" to the
original Bereshit Rabba, however, is exceedingly difficult.
We do not have basic information about the origin of the
document.[2] Who produced it? Was it a man or a group of
men?[3] Was this man (or men) a creative author or merely a
mechanical compiler, or was he a combination of both?[4] Without such information, statements concerning the intention

---

[1]Paul Maas, Textual Criticism (Oxford, 1958), p. 1.

[2]In his Introduction, pp. 93-96, Albeck deals primarily
with the name of the midrash and the date of its composition.

[3]For arguments on why R. Hoshayah could not have been
the author of Bereshit Rabba, see T.A., p. 1, note 1, and
Albeck, Introduction, p. 94.

[4]H. Freedman, in the Introduction to his translation
of Bereshit Rabba, suggests that the midrash was "edited."
This term is not particularly useful since we still do not
know who wrote or compiled the material which an unknown
editor may have edited. H. Freedman, Midrash Rabba (London,
1939), Genesis I, p. XXIX.

of the author-compiler or the purpose of the document must remain speculative. Similarly, arguments in favor of a particular textual reading can be justified only by recourse to the manuscripts themselves rather than to basic notions of an author's outlook or style.[5]

The second difficulty in establishing the "original" stems from the flexibility of scribes in copying the text of Bereshit Rabba. In contrast to the rigidly prescribed rules for copying the Bible, no standards existed for copying rabbinic documents.[6] Scribes changed or added to the text almost at will.[7] In addition, the scribes of some manuscripts other than Vat. 30 alternated from one exemplar to another while copying (contamination).[8] Contamination of the textual tradition makes it nearly impossible to construct a reliable pedigree for the manuscripts of Bereshit Rabba.[9]

Nevertheless, some guidelines exist for reconstructing "a text as close as possible to the original." Lerner and

---

[5]The importance of mastering an author's style is stressed by Maas, pp. 10 and 14.

[6]Lutski, "Introduction," p. 72 in Finkelstein, Sifra or Torat Kohanim.

[7]Changes of spelling and style have already been demonstrated within Vat. 30 itself, in the work of Scribe B.

[8]For example, the Munich manuscript was copied in part from an exemplar similar to the Paris manuscript; Oxford manuscript #2 was copied in part from an exemplar similar to Oxford manuscript #1 and in part from the Venice edition. See Albeck, Introduction, p. 137.

[9]Maas, p. 7.

Albeck have shown that this midrash utilized written documents for source material.[10] Albeck accurately described
Bereshit Rabba as an exegetical midrash, the majority of
whose chapters commence with one or more proems.[11] Finally,
Kutscher and others have revealed what the original language
of Bereshit Rabba must have been.[12]

On the basis of these guidelines, literary and linguistic, it is evident that the judgement first pronounced by
Theodor and confirmed by Albeck remains essentially correct:
Vat. 30 alone reflects the archetype of Bereshit Rabba manuscripts.[13] All other manuscripts are descended from a later
form of the midrash. They testify to an important split in
the tradition in which original material from Chapters
95 - 97 and elsewhere disappeared. The gaps left by these
chapters were later filled with selections taken primarily
from the Tanchuma.[14] Even Vat. 60, which may predate Vat.
30 by a century or more, represents the later version.[15]
While it does not contain the added Tanchuma material, it

---

[10]See Chapter III, note 68. Although our midrash preserves material which may have been oral originally, there
is no evidence that an "oral" Bereshit Rabba ever existed.

[11]Albeck, Introduction, pp. 1-18.

[12]For the literature, see Chapter III, note 29.

[13]See Chapter I, notes 17, 18, and 21.

[14]Ibid., note 19.

[15]Cassuto, p. 87, dates this codex c. 10th century.

lacks the original Chapters 95 - 97, the concluding Chapters 98 - 101, and the passage from Vat. 30 at the end of Chapter 94. Consequently, Vat. 60 is a witness to the earliest form of the midrash after the split occurred, but before the additions were brought into the tradition.

From a linguistic perspective also, Vat. 30 represents the earliest form of the midrash. Kutscher has shown that the Aramaic of Vat. 30 is less altered and therefore closer to the original than the Aramaic of the London manuscript; Scribe B's revisions do not change that view appreciably.[16] In general, Vat. 30 contains a significantly larger number of Palestinian dialect and spelling features than any of the other manuscripts.[17] The criterion of language is also helpful in evaluating fragments, abstracts, and citations of Bereshit Rabba. The mere fact that a fragment was found in the Cairo Geniza is not an automatic guarantee of its date or textual significance.[18] For example, many of the characteristics of the "group" are found in the Lewis-Gibson fragment, and in the Taylor Palimpsest; to these, the fragments published by Ephraim Levine and later by Albeck may

---

[16]Kutscher, "Studies," pp. 8-10.

[17]Theodor listed numerous Palestinian examples from the London manuscript, but they are much less frequent than in Vat. 30. See Chapter I, note 8, for the reference.

[18]The Geniza documents cover a period of at least five hundred years; see Goitein, pp. 1-28 and especially p. 9 where he mentions a "bill of divorce made out in Bombay as late as 1879" which was deposited in the Geniza.

be added.[19] On the other hand, the Adler collection of the
Jewish Theological Seminary contains Geniza fragments which
reflect the language of the later manuscripts.[20]

From the literary and linguistic evidence relating to
Vat. 30, it is clear that the diagram of Bereshit Rabba
manuscripts constructed by Albeck should be modified.[21]
In his diagram, Albeck does not properly represent his own
statement that "from an exemplar like this [Vat. 30] , the
other manuscripts separated into three branches."[22] Instead, he shows two main branches descended from the original
Bereshit Rabba, one represented by Vat. 30, and the other
by the Paris and Munich manuscripts. In addition, Vat. 60
was unknown to both Theodor and Albeck and its position is
consequently not indicated.[23] Finally, the diagram claims

---

[19]Ephraim Levine, "A Geniza Fragment of Genesis Rabba,"
JQR, XX (1908), 777-783; Albeck, Register, pp. 146-150.

[20]I am indebted to Dr. Menahem Schmelzer, Librarian of
the Jewish Theological Seminary, for permitting me to examine
Geniza fragments of Bereshit Rabba from the Adler collection.
From a cursory examination, it appears that the bulk of the
fragments, covering material from Chapters 28-29, is in a
rabbinic hand. One leaf is in the square script and contains
a section of Chapter 1,3 and Chapter 4,4. In the latter is
found, for example, the word בורייא, see T.A., 27, variants
to lines 9-10 and my samples, Chapter IV, f. 3, lines 21 and
23 and variants.

[21]Albeck, Introduction, p. 137.

[22]Albeck, Introduction, p. 137.

[23]The neglect of Vat. 60 is somewhat surprising in that
it is listed in Assemani and correctly identified there
(p. 46). In addition to the omission of Vat. 60, the position of the Geniza fragments is also not indicated in the
diagram. In reconstructing the original text of Bereshit
Rabba, Geniza fragments with Palestinian characteristics are
preferable to Vat. 30, especially in those parts written by
Scribe B.

to represent the pedigree of the manuscripts. Because of the liberty taken by scribes in copying the text, manuscript contamination makes it impossible to construct an accurate pedigree.[24]

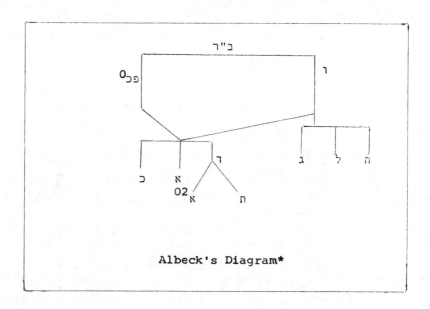

Albeck's Diagram*

*(The manuscripts are referred to hereafter according to the designation given them by Theodor and Albeck: Vat. 30, (ו); Vat. 60, (²ו); London, (ל); Stuttgart, (ג); Paris, (פ); Munich, (כ); Oxford, (א); Constantinople edition, (¹ד); Venice edition, (²ד); Midrash Hahamim, (ח); Yemen, (ת); Geniza Fragments, (ז)).[25]

---

[24]See note 9 above.

[25]For the full reference to each manuscript, see T.A., "Table of Signs in the Variant Readings," preceding p. 1, and Albeck, Introduction, pp. 105-136. Kutscher designated Vat. 60 as ²ו.

The diagram I am presenting here is not intended to
indicate the pedigree of the manuscripts. Rather, it suggests in a general way the relationship of the manuscripts
to each other. Manuscripts ת,ח,ד,א,כ,פ,ג,ל, contain additional material and lack original passages.[26] Each has
distinct scribal and linguistic characteristics.[27] Some
of the manuscripts share more characteristics and additional
material in common than others. This permits us to place
the manuscripts in groups, and retain Albeck's basic organ-
ization.[28] The first editions (ד) contain both the
additions and original material from the concluding chapters
of Bereshit Rabba. Consequently, one must assume the transmission of the original material directly from a Vat. 30
type exemplar.[29] This assumption would also explain the
existence of the original Chapters 95 - 97, albeit in a

---

[26]For the additions not found in Vat. 30, see above,
Chapter 2, p. 19.

[27]Albeck has briefly listed the distinctive characteristics of each manuscript in his Introduction, pp. 104ff.

[28]Common features must be divided into two parts:
scribal characteristics and additional material. When one
manuscript was copied in part from an exemplar similar to
another, as in the case of the Paris and Munich manuscripts,
then these should naturally be joined by a connecting line.

[29]Printers were responsible for the combination of
the original material and the additions in the first edition.
Only the Yemenite manuscript contains them in combination,
and it was copied from the Venice edition.

revised form, in the Midrash Haggadol.[30]   In the diagram
this transmission is represented by a broken line.

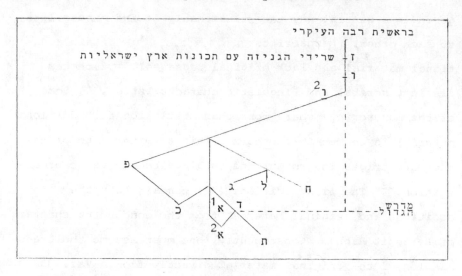

Although Vat. 30 as a whole represents the <u>archetype</u>
of the original Bereshit Rabba, there is no reason to
expect that every letter, word, or phrase mirrors the
original.[31]   Five centuries intervened between the creation
of Bereshit Rabba and the composition of Vat. 30. During
that period mistakes due to scribal error or ignorance

---

[30]See Albeck, <u>Introduction</u>, p. 108. For a discussion
of the methodology of the author of the Midrash Haggadol
in revising his source material, see <u>Mekhilta D'Rabbi Sim'on
b. Jochai</u>, ed. J. N. Epstein and E. Z. Melamed, (Jerusalem,
1955), Introduction, pp. 47ff.; a concise English summary
of the relevant material appears in an article by Dr. Eugene
Mihaly, "A Rabbinic Defense of the Election of Israel,"
<u>HUCA</u>, XXXV (1964), pp. 137-140.

[31]However, on the importance of the <u>archetype</u>, see
Maas, pp. 2-3.

entered the exemplars from which Vat. 30 itself was ultimately descended. In addition, scribes may have made some
minor alterations in the text, to clarify a difficult reading, or to reword a passage to fit contemporary linguistic
usage. The other manuscripts of Bereshit Rabba are needed
to reconstruct the text of the original where Vat. 30 is
damaged, lacking or incorrect, and to set the record
straight where a reading from Vat. 30 has been questioned.
The relationship of the other manuscripts to each other is
useful in describing the later development of the text as
a whole and in establishing the text and versions of the
major additions which do not appear in Vat. 30.

Examples

Suspected readings.--In his Introduction, Albeck lists
three passages from Vat. 30 which he considers to be additions (pp. 608,2; 779,4; 1180-1183), and two more which are
possible additions (pp. 186,7; 872,3).[32] Elsewhere in the
Introduction, he expresses hesitation about one of these
passages, pp. 1180-1183, and is unsure whether it is an
addition or from the original Bereshit Rabba.[33] Since no
new material containing that passage has been discovered,

---

[32]Albeck, Introduction, p. 108.

[33]Ibid., p. 104. He writes: וספק הוא אם המאמרים האלו
נוספו בכי"ו ובדפוסים ואינם מב"ר, או שהם מב"ר ונשמטו בשאר הכי"י.

89

such doubts cannot be resolved.[34] However, new manuscript
material is available to the other four. With the broader
perspective which the new evidence offers, it is possible
to test the adequacy of Albeck's judgement.

Example 1.--Vat. 30, ff. 88,23-88v,9 to T.A., 608,11-
610,2.

ויקרא מלאך יי אל אברהם שניה וגו ויאמר בי נשבעתי מה

צורך היה לאותה השבועה אמ לו השבע לי שאין את מנשה

אותי ואת יצחק בני לאחר שישוור את אגום והשביר את

בנו עמו ד׳ א׳ מה צורך לשבועה הזאת ר לוי בשם ר חמא ביר

חנינה אמ לו השבע לו שאין מנסה אותי עוד מעתה למלך   א

שהיה נשאוי למטרונה ילדה ממנו בן שיני וגרשה שיני   א

וגרשה שלישי וגרשה וכיון שילדה ממנו בן עשירי נתכסו

כולם ואמרו לו השבע לנו שאין את מגרש את אימינו עוד

מעתה כך כיון שנתנסה אברהם ניסיון עשירי אמ לו השבע

לי שאין את מנסה אותי עוד מעתה אמ ר חנין כי יען אשר

עשית את הדבר הזה אלא זה נס האחרון שהוא שקול כנגד

הכל שאילולי שקיבל עליו נס הזה האחרון איבד את כל מה

שעשה   θ

The suspect passage is:

לאחר שישוור את אגום והשביר את בנו עמו

However, it is also found in

1. Lewis-Gibson, Plate III, Fragment III:

לאחד שישוור את אגוס והשביר את בנו עימו

---

[34]It should be noted, however, that this passage from
Vat. 30 is of a piece linguistically with the rest of the
manuscript. Kutscher published a section of it, the story
of Serah b. Asher, among his examples of Galilean Aramaic
in Rosenthal, An Aramaic Handbook, I/1, p.67.

2. Vat. 60:

לאחד ששוור את אגום והישוור אה בנו עימו

and in a later, expanded form in

3. the Constantinople edition:

משל לאחד ששוור את אגינו שבולת נהר והקפיץ גם בנו עמו

4. the Venice edition:

משל לאחד ששמר את אגינו שבולת נהר והקפיץ גם בנו עמו

It is not found in the other manuscripts.

By comparing manuscripts and utilizing linguistic
tools, it is possible to establish the "original" mašal and
to understand its function in the context of the total passage. In Vat. 30, 60, and the Geniza fragment, the abbreviated introduction to a mašal is used, merely the preposition
ל; the printed editions quote the fuller formula: Mašal
l. . . . .[35] In Vat. 30, the reš in לאחר should be amended
to daleth לאחד.[36] In the reading שישוור of Vat. 30 and the
fragment, the yod is a mater lectiones for segol; the form
is kal, third person masculine singular perfect, šwwr, "to
leap," and agrees with Vat. 60 and the Constantinople

---

[35]In general, Vat. 30 uses the shortened form while
the later manuscripts and editions use the fuller formula.
For examples, see the variants to T.A., 280,8; 365,6; 401,5;
681,10; 1005,1. The complete formula was probably משל למה
הדבר דומה ל ..., which is not common in the manuscripts;
however, see T.A., 159,7-8, where it appears in the London
manuscript and the editions, but not Vat. 30.

[36]The reš and the daleth are often indistinguishable
in the manuscripts. This confusion has a long history and
may be found even in ancient Aramaic inscriptions.

91

edition.[37]   In the Venice edition, **šmr** is a printer's error;
it has been transmitted in all subsequent editions.[38]   In the
fragment, אגוס should be corrected to read with Vat. 30 and
60 אגוס; **samekh** and final **mem** are often indistinguishable in
the manuscripts.   To my knowledge, neither אגום nor אגינו of
the printed editions has been satisfactorily explained.[39]   In
the editions, שבולת הנהר, "the current of the river," is an
interpretation of the preceding word אגינו, and may be close
to the original meaning.   A possible origin of אגינו/אגום is
the Greek, $\alpha\gamma\omega\gamma os$ "an aquaduct"; this word is also found in
Syriac, ܐ meaning "a water course," "canal," and "aqua-
duct."[40]   The root of **hšbyr** is also **šwwr**; the interchange of
waw and **bet** is typical in Palestinian orthography and is
concretely reflected in the fragment where a **waw** is placed
above the **bet**.[41]   In the editions, **hqpyz** is commonly

---

[37]See the root **šwwr** in Jacob Levy, Neuhebräisches und
Caldäisches Wörterbuch (Leipzig, 1889), IV, p. 524 and
Marcus Jastrow, A Dictionary (reprinted New York, 1950),
p. 1530. This root is also well attested in Syriac, J. Payne
Smith, A Compendious Syriac Dictionary (Oxford, 1903), p.568.
It is not found in Hebrew. Our **mašal**, however, is entirely
in Hebrew, the Aramaic root having been Hebraised. The process of transforming or translating Aramaic into Hebrew in
the manuscripts of Bereshit Rabba has not been studied; it
seems to parallel the general tendency to "modernize" the text.

[38]This error accounts for some of the unusual interpretations of the **mašal** offered by the commentators.

[39]See the previous note and T.A., 608, note to line 12.

[40]Henry George Liddell and Robert Scott, A Greek-
English Lexicon (Oxford, 1968), p. 18; Payne Smith. p. 3.

[41]See also Kutscher, "Researches," p. 10; Sokoloff, p.
6; and Epstein, Mavo, pp. 1223-1226.

recognized synonym of hšbyr.[42] Thus the original reading
is to be rendered: "This may be compared to one who has
leapt over an aquaduct (or canal) and made his son leap
with him."[43]

Understood in this way, the mašal fits perfectly the
sense and the structure of the comment to Gen. 22,15-16.
These verses appear at the conclusion of the Aqedah story.
The rabbis consider the oath mentioned in Gen. 22,16 to
be superfluous and seek its non-explicit implications.
In the first interpretation, Abraham asks God not to test
"me or my son Isaac." The mašal quoted above offers a
concrete image of a man saving himself and his son. In
the second interpretation, Abraham asks God to promise
that "you are not going to test me again from now on."
Again a mašal is brought which suggests that the trial
just completed was the last in a long series; Abraham had
had enough. Consequently, the passage may be seen as a
whole composed of two main parts with the same formal
features: the   question,   the   demand,   and   the   mašal.[44]

---

[42]See Levy, IV, p. 356 and Jastrow, p. 1403, where
this example is cited.

[43]Other rabbinic passages where šwwr is used in the
sense of "leaping" into or over a river are Talmud Bavli,
B.M. 84a and Shabbat 110a.

[44]The concluding statement of R. Hanin merely emphasizes that this last trial was the most decisive of all
and validated the previous experiences.

The text as contained in Vat. 30, 60, and the fragment
is not without error.[45] Nevertheless, these manuscripts
reflect the original version of the passage. They permit
us to understand the changes which entered the text in the
course of transmission. Scribes who did not understand the
first mašal simply excluded it from the other manuscripts.
Manuscripts גא[21] omit the first interpretation entirely,
and א[2] improperly utilizes Abraham's first demand to commence the passage. In the printed editions, a composite
demand opens the first interpretation:

השבע לי שאין את מנסה אותי מעתה ולא את יצחק בני

while the second interpretation preserves the proper text.

Example 2.--Vat. 30, f. 115v,10-18 to T.A., 778,6-
779,4.   ⊖   ויפגע במקום

צלי במקום צלי אמ ר יהושע בן לוי האבות הראשונים התקינו
שלש תפילות אברהם התקין תפילת השחר שנ' וישכם אברהם
בבקר אל המקום   ואין עמידה אלא תפילה הכ' דת' ויעמד
פינחס ויפלל ותעצ המגפה   יצחק תיקן תפילה שלמנחה ויצא יצ
לשוח וגו ואין שיחה אלא תפילה שנ' תפילה לעני כי יעטף וכך
הוא או ערב ובקר וצהרים וגו   יעקב התקין הפילה שלערבית
שנ ויפגע במקום ואין פגיעה אלא תפילה שנ ואתה אל תתפלל
בעד העם הזה וגו וכן הוא או ואם נביאים הם ואם יש דבר יי וג

The suspect passage is a biblical verse, Jer. 27,18:

.וכן הוא או' ואם נביאים הם ואם יש דבר יי וג'

---

[45]The following emendations should be made:
:ילדה ממנו בן שיני (3 .השבע לי: השבע לו (2 .לאחר: לאחד (1
.ילדה ממנו בן ראשון. (4 נתכסו: נתכנסו.

94

But it is also found in:

1. Vat. 60,

אם נביאים הם ואם יש דבר יי אתם יפגעו נא ביי צב'

2. the Constantinople edition,

וכן הוא אומ' ואם נביאים הם ואם יש דבר וגו

3. and the Venice edition,

וכן הוא אומר ואם נביאים הם ואם יש דבר יי אתם יפגעו נא
ביי צבאות

In Vat. 30, 60, and the editions, Jer. 27,18 is
quoted in the context of a comment on ויפגע במקום in Gen.
28,11. These words provide a pretext for the citation of
various traditions explaining the origin of the three
daily prayer services. The opening tradition traces
the institution of these prayers to the Patriarchs and
specifically the evening service to Jacob. For the Jacob
example, proof is brought from Jer. 7,16 and 27,18 in which
the root פגע is found to mean התפלל, "to pray."
This meaning is applied to ויפגע in the Genesis verse,
and the following word מקום is taken as a designation
of God. Thus Gen. 28,11 is translated midrashically, "And
Jacob prayed to the All-present One."

Since Jer. 7,16 clearly provides proof for the meaning of ויפגע , why cite additional support from Jer.27,18?
Is there any further nuance or association which this second
verse conveys? Questions such as these and the omission of
Jer. 27,18 from other manuscripts of Bereshit Rabba must

have led Albeck to conclude that the verse was a later addition. In this case, the fact that Vat. 60 also contains the suspected reading might only signify that the verse was added soon after the completion of Bereshit Rabba.

A solution to the problem may be provided by an analysis of the parallels to our passage cited by Theodor.[46]

Bab. Tal., Berachot 26b	Pal. Tal., Berachot 7a
... ר׳ יוסי ב"ר חנינא אמר	רבי יב"ל אמר
תפילות אבות תקנום	תפילות מאבות למדום
... יעקב תקן תפלת ערבית	... תפילת ערב מיעקב אבינו
שנאמר ויפגע במקום וילן שם	ויפגע במקום וילן שם
ואין פגיעה אלא תפילה	ואין פגיעה אלא תפילה
שנאמר אל תתפלל בעד	כמה דתימר יפגעו נא
העם הזה ואל תשא בעדם	בה׳ צבאות. ואומר אל
רנה ותפלה ואל תפגע בי.	תשא בעדם רינה ותפילה
	ואל תפגעו בי

In his Commentary, Ginzberg examines the terminology of these parallels and argues convincingly that the version of the Palestinian Talmud was earlier than that of the Bavli.[47] He also notes that the versions in Bereshit Rabba and the Bavli are almost identical but quite distinct from the Palestinian Talmud.[48]

In two significant points, however, Bereshit Rabba is closer to the Palestinian Talmud than to the Bavli: the

---

[46]T.A., 778, parallels to lines 6, and 779, parallels to line 4.

[47]Ginzberg, A Commentary, p. 24 : ... ונוסח הוא ברור ... המקורי הוא בירושלמי זו הגדה.

[48]Ibid.

name of the sage to whom the passage is attributed, and the
proof-texts cited in the example dealing with Jacob. Both
the Palestinian Talmud and Bereshit Rabba quote the passage
in the name of R. Joshua b. Levi, while the Bavli ascribes
it to R. Joshua b. Hanina. Ginzberg notes the difficulties
in determining precisely who the author was, but suggests
that the tradition of the Palestinian documents is correct.[49]
The second area of agreement between the Palestinian Talmud
and Bereshit Rabba as transmitted by Vat. 30, 60, and the
editions is that both cite Jer. 7,16 and 27,18. However,
the Palestinian Talmud reverses the order and uses Jer. 27,
18 as the primary proof-text instead of Jer. 7,16.

Because of the differences between the Palestinian
Talmud and Bereshit Rabba, it cannot be argued that the
former, as we now have it, served directly as the source for
Bereshit Rabba.[50] On the other hand, the transmission of
the author's name and the two proof-texts preserved in Vat.
30, 60, and the editions suggests that these manuscripts
have retained significant features of the original passage.
If another rabbinic source could be found which also contained the two proof texts, there would be additional
confirmation that these three manuscripts contain a unique

---

[49] Ibid.

[50] For the problem of the relationship between Bereshit
Rabba and the Palestinian Talmud in gereral, see the references in Chapter III, note 68.

transmission of original details.

Such a source does exist. Both Jeremiah verses appear in an anonymous comment to Ex. 14,10 in the Mekilta.[51] The Mekilta mentions that when the Israelites at the Red Sea "cried out unto the Lord," they "seized the occupation of their fathers" in praying for help. The example of Jacob, Gen. 28,11 (supported by Jer. 7,16 and 27,18), is the third illustration showing that the Patriarchs prayed. If the Mekilta is a Tannaitic midrash, as most scholars think, then the use of the two Jeremiah verses in association with Gen. 28,11 precedes the Palestinian Talmud; if the Mekilta is a "post-talmudic compilation," as has recently been suggested, then it attests to a tradition already in existence by the 7th century A. D.[52] In either case, the problem is no longer whether Jer. 27,18 is a late addition in Vat. 30. The use of this verse in the Palestinian Talmud and the Mekilta obviates such a judgement. A more difficult and perhaps unanswerable question is, why do Vat. 30, 60, and the editions utilize

_____

[51]Jacob Z. Lauterbach, ed., Mekilta (Philadelphia, 1949), I, pp. 206-207; H. S. Horovitz, and I. A. Rabin, editors, Mechilta D'Rabbi Ismael (Jerusalem. 1960), p. 92. However, see also M. Friedmann (Meir Ish Shalom), ed., Sifre (Vienna, 1864), p. 70b; Bavli Sota 14a; Bavli Sanhedrin 95b; and Bavli Ta'anit 7b; where the proof that פגיעה means תפלה is Jer. 7,16 only.

[52]Ben Zion Wacholder, "The Date of The Mekilta De-Rabbi Ishmael," HUCA,XXXIX (1968), p. 117, note 1, and p. 118.

the Bavli form of the passage while preserving these few
original details?[53]

Example 3.--Vat. 30, f. 16,19-26 to T.A., 186,4-8.

The entire passage corresponding to T.A., 186,4-8 from
Vat. 30 is presented here; it is a comment on Gen. 3,14.
The words in brackets were added by a later hand in spaces
left by Scribe B.

על גחנך תלך בשעה שאמ לו הקבה על גחונך תלך ירדו
מלאכי שרת וקצצו ידיו ורגליו והיה קולו הולך מסוף העולם ועד סופו
בא נחש ללמד על חילתה שלבבל ונמצא למד ממנה קולה כנחש ילך
[ר יודן ור חונא חד מנהן א] אתה נדמיתה לבריותיי שיהיו [מהלכין]
גיחוניהם על מיתיהם כך אף אתה על גחנך תלך ואחרין אומ את גרמת
לבריותי שיהיו מיעיהן על כתיהם כך אף את על גחנך תלך [אמ ר אלעזר]
[אף קללתו שלהקבה יש בה ברכה אילו שאמ לו הקבה על גחנך תלך היאך]
היה בורח לכותל וניצול לחור וניצול

The line in question is:

ואחרין אומ אה גרמת לבריותי שיהיו מיעיהן על מתיהם כך אף את על
גחנך תלך

It appears in a comment to Gen. 3,14 treating the
significance of God's punishment of the Serpent by making
him crawl on his belly. The line also is found in Vat. 60
and the Munich manuscript.[54] In Vat. 60, however, it has

_____

[53]The answer given by Ginzberg (A Commentary, p. 24),
that the "way of the aggadah was 'to be fruitful and multi-
ply,'" does not add to our understanding of the literary
development of particular aggadic passages.

[54]I was unable to obtain a copy of the Munich manuscript and had to rely on Theodor's variants for this passage.

been added between the lines and in the margin by the original scribe of the manuscript and not by a later hand. The
gloss was probably copied from an exemplar other than the
one used for the manuscript as a whole.

From the formula by which the suspected line from Vat.
30 is introduced and from a close analysis of the wording,
it is possible to determine the function of the line in the
passage as a whole. The line is quoted as the second of two
differing opinions in a controversy between R. Yudan and
R. Huna. Preceding the first opinion is a typical introduction indicating that a controversy between the two sages
is to follow: ר׳ יודן ור׳ הונא חד מנהון אמר (T.A., 186,7).
However, only in Vat. 30, 60, and the Munich manuscript
does the second opinion actually appear. The absence of
the expected continuation in the other manuscripts and the
editions caused Theodor to remark, "It seems that a complete passage is lacking here."[55] Is the suspected passage
in Vat. 30 the original second opinion?

Unfortunately, the introductory words of the line as
it is found in Vat. 30 do not conform to the expected
patterns of these controversies. The usual formulations are:

חד מנהון א׳ (חד א׳) ... וחד מנהון א׳ (וחד א׳)
חד מנהון א׳ (חד א׳) ... ואוחרן א׳ (וחורן א׳)

Instead, in Vat. 30, אחרין appears to be plural,

---

[55]T.A., 186, note 7.

"others."[56] The verb which follows, אומ׳, may also have

been abbreviated from the plural אומרין; in addition, it is

Hebrew rather than Aramaic.

Even more serious than the problem of these intro-

ductory words is the fact that the reading in Vat. 30 is

incomplete. A syntactical comparison of the first and the

second opinions in the controversy suggests that the second

opinion is lacking a verb:

1. <u>T.A.</u>, 186,67:

אתה גרמתה לביריותיי שיהו מהלכים גחונים על מיתיהם

2. Vat. 30:

על מתיהם [   ] שיהיו מיעיהן לבריותי גרמת את

The first opinion states that the Serpent was forced to

walk on his belly (גחונך) because he caused people to "go

bent" (מהלכים גחונים) in sorrow over their dead. In the

second opinion, the word מיעיהן, "their intestines" or

"their bowels,"is linked midrashically with "belly" (גחון).

However, because no verb appears in connection with מיעיהן,

it has not been possible to derive the precise meaning of

the sentence.

These difficulties of the Vat. 30 reading can now

be dismissed because of the previously unknown gloss in

---

[56]The precise form of the pronoun is not completely
decisive since numerous alternate forms may appear in
Jewish Palestinian Aramaic. See Rosenthal, <u>An Aramaic
Handbook</u>, I/2, p. 53.

Vat. 60. The full text in Vat. 60 reads:[57]

וחוריה א׳ את גרמת לבירויתיי שיהיו מיעיהן מִתַעַנִין עַל מיתיהן אף
אַת על גחונך תלך

Here the introductory formula is in the singular and in
Aramaic; more important, the missing verb appears. The root
of מתענין is ענה; in <u>hitpael</u> it has the meaning "to be
afflicted, to suffer."[58] Consequently, the passage should
be translated, "And the other said, 'You caused my creatures'
bowels to be afflicted over their dead, (thus) you shall
crawl on your belly.'" In this complete form the line contains a suitable comment to Gen. 3,14 and offers an appropriate contrast to the image projected in the first opinion
of the controversy. Since the corrected line fulfills
formal expectations and conceptual needs, there is no longer
any reason to doubt that Vat. 30, as corrected by Vat. 60,
echoes the reading of the original Bereshit Rabba.

In addition to the line which Albeck questioned, it
should be noted that the entire comment on Gen. 3,14 in
Vat. 30 is problematic. Textual difficulties are found
even in the first opinion of this controversy. The word

---

[57]This gloss was exceedingly difficult to read from
the Xerox copy of the manuscript. A close examination of
the microfilm brought the full reading to light. The first
two letters of מְתַעַנִין are dotted because they were written
in the binding of the manuscript and remain almost illegible;
nevertheless, enough of their shape is distinguishable to
make this reading a certainty.

[58]Jastrow, p. 1093, Levy, III, p. 669.

גרמתה has been corrupted to נדמיתה because of the similarity of נ-ג and of ר-ד; גחונים has been contaminated by the
adjoining word מיתיהם to read גיחוניהם. The numerous
words, phrases, and even an entire line which were added
by a later hand in Vat. 30 (indicated by brackets) suggest
that the exemplar from which Vat. 30 was copied was
extensively damaged or defective in the folio containing
this passage.

   Example 4.--Vat. 30, f. 131,4-131v,2 to T.A., 872,2-

874,5.   ⊖   עד הגל הזה וגו לרעה אין את

עלי לטובה את עובר עלי לרעה אין את עובר עלי עובר
אתה עלי לפרגמטיה   ⊖   בשעה ששילח דוד את יואב
לארם נהרים ולארם צובה פגע באדומים וביקש לזנבן א
הוציאו לו אסטליות שלהם רב לכם סב את ההר הזה וגו פגע
במואביים וביקש לזנבן והוציאו לו אסטליות שלהם אל תצר
את מואב שילח אצל דוד אם לו פגעתי באדומיים ובקשתי
לזנבן זהוציאו לי אסטליות שלהם אל תצר את מואב באותה
שעה לא נהג דוד בעצמו מלך אלא   עמד והעביר א
פורפירו מעליו ועטרה מעל ראשו ונתעטף טליתו והלך לו
אצל סנהדרין אם להם רבותיי לא באתי לכן אלא לילמד ואם
נותנין אתם לי רשות אני מלמד שילחתי את יואב לארם נהרים
ולארם צובה ופגע באדומיים וביקש לזנבן והוציאו לו את
אסטליות שלהם רב לכם סב ולא הם פרצו את הגדר תחילה
ויאסף אליו את בני עמון ועמלק פגע במואביים וביקש א
לזנבן והוציאו לו אסטליות שלהם אל תצר את מואב   ולא
הם פרצו את הגדר תחילה וישלח מלאכים אל בלעם וגו
ועתה לכה נא ארה לי   כמה איגרות כתב ר אייבו אם שתי
איגרות כתב אחת למואביים ואחת לאדומיים ר חנינה אם
איגרת אחת כתב הדה היא וישב יואב וגו חזר ולמד
שלאדומיים ושלמואביים הדה היא למנצח על שושן עד

                        103

לעדה שהיא משיחה בלשונו שלאל מכתם לדוד ללמד מכות

ותמות לדוד בהצותו את ארם נהרים וגו כתוב אחד אומ

שמונה עשרה וכת אחר או שנים עשר אלא שתי מלחמות

היו אחת שלשנים עשר ואחת שלשמונה עשר ⊖

הערה בשוליים לשורה 8: רב לכם סב את ההר פגעתי במואביים וביקשתי

לזנבן הוציאו לי אסטליות שלהם

This passage deals with Gen. 31,52. It consists of
two parts, a shorter and a longer interpretation.

The shorter passage relates directly to the biblical
verse: Laban takes an oath that neither he nor Jacob will
cross the boundary mark with hostile intent; the midrash
adds, however, that Jacob may cross with good intent. The
longer passage is indirectly connected to the verse because
of the mention of "mound" and "pillar." The Amonites and
Moabites reputedly produced for Joab a "stele" upon which
were inscribed the words of the Torah stating that Israel
should refrain from attacking these people.

Albeck has suggested that the shorter interpretation
in Vat. 30 contains a late addition:

לרעה אין את עובר עלי לטובה את עובר עלי

This line is also found in:

    1. Vat. 60:

לרעה אין את עובר עלי אבל את עובר עלי לטובה

    2. the Midrash Haggadol (p. 554):

לרעה אין אחה עובר עלי לטובה את עובר עלי

In addition, Vat. 60 also contains the line immediately
following:

לרעה אין את עובר עלי עובר את עלי לפרקמטיא

A crucial question in determining whether the suspected line is actually an addition is, why are both the first and the second lines repeated in Vat. 30 and 60? In light of the second line, found in all witnesses except the Midrash Haggadol, the first line seems superfluous. On the other hand, the use of the first line in Vat. 30 and 60 makes the repetition of the second line in these two manuscripts also superfluous. Consequently, a decision has to be made as to which of the two lines is actually the addition and which is the original.

It has generally been accepted that the second is the original because it is attested in all of the manuscripts, in the editions, and in Rashi.[59] The quantity of witnesses, however, should not be decisive in this regard. The first line is found in Vat. 30, 60 and the Midrash Haggadol, each of which has been shown to be a reliable carrier of other original readings. It is also attested to in the 11th century aggadic commentary Lekach-Tob, which transmits a condensation of both lines into one:[60]

לרעה לא תעבור, אבל אתה עובר לטובה ולפרגמטיא

---

[59] It is also found in the commentary of Behya to Gen. 31,52.

[60] Rabbi Tobia ben Elieser, Lekach-Tob, ed. Solomon Buber, (Wilna, 1884), p. 81b (162).

More decisive than the use of witnesses for determining which of the lines is original is a close examination of the single difference in reading between the two lines. Gen. 31,52 stresses that Jacob is not to cross "this mound and this pillar" to Laban לרעה "with hostile intent" or "for harm." The midrash plays on לרעה by suggesting that Jacob can cross if he has other intentions. The natural antonym for לרעה is לטובה, "with beneficial intent" or "for good," and not לפרגמטיא, "for trade." Consequently, לפרגמטיא may be understood as a later addition, the purpose of which was to amplify or render more explicit the general term, לטובה. It is not logical to assume that the derivative concept "trade" should precede the primary and natural interpretation.

Vat. 30 also reflects a version of the second and longer comment to Gen. 31,50, which is more original than that contained in the other manuscripts. In our passage only Vat. 30 and the printed editions carry the full text of Joab's message to David. In place of the complete message, the other manuscripts read with the London manuscript (T.A., 873,1-2): שולח אל דוד כל המורע.

While it is a generally accepted critical principle that a briefer version is earlier and a more elaborate text later, this principle does not apply here. In narrative passages, complete repetition is stylistically typical of the original Bereshit Rabba.[61] Further, the

scribes of all manuscripts of Bereshit Rabba do abbreviate

and abridge. The fact that the other manuscripts transmit

an abridgement of our passage suggests that a more complete

version must have once existed. This complete and earlier

version is represented in Vat. 30.

Possible unique readings.--In addition to the four

passages attested in new manuscript material, Vat. 30 con-

tains possible unique readings which have no support in

any other witness. The compatibility of such readings

with the meaning and imagery of the passages in which they

appear will determine their acceptability. Three of these

readings are presented here; none of them is to be found

in Theodor's variants.

1. Vat. 30, f. 16,19-21 to T.A., 186,4-6.

על גחנך תלך בשעה שאמ' לו הקבה על גחונך תלך ירדו
מלאכי שרת וקצצו ידיו ורגליו והיה קולו הולך מסוף העולם ועד סופו
בא נחש ללמד על חילתה שלבבל ונמצא למד ממנה קולה כנחש ילך

This passage is the opening comment in a series of

interpretations (quoted above, example #3) on Gen. 3,14.

It pictures the dismemberment of the Serpent by the

ministering angels and the power of his anguished cry.

Theodor indicates the problems emerging from different

<hr>

[61]See for example Vat. 30, f. 4v-5 to T.A., 32, 1-11
and the repetition of the passage, Vat. 30, f. 24v to T.A.,
260,2-12, in Appendix II, Sample 1.

readings of this passage in various rabbinic sources.
According to him all the manuscripts of Bereshit Rabba
state that the cry of the Serpent came to throw light on
מפלתה שלבבל, "the downfall of Babylon," while the editions,
the Yalkut, and the Baraitha of the 32 Middot reads, מפלתה
שלמצרים, "the downfall of Egypt."[62]

The biblical chapter, Jer. 46, from which verse 22 is
quoted in this passage deals with the defeat of Pharoah Neco
at Carchemish by Nebuchadrezzar of Babylon in 605 B.C. The
serpent mentioned in the Jeremiah verse clearly refers to
Egypt. Consequently, the proof-text would seem to support
the reading, מפלתה שלמצרים, found in the editions, the
Yalkut, and the Baraitha of the 32 Middot.

Unnoticed by Theodor, however, was the unique reading
in Vat. 30, חילתה שלבבל. As previously mentioned, the
folio on which this passage appears contains numerous
omissions and errors. Nevertheless, חילתה cannot be
explained away on the basis of any of the more well known
scribal errors. The word appears to be a feminine noun
with a third person singular feminine suffix serving as
an anticipatory pronoun; it is related to the masculine
חיל, and means "strength," "power," or "army."[63] Thus, חילתה
שלבבל is probably to be translated, "the power of Babylon."

---

[62]T.A., 186, note 4.

[63]Only the masculine form is attested; see Jastrow,
p. 455-456.

The source of this reading may be the continuation of Jer. 46,22, כי בחיל ילכו, "for they march in force," a reference to the Babylonians coming against the Egyptians.[64]

Such an association would be appropriate to the midrashic interpretation as a whole. The passage states that when the ministering angels cut off the Serpent's hands and feet, his voice reverberated from one end of the world to the other. The intensity of that sound comes to "throw light" on the sound made by the marching Babylonian army. Taking the entire Jeremiah verse as referring to Babylon, the midrash pictures the Babylonian army as a noisy serpent, the sound of whose slithering movement fills the whole world, and the sound of the dismembered Serpent's voice being as loud as the army of Babylon on the march.[65]

If this interpretation is correct, then the passage emphasizes the power of the Serpent's voice rather than his anguish or Egypt's misery at her own downfall. The reading in all other Bereshit Rabba manuscripts retains at least one part of the original phrase, שלבבל.[66] The phrase,

---

[64]This is precisely the image which emerges from the Targum Jonathan to this verse: קל ניקוש זינהון כחויין זחלין ... See Alexander Sperber, The Bible in Aramaic (Leiden, 1962), III, p. 240.

[65]See previous note.

[66]The word מפלתה, "downfall," may have replaced חילתה when the meaning of the original interpretation was lost. Subsequently, the reading was changed to מפלתה שלמצרים to bring it in line with the plain meaning of the Jeremiah passage.

מפלתה שלמצרים, of the editions, the Yalkut, and the Baraitha
of the 32 Middot is late. Albeck and others have already
shown that the Baraitha of the 32 Middot could not have been
a source for Bereshit Rabba. This passage offers additional
confirmation of that judgement and indicates that Theodor's
view, that the source of this passage was the Baraitha of
the 32 Middot, is incorrect.[67]

2. Vat. 30, f. 10,10-11 to T.A., 152,5.

ויש אומ' אף ממעט את האדם

This reading occurs in a passage commenting on the
words לא טוב in Gen. 2,18 (T.A., 151,4-152,6). The
various interpretations offered to the verse emphasize that
it is "not good for man to be alone," and that he should
marry. The concluding interpretation, as it appears in all
other witnesses, suggests that if a man does not marry and
reproduce, he "diminishes the image of God" (ממעט את הדמות)
Proof for this assertion is derived from Gen. 9,6b-7, ". . .
for in the image of God was man created. Be fruitful, then,
and increase. . . ."[68] Although Vat. 30 retains the same
proof-texts, it offers a different reading, ממעט את האדם.

The phrase from Vat. 30 is linguistically plausible
and may be translated "diminishes man"; however, it is not

---

[67]Theodor, T.A., 186, note 4; Albeck, Introduction,
p. 66 and Hadrashot, p. 268, note 11.

[68]The notion that man was created in God's image is
also found in Gen. 1,27; 5,1,2. In the latter, צלם and
דמות are used interchangeably.

acceptable. The exegesis of Gen. 9,6b-7 stresses that man

was created in the image of God and that by refusing to

reproduce he diminishes the image. This is apparent from

the repetition of our comment in a later passage dealing

directly with Gen. 9,6 (T.A., 325,3-327,2). In this repeti-

tion, our comment follows a statement by R. Akiba that one

who sheds blood "diminishes the image." In the repetition,

however, Vat. 30 along with all other witnesses reads

הדמות;   the word   האדם does not appear. From the

exegesis of the proof-text and from the absence of   האדם

in a repetition of the same passage in Vat. 30, it is clear

that   האדם must be rejected.

What was the source of this reading in Vat. 30? Its

origin in the manuscript can be traced to a scribal error.

The scribe may have carried over the word   אדם from the

immediately preceding interpretation (Vat. 30, f. 10,9-10;

T.A., 152,4-5):   ר׳ חייא בר גומרי אמ׳ אף אינו

אדם שלם ᵇ ויברך אתם ויקרא שמם אדם.   It is also possible

that he looked ahead to the proof-text where the biblical

designation elohim may have been abbreviated in the exemplar

אדים.[69] He may have misread this abbreviation and in-

serted it in the interpretation. In either case, the scribe

first copied down   אדם in an undetermined form and later

---

[69]In Vat. 30, the abbreviation אדים is found throughout the work of the "group"; for example, ff. 2v and 4v. In
all likelihood, it was one of the standard abbreviations in
the exemplar. Scribe B, however, preferred אי׳ם.

111

added the definite article. This is clear from the manuscript because the <u>he</u> is inserted carefully into the space
between את and אדם, and the two words appear together,
אתהאדם. The scribal error responsible for this reading,
contamination from a nearby word, is not uncommon in the
work of Scribe B.[70]

    3. Vat. 30, f. 25v,23-24 to <u>T.A.</u>, 266,5-6.

כאנש דאמ' אימחיק שמיה דפלן דאפיל ברי בגו אשא

In contrast to Vat. 30, the other witnesses read:

כאינש דאמר אימחוק שמיה דפלן דאפיק ברי לתרבות בישא

By comparing both versions of this Aramaic proverb,
it is possible to delineate the differences between them
and determine whether one or the other is more suitable to
the passage in which it appears. In Vat. 30, אימחיק is
probably <u>ithp'el</u>, third masculine singular, imperfect (or
jussive), from the root <u>mhq</u>, "to be blotted out"; the <u>taw</u>
has been assimilated, the <u>yod</u> strengthened with an <u>alef</u>,
and the <u>mem</u> doubled.[71] This analysis of the verb is
supported by the reading of the editions, יתמחיק, against
the other witnesses, אימחוק. The verb אפיל is <u>aph'el</u>,
third masculine singular, perfect, from <u>nfl</u>, "to cause to

---

[70]See, for example, the passage Vat. 30, f. 28v, 16-24
to <u>T.A.</u>, 272,5-273,4 quoted below in the section dealing
with obvious errors and inaccuracies.

[71]Jastrow, p. 764. For the use of the <u>alef</u> with or
without the <u>yod</u> in this imperfect/jussive form, see <u>T.A.</u>,
2,6-7 and variants and note to the end of line 6, אתפרכן.

fall."[72] The preposition גו is very common in Aramaic,

meaning "in" or "into."[73] The noun אשא, vocalized אֶשָּׁא,

is feminine absolute, "fire."[74] Thus, the Vat. 30 version

is to be translated, "Like a man who says, 'May the name of

So-and-So, who caused my son to fall into a fire, be blotted

out.'"

Except for the editions, the other witnesses read

אימחוק, p'al, first person singular, imperfect. The verb

אפיק is attested in all manuscripts and editions except

Vat. 30; it is aph'el, third masculine singular, from nfq,

"to bring out" or "to lead."[75] The concluding words of the

line according to the better reading of Vat. 60 and the

Stuttgart manuscript are לתרבו בישה, the feminine noun

absolute with the adjective also in the absolute state;

"a bad life," "Unzucht verführte."[76] This version may be

translated, "Like a man who says, 'I will blot out the name

of So-and-So who led my son into a bad life.'"

Since both versions are linguistically plausible, is

one more suitable than the other for the context in which

---

[72]Jastrow, p. 924.

[73]Jastrow, p. 216; Rosenthal, An Aramaic Handbook,
I/2, p. 56.

[74]Jastrow, p. 126; Rosenthal, An Aramaic Handbook,
I/2, p. 55.

[75]Jastrow, p. 926.

[76]Jastrow, p. 1695; Levy, IV, 667.

it occurs? The proverb appears in one of the interpretations
brought to explain the words   מאדם ועד בהמה   in Gen. 6,7;
Vat. 30, 25v,19-24 to T.A., 226,3-7:

אמ ר אלעזר הכל קראו תיגר

על הכסף ועל הזהב שיצאו עמהם ממצרים כספך היה לסיגים סבאך

מהול   וכסף הרביתי לך וזהב עשו לבעל כספם וזהבם עשו להם עצבים

למען יכרת ר הונא ר ירמיה בש ר שמוא בר רב יצחק למען יכרת למען

יכרתו

אין כת' כן אלא למען יכרת כאנש דאם אימחיק שמיה דפלן דאפל בר בגו

אשא

The problem which the midrash treats in Gen. 6,7 is why God
determined to blot out the beasts along with man in the
Generation of the Flood. In the introductory comments, the
answer is given that the beasts were partially responsible
for man's sinfulness and should be punished (T.A., 265,2-
266,1). The underlying idea, that whatever brings man to sin
should be destroyed, leads to an analogous interpretation
concerning the wealth of the Generation of the Flood which
God caused to perish (T.A., 266,1-266,3). Immediately after-
ward, our passage (wrongly attributed to R. Elazar in Vat.30)
is quoted. It is concerned with the gold and silver which the
Israelites brought from Egypt and made into idols. Through
the exegesis of Hosea 8,4, in which the singular form of the
verb יכרת is emphasized, it is suggested that this silver
and gold was to be destroyed. Our proverb is cited to
reinforce the notion that whatever leads man astray is
punished.

114

From this analysis, it appears that both versions of the proverb are suitable to the context. It may be argued that the phrase "into a bad life" of the other witnesses is more appropriate to the sin of idolatry than "into a fire"; however, the difference is not significant. The former expresses in a general way the evil into which the son was led, while the latter speaks of the fate which he ultimately met. More important, in both versions the man responsible for the son's downfall is the prime concern of the proverb.

To the two versions in Vat. 30 and the other witnesses, a third may be added. It is found in the Palestinian Talmud, Sanhedrin 25a, and is as suitable to the context as those of Bereshit Rabba:[77]

כאינש דמר שחיק טימייה דפלן דאפיק בריה לעבדא בישא

It is impossible to determine precisely how these differing versions came into being.

Obvious errors and inaccuracies.--Vat. 30 also contains textual material which reveals scribal errors or inaccuracies and is lacking in some detail. Two typical examples are offered here of defective passages, both taken from Scribe B.

---

[77]"Like a man who says, 'I'm going to crush the bones of So-and-So who led his (my?) son to a bad deed.'" For the form עבדא, see Payne-Smith, p.397. ܥܒܕ and ܥܒ݂ܕܐ.

1. Vat. 30, 28v,16-24 to <u>T.A.</u>, 272,5-273,4.

This passage is a comment on the words איש צדיק in
Gen. 6,9.

איש צדיק בכל מקום שנ איש צדיק ממחה הוא שכל
מאה ועשרים שנה נוטע ארזים וקוצצן אמרון ליה למה כדין אמ לון
כן אמ מריה דעלמא דהוא מייתי מבולא על עלמא אמרון ליה אין   א
אתא   מבולא לא אתא אלא על ביתיה דאבוה דההוא גברא
הד ה לפיד בוז לעשתות שאנן נכון למוע רגל אמ ר אבא בר כהנא
אמ הקבה פרחא חד עמד לי בדור המבול זה נוח ואינון אמ כדין ליה
לפיד ליה בוז שהיו מבזים עליו וקרו ליה בוזה סבא לעשתות שאנן
שהיו קשין כעשתות נכון למועדי רגל שהיו מוכנין לשני שבריים
שבר מלמעלן ושבר מלמטן

The first part of the passage states that Noah is a righteous
man warning a generation which rejects and despises him. In
the second part, the verse Job 12,5 is applied by R. Abba
to Noah. Again, this biblical character is pictured as a
preacher chastising his fellow men but rejected by them.

This second part in Vat. 30 contains errors. The
notable departures from the other manuscripts are

Vat. 30	Others
פרחא חד עמד לי	כרוז אחד עמד לי
ואינון אמ׳	תמן אמ׳
כדין ליה	כרוז ליה

These deviations derive from similarity of letters and
contamination of one phrase by another. Noah's contempo-
raries first respond to his planting and cutting of cedars

116

by asking, למה כדין, "Why [are you acting] like this?" In writing the second part, Scribe B recalls כדין which he reads instead of כרוז. He places this new reading again in the mouth of Noah's antagonists, ואינון אמ׳ כדין ליה. The words כרוז אחד are corrupted to פרחא חד because of the similarity of pe and kaph, the extension of the roof of the zayin to touch the top of the waw forming a het, and the misplacement of the alef. Consequently, the scribe does not realize the extent of his revision. The meaning of the whole passage depends on linking the words כרוז, לפיד, ממחה, to convey the idea of a chastising preacher; thus, the reading in Vat. 30 leads to confusion.[78] In spite of these errors, Vat. 30 does not contain the later addition to this passage found in many of the other manuscripts.[79]

2. Vat. 30, f. 10,12-16 to T.A., 152,7-155,5.

This passage is an interpretation of Gen. 2,18; it appears in Vat. 30 in an abbreviated form.

אעשה לו עזר כנגדו אם זכה עזר ואם לא זכה כנגדו ר יהושע בר
נחמיה אם זכה כאשתו שלר חנניה בן חכינאי ואם לא כאשתו
שלר יוסי הגלילי ר יוסי הגלילי הוה נשים לביתא דאחתיה והות
מבזה יתיה אמרון ליה תלמידוי שיבקה אמ לית לי מן הן נתן לה
פרנה אמרון ליה כולי דכת באשרי משכיל אל דל דויקרא

---

[78]For Theodor's explanation of this passage, see T.A., 272, notes 5-6, and 273, notes 2-4.

[79]T.A., 273, variants to line 1, גברא.

117

The passage is composed of three parts:

    a.   an anonymous interpretation of the words עזר כנגדו.

    b.   a comment by R.Joshua b. Nehemiah.

    c.   a story concerning R. Jose the Galilean.

A longer and a shorter version of the R. Jose story appear
in the manuscripts of Bereshit Rabba.[80] Both versions conclude with Is. 58,7, interpreted to mean "do not hide your-
self from showing mercy to your divorced wife in her distress."
In Bereshit Rabba, the story is quoted merely because of
its reference to the nasty wife of R. Jose the Galilean.

    Vat. 30 contains the short version, and this version
is itself abbreviated. Rosenthal points out that the scribal
notation in Vat. 30 refers to Leviticus Rabba; yet Leviticus
Rabba contains the longer and not the shorter version.[81]
This reference is not surprising because the shorter version
is attested only in some Bereshit Rabba manuscripts; it does
not appear in any other early midrashic work.[82] More important, the small portion of the text given in Vat. 30 contains
the phrase   הוה נשים לביתא דאחתיה, which does not make
sense. Other manuscripts transmitting this version suggest

---

[80]The London manuscript contains both: the longer,
T.A., 152,8-154,7; and the shorter, T.A., 154,7-155,5.

[81]Rosenthal, p. 302-303, and note 96; the passage is
found in Leviticus Rabba 34,14; Margulies edition, pp. 802ff.

[82]It is, however, found in the Yalkut and the Aruch;
see T.A., 152, note 8. The parallel in the Palestinian
Talmud, Kethubot 34b, represents a third version which is
closer to the short version of Vat. 30.

that the line should be read הוה נשיב לברתא דאחתיה.
Since sin and samekh are interchangeable in the Palestinian
dialect, נשיב is the same as נסיב; the text is to be
rendered, "was married to his sister's daughter."[83] Scribe
B wrote the passage and we may assume that the original
spelling of לברתא was לברתה, as in the London and Paris
manuscripts and the Yalkut.[84]

Conclusion

No autograph manuscript written by the author or
compiler of Bereshit Rabba has survived from antiquity. The
manuscripts in our possession are based on an unknown number
of exemplars ultimately descended from the original. Comparison of the various surviving witnesses indicates that
Vat. 30 as a whole most closely represents this original.
It was copied by four to six scribes from the same exemplar,
probably in Egypt in the tenth or eleventh century. One of
the scribes made significant orthographic and linguistic
changes in the text.

Close analysis of the readings in Vat. 30 suggests that
this manuscript contains few if any later additions. The
four passages suspected by Albeck are probably from the
original Bereshit Rabba, of whose language and style they
are typical. This judgement is confirmed even in those

---

[83]Sokoloff, p. 8.

[84]See T.A., 154,8 and variants.

readings where the text of Vat. 30 is faulty and needs correction from other manuscripts.

In addition, Vat. 30 contains unique readings unattested in any other witness. The few examples surveyed here indicate that each case must be examined separately to determine its acceptability. Some readings which appear to be unique can be traced to scribal error and must be rejected.

The fact that Vat. 30 represents the original Bereshit Rabba does not mean that its text is adequate in every detail. Scribal errors, defects in the exemplar, and missing sections require the constant comparison of Vat. 30 with other manuscripts of Bereshit Rabba. Only by such comparison can the original be adequately reconstructed. Nevertheless, on literary and linguistic grounds, Vat. 30 should be used as the basic manuscript for a new edition of Bereshit Rabba.[85]

---

[85]Sokoloff has prepared the entire text of Vat. 30 on IBM cards and a type-out has been made. As far as I know, it is not yet available for public distribution. For the details, see Sokoloff, p. 5.

CHAPTER VI

SAMPLE CHAPTERS FROM VAT. 30

The sample chapters presented here represent the work
of four scribes in Vat. 30: Scribe A, Chapter 4; Scribe B,
Chapter 46; Scribe C, Chapter 67; and Scribe D, Chapter 81.
Each selection has been transcribed with the aim of preserving the scribe's original layout. No attempt has been made
to correct errors or to indicate the source of biblical
verses. Marginal notes and glosses are placed in approxi-
mately the same position as in the manuscript, as are words
appearing between the lines. A pencil mark above a letter
(´) or a typed apostrophe (') represent the original abbreviation or correction sign of the scribe. A single alef at
the end of a line symbolizes the alef-like sign used by
scribes to mark the left hand margin. Brackets [   ] indicate
a word added by a later scribe. Dots below letters signify
an unclear but probable reading; a dot above a letter indicates that it was added by a later scribe. An attempt has
also been made to transcribe the names of God just as they
appear in the manuscript. However, the alef and lamed of
elohim are often written as one letter by the scribes; in
addition, the he is often deleted. In the abbreviation א׳׳מ

121

the _alef_ represents the combination of _alef_ and _lamed_.
Finally, each line of the text has been numbered.

Variants to the four chapters have been added from
eight manuscripts and printed editions. They are indicated
by the signs used in the Theodor-Albeck edition. Instead
of placing the variants at the bottom of each page, they
appear here after each folio and are numbered according to
the line numbers of the folio. The line number appears first,
then the word from Vat. 30, followed by a perpendicular line
(|); variants follow this line, with the sign of the manu-
script from which each is taken. A comma separates variants
to the same word and a period indicates the end of all the
variants to that word. Where other manuscripts contain
additional words or phrases, these appear with a plus sign
(+). The position of the plus sign suggests where the
reading from Vat. 30 is to be placed in relation to the
addition from the other manuscript: + before the additional
word when the reading from Vat. 30 precedes that word, +
after the additional word when the reading from Vat. 30
follows that word. The Hebrew letter _het_ signifies that a
manuscript lacks the word cited; if a manuscript lacks an
entire passage, it will be mentioned in parentheses. Since
the variants are arranged on a word by word basis, it is
often necessary to scan the surrounding words and variants
to obtain a complete picture of the way another manuscript
conveys a phrase or passage.

122

11 פרשתה ד׳ ⊕

12 ויאמר א׳ים יהי רקיע בתוך המים וג׳ המקרה במים

13 עליותיו וג׳ בנוהג שבעולם מלך בשר ודם בונה פלטין א

14 ומקרה בעצים ובאבנים ובעפר אבל הק׳בה לא קירה את

15 עולמו כולו אלא במים המקרה במים עליותיו וגו ויאמר

16 א׳דים יהי רקיע בתוך המים ⊕ כל רבנן אמרין

17 לה בשם ר׳ חנניה ר׳ פינחס ר׳ יעקב בר בון בשם ר שמואל

18 בר נחמן בשעה שאמר הק׳ב׳ה יהי רקיע בתוך המים גלדה

19 טיפה האמצעית ונעשו שמים התחתונים ושמי שמים

20 העליונים רב אמ׳ לחים היו שמים ביום הראשון ובשני קרשו

21 רב אמ׳ יהי רקיע יחזק הרקיע ר׳ יודה ביר׳ סימון אמ׳ יעשה

22 מטלת הקריע הכ׳ דת׳ וירקעו את פחי הז אמ ר חנניה יצאת

23 אש מלמעלן וליחכה את פני הרקיע ר יוחנן כשהיה מָגִיעַ

24 לפסוק הזה ברוחו שמים שפרה היה אום יפה לימְדָנִי ר א

25 חנניה אמ ר יודן בר שמעון יצאה האש מלמעלן וַלְיְהֵטה

123

11: פרשתה| פרשתא לו[2]א[1], פרשה ד[21]. ד´| ג´ ל.

12: ויאמר| ויא´ לו[2]. אים| אדים ו[2], אלהים ד[21], אלקים ח.
רקיע|רק´ ו[2]. בתוך| בת´ ו[2], וגו´ ל, ח´ ד[21]. המים| המ´ ו[2],
ח´ לד[21]. וגו´| ח´ לו[2]א[1]חד[21]. המקרה| כת´ + ל, כתי´ + א[1],
כתיב + ד[21]. במים| במ´ ו[2].

13: עליותיו| עליות´ ל, עלי´ ו[2]. וגו´| ח´ ו[2]א[1]ד[21].
בנוהג| מנהג ח. שבעולם| העו´ ל, שבעו´ ו[2], העולם ח.
בשר ודם| בש´ וד´ ל, בשר וד´ ו[2], בש ו´ א[1]. פלטין| פלאטין ל,
פלטרין א[1].

14: בעצים| באבנים לד[21]ח. ובאבנים| ובעצים לד[2], ובעצי´ ד[1],
ובעפר ח. ובעפר| ובעצים ח. הקבה| הק´ ל, הקב´ ו[2], הבֿה א[1]ד[1].
קירה| קרה לו[2]ד[21]. את| ח´ ל.

15: כולו| ח´ לו[2]א[1]חד[21]. אלא| אל´ ו[2]. המקרה| המ´ ו[2]; שנ´ +
לו[2]ד[1]ח, שנא´ + א[1], שנאמר + ד[2]. במים| במ´ ו[2]. עליותיו| וגו´
ל, עלי´ ו[2]. וגו´| וג´ ל. וגו´| ו[2], ח´ א[1]ד[21]ח, (ראה המילה הקודמת ל).
ויאמר – המים| (הפסוק הזה מופיע כאן בו[2]ד[21], בהתחלת המאמר הבא
בלא[1]ח). ויאמר| ויא´ ל.

16: אדים| אים לא[1], אלקי´ ח. בתורך| וגו´ ל, ח´ ח.
המים| ח´ לח. כל| ח´ לד[2]ח. רבנן| רבנין לו[2].
אמרין| אמ´ ל, אמרי א[1]ח.

17: לה| (ח חסר מכאן עד...בשעה). בשם ר´| בש´ ר´ ל, בשׁר ו[2]א[1].
חנניה| חנינא לד[2], חנינ´ ו[2], חנין א[1], חנינה ד[1], ר´| ור´ א[1]ד´,
ורבי ד[2], פינחס| פנחס א[1]ד[2]. ר´| ור´ ו[2]ד[1], ורבי ד[2], יעקב| יעק´
ו[2]. בר| ח´ ו[2]א[1]. בון| אבון ד[21], ח´ ו[2]א[1].

בשם ר׳ שמואל| בש׳ ר׳ שמו׳ ל, בש׳ ר׳ שמואל ו[2], בשרׂש א[1], בשם רבי
שמואל ד[2].

18: בר נחמן| בֹֿש א[1]. בשעה| בשׂע׳ ו[2]. שאמר| שא׳ לו[2], שאמ׳ א[1]ד[21].
הקבה| הק׳ לו[2], הבֿה א[1]. יהי רקיע בתוך המים| יהי רק׳ בתוך ה׳ ו[2].
גלדה| גלה ד[21].

19: שמים| השמים א[1]ד[21]. התחתונים| התח׳ ו[2]. ושמי| שמי ו[2].
שמים| השמים א[1].

20: העליונים| העליונ׳ ו[2], עליונים א[1]. רב| רבנ׳ ו[2].
אמ׳| אמר ד[2]. לחים| לחים׳ לחיים ל, לחין א[1]. שמים| ל׳, מעשים לו[2],
מעשיהם ד[21]ח, ח׳ א[1]. ביום הראשון| ל׳, ח׳ לו[2]ח.

21: רב אמ׳| ל׳, ח׳ לו[2]א[1]ד[21]ח. ר׳| רבי ד[2]. יודה| יהוד׳ לד[1],
יהודה ו[2]ד[2]ח. בירן| בר לו[2]ד[21], אום׳ ח. סימון| ל׳, סימ׳ ו[2],
ח׳ ל. אמ׳| א׳ לו[2].

22: מסלת| מטלית ד[21]ח. הרקיע| לרקיע לו[2]ד[21]ח. הכ׳| היך מה
לד[21], הוא כ׳ ו[2], כמה ח. דת׳| דאת א׳ ל, ד׳ א׳ ו[2], דאת אמ׳ ד[1]ח,
דאת אמר ד[2]. הז׳| הזהב וגו׳ ל, הז׳ וק׳ פת׳ ו[2], הזהב ד[21]ח.
אמ׳| א׳ לו[2]ח, אמר ד[2], ח׳ א[1]. ר׳| רבי ד[2]. חנניה| חנינא לא[1]ח,
חני׳ ו[2], חנינה ד[1], חנינ׳ ד[2]. + אמ׳ א[1]. יצאת| יצאה ד[21],
יצאתה ח.

23: אש| האש לד[21]. מלמעלן| מלמעלה לו[2]א[1]ד[21]ח. וליחכה| ולחכה
א[1]. את| ח׳ ל. ר׳| רבי ד[2].

24: הזה| זה ו[2]ד[21], ח׳ ל. שפרה| ח׳ ל. אום׳| או׳ לו[2], אומר
ד[2]ח. לימ...| לימדני לו[2]ח, לימדנו ד[21]. ר׳| רבי ד[2].

125

25: חנניה| חנינא לח, חני׳ ו², חנינה ד²¹. אמ׳| א׳ ל, וא׳ ו².
ר׳| רבי ד². שמעון| שמע׳ לו². יצאת| יצאה ד¹. האש| אש ו².
מלמעלן| מלמעלה לד². ...טה| ולהטה ל, וליהטה ו²ד²¹.

1 את פני הרקיע ר׳ ברכיה ר׳ יעקב ר׳ אבונה בשם ר׳ אבא בר
2 כהנא בא מעשה בראשית ללמד על מתן תורה ונמצא למד
3 ממנה כקדוח המסים כקדוח אש חמסים המיסו אמתי
4 חצה אש בין העליונין לתחתונים לא במתן תורה אתמהא כך
5 היה בבריתו שלעולם ר׳ פינחס בשם ר׳ הושעיה כחלל שבין
6 הארץ לרקיע כך יש בין רקיע למים העליונים יהי רקיע בתוך
7 המים ביניים ובינתיים אמ׳ ר׳ תנחומא אנא אמרת טעמה אילו
8 נאמר ויעש אים את הרקיע ויבדל בין המים אשר על הרקיע
9 הייתי אומ׳ על גופו שלרקיע המים נתונים כשהוא אומר בין
10 המים אשר מעל לרקיע הוי המים העליונים תלוין במאמר
11 אמ׳ ר׳ אחא כהדן קנדילה ופירותיהן אילו הגשמים ◗
12   כותי אחד שאל את ר׳ מאיר אמ׳ לו איפשר המים
13 העליונין תלויין במאמר אמ׳ לו הין אמר לו הבא לי אפרכס*
14 הביא לו אפרכס* נתן עליה טס שלזהב ולא עמדו מים טס
15 שלכסף ולא עמדו מים וכיון שנתן אצבעו עמדו מים אמ׳ לו
16 אצבעך אתה נותן אמ׳ לו מה אם אני שאני בשר ודם אצבעי
17 מעמדת מים אצבעו שלהקׁבׄה על אחת כמה וכמה הווי או׳
18 המים העליונים תלוים במאמר אמ׳ לו איפשר אותו שכתוב
19 בו הלוא את השמים ואת הארץ וגו׳ היה מדבר עם משה מבין
20 שני בדי הארון אמ׳ לו הבא לי מראות גדולות הביא לו מראות
21 גדולות אמ׳ לו ראה בובייה שלך בהן ראה אותה גדולה אמר
22 לו הבא לי מראות קטנות הביא מראות קטנות אמ׳ לו ראה
23 הבובייה שלך בהן ראה אותה קטנה אמ׳ לו מה אם אתה
24 שאתה בשר ודם אתה משנה את עצמך בכל מה שתרצה
25 מי שאמר והיה העולם על אחת כמה ואחת כמה אתמהא

---

*הערה: בשוליים לשורות 13 – 14; נ׳ א׳ ארפכס

1: את| ח׳| לד[2]. הרקיע| הר׳ ו[2]. ר׳| רבי ד[2]. ברכיה| ברכ׳ ו[2].
ר׳| ור׳ ו[2]א[1], ח׳ ד[21]. יעקב| יעק׳ ו[2], ח׳ ד[21]. ר׳| בר לו[2]א[1],
ח׳ ד[21]. אבונה| אבינא לו[2], חנינא א[1], ח׳ ד[21]. בשם ר׳| בש׳ ר׳
לו[2], בש̃ר א[1]. אבא| אבה ל, אב׳ ו[2].

2: כהנא| + אמ׳ א[1]ד[21]. בראשית| בראש׳ ו[2]. ללמד| ללמוד ל.
תורה| תו׳ ו[2]. ונמצא| ונימצא (?) ו[2].

3: כקדוח המסים| ח׳ לו[2]א[1]ד[21]. כקדוח| שנא׳ + א[1]. חמסים| חמס׳
ו[2], המסים א[1], חמסי׳ ד[2]. המיסו| הימיסו ל, המי׳ ו[2], המיסה א[1],
ח׳ ד[21]. אמתי| אימתי לד[21], אמתי ו[2], אימת א[1].

4: אש| האש לו[2]ד[21]. העליונין| העליונים לא[1]ד[2], העליו׳ ו[2]
העליוני׳ ד[1]. לתחתונים| לתחת׳ ו[2]. תורה| תור׳ ו[2]ד[21].
אתמהא| ח׳ א[1].

5: היה| הייתה ד[21], ח׳ א[1]. בבריחתו| בבריתו א[1]. שלעולם| של
עולם א[1]ד[21], שלעו׳ לו[2]. ר׳| רבי ד[2]. פינחס| פינח׳ ו[2], פנחס
א[2]ד[1]. בשם ר׳| בש׳ ר׳ ו[2], בש̃ר א[1], בשם רבי ד[2], ר׳ ח.
הושעיה| יהושעיה ל, הושעיא ו[2]ד[2]ח; + א׳ ו[2], + אמ׳ א[1]ד[1]ח, +
אמר ד[2].

6: רקיע| הרקיע א[1]ד[21]. העליונים| העליו׳ ו[2].
יהי רקיע בתוך המים| יהי רק׳ בתו׳ הם׳ ו[2]; שנ׳ + ח.

7: ביניים| בינס א[1]. ובינתיים| ובינתים ו[2]ח, ובנתים א[1]ד[21].
אמ׳ ר׳| אז̃ א[1], אמר רבי ד[2]. תנחומא| תנחום א[1]. אמרת| אמ׳ לו[2],
אמרית א[1], אמרי ד[21], אימר ח. טעמה| **טע׳** ל, **טעמ׳** ו[2], טעמא
א[1]ד[21]ח. אילו| אלו א[1]ד[21].

8: נאמר| נא׳ ו[2]ח, נאמ׳ לא[1]ד[1]. אים| אדים ו[2]. את| א׳ ו[2].
הרקיע| הרק׳ ו[2]. ויבדל| ויבד׳ ו[2]. המים| המ׳ ו[2]. אשר| אש׳ ו[2].
על| מעל א[1°]. הרקיע| הרק׳ ו[2], לרקיע א[1].

9: אומ׳| או׳ לו[2], אומר ד[21]. כשהוא| וכשהוא ו[2]ד[21].
אומר| או׳ לו[2], אומ׳ א[1]ד[1]. בין| ובין לד[21].

10: המים| המ׳ ו[2]. אשר| אש׳ ו[2]. מעל| מע׳ ו[2]. לרקיע| לרקי׳ ו[2].
הוי| האוי ו[2]; + אומ׳ א[1]ח. תלויין| תלוים לא[1], תלואים ו[2],
תלויים ד[21], תלויין ח.

11: אמ׳| א׳ לו[2]א[1]ד[21]. ר׳| רבי ד[2]. כהדן| כהדין לא[1]ד[21].
קנדילה| קנדילא לו[2]א[1°]ד[21]. אילון| אלו לד[21].
הגשמים| גשמים לו[2]ד[21]; מימי + ד[1], מי + ד[2].

12: אחד| א׳ א[1]ד[1]. ר׳ מאירן| ר׳ מ א[1], רבי מאיר ד[2]. אמ׳| לו| א׳
לו לו[2], אל̃ א[1], אמר לו ד[2]ח. איפשר| אפשר לד[21], אפש׳ ו[2].

13: העליונין| העליונים לו[2]א[1°]ד[21]ח. תלויין| תלויים לא[1°]ח,
תלואים ו[2], תלויים ד[21]. במאמר| במאמ׳ ד[1]. אמ׳| לו| א׳ לו לו[2],
אל̃ א[1], אמר לו ד[2]ח. היין| הן לו[2]א[1]ד[2]ח. אמר לו| א׳ לו ל, וא׳
לו ו[2], אל̃ א[1], אמ׳ לו ד[1]. אפרכס| ארפכס לו[2]ח (ובגליון של ו נ"א
ארפכס.)

14: אפרכס| ארפכס לו[2], (ובגליון של ו שוב נ"א ארפכס.)
טס| (טס של – כיון שנתן ח׳ בא[1].)

15: מים| ח׳ ל. וכיון| כוון ל, כיון ו[2]ח. אמ׳| לו| א׳ לו לו[2],
אל̃ א[1], אמר לו ד[2].

16: אתה| את ו'ד²¹. נותן| (כ"י ג מחיל כאן). אם לו| א' לו לו²
אל א'¹, אמר לו ד²ח. מה| ומה גח. אם| ח' לגו²א'¹ד²¹ח.
אני| ח' לא'¹. בשר ודם| בש' וד' ל, בשר וד' ו² בשׂו א'¹.

17: מים| המים לא'¹, את + א'¹. שלהקבה| שלהק' לו² שלהבה א'¹.
על אחת כמה וכמה| על א' כ' וכ' ו², עאכׁו א'¹. הווי| הוי לגו²
א²ד²¹ח. או'| אומ' א'¹ח, ח' לגו²ד²¹.

18: העליונים| העליו' ו². תליום| תליין ג, תלואים ו², תליים
א'¹ד²¹, + הם א'¹. אמ' לו| א' לו' לו², אל א'¹, אמר לו ד².
איפשר| אפשר ו²ד²¹. שכתוב| שכת' לגו², שכתב א'¹, שכתו' ח.

19: בון| ח' לא'¹. הלוא| הלא לגו²ד²¹ח. השמים| השמי' ו².
ואת| וא' ו². הארץ| האר' ל, הא' ו². וגו'| ח' ל, אני מלא נאם
י' ו², אני מלא ד²¹.

20: שני| + הכרובים בין א'¹. הארון| ארון לגו²ח. אם לו| א' לו
לו², אל א'¹ד². הביא| ח' א'¹ד²¹. לו| לה ג, ח' א'¹ד²¹.
מראות| ח' לא'¹ד²¹.

21: גדולות| גדול' ו², ח' לא'¹ד²¹. אמ' לו| א' לו לו², אל גא'¹,
אמר לו ד². בוביה| בוביא לג, בוביה ו², בבואה א'¹ד²¹, בובאה ח.
בהן| ח' ל. אמר לו| אל גא'¹, א' לו ו², אמ' לו ד', ח' ל.

22: הבא| הביא ד'¹. הביא| הבא ח, ח' גא'¹. לו| ח' גא'¹.
מראות| מרא' ו², ח' לגא'¹. קטנות| קט' ו², ח' לגא'¹.
אמ' לו| אל גא'¹, א' לו ו², אמר לו ד²ח, ח' ל.

23: הבובייה| בוביא לג, בוביה ו², בבואה א'¹ד²¹ח. בהן| ח' ל.
ראה| כך + ג. אמ' לו| א' לו לגו², אל א'¹, אמר לו ד².
מה| ומה גא'¹ח, ח' ל. אם| ח' גו²א'¹ח. אתה| את ג, ח' לא'¹.

24: שאתה| שאת ג.   בשר ודם| בש׳ וד׳ ל, בשר וד׳ ר׳, בשׂוֹ א[1].
אתה| את ג, ח׳ לא[1].   משנה| מטה א[1].   את| ח׳ לו[2]ד[21]ח.
עצמך| מראך ל°ג, + לכמה גוונים א[1].   מה| ח׳ ל.   שתרצה| שאתה
רוצה א[1].

25: שאמר| שא׳ לו[2], שאמ׳ גא[1].   העולם| העו׳ לו[2], + ברוך הוא
ד[21].   על אחת כמה ואחת כמה| על אחת כמה וכמה לגד[21]ח, על אבֿוֹבֿ ר[2],
עאכוֹ א[1].   אתמהא| ח׳ גא[1]ד[21]ח.

1 הווי כשהוא רוצה הלא את השמים ואת הארץ   וכשהוא
2 רוצה היה מדבר עם משה מבין שני בדי הארון אמ ר א
3 אנינא בר סוסיי פעמים שאין העולם ומלואו מחזיקין א
4 כבוד אלהותו ופעמים שהוא מדבר עם אדם מבין סערות
5 ראשו הדה היא ויען ייי את איוב מן סערה מבין סערות
6 ראשו אמ לו איפשר פלג אים מלא מים מששת ימי ברא
7 בראשית ולא חסר כלום אתמהא אמ לו הכנס רחוץ ושקול
8 עצמך משתיכנס הלך ושקל עצמו ולא חסר כלום אמ לו א
9 כל אותה הזיעה שיצאת לא ממך יצאת אמ לו הין אמ לו מה
10 אם אתה שאתה בשר ודם לא חסר מעיינך כלום מעיינו
11 שלהקב̇ה̇ על אחת כמה וכמה הווי פלג אים מלא מים
12 מששת ימי בראשית ולא חסר כלום אמ ר̇ יוחנן נטל הק̇ב̇ה̇
13 כל מי בראשית ונתן חציים ברקיע וחציים באוקיינוס
14 הדה היא דכ̇ פלג אים מלא מים פלג̇י̇ה הרקיע דומה לבריכה
15 ולמעלה מן הבריכה כיפה ומחמת בריכה כיפה מזעת
16 והיא מזעת טיפות עבות והן יורדין לתוך מים המלוחים
17 ואינן מתערבין אמ ר̇ יונה ואל תתמה הדן יורדנוס עבר
18 בימה דטבריה ולא מתערב ביה מעשה ניסין יש בדבר
19 אדן כובר חטין או תבן בכברה עד שלא ירדו שתים ושלש
20 אצבעות הן מתערבין ואילו מהלך כמה שנים ואינן מתערבין
21 ר̇ יודן בר שמעון אומ̇ שהוא מורידן במידה כי יגרע נטפי
22 מים הכמה דתמר ונגרע בערכך כעוביה שלארץ כן עוביו
23 שלרקיע היושב על חוג הארץ וחוג שמים יתהלך חוג חוג
24 לגזירה שווה ר̇ אחא בשם ר̇ חננה אמ כטעם הזה ר̇ יהושע
25 בי̇ר̇ נחמיה אמ̇ שתים בשלוש אצבעות פזי אמ̇ המים

1: הווי| הוי לגד[21], האוי ו[2], ח׳ א[1]. השמים| השמ׳ ו[2], השמי׳
ד[2]. ואת| וא׳ ו[2]. הארץ| הא׳ לו[2]; + מלא ל, + מלא נא׳ יי ו[2],
+ אני מלא גא[1]ד[21]. וכשהוא רוצה| וכשרוצה ל.

2: היה| ח׳ לגו[2]א[1]ד[21]. שני| ח׳ ל; + הכרובים שני א[1].
הארון| ארון לו[2]. אמ׳ ר׳| א׳ ר׳ לגו[2]א[1].

3: אנינא| אניא ל, אמינא ג, חנינא א[1]ד[21]. בר| בן ו[2].
סוסיי| סיסיי ג, אסי א[1], איסי ד[21]. פעמים| פעמ׳ לו[2].
העולם| הים ו[2]. מחזיקין| מחסר א[1].

4: כבוד| כבודו ל. אלהותו| אלהינו א[1], ח׳ ל. ופעמים| פעמ׳ לד[1],
ופעמ׳ ו[2], פעמים ד[2]. שהוא מדבר| שמדבר ל, שהוא מדב׳ ו[2], עם
אדם א[1]. עם אדם| הוא מדבר א[1]. מבין| ומבין א[1].
סערות| שערות לגא[1]ד[1], שערו׳ ד[2].

5: הדה היא| ה̃ ה̃ ד ל[°]ד[21], הד׳ ה׳ דכת׳ ו[2], (לגא[1] חסרים מכאן
עד...אמ׳ לו, ול הושלם בין השורות). ייין| י׳ ל[°] יי׳ ו[2], יי ד[21],
את| א׳ ו[2], סערה| הסערה ל[°], הסע׳ ו[2], וגו׳ ד[1], השערה וגו׳ ד[2],
מבין| האוי + ו[2]. סערות| שערות ד[21].

6: אמ׳ לו| א׳ לו לגו[2], אל א[1], ועוד שאלו אמר לו ד[21].
איפשר| אסר לגו[2]ד[21]. אים| אדים ו[2], אלהים ד[21]. מלא| מלי ו[2].
משמת| משמ׳ ו[2].

7: בראשית| ברא׳ ל, בראשי׳ ד[2], מעשה + ג. אתמהא| ח׳ גא[1].
אמ׳ לו| א׳ לו לו[2], אלֿ א[1], אמר לו ד[2]. הכנס| היכנס לגו[2].
רחוץ| ורחוץ א[1]ד[21], למרחץ + א[1].

8: משתיכנס| א[1], עד שלא תיכנס (תכנס ד[21]) לגו[2]ד[21], + ושקול
עצמך משיתכנס (משתיכנס ג, שי שימכנס ו[2]) לגו[2], + וקודם שתכנס
(שנכנס א[1°]) א[1], + ומאחר שתכנס ד[21]. ושקל| ורחץ וקדם + א[1],
כיון שיצא + ד[21]. ולא| לא לד[21]. אמ׳ לו| א׳ לו לו[2], אל א[1],
אמר לו ד[2].

9: כל| היכנס + ג (הנקודות מהוות סימן למחוק). הזיעה| זיעה גא[1].
שיצאת| שיצאה א[1]. יצאת| היתה ג, יצאה א[1]. אמ׳ לו| א׳ לו לו[2],
אל א[1], אמר לו ד[21]. היין| הן א[1]ד[21]. אמ׳ לו| א׳ לו ו[2], אמר לו ד[2],
ח׳ לא[1]. מה| ומה לגו[2]ד[21].

10: אם| ח׳ לא[1]ד[21]. אתה| את גו[2], ח׳ א[1]. שאתה| שאת גו[2], ח׳ ל.
בשר ודם| בש׳ ודם ל, בשר וד׳ ו[2], בן אדם א[1]. מעיינך| מעינך
לא[1]. מעיינו| מעינו לא[1].

11: שלהקבה| שלהק׳ לו[2], של הבה א[1]. על אחת כמה וכמה| (כמ׳ ד[1]),
על אכוב ו[2], עאכו א[1]. הווי| הוי לגא[1]ד[21], האוי ו[2]. אים| אדים
ו[2], אלהים ד[21]. מלא| מל׳ ו[2]. מים| מ׳ ו[2].

12: משמת| ולא א[1]. ימי| חסר א[1]. בראשית| בראש׳ לו[2], כלום א[1],
ולא| משמת א[1]. חסר| חס׳ ו[2], ימי א[1]. כלום| כל׳ ו[2], בראשית
א[1], ח׳ ל. אמ׳ ר׳| א׳ ר׳ לגו[2]א[1]. הקבה| הק׳ לגו[2], הבה א[1].

13: מי| מימי ד[21]ח. בראשית| בראשית ברא׳ ל, בראש׳ ו[2]. ונתן| ונתנם
גו[2]ד[21]. חציים| חצים א[1]. וחציים| וחצים גא[1].
באוקיינוס| באוקינוס ל, באוקיאנוס א[1].

14: הדה היא דכ׳| ה ה ד לד[21], הד׳ דכת׳ ג, הדא היא ו[2], היינו
דכת׳ ח. אים| אדים ו[2], אלים א[1], אלהי׳ ד[1], אלהים ד[2] אלק׳ ח,
ח׳ ל. מלא| ח׳ לגו[2], וגו׳ ח. מים| ח׳ לגו[2]ח.

פליגיה| פלגא לד[21], פלגה ו[2]ח, פלג א[1], ח´ ג.

15: כיפה| ח´ א[1]. ומחמת| ח´ א[1]. בריכה| הבריכה לג, ח´ א[1].
כיפה| ח´ א[1]. מזעת| מזיעת ו[2] ח´ א[1].

16: והיא| טפה א[1]ד[21], ח´ ד[21]. מזעת| מוזעת ל, מזיעת ו[2], ח´ ד[21].
טיפות| טיפים לגד[21], טפים ו[2], טפות א[1]. יורדין| יורדים ו[2].
מים| המים א[1]. המלוחים| המלוחין א[1].

17: ואינן| ואין ל, ח´ ג. מתערבין| מתערבות ו[2], ח´ ג.
אמ´ ר´| א´ ר´ לגו[2]א[1], אמר ר´ ד[21]. ואל| אל לגד[21].
הדן| הדין גא[1]ד[21]. יורדנוס| ירדנה לגו[2], ירדנא ל[ס]א[1]ד[21].

18: בימה| בימא לגא[1]ד[21]. דטבריה| דטבריא לגו[2]ד[21], של טבריה
א[1]. ניסין| ניסים לגא[1], נסים ו[2]ד[21].

19: אדן| אדם לגו[2]א[1]ד[21]. חטין| חטים לגו[2]א[1]ד[21], חיטים ד[1].
או תבן| ח´ ג. ושלש| ושלוש ל, שלש ג, ושל´ ו[2], ג´ א[1].

20: אצבעות| אצבע´ ו[2]א[1]. הן| הם א[1], ח´ גו[2]. מתערבין| מתערב´
ל, מיתערבין ו[2]. ואילו| אלו א[1], ואלו ד[21]. מהלך| מהלכין +
א[1]ד[21]. ואינן| ואין גד[21], אינן ו[2], ואינם א[1].
מתערבין| מיתערבין לו[2], מתערבי´ ד[21].

21:ר´| רבי ד[2]. בר| בן| בשם ר´ ג, ברש א[1]. שמעון| שמע´ לגו[2],
ראה המלה הקודמת א[1]. אומ´| או´ ל, אמ´ ג, א´ ו[2], אומר ד[2].
שהוא| שהן ו[2]. מורידן| מורידין ו[2], מורדן א[1]. במידה| במדה
גו[2]א[1]ד[21]. כי| ואל לו[2], שנא´ + א[1], שנ´ + ד[21].

22: מים| + יזוקו מטר לאידו א[1]. הכמה דתמר| הך מה דאת א´
(אמ´ ד[1], אמר ד[2]) לד[21], הכמדתמר ג, הא כ ד א וֹ[2].

בערכך| מערכך לגו²א¹ד²¹ . כעוביה| כעביו א¹ . שלארץ| של רקיע
א¹ . כן| כך לגו²ד²¹, ח׳ א¹ . עוביו| עובי לו², עביו א¹,
עוביה ד²¹ .

23: שלרקיע| של רקיע גד²¹, שלארץ א¹ . היושב| שנ׳ + ג, שנא׳ +
א¹ד¹, שנאמר + ד² . הארץ| + וגו׳ ד²¹ . וחוג| וכתי׳ + א¹ .
יתהלך| מתהלך לו²ד¹ . חוג| וחוג ד²¹ .

24: לגזירה שווה| גזירה שוה לגו², לגֿשֿ א¹, לגזירה שוה ד²¹ .
ר׳| רבי ד², אמ׳ + ד²¹ . בשם ר׳| בש׳ ר׳ ו², בשר א¹ .
חננה| חננא לגו², חנינא א¹ד², חנינה ד¹ . אמ׳| א׳ לו², ח׳ ד²¹ .
כטעם| כטס לגו²א¹ד¹ . ר׳| רבי ד² .

25: ביר| בר לגו²ד²¹, בן א¹ . נחמיה| גמליאל א¹ . אמ׳| א׳ לו²,
אומ׳ ג, אמר ד²¹ . שתים| בשתים גד², כשתים ד¹, ח׳ ל .
בשלוש| בג׳ ל, שלש ג, בשלש ו², וג׳ א¹ ושלש ד²¹ .
אצבעות| אצבעו׳ ו² . פזי| בן + לגו², ר יהודה בן + א¹, ר׳
(רבי ד²) שמעון בן + ד²¹ . אמ׳| א׳ לו², או׳ ג, אמר ד² .

העליונים יתר על התחתונים כשלשים כסיסטיות בין מים   1

למים למד תלתין רבנן אמ̇ מחצה למחצה   ⊙   2

ויעש א̇ים את הרקיע זה אחד מן המקריות שהרעיש בן   3

זומה את העולם ויעש אתמהא הלא במאמר בדבר יי̇י   4

שמים נעשו וברוח פיו וג̇ו למה אין כח̇ בשני כי טוב ר̇ יוחנן   5

תני לה בשם ר̇ יוסי ביר̇ חלפתה שבו נבראת גהינם כי ערוך   6

מאתמול תפתה יום שיש בו אתמ̇ול ואין בו שלשום ר̇ חנניה   7

אמ̇ שבו נבראת המחלוֹ̇קת ויהי מבדיל בין מים למים אמ̇ ר̇   8

טב יומא ומה מחלקוֹ̇ת שהיא לתיקונו שלעולם ולישובו   9

אין כח̇ בה כי טוב מחלקוֹ̇ת שהיא לערבובו על אחת כמה   10

ואחת כמה אתמהא אמ̇ ר̇ שמוא̇ל בך נחמן לפי שלא נגמרה   11

מלאכת המים לפיכך כח̇ בשלישי שני פעמים כי טוב אחד   12

למלאכת המים ואחד ליו̇ם   מטרונה שאלה את ר̇ יוסה   13

אמרה לו אין כתוב בשני כי טוב אמ̇ לה אפעלפיכן חזר   14

וכללן כולן בסוף וירא א̇ים את כל אשר עשה והנה טוב מאד   15

אמרה לו משל ששה בני אדן באין אצלך ואתה נותן לכל   16

אחד מנא ולאחד אין את נותן לו מנא ואת חוזר ונותן לכולם   17

מנא לא נמצא בכל אחד מנא ושתות אתמהא וביד אחד   18

שתות אתמהא חזר ואמר לה כי̇י דמר ר̇ שמואל בר נחמן   19

לפי שלא נגמרה מלאכת המים לפיכך כתוב שׁ̂לישי שני   20

פעמים כי טוב אחד למלאכת המים ואחד למלאכת היום   21

ר̇ לוי בשם ר̇ תנחום בר חנילייכ̂ח̂ מגיד מראשית   22   ⊙

אחרית מתחילת ברייתו שלעולם צפה הק̇ב̇ה̂ משה קרוי   23

כי טוב ועתיד ליטול את שלו מתחת ידיהם לפיכך לא כתב   24

בהם כי טוב ר̇ יצחק בשם ר יהושע בן לוי למלך שהיה   25

1: העליונים| העליוני׳ ד^{21}. יתר| יותר ו^{2}א^{1}, יתירין ד^{21}.
כשלשים| כל׳ לא^{1}. כסיסטיות| כסיסטיאה ל, גסיסטיות ג,
כסיסטיאות א^{1}, כסיסטאות ד^{21}, מילין ל°.

2: למד| ח׳ א^{1}. רבנן| רבנין לגו^{2}א^{1}. אמ׳| מרין ג, אמרין
ו^{2}ד^{21}, אמרי א^{1}. למחצה| על מחצה א^{1}ד^{21}.

3: אים| אהים ג, אדים ו^{2}, אלים̃ א^{1}. הרקיע| הרק׳ ו^{2}. אחד| א׳ א^{1}.
המקריות| המקראות (המקראו׳ ד^{2}) גד^{21}, המקומות א^{1}.

4: זומה| זומא לגו^{2}א^{1}ד^{21}. העולם| העו׳ ל. אתמהא| אתמ׳ ג,
ח׳ א^{1}. הלא| והלא ד^{21}. במאמר| המאמ׳ ד^{2}; + הן לגו^{2}ד^{21}.
בדבר| הוא + לו^{2}, שנא׳ + גא^{1}, הוי + ד^{21}. ייי| יי׳ לו^{2}, יי
גא^{1}ד^{21}.

5: שמים| שמ׳ ל, שמי׳ ד^{2}. וברוח| ובר׳ ו^{2}, ח׳ א^{1}. פיו| ח׳ א^{1}.
וגו׳| כל צבאם לגו^{2}ד^{21}, ח׳ א^{1}. אין| בשני ח. כת׳| כתוב לד^{2},
כתי׳ א^{1}ד^{1}, אין ח. בשני| בשיני גו^{2}, כתי׳ ח. ר׳| ח׳ א^{1}ח.
יוחנן| יוח׳ ו^{2}, ח׳ א^{1}ח.

6: תני| ותני לגו^{2}, רנן (?) א^{1}, ח׳ ח. לה| ח׳ ח. בשם| בש׳
לו^{2}, בשר̃ א^{1}, אמ׳ ח. ר׳| (ראה המלה הקודמת א^{1}). ביר| בר לגד^{21}ח,
בן ו^{2}א^{1}. חלפתה| חלפתא לו^{2}א^{1}ד^{21}ח, חלפת׳ ג. נבראת| נברא א^{1}.
גהינם| גיהנם ל, גיהינם ג. כי| שנ׳ + גו^{2}ח, שנא׳ + א^{1}ד^{2},
שנאמר + ד^{1}.

7: מאתמול| מאתמו׳ ו^{2}. תפתה| תפת׳ ו^{2}. שיש| ח׳ א^{1}.
בו| שבו א^{1}, לו ח. אתמול| אתמל ג, את...א^{1}. בו| לו ח.
ר׳| רבי ד^{2}. חנניה| חנינא לא^{1}ח, חנינה גד^{21}, חנ׳ ו^{2}.

8: אמ׳ | א׳ לו[2], אומ׳ א[1], אמר ד[2]. נבראת| נברא א[1], נברא׳ ד[2].
מחלוקת| מחלקת ל. ויהי| שנא׳ + א[1], שנ׳ + ד[21]. למים| למי׳
ר[2]א[1]ד[2]. אמ׳ ר׳| א׳ ר׳ לו[2]א[1], אמ׳ גח, אמר רבי ד[2].

9: סב יומא| טביומי לגו[2]א[1]ד[21], טבי ח. ומה| אם לגד[21].
מחלֹקֹת| מחלוקת לגו[2]א[1]ד[21]ח. שהיא| שהוא לגח.
לתיקונו| לתיקון לא[1], לתקונו ד[21]. שלעולם| העולם לא[1],
שלעו׳ ר[2]. ולישובו| ולישבו ר[2], וליישובו שלעולם א[1].

10: כת׳| כתי׳ א[1], כתו׳ ח, ח׳ ד[21]. בה| בו גח, כאן א[1].
מחלֹקֹת| מחלוקת לגו[2]א[1]ד[21]ח. שהיא| שהוא לח.
לערבובו| לעירבובו לגו[2]ח, לערבובי העולם א[1].
על אחת כמה ואחת כמה| על אחת כמה וכמה לגד[2]ח, על א׳ כ׳ וכ׳ ר[2],
עאכו׳ א[1], על אחת וכמה ד[1].

11: אתמהא| אתמ׳ ג, ח׳ אד[21]ח. אמ׳ ר׳| א׳ ר׳ גו[2]ד[2], ארשב̃ן א[1].
שמוא׳| שמוא׳ ג, שמואל ו[2]ד[21]ח (ראה המלה הקודמת א[1]).
בר| בן ח, ח׳ ד[21], (ראה לעיל אמ׳ ר׳ א[1]). נחמן| נחמני גח, ח׳
ד[21], (ראה לעיל אמ׳ ר׳ א[1]).

12: מלאכת| מלאכ׳ ו[2]. לפיכך| לפי׳ א[1], לפיכ׳ ד[1]. כת׳| כתב
א[1]ח, כתי׳ ד[1], כתוב ד[2]. בשלישי| בג׳ א[1]. שני| ב׳ ו[2], כי
א[1]ד[21]. פעמים| פעמ׳ לו[2], טוב א[1]ד[21]. כי טוב| שני פעמים
א[1]ד[21]. אחד| א׳ א[1]ד[1].

13: ואחד| וא׳ א[1]. היום| ליום ו׳, של יום ד[21], למלאכת +
לגו[2]א[1]ח, למלאכתו + ד[21]. מטרונה| מטרונא ח, מטרונ׳ ד[1]; שאלה +
ד[21]; + אחת א[1]ח, + א׳ ד[1], + אח׳ ד[2]. שאלה| (ד[21], ראה המילה
הקודמת). את| ח׳ ר[2]. ר׳| ח׳ ר[2]. יוסה| יוסי לא[1]ד[21]ח,ח׳ ר[2].

14: אמרה לו| אל א[1], ח' לח. אין| למה + לו[2]א[1]ד[21], בשני ח.
כתיב| כת' לו[2], כתי' א[1]ד[1], אין ח. בשני| בשיני לו[2], כתו' ח.
אמ' לה| א' ליה ל, א' לה ו[2], אל א[1], אמר לה ד[2].
אפכלפיכן| אעכלפי כן ל, אף על פי כן ו[2], אעפכ א[1]ד[21], אעפי כן ח.

15: וכללן| וכללו א[1]. כוללן| כולם לו[2], ח' א[1]ח. בסוף| בסוף
א[1]. וירא| שנ' + ו[2]ד[1]ח, שנא' + ד[2]. אים| אלהים ד[21], אלקי' ח
אשר| אש' ו[2].

16: אמרה לו| אמ' לו לו[2], ואמרה לו ח. משל| משל למהד א[1].
ששה| לששה א[1]. אדן| אדם ו[2]א[1]ד[21]ח. באין| באים ו[2]א[1].
אצלך| אצ' ו[2]. ואתה| ואת ד[21]ח. נותן| נותנת ח.

17: אחד| אחד ואחד לד[2], א' וא' א[1]ד[1]. מנא| מנה ו[2]א[1]ד[21]ח.
ואחד| ולא' א[1]ד[1]. אין| אי א[1], לא ח. את| אתה לא[1], ח' ח.
נותן| תתן ח. לו| ח' לו[2]א[1]ד[21]ח. מנא| מנה ו[2]ד[21]ח, ח' לא[1].
ואת| ואתה א[1], ח' ל. חוזר| ותחזור ל, חוזרת ח.
ונותן| ותתן ל, ונותנת ח. לכולם| לכלן א[1], לכלם ח.

18: מנא| מנה ו[2]א[1]ד[21]ח. נמצא| נמצ' ד[1]. בכל| ביד כל לו[2]ד[21]ח,
לכל א[1]. אחד| א' א[1]ד[1]. מנא| מנה ו[2]א[1]ד[21]ח. אתמהא| ח' א[1]ד[21]ח.
וביד| (ראה המלה הבאה א[1]). אחד| ולא' א[1], א' ד[1].

19: שתות| רק + ח. אתמהא| ח' ו[2]א[1]ח. ואמר| וא' לו[2].
כיי| כההיא לו[2]ד[21]ח, ח' א[1]. דמר| דא' לו[2], דאמ' א[1]ד[1]ח,
דאמר ד[2]. ר' שמואל| ר שמוא' לו[2], רשב"ן א[1]. בר| בן לח,
(ראה המלה הקדמת א[1]). נחמן| נח' ו[2], נחמני ח (ראה המלה
הקודמת א[1]).

140

20: נגמרה| + בו ח.   המים| + וכו׳ ח.   לפיכך| לפי א[1]ד[1],
(לפיכך...היום ח׳ ח). כתוב| כת׳ לו[2], כתב א[1], כתי׳ ד[1], כתיב
ד[2].   שני| ב׳ לד[21], כי א[1].

21: פעמים| פעמ׳ לו[2], טוב א[1].   כי טוב| שני פעמים א[1].
אחד| א׳ ד[1], אחת ד[2], ח׳ א[1].   למלאכת| ח׳ א[1].   המים| ח׳ א[1].
ואחד| וא׳ לד[1], ואחת ד[2], ח׳ א[1].   למלאכת| ח׳ א[1].   היום| ח׳ א[1].

22: ר׳ לוי| רש א[1], רבי לוי ד[2]; אמ׳ + ח.   בשם ר׳| בש׳ ר׳ לו[2],
בשׂר א[1], בשם רבי ד[2].   תנחום| תנחומא א[1].   בר| אמ׳ א[1], ח׳ ח.
חניליי| חנילאי לד[21], חלינאי ג, חבילאי ר[2]; + א׳ ר[2], + אמ׳ ד[21].
כת׳| כתיב ר[2]ד[21], כתי׳ ח, ח׳ א[1].   מראשית| מראש׳ ר[2].

23: אחרית| אח׳ ר[2].   ברייתו| ברית ל, בריתו גא[1].
שלעולם| העולם ל, של עולם גא[1], שלעו׳ ר[2].   הקבה| הק׳ לו[2],
הבה א[1].   משה| במשה ר[2].   קרוי| שקראוי ר[2].

24: כי טוב| טוב ד[21].   ידיהם| ידיהן ג, ידן א[1].   לפיכך| לפי׳
א[1]ד[1].   לא| (א[1] חסר מכאן עד סוף הפרשה).   כתב| כת׳ לד[2],
כתי׳ ד[1].

25: בהם| בהן ח.   ר׳| רבי ד[2], ח׳ ח.   יצחק| סימון לגו[2]ד[21],
ח׳ ח.   בשם| בש׳ לו[2], ח׳ ח.   ר׳| רבי ג.   יהושע| יהוש׳ ר[2].
לוי| + א׳ ר[2]ד[1], + אמר ד[2], + אמ׳ ח.   למלך| משל + חד[21].

141

1 שהיה לו ליגיון קשה אם המלך הואיל וליגיון זה קשה לֹא

2 יִכֹתֹב שמי עליו כך אם הֹקֹבֹה הואיל והמים הללו בהם לקו

3 דור אנוש ודור המבול ודור הפלגה לפיכך אל יכתב בהן

4 כי טוב ⊕   ויקרא אֹים לרקיע שמים רב אֹמ אש   א

5 ומים רֹ לוי אֹמ אש ומים רֹ אבא בר כהנא בשם רב נטל

6 הקבה אש ומים ופתכן זה בזה ומהן נעשו שמים שמים

7 שהן שמים מעשיהן שלבריות אם זכה יגידו שמים

8 צדקו ואם לאו יגלו שמים עונו שמים שהבריות משתממין

9 עליהן לאמר שלמים הן שלאש הן אתמהא שלמים   א

10 אתמהא רֹ פינחס בשם רֹ לוי הוא אתא וקם עליה המקרה

11 במים עליותיו הווי שלמים הן סֹמים מה סמים הללו   א

12 מהן ירוקין מהן אדומין מהן שחורין מהן לבנים כך הן

13 שמים פעמים ירוקין פעמים אדומין פעמים שחורין

14 פעמים לבנים רֹ יצחק שא מים טעון מים לחלב שהיה

15 נתון בקערה עד שלא תרד לתוכו טיפה אחת של מסו

16 הוא מרפרף כיוון שהוא יורדת לתוכו טיפה אחת של מסו

17 מיד הוא קופה ועומד כך עמודי שמים ירופפו עמדו   א

18 שמים ניתן בהן את המסו ויהי ערב ויהי בקר יום שני ואתייה

19 כההיא דמר רב לחים היו שמים ביום הראשון ובשני קרשו

142

1: ליגיון| לגיון לגד[21]ח. אמ'| א'| לו[2], אמר ח.
וליגיון| ולגיון לגד[21]ח. לא| אל לגו[2]ד[21]ח.

2: יכתב| יכתב לגד[21]ח, יכתוב ?| ו[2]. כך| לפיכך ג. אמ'| א'| לו[2],
אמר ד[21]ח. הקבה| הק' לגו[2]. והמים| המים לגו[2]. בהם| לקו ד[21].
לקו| ילקו ג, בהם ד[21].

3: אנוש| המבול ד[21]. המבול| אנוש ד[21]. ודור| ח' ח.
הפלגה| ח' ח. לפיכך| לפי' ד[1]. יכתב| יכת' ד[1]. בהן| בהם לו[2]ח.

4: ויקרא| ויק' ו[2]. אים| אהים גו[2], אלהים ד[21]. לרקיע| לרק'
ו[2]. שמים| שמ' לו[2]. אמ'| א'| לו[2], אמר ד[2].

5: ר'| גו[2], (לד[21] חסרים מכאן עד... ר' אבא...). אמ'| א'| ו[2].
כהנא| כה' ו[2], כהנ' ד[1]; + א'| ו[2], + אמ' ד[21]ח. בשם| מש' לו[2],
משו' ד[1], משום ד[2], משם ח.

6: הקבה| הק' לו[2], הב'ה ד[1]. ומהן| ומהם ג. שמים| שמ' לו[2].
שמים| + כת' לגד[1]ח,+כתי' ד[2].

7: שהן| שהם ח. מעשיהן| מעשיהם לח. אם| + אדם ח.
יגידו| הגידו לגו[2]ד[21]ח. שמים| שמי' ו[2].

8: יגלו| יגידו ?| ו[2]. שמים| שמי' ד[2]. עונו| עוונו ל.
שמים| שמי' ד[2]; ד"א + ד[21]. שהבריות| שהבריו' ד[21].
משתממין| משתוממין ל, משתמשין ?| ו[2], משתוממי' ד[21], משתוממים ח.

9: עליהן| עליהם ח. לאמר| לומר גו[2]ח. שלמים| שלמה לגו[2]ד[21]ח.
הן| הם ח. שלאש| שלאש שלמים ג. הן| ח' לגו[2]ד[21]ח. אתמהא| או' ח,
ח' ד[21]. שלמים| ל, של אש ג, ח' ל, + הן ל°ד[21].

10: אתמהא| ח' לח.   פינחס| פנחס גד^2.   בשם| בש' לו^2.   לוי| +
אמ' ד^1, + אמר ד^2.   עליה| עליו ד^{21}.   המקרה| המק' ל.

11: עליותיו| עליו' ל, עלי' ו^2.   הווי| הוי לגד^{21}, האוי ו^2.
סֿמים| סמים לגו^{2}ד^{21}ח, שמים הן + ח.

12: מהן| מהם ו^{2}ח.   ירוקין| ירוקים ו^{2}ח.   מהן| מהם ו^{2}ח, ומהן
ד^1, ומהם ד^2.   אדומין| אדומים לגו^{2}ד^{21}ח.   מהן| מהם ו^{2}ד^{21}ח.
שחורין| שחורים לו^{2}ח, שחורי' ד^{21}.   מהן| מהם לו^{2}ד^{21}ח.
הן| הם גח.

13: שמים| השמים ו^{2}ח.   פעמים| פעמ' ג; כך שמים + ד^{21} (ו^2 מכאן
ועד סוף הפרשה כמעט ואי אפשר לקרוא).   ירוקין| שחורים ל,
ירוקים ח; + וכו' ד^{21}.   פעמים| פע' ל, פעמ' ג.
אדומין| אדומים לגח.   פעמים| פע' ל פעמ' ג.   שחורין| ירוקין ל,
שחורים גח.

14: פעמים| פע' ל.   יצחק| + א' ל, + אמ' גד^1, + אמר ד^{2}ח.
שאן| שמים + ד^{21}.   טעון| ח' ג.   מים| ח' לג.   לחלב| משל + ח.
שהיה| שהוא ג.

15: אחת| ח' ג.

16: כיוון| כיון לגד^{21}ח.   שהוא יורדת| שתרד ל, שיורד גח,
שירד ד^{21}.   אחת| ח' ח.

17: ירופפו| לֿ°, ח' ל.   עמדו| עמודי ג, עָמְֿדו ח, ח' ל; כך + ד^{21}.

18: שמים| ח' ל.   ניתן| נותן לג, עד שניתן ח.   בהן| בהם לד^{21}ח.
יום שני| ח ג.   ואתייה| אתיא לגח, אתייא ד^{21}.

144

19: כההיא דמר| כההיא דא׳ (דאמ׳ גח) לגח, כדאמ׳ ד[21].

שמים| מעשים ל, מעשיהן ג, מעשיהם ח, ח׳ ד[21].

ביום הראשון| בראשון ד[21], ח׳ לגח.

64

BERESHIT RABBA, CHAPTER 46

SCRIBE B

5 ויהי אברם בן תשעים שנה ותשע   פרשתא   מו

6 שנים   כענבים במדבר מצאתי יש֗ אמ֗ ר֗ יודן התאינה הזו כתחלה

7 אותה שנים שנים אחת אחת אחר כך שנים שנים אחר כך שלש

8 שלש עד שאורים אותה בסלים ומגרופיות כך כתחילה אחד היה

9 אברהם וירש את הארץ אחר כך שנים אברהם יצחק אחר כך

10 אברהם יצחק וי֗צחֹ ויעקב עד ובני יש פרו ויש֗   אמ֗ ר֗ יודן מה

11 התאנה הזו אין לה פסולת אלא עוקצה בלבד העבר אותו ובטל

12 המום כך אמ֗ הקֹבֹ֗ה לאברהם אין בך פסולת אלא הערלה הזו העבר

13 אותה ובטל המום התהלך לפני והיה תמים   לכל זמן ועת לכל חפץ

14 תחת השם   זמן היה לאבינו אברהם שניתנה לו מילה בעצם היום הזה֗

15 נמול אברהם   זמן היה שתחפול מבניו במדבר כי מולים היו כל העם

16 היוצ֗ וכל הע֗ היל֗ במ֗ בד֗ בצ֗ מֹ לא מלו   בן ארבעים ושמונה שנה

17 היה אברהם בשעה שהכיר את בוראו אלא שלא לנעול דלת בפני

18 הגרים נימול בן שמונים וחמש שנה היה אבינו אברהם בשעה שנדבר

19 עמו בין הבתרים אלא כדי שיצא יצחק מטיפה כשירה וקדושה נימול

20 בן שמונים ושש שנה היה אברהם בשעה שנולד ישמעאל   אמ֗   א֗

21 ריש לקיש קנמון אני מעמיד בעולם מה הקנמון הזה כל זמן שאתה

22 מזבלו ומ֗עבֹרו ומעדרו הוא עושה פירות כך שצרור דמו משבטל

23 יצרו משבטלה תאוותו אמ֗ אם חביבה היא המילה מפני מה לא

24 נתנה לאדם הראשון אמ֗ לו הקבֹ֗ה אברהם דייך אני ואת בעולם אם

25 אין את מקבל עליך למול דיי לעולמי דיי כן דייה לערלה עד כן דייה

26 למילה שתהא עגומה עד כן א֗   עד שלא מלתי היו באים ומזדווגים

146

5: פרשתא| פרשת׳ לא[2], פרשה גד[21], ח׳ ח. מ׳ו׳| מ׳ז׳ ג, מ׳ד׳ א[1],
ח׳ ח. תשעים| תשעי׳ ד[2]. שנה| וגו׳ ל. ותשע| וגו׳ ר[2], ח׳ לא[1].

6: שנים| ח׳ לו[2]א[1]. כענבים| כענב׳ ר[2]; כתוב + א[1], נאמ׳ + ח.
יש׳| ישר׳ גו[2]א[2], ישרא׳ א[1], ישראל ד[21], אבותיכם ח; + וגו׳ ל, +
כביכורה בתאינה בראשתיה ראיתי אבותי׳ ג, + כב׳ בתא׳ ברא׳ מצ׳ אב׳
ר[2], + כבכורה כתאינה בראשית׳ וגו׳ ד[1], + כבכורה בתאנה בראשיתה
וגומר ד[2], + כתאינה בראשיתה ח. אמ׳ ר׳ יודן| ר׳ יודן אמ׳ ל, א׳
ר׳ יודן גו[2]א[21]ד[1], אמר רבי יודן ד[2]. התאינה| התאנה לא[21], תאינה
ג. הזו| זו לגח, הזאת א[2], ח׳ ו[2]. כתחלה| כתחילה לגו[2], בתחלה
א[21]ח, בתחילה ד[21]; + אורים לגו[2]א[2]ד[21]ח, + אורין א[1], (ח׳ ו).

7: שנים שנים| ח׳ לגו[2]א[21]ד[21]ח. אחת אחת| אחת א׳ א[1]. אחר כך|
ואחרכך לגו[2], ואחכ א[21], ואחר כך ד[21], ואחר ח. שנים| שתים לו[2]
א[1]ד[21]ח, ב׳ א[2], ח׳ ג. שנים| שתים ל, ח׳ גו[2]א[21]ד[21]ח. אחר כך|
ואחרכך ל, ואח׳ כך ו[2], ואחכ א[21], ואחר כך ד[21], ואחר ח, ח׳ ג.

8: שלש| שלוש ו[2], ג׳ א[1]ד[21], שלשה ח. שלש| ח׳ לגו[2]א[21]ד[21]ח.
שאורים| שאורי׳ א[1]ד[1], שאורין ח. אותה| ח׳ ל. בסלים| בסלין ו[2].
ומגרופיות| ובמגרפות לא[2], ובמגריפות גו[2]ד[21]ח, ומגרפות א[1].
כתחילה| כתחיל׳ ו[2], בתחלה א[21]ד[21]ח. אחד| א׳ א[2]ד[1].

9: וירש| ויירש ג, ח׳ לא[21]ח. את| ח׳ לא[21]ח. הארץ| ח׳ לא[21]ח.
אחר כך| ואחרכך לו[2], ואחר כך גד[21], ואחכ א[2], ואחר ח, ח׳ א[1].
שנים| ב׳ ר[2], ח׳ לא[1]. אברהם| ח׳ ר[2]א[1]. יצחק| ויצחק לד[21]ח, ח׳
ר[2]. אחר כך| ואחרכך ל, ואחר כך גד[21], ואח׳ כך ר[2], ואחכ א[21],
ואחר ח; + שלשה גח, + ג׳ ר[2]א[2]ד[21].

10: אברהם| עד + ד[21], ח׳ א[1]. יצחק| ח׳ א[1]. ויעקב| ח׳ א[1].
עד| וא"חכ ד[1], ואח"כ ד[2], (וראה לעיל "אברהם" בד[21]). ובני| ח׳
א[21]. יש׳| ישר׳ גו[2], ישראל ד[21]ח, ח׳ א[1]. פרו| שפרו א[21].

147

ויש׳| וישרצו לגא[21]°[21]ד[21]ח, וישר׳ ר[2]; + וירבו וגו׳ ל, + וירבו
ויעצמו ג, + וירב׳ ויעצ׳ במ׳ מא׳ ר[2], + וירבו ויעצמו במאד מאד
ד[21]. אמ׳ ר׳| א׳ר׳ גו[2]א[21], אמר רבי ד[2]. מה| ח׳ ג.

11: התאנה| התאינה לו[2]ח, תאנה א[21]. הזו| זו לח, זאת א[2].
לה| בה ר[2]א[21]. עוקצה| ערלב א[2]. בלבד| בלב׳ ד[1], ח׳ א[21].
אותו| אותה לא[21]ח. ובטל| + אותו ר[2].

12: אמ׳| א׳ גו[2], אמר ד[21], (אמ׳...המום ח׳ בא[2]). הקבה| הק׳ ר[2],
הבה א[1]ד. לאברהם| לאבינו אברהם ר[2]. בך| לך ג, בה ח.
הערלה| ערלה ל, העורלה גד[1], עורלה ר[2]א[1]. הזו| זו ר[2]א[1]ח, ח׳ ד[21],
+ בלבד ר[2].

13: ובטל| + אותו ר[2]. התהלך| ההד + א[1]. לכל| כתיב + א[1], עת +
א[2]. ועת| וגו׳ ר[2]. לכל| ח׳ ר[2]. חפץ| ח׳ ר[2].

14: תחת| ח׳ ר[2]. השמי׳| השמים לגא[21], ח׳ ר[2]. היה| + לו גח.
לאבינו אברהם| לאברהם ל, לאברהם אבינו גא[21], לאברה׳ (לאברהם ד[2])
אימתי ד[21]. שניתנה| שנתנה ל, שתינתן ר[2]. מילה| המילה לו[2].
בעצם| זמֹ| + ל, שנ׳ + גו[2]ד[21].

15: נמול| נימול לו[2]א[2]ד[21]. אברהם| + וישמעאל בנו ד[21]. תיה| +
להם לבניו ר[2]ד[21], + לאברהם א[2]. שתפול| שימול א[2], שנמולו ד[21].
מבניו| לפניו לג, מהן, ר[2], לבניו לימול א[1], אותם א[2], ח׳ ד[21]
(וראה לעיל, "היה", ההוספות בו[2]ד[21]). במדבר| ב׳ ר[2]ד[1], שתי ד[2],
ח׳ א[1]; + פעמים אחת במצרים ואח׳ במדבר ר[2], + פעמי׳ א׳ במצרי׳
ואח׳ במדב׳ ד[1], + פעמים אחד במצרים ואחד במדבר ד[2]. כי| כשנ׳ +
ג, שנא׳ + א[2], שנ׳ + ד[1], שנאמר + ד[2]. העם| הע׳ ג.

16: היוצ׳| היוצאים לגא[21]ד[2], היוצאי׳ ד[1], וגו׳ ו[2]. וכל| ממצרים
לא[1], וגו׳ א[2], ח׳ גו[2]ד[21]. הע׳| וגו׳ ל, ח׳ גו[2]א[21]ד[21]. היל׳ במ׳
בד׳ בצ׳ ממ׳ לא מלו| ח׳ לגו[2]א[21]ד[21]. בן| ימול + לו[2]א[21]ד[21]
וימל + ג, בן תשעים ותשע שנים ימול + ח. ארבעים ושמונה| מ׳ח׳
לו[2]א[21]ד[21], ארבעים ושמנה גח. שנה| ח׳ ל.

17: היה| ח׳ לו[2]א[21]ח. אברהם| ח׳ לגו[2]א[21]ד[21]ח. בשעה| ח׳ ד[21].
שהכיר| שהכי׳׳ ד[1], כשהכיר ד[2]. אלא| אל׳ ו[2]. לנעול| תנעול ל,
ינעול א[21], לינעול ו[2]. דלת| ח׳ ו[2].

18: הגרים| גרים לגא[21], גירים ו[2], הגרי׳ ד[1]. נימול| ימול לא[21],
וימל ג, יָמּול ו[2], ואם תאמ׳ (תאמר ד[2]) היה לו לימול ד[21].
שמונים וחמש| פ׳ה׳ לו[2], שמנים וחמ׳ ג, ע׳ה׳ א[21], פו"ה ד[1],
שמונים וחמשה ד[2], שבעים וחמש ח. שנה| ח׳ לח. היה| ח׳ לגו[2]א[21]
ד[21]ח. אבינו אברהם| ח׳ לגו[2]א[21]ד[21]ח. שנדבר| שנידבר לו[2],
שדיבר א[1].

19: עמו| ח׳ ל, + הבֿה א[1]. הבתרים| הבתרי׳ ו[2]. כדי| ח׳ ו[2].
שיצא| כשיצא ו[2]. מטיפה| מטפה א[1]. כשירה| ח׳ לגו[2]א[21]ד[21]ח.
וקדושה| קדושה לו[2]א[21]ד[21]ח, קדוש׳ ג. נימול| ימול לו[2]א[21]ד[21],
וימל גח.

20: שמונים ושש| פ׳ו׳ לו[2]א[21], שמנים ושש גח, פ׳וו ד[1].
שנה| שנים ד[21] ח׳ ל. היה| ח׳ לגו[2]א[21]ד[21]ח. אברהם| ח׳ לגו[2]
א[21]ד[21]ח. ישמעאל| ישמע׳ ג.

21: אמ׳ ריש לקיש| אמ׳ ר׳ שמע׳ בן לקיש ל, א׳ ר׳ שמע׳ בן לקיש
ג, א׳ ר׳ שמע׳ בן לק׳ ו[2], ארל א[1], אמ׳ רֿל א[2], אמ׳ ר׳ שמעון ח.
קנמון| קינמון לו[2]. מעמיד| בעולם א[1], מוליד א[2]. בעולם| מעמיד
א[1]. מה| ומה ג ח. הקנמון| קינמון לו[2], קנמון גא[21]ד[21].
הזה| זה א[21]. שאתה| שאת גו[2].

22: מזבלו| מבולו א^{2}, מְעַדְרו ח. ומעדרו| ומזבלו ח. כך| + דמי
מילה א^{21}. שצרור| משצרר לג, שצרו ר^{2}ח, משנצרר א^{1}ד^{21}, ח׳ א^{2}.
דמו| ח׳ א^{2}. משבטל| מה שבטל ל, מי שביטל ר^{2}ח, משביטל א^{1},
שבטל א^{2}.

23: משבטלה| שֶׁמשבטלה א^{1}, מליל שבטל א^{2}, משבוטלה ד^{21}, משביטלה ח.
תאותו| תאוותו ל; + משקשר דמו ד^{21}. אמ׳| א׳ גו^{2}, אמר ד^{2}, ח׳ ח.
היא| ח׳ ל. המילה| המלה א^{1}. מפני מה| למה לגו^{2}א^{21}.

24: נתנה| ניתנה לו^{2}א^{2}ד^{21}ח. אמ| א׳ גו^{2}, אמר ד^{21}ח. לו| ח׳
א^{21}. הקבה| הבֿ א^{21}ד^{1}. אברהם| דייך א^{21}, לאברהם ד^{21}, ח׳ גו^{2}.
דייך| אברהם א^{21}. ואת| ואתה ל ד^{21}ח. אם| ואין ג, ואם ר^{2}א^{21}ד^{21}ח.

25: אין את| אינך ל, את ג, לא א^{21}, אין אתה ח. מקבל| תקבל א^{21}.
עליך| ח׳ א^{21}. למול| המילה א^{21}, לימול ד^{21}ח. דיי| דיו לא^{21}ד^{21},
דייו גו^{2}, די ח. כן| כאן לגו^{2}א^{21}ד^{21}ח. דייה| ודייה לגו^{2}א^{21}
ד^{21}ח. לערלה| לעורלה לגו^{2}. עד כן| עד כאן לגו^{2}א^{1}ד^{21}ח, עֿל א^{2}.
דייה| ודייה לגו^{2}א^{21}ד^{21}ח.

26: שתהא| שהיא ג. עד כן| עד כאן לגו^{2}א^{1}ד^{21}ח, עֿל א^{2}. אמ׳| אמ׳
לא^{21}ד^{1}, אמר ד^{2}ח; + אברהם ל. מלתי| + לא ח. באים| באין גא^{21}ח.
ומזדווגים| ומזדוגים ל, ומזדווגין גא^{21}ח, ומיזדווגים ר^{2},
ומזדוגי׳ ד^{1}.

1 לי תאמר שמשמלתי באים ומזדווגים לי אמ לו הקבה דייך שאני אהיך

2 דייך שאני פטרונך ולאלעׄ לך לעצמך אלא דייו לעולמי שאני אוהו

3 שאני פטרונו רב נתן בשׄ אחא רׄ ברכיה בשׄ ר יצחק אני אמ רׄ שדי

4 אני שאמרתי לשמים דיי ולארץ דיי שאילולי שאמרתי לשמים

5 ולארץ דיי היו נמתחים והולכים תני משם רׄ אליעזר בן יעקב אני
    הוא

6 שאין העולם ומלואו באלהותו תרגם עקילס אכסיוס ואיקנוס אמ   ר

7 לוי למטרונה שאמׄ לה המלך עברי לפניי עברה לפניו ונתכרכמו
    פניה אמׄ

8 תאמר שנמצא בה ממום אמׄ לה המלך אין בך מום אלא צפורן אצבע
    קטנה

9 שליך גדולה מחברתה קימאה העבירי אותו ובטל המום כך אמ הקבה

10 לאבינו אברהם אין בך פסולת אלא הערלה הזו העבר אותה ובטל המום

11 התהלך לפני והיה תמים ואתנה בריתי ביני וביניך וארבה אותך
    במאד מאד

12 רׄ הונא בשׄ בר קפרא ישב אברהם ודן גזירה שוה נאמׄ ערלה באדם
    ונאמׄ ערלה

13 באילן מה ערלה שנאמׄ באילן אל מקום שהוא עושה פירות אף ערלה
    שנאמׄ

14 באדם אל מקום שהוא עושה פירות אמׄ רׄ חנינא בן פזי וכי כבר
    נתנו גזירות

15 שוות לאברהם אתמׄ אלא ואתנה בריתי ביני ובׄ וארׄב אותך ואתנה
    בריתי

16 ר ישמעאׄ ור עקיבה רׄ ישמעאׄ אמׄ אברהם כהן גדול היה שנׄ נשבע יׄי
    ולא

17 ינחם אתה כהן לעולם ונאׄ לו ומלתם את בשר ערלתכם והיה לאות
    ברית

18 אם ימול מן האוזן אינו כשר להקריב מן הפה אינו כשר להקריב
    מן הלב אׄ

19 אינו כשר להקריב ומאיכן ימול ויהיה כשר להקריב הוי אומׄ זו
    ערלת הגוף

151

20 ר׳ עקיבה אומ׳ ארבעה ערלות הם נאמ׳ ערלה באוזן והנה ערלה אזנם ונאמ׳

21 ערלה בפה הן אני ערל שפתים ונאמ׳ ערלה בלב וכל בית יש ערלי לב ונאמ׳

22 לו התהלך לפני והיה תמים אם ימול מן האוזן אינו תמים מן הפה אינו תמים

23 מן הלב אינו תמים ומאיכן ימול ויהיה תמים הוי אומ׳ זו ערלת הגוף מקרא

24 אמ׳ ובן שמנת ימים ימול לכם כל זכר מן האוזן אינו שומע מן הפה אינו

25 מדבר מן הלב אינו חושב ומאיכן ימול ויהיה יכול להשיב הוי או׳ זו ערלת

26 הגוף אמ ר׳ תנחומה מיסתברא הדה דנקרא ערל זכר וכי יש ערל נקבה

1: לי| עצלי ו[2]. תאמר| תאמ' גד[1]. שמשמלתי| משמלתי לגא[21]ד[21],
משלא מלתי ו[2], משאמול ח; + אין ל, + הן גו[2]ד[21]ח. באים| באין גו[2]
ח, יבואו א[21]. ומזדווגים| ומזדווגין גח, ומזדוג' ו[2], ויזדווגו
א[21]. לי| ח' ג. אמ' לו| א' לו גו[2], אֹל א[21], אמר לו ד[2]ח; +
אברהם לו[2]ד[21]ח. אהיך| א', אביך א[1], אלוהיך ד[1], אלוהך ח, ח' א[2].

2: דייך| ח' א[2]. שאני| ח' א[2]. פטרונך| פיטרונך ג, פֿטרונך א[2].
ולא לע| ולא לגו[2]א[21]ד[21]ח. לעצמך| לעצמ' ד[1]. אוהו| אודו לג,
פטרונו ו[2]א°[2]ח, אלוהו א[1]ד[21], פֿטרונו א[2]. + דיו לעולמי לגא[1]ד[21].

3: שאני| ח' ו[2]א[2]ח. פטרונו| ח' ו[2]א[2]ח. רב| ר' לגא[21]ד[1], רבי ד[2],
רב - בש' ח' ח. בש'| בשם ג, אמ' א[1], אום' א[2], ח' ד[21]. ר'| ור'
ד[21], ר' -- יצחק ח' א[21]. ר| ור' ד[21]. בש'| בשם גד[21]. ר'| רבי
ד[2]. יצחק| יצ' ו[2]. אמ ר'| א' לגו[2], אל א[21]ד[21]ח.

4: אני| + הוא לגו[2]א[1]ד[21]. שאמרתי| אמרתי א[2]. לשמים| לעולם
לגא[21], לעולמי ד[21]. דיי| די א[21]ח, ח' ד[21]. ולארץ| ולשמים
גד[2], ולשמי' ד[1], לשמים ח, ח' לא[21]. דיי| די ד[21]ח, ח' לא[21]; +
ולארץ דיי גד[21], + לארץ די ח. שאילולי| ואילמלא ל°, אם לא א[21],
שאלולי ד[21], ואילולי ח, ח' לו[2]. שאמרתי| ל°, אמרתי גא[21], ח' לו[2].

5: לשמים| לעולמ' ל°, לי א[1], להן א[2], להם ד[21]; + דיי ל°גא[1], +
די, א[2]ד[21]ח, ח' לו[2]. ולארץ| ח' לו[2]א[21]ד[21]. דיי| די ח, ח' לו[2]
א[21]ד[21]; + עד עכשיו לו[2]ד[21], + עד עתה א[21], עד עכשו ח.
נמתחים| מותחים לג, מותחין א[21], נמתחי' ד[21], מתוחים ח.
והולכים| והולכין א[21], והולכי' ד[21]; השמים והארץ +, + עד
שיחיו המתים ג. תנ'| תאני ג, תניא ד[21]. מּשׁם| מש' לו[2], משום
גח, בשם א[1], בש"ר א[2], משו' ד[1]. אליעזר| אליע' ר[2], אלעזר ד[21]ח.
בן יעקב| בן יע' ו[2], ב"י א[1].

6: העולם| העול׳ ד[1]. ומלואו| + כדיי ל, + כדי גו[2]א[1]ד[21]ח, +
כדאי א[2]. באלהותי| ל, לאלהותו ג, באלהותו ו[2]א[21], לאלהותי ד[21].
תירגם| תירגם ג. אכסיוס| אקסיוס ל, אכיוס גו[2], אכסיוס ד[2].
ואיקנוס| ואנקיוס גא[1], ואיקיליס (?) א[2], ואנקום ד[1], ואנקום ד[2].
אמ׳ ר׳ לוי| א׳ ר׳ לוי ו[2], רֿל אמ׳ א[1], ר׳ לוי אמ׳ א[2], אמ׳ רבי
לוי ד[2].

7: למטרונה| למטרונא ח, משל + א[1]ח. שאמ׳| שא׳ גו[2], שאמר ד[2]ח.
לה| ח[1] ד[21]. עברי| עיבר׳ ו[2]. לפניי| לפני לגו[2]א[21]ד[21]ח.
עברה| ועברה לגא[2]ד[21]ח, ועיברה ו[2]. ונתכרכמו| ונתככ׳ א[1].
אמ׳| אם ל, אמרה גו[2]א[1]ד[21], אמֿ א[2], ואמרה ח.

8: שנמצא| שנימצא ל, שמצא א[2]. בה| בי לגו[2]א[21]ד[2]ח, בו ד[1].
ממום| פסולת לגו[2]א[1]ד[21]ח, פסלית (?) א[2]. אמ׳| א׳ ו[2], אמר ד[2].
בך| לך ל, ביך ו[2]. מום| פסולת לגו[2]א[1]ד[21]ח, פסלת (?) א[2].
צפורן| ציפורן ל, צפרן א[1]. אצבע| אצבער א[21], של אצבע ד[21]ח.

9: שליך| שלך לח, ח׳ א[1]. גדולה| גדל א[2]. מחברתה| ח׳ לגו[2]
א[21]ד[21]ח. קימאה| קימעה לו[2]א[21], קימעא גד[21]ח. העבירי| העיברי ג.
אותו| אותה ו[2]. המום| + ממך א[21]. כך| (א[21] חסרים מכאן ועד
התהלך לפני...) אמ׳| א׳ גו[2]ד[1], אמר ד[2]ח. הקבה| הק׳ ו[2].

10: לאבינו| לאברהם ד[21]ח.אברהם| אבר׳ ו[2], אבינו ד[21]ח.
פסולת| פסו׳ ו[2]. הערלה| הערולה גו[2]. הזו| הזאת ד[21].
ובטל| ובט׳ ו[2].

11: התהלך| שנ׳ + ג, ההֿד + א[2]. והיה| וה׳ ו[2]. תמים| תמ׳ ו[2].
ואתנה| ואתנ׳ ד[1]. ביני| וגו׳ ל. ובינך| וביניך ד[21], ח׳ ל.
וארבה| וגו׳ ד[1], וגומר ד[2], ח׳ לו[2]א[21]. אותך במאד מאד| ח׳
לו[2]א[21]ד[21].

12: ר' | אמ' רב ד²¹ , ח' ח. הונא | חונא ו², ח' ח. בש' | בשם ג,
אמ' א²¹, ח' ח. בר| ח' א²¹. קפרא| קפרה ו², + (אמ' ח), ח' א²¹.
אברהם| ארם א², + אבינו ו²ח. ודן| ודרש ו². בגזירה שוה| גזירה
שוה גד²¹ח, מקל וחו' ר², בגש̃ א¹, גש̃ א². נאמ'| נאמרה גו²ד²¹,
נאמר ח, + כאן ל. ערלה| עורלה ו². באדם| באלן ג, באילן ו²א²
ד²¹ח, ח' ל. ונאמ'| ונאמרה גו²ד²¹, ונא' א². ערלה| עורלה ו².

13: באילן| באדם גו²א²ד²¹ח. ערלה| עורלה ו². שנאמ'| שנאמרה
ו²ד²¹, שנא' א², שנ' ח. אל| אינו אלא א¹, ח' לגו²ד²¹ח.
מקום| במקום גח, ממקום א²¹ד²¹. שהוא עושה| שעושה לח.
שנאמ'| שנ' לו²ח, האמורה ג, שנאמרה א¹ד²¹, שנא' א².

14: אל| אינו אלא א¹, ח' לגו²א²ד²¹ח. מקום| במקום גח, ממקום
א²¹. שהוא עושה| שעושה ל. אמ' ר'| אמ' ר' ליה ר' לד¹ח, אמ' לו ר'
ג, א' ר', ו², אל̃ ר א¹, אמר ליה רבי ד². חנינא| חנינה לגא¹,
יוח' ו², חנינ' ד¹. בן| בר א¹ד²¹, ח' לח. פזי| פפא א¹, ח' לח.
נתנו| ניתנו גא², היה אבינו אבר' יודע קלין וחומרין ו².
גזירות שות| גש̃ א¹, גזירו' שות א², וגזירות שות ר².

15: לאברהם| ח' ו². אתמ'| אתמהא לא²¹ד²¹, ח' ח. אלא| ח' א²; +
רמז רמזה לו אמרה לו ו², + רמז רמזה לו א¹ד²¹. ואתנה| ח' א².
ואתנ' ו². בריתי| ח' א². ביני| ח' א². ובי'| ובינך לגח,
וביניך א¹ד²¹, ח' א². וארב'| וארבה לו²א¹ד²¹ח, ח' גא², וג' +
ו². אותך| ח' דא²; + במאד מאד מאי וארבה אותך במא' מאד ל, +
במא' מא': ו², + במאד מאד ד²¹, + במאד מאד במקום שהיה פרה ורבה
א¹, + במאד מאד מזה הפסוק ידע ח, ח' גא². ואתנה בריתי| ח' גא²¹
ח; + ביני ובינך ל, + בי' ובי' אל̃ מקום שהוא פרה ורבה ו², +
ביני ובינך במקום שהוא פרה ורבה ד²¹.

155

16: ר׳| רב׳ ד[21]; אתנה בריתי ונאמ׳ נימלתם את בשר ערלתכם + א[1],
| ונמלתם את בשר ערלתכם + א[2]. ישמעא׳| ישמעאל לא[21]ד[21], ישמע׳ ג.
ור׳ עקיבה| ור עקיב׳ ג, ור׳ עק׳ ו[2], ור׳ עקיבא א[1]ד[21], ורׄע א[2].
ר׳| רב׳ ד[21]. ישמעא׳| ישמעאל לא[21]ד[21], ישמע׳ ג, ישמ׳ ו[2].
אמ׳| או׳| לא[2], א׳ גו[2], אומ׳ א[1]ד[2], אומר ד[1]. אברהם| אבר׳ ג,
אברם א[1]. כהן גדול| כוהן גדול ו[2], כֹׄ א[2]. שנ׳| דכתי׳ ו[2], ההדֿ
א[1], שנא׳ א[2], שנאמ׳ ד[21]. ולא| לא ו[2].

17: אתה| וגו׳ ו[2], ח׳ א[2]. כהן| ח׳ ו[2]א[2]. לעולם| ח׳ ו[2]א[2]; +
על דברתי מלכי צדק ל, + לֹׄא דברתי אֹו מלכי צדק ג, + על דברתי
מלכי צדק וגו׳ א[1], + וגו׳ ד[21]. ונא׳| ונאמ׳ לא[1]ד[1], נאמר ג,
א׳ ו[2], ונאמר ד[2]. ומלתם| ונמלתם ד[21]. ערלתכם| ערל׳ ו[2].

18: אם| ח׳ א[1], מאיכן ימול + ו[2], מהיכן ימול + א[1]ד[21].
ימול| ח׳ א[1]. האוזן| האזן א[1], + עדיין ו[2]. כשר| כש׳ א[2].
להקריב| להקרי׳ ד[1]. מן הפה| אם ימול + ו[2], + עדיין ו[2].
מן הלב| אם ימול + ו[2], + עדיין ו[2].

19: להקריב| להריב ד[1]. ומאיכן| מאיכן לו[2], מהיכן גא[21]ד[21].
ויהיה| ויהא לגא[21]. הוי| הווי ו[2], ח׳ א[2]. אומ׳| או׳ לגו[2],
אומר א[1]ד[2], ח׳ א[2]. זו| את גא[2].

20: ר׳ עקיבה| ר׳ עקיב׳ ג, ר׳ עקי׳ ו[2], ר׳ עקיבא א[1]ד[1]ח, רׄע א[2],
רבי עקיבא ד[2]. אום׳| או׳ ו[2], אמ׳ א[1], אומר ד[2], ח׳ ג.
ארבעה| ארבע לגח, ד׳ ו[2]א[2]ד[21], ג׳ א[1]. הס| הן לגו[2]א[21]ד[21].
נאמ׳| נאמרה גו[2]ד[21]ח, נאמר א[1]. באוזן| באזן א[1]ח; + אֿנאמ׳ ל, +
שנ׳ גח, + שנאמ׳ א[1]. והנה| הנה גו[2]א[1]ד[21]ח, ח׳ א[2]. ערלה| עריללה
ו[2], וערלה א[2]. ונאמ׳| נאמרה גד[21], ונא׳ א[1].

21: בפה| + שנ׳ גח, + שנאמ׳ א׳. הן| ח׳ ר׳א[21]. אני| ואני
ר׳א[21]ד[21]ח. שפתים| שפתי׳ ד׳. ונאמ׳| נאמ׳ גו[2], ונא׳ א[2],
ונאמר ד[21]. בלב| + שנא׳ א[1], + שנ׳ ח. יש׳| ישר׳ ג, ישראל א[21]
ד[21]ח. ונאמ׳| נאמ׳ ר[2]. לו| ח׳ א[2], ערלה בגוף וערל זכר וכת׳ ר[2].

22: תמים| תמי׳ ר[2]. אם| ח׳ לא[2], מאיכן ימול + ר[2]. ימול| ח׳
לא[2]. מן| ח׳ לא[2]. האוזן| האזן א[2]ח, ח׳ לא[2]; + עדיין ר[2].
אינו| ח׳ לא[2]. תמים| תם א[1], שומע ח, ח׳ לא[2]. מן הפה| מהפה א[2],
ח׳ ל, אם ימול + ר[2], + עדיין ר[2]. תמים| תם תמ׳ ג, תם א[1], מדבר
ח, ח׳ ל.

23: מן הלב| מהלב א[2], ח׳ ל, אם ימול + ר[2], + עדיין ר[2].
אינו| כך א[2], ח׳ ל. תמים| תמ׳ ג, תם א[1], ח׳ לא[2]. ומאיכן|
מאיכן לו[2]ח, ומהיכן גא[2]ד[21], מהיכן א[1]. ויהיה| ויהא לא[21], והיה
ר[2]. תמים| תם א[1]. הוי| הווי ר[2], ח׳ ח. אומ׳| א׳ ל, או׳ גו[2],
אומר א[2]ד, ח׳ ח. זו| זה לא[1]. מקרא| נקרא ל, נקרא ג, נגדה ר[2],
ר יצחק א[2], נקדה ח, ח׳ א[1].

24: אמ׳| א׳ ר[2], אומ׳ א[2], ח׳ גא[1], + כת׳ ר[2]. ובן| בין ר[2], בן
א[2], ח׳ א[1]. שמנת| שמונת ר[2]א[2], ח׳ א[1]. ימים| ח׳ א[21]. ימול| ח׳
א[1]. לכם| ח׳ א[21]. כל| ח׳ א[21]. זכר| ח׳ א[21]; + לדורותיכם גד[2],
+ לד׳ ר[2], לדורותיכ׳ ד[1]. מן| אם ימל + ל, אם ימול + גא[2]ד[21],
מאיכן ימול אם ימול + ר[2]א[1], אמ׳| אם ימול+ה. האוזן| האזן א[1]ח,+
עדיין ר[2]. מן| אם ימול + ר[2]. הפה| + עדיין ר[2].

25: מדבר| יכול לדבר ר[2], מדב׳ ד[1]. מן| אם ימול + ר[2]. הלב| +
עדיין ר[2]. חושב| מחשב גח, יכול לחשב ר[2]. ומאיכן| מאיכן לו[2],
ומהיכן ג, מאין א[1], מהיכן א[2]ד[21], ומהיכן ח. ויהיה| ויהא גא[21].
יכול| ח׳ גו[2]. להשיב| לחשוב לא[21]ד, מחשב ג, שומע ומדבר וחושב
ר[2], לחשב ח. הוי| הווי ר[2], ח׳ לד[21]. או׳| אומ׳ גא[21]ח, ח׳ לד[21].
זו| זה א[1].

26: אמ׳ ר׳ | א׳ ר׳ גו²א²‎, אר~א¹. תנחומה| תנחום׳ לגד¹,
תנחומא ו²א²ד²ח, תנחום א¹. מיסתברא| מסתברא לגו²א²¹ח, מאין
ימול + א¹. הדה| הדא לגא²¹ד²¹ח, ח׳ ו². דנקרא| דנקדה לח,
דנגדה ג, דקרא א¹, מקרא ד²¹; + דכתיב ג, + דכתיב ג, + כת׳ ו², דכחי׳ ח.
ערל| וערל לגו²א¹ד²¹ח. זכר| + אשר יא׳ ימול את בשר ערל׳ ר׳
יודן בש׳ ר׳ יצחק ר׳ ברכיה בש׳ ר׳ יצ׳ ותני לה בש׳ ר׳ יוסי בן
חלפתא וערל זכר ו². יש| ח׳ א²¹. נקבה| נקיבה ר²ד²¹ח.

1 אלא ממקום שהוא ניכר אם זכר אם נקבה משם מוהלים אותו   ויפל

2 אברהם על פניו וידבר אתו א͏ים ר͏ פנחס בש͏ם ר͏ לוי ש͏ני פעמים נפל אברהם

3 על פניו וכנגדן ניטלה מילה מבניו אחת במדבר ואחת במצרים במצ͏ בא

4 משה ומלן במדבר בא לו יהושע ומלן אני הנה בריתי אתך והיתה לאב א͏

5 דילמא ר͏ אבא ר͏ ברכיה ור͏ אבא בר כהנא אמ͏ ר͏ שמואל בר אמי לו הון א͏

6 יתבין מקשין מנין נוטריקון מן התורה מן הכא והיתה לאב דהוה חסיר

7 ר͏אש   ולא יקרא עוד שמך אברם והיה שמך אברהם בר קפרא אמ͏ כל

8 מי שהוא קורא לאברהם אברם עובר בעשה אמ͏ ר͏ לוי בעשה ולא תעשה

9 ש͏נ ולא יקרא בלא תעשה והיה שמך אברהם בעשה והרי אנשי כנסת

10 הגדולה קראו אותו אברם ש͏נ אתה הוא הא͏ים אשר בחרת באברם שנייה

11 היא שעד שהוא אברם בחרת בו דכוותה הקורא לשרה שרי עובר

12 בעשה אלא הוא שנצטוה עליה דכוותה הקורא ליש͏ יעקב עובר בעשה

13 תני לא שעיקר שם יעקב אלא אם יש͏ יהיה שמך יש͏ עיקר ויעקב טפילה

14 ר. זבדיה בש͏ ר͏ אחא מכל מקום יעקב שמך אלא כי אם ישרא͏ יהיה שמך א͏

15 יעקב עיקר וישרא͏ מוסף עליו ונתתי לך ולזרעך אחריך את ארץ מגוריך

16 את כל ארץ כנען ר͏ יודן אמ͏ אילו חמש ר͏ יודן אמ͏ אם מקבל בניך אלוהותי

17 אני הווה להן לא͏וה פטרון ואם לאו איני הווה להן לא͏וה פטרון אם מקבלין

18 בניך אלוהותי הן נכנסין לארץ ואם לאו אין נכנסין לארץ אם מקיימין א͏

19 בניך את המילה הן נכנסין לארץ ואם לאו אין אתם נכנסין לארץ ר͏ ברכיה

20 רֿ אעֿזר רֿ חלבו בשֿ רֿ אבין בר יוסי כתֿ וזה הדבר אשר מֿל יהושע
אמר

21 להן יהושע אמֿ להם מה אתם סבורים שאתם נכנסין לארץ ערלים כך

22 אמֿ הקֿבֿה לאברהם ונתתי לך ולזרעך אחריך על מנת ואתה את בריתי

23 תשמור ואתה את בריתי תשמר רֿ הונא אמֿ רב ורֿ יוחנן רב אמֿ ואתה

24 למהול שיהא מוהל רֿ יוחנן אמֿ המֿל ימול מיכן למהול שיהא מוהל

25 תנֿי ישראֿ ערל אינו מוהל קל וחומר גוי ערל ונמלתם את בשר
בֿערלתכם

26 כנומי היא תלויה בגוף מעשה במונבז ובזויטוס בניו שֿלתלמי המלך

1: שהוא| שהן ר[2]. ניכר| רואין אותו ויודעין ר[2], ניס (?) א[1].
אם| שהיה א[1]. זכר| נקבה א[1]; + הוא לגו[2]. אם| ואם ר[2], או א[1].
נקבה| נקיבה ר[2]ד[21], זכר א[1]; + היא לא[2], + הוא ר[2]ח. משם| משום א[1],
ח[1]. מוהלים| אותו א[1], מאותו א[2]. אותו| אתו ל, מקום א[21].
ויפל| ויפול א[21]ד[21]ח.

2: אברהם| אברם לגד[21]. על| וגו׳ ר[2]. פניו| ח׳ ר[2].
וידבר| וגומ׳ ל, ח׳ ר[2]ח[21]. אתו| ח׳ לו[2]א[21]. אים| אלהים גד[2],
אלהי׳ ד׳, ח׳ לו[2]א[21]ח; + לאמ׳ ד[1], + לאמר ד[2]. ר׳| ח׳ א[21].
פנחס| פינחס לו[2]ד[2], פינח׳ ד[1], ח׳ א[21]ח. בש׳| בשם גד[2], ח׳ א[21]ח.
ר׳| ח׳ א[21]. לוי| ח׳ א[21]; + אמר ח. שני| שתי גד[21], ב׳ ר[2]א[2]°.
פעמים| פעמ׳ ר[2]א[1]ד[1]; + כתיב ד[21]. נפל| באברהם ד[21].
אברהם| אברם ר[2], נפילה ד[21].

3: וכנגדן| כנגד כן לגו[2]א[21]. כנגדן ד[21]. ניטלה| נטלה ד[21].
מילה| משה א[1], המילה ח, ח׳ ג. אחת| חד א[2], א׳ ד[1], אחד ד[2], ח׳
א[1]; שתי פעמי׳ + ד[1], שתי פעמים + ד[2]. במדבר| במצרים ר[2]א[21]ד[2]ח,
במצרי׳ ד[1]. ואחת| אחד א[1], וחד א[2], וא׳ ד[1], ואחד ד[2].
במצרים| במצר׳ ג, במדבר ר[2]א[21]ד[21]ח. במצרים| במצר׳ גד[1].
בא| מלן א[21].

4: ומלן| ח׳ א[21]. בא| מלן א[21]. לו| ח׳ לגו[2]א[21]ד[21]ח.
ומלן| ח׳ א[21].

5: דילמא| דלמא ל, דלמה גו[2], ח׳ א[21]ד[21]ח. ר׳| ח׳ א[21]ד[21]ח. רבי ד[2], ח׳ ר[2]א[2]
ח. אבא| ח׳ ר[2]א[21]ח. ר׳| ור׳ לגד[1], ורבי ד[2], ח׳ ח.
ברכיה| ברכ׳ ג, ח׳ ח. ור׳| ח׳ ד[2]ח. אבא| אב׳ ר[2], ח׳ ד[21]ח.
בר| ח׳ ד[21]ח. כהנא| כהנ׳ ג, כה׳ ר[2], ח׳ ד[21]ח. אמ׳| ח׳ לגו[2]א[21]
ד[21]ח. ר שמואל בר אמי| (ור׳) לגו[2]ד[1] (ורבי) ד[2], ורשבֿן אבין א[1],
ור׳ ישמעאל א[2], ר׳ שמואל אמ׳ ח. לו| ח׳ לגו[2]א[21]ד[21]ח. הוון| הוו
ל, הוון גו[2]ד[21], הויין א[1], הוויין א[1], ח׳ ח.

6: יתבין| ח' א[21]ח. מקשין| מקשיין גו[2], מקשי' א[1], ומקשין ד[21],
ח' ח. מנין| מניין גו[2]. נוטריקון| נוטריקון נוטרייקון ג, נוטריקו' ד[1],
לנוטריקון ח; + שהוא ו[2]. התורה| התור' ד[1]. מן הכא| מן ו[2]
מהכא א[21], שנא' ד[21]. והיתה| והיית גו[2]א[21]ד[21], ח' ח. לאב| + הם
לגו[2], + המון גוים אברהם א[1], + המון אב הם א[2], + המון גוים לאב
הם ד[21], + לאב הם ח. ההוה| ההוא גו[2]א[21], ח' ח.
חסיר| חסר לגו[2]א[21], ח' ח.

7: ראש| ריש גו[2]א[21]ד[21], ח' ח. ולא| (כל המאמר ח' ח). עוד| + את
לגו[2]ד[21]. אברם| ח' א[1]. יהיה| ח' א[21]. שמך| שמ' ו[2], ח' א[21].
אברהם| ח' א[1]. בר קפרא| בר קפ' ו[2], בק̃ א[1]. אמ'| א' גו[2], אומ'
א[1], אמר ד[2].

8: שהוא קורא| שקורא לא[21]. בעשה| בלא תעשה א[21]ד[21].
אמ' ר' לוי| א' ר' לוי גו[2]א[21], ארל̃ א[1], ר' לוי אמ' ד[1], רבי לוי
אמר ד[2]. ולא| ובלא לו[21]א[21].

9: שנ'| בלא תעשה א[2], ח' לגו[2]א[1]ד[21]. יקרא| יק' ו[2]; + עוד את
שמך ל, + עוד את שמך אבר' ג, + עוד את שמך אברם ו[2]ד[21], + עוד
שמך אברם עובר א[1],+שמך עוד א[2]. בלא| ח' א[2]. תעשה| ח' א[2].
והיה| בעשה + א[2]. שמך| שמ' ו[2]. בעשה| עשה א[1], ח' א[2].
אנשי| ח' גא[1]. כנסת| כנס' א[2].

10: הגדולה| הגדו' א[2]. קראו אותו| קראוהו לא[21]. שנ'| שנאמ'
א[1], שנא' א[2]ד[2], ח' לו[2]. אתה| ח' לא[1]. הוא| ח' לא[1]; + יי גו[2],
+ ייא̃ א[21]ד[21]. האים| האלהים גו[2]א[2]ד[2], האליx̃ א[1], האלי' ד[1].
באברם| + והוצאתו מאור (מאו' ד[2]) כשדים ושמחה (ושמח ד[21]) שמו
אברהם גד[21], + וג' ו[2]. שניה| שניה לא[1]ד[21], שמא ו[2]; דלמא + ד[21].

11: היא| ח' ו^{2}א^{2}. שעד| עד א^{21}. בחרת| בחרתה לו^{2}; אשר + א^{1}.
דכוותה| דכותה גא^{2}(ו^{2}א^{1} חסרים מכאן עד "עליה"). הקורא| הקור'
ד^{1}.

12: הוא| ח' ד^{21}. שנצטוה עליה| שנצטוו' (שנצטווה ד^{2}) עליה ד^{21},
אינו קורא שנא' ויאמר יי' אל אברם שרי אשתך לא תקרא את שמה שרי
כי שרה שמה א^{2}. דכוותה| ודכותה ר^{2}, ודכוות א^{1}, דכותה א^{2}.
הקורא| קורא א^{2}, הקור' ד^{1}, ח' ל. ליש'| ליסר' ג, לישראל א^{21}
ד^{21}.

13: תני| ח' ל. שעיקר| שיעקר גו^{2}, שעקר א^{2}, שיעקו' ד^{1}, שיעקב
ד^{2}. יעקב| יעק' ר^{2}; + ממקומו ד^{21}. אלא| + כי גו^{2}א^{2}ד^{21}.
אם| ח' ל. יש'| ישר' גו^{2}, ישראל א^{21}ד^{21}. יהיה| יה' ר^{2}, ח' ל.
שמך| ח' ל. יש'| ישר' גו^{2}, ישראל א^{21}ד^{21}, ח' ל. עיקר| ח' ג.
טפילה| טפל ל, אפלה א^{21}.

14: ר'| רבי ד^{2}. זבדיה| זבידא ל, זכריה גא^{21}, זכרה ו^{2}, זבדא
ד^{21}. בש'ר'| בשם ר' גד^{2}, בשׁר א^{1}, ר' א^{2}. אחא| + אמ' א^{1}, בשׁר
א^{2}. מכל מקום| מׁמ א^{21}, מכל מקו' ד^{21}. יעקב| שמך א^{1}.
שמך| יעקב א^{1}, לא יקרא יעקב א^{2}. אלא| ח' ו^{2}א^{2}ד^{21}. ישרא'| יש'
ל, ישר' גו^{2}, ישראל א^{21}ד^{21}. יהיה| ח' ד^{21}. שמך| שמ' ל, ח' ד^{21}.

15: עיקר| עקר א^{2}. וישרא'| ויש' ל, וישר' גו^{2}, וישראל א^{21}ד^{21}.
מוסף| טפילה ל, מוסיף גו^{2}; טפלה + א^{21}. עליו| ח' ל.
ולזרעך| ולזרע' ר^{2}. את| וגו' ל, וג' ר^{2}, ח' א^{21}. ארץ| ח' לו^{2}
א^{21}. מגוריך| מגוריי ג, ח' לו^{2}א^{21}.

16: את כל ארץ כנען| ח' לגו^{2}א^{21}ד^{21};+וגו' והייתי להם לאלקי' ח.
אמר| אמ' לא^{2}ד^{21}, א' גו^{2}, אום' א^{1}. אילו| ח' לגו^{2}א^{21}ד^{21}.
חמש| שלש א^{1}. ר'| אר א^{21}, ח' גד^{21}. יודן| ח' גד^{21}.

אמ׳| א׳ ו^2, אום׳ ח, ח׳ גא^{21}ד^{21} . אם| אמ׳ הבֿה לאברהם אברם

(אברם ח׳ בא^2) + א^{21} . מקבל׳| מקבלין לגו^{2}ד^{2}ח, מקבלי׳ ד^1,

יקבלו א^{21} . אהׄותי| אלהותי גו^{2}א^{21}ד^{21}ח . אני| אם ו^2 .

17: הווה| היה א^1, אהיה ד^{21}, הוא ח . להן| להם לג׳ו^{2}א^{21}ד^{21}ח .

לאוה| לאלה ו^2, לאלוה לאלוה א^1, לאלוה א^{21}ד^{21}, לאלקים ח .

פטרון| פטרין א^2, ולפטרו׳ ד^1, ולפטרון ד^{21} ופטרון ח . ואם| אם ל .

איני| אני א^1, לא ד^1; + אני ו^2 . הווה| הוה לח, אהא א^1, אהיה

ד^{21} . להן| להם לג׳ו^{2}א^{21}ד^{21}ח . לאוה| לאלה ל, לאלוה א^{21}ד^{21}ח,

ח׳ ו^{2}א^1 . פטרון| פטרין א^2, ופטרון ד^{21}ח .

מקבלין| נכנסין לגו^{2}א^{21}ד^{21}ח, נכנסים א^1 .

18: אלהותי| לארץ לגו^{2}א^{21}ד^{21}ח, בארץ א^1 . הן| הם ח, ח׳ לגא^{21} .

נכנסין לארץ| מקבלין עליהם אהׄותי ל, מקבלין אלהותי גו^{2}ד^{21},

יקבלו אלהותי א^{21}, מקבלים אלהותי ח . אין| אינן ו^{2}א^{21}, אינם

ד^{21}ח . נכנסין| מקבלין לגו^{2}א^{21}ד^{21}, מקבלים ח . לארץ| אהׄותי ל,

אלהותי גו^{2}א^{21}ח, ח׳ ד^{21} . מקיימין| מקבלין ל, יקיימו א^{21},

מקבלים ח .

19: בניך| ח׳ ל . את| ח׳ א^1 . הן| הם גח, ח׳ א^{21} .

נכנסין| מקבלין ל, יכנסו א^{21}, נכנסי׳ ד^{21}, מקבלים ח .

לארץ| אהׄותי ל, לארץ ישראל א^{21}, אלהותי ח . אין| אינן גו^2,

אינם א^{1}ח . אתם| ח׳ לגו^{2}א^{21}ד^{21}ח . נכנסין| מקבלין ל, נכנסי׳

ד^{21}, מקבלים ח . לארץ| אהׄותי ל, לארץ ישראל א^{21}, אלהותי ח; +

אם מקבלין (בגליון של ל מקיימין) (מְקֵבְֿלֵי מקיימים ח) בניך את

המילה יכנסו (הם נכנסין ח) לארץ ואם לאו אין (אינם ח) נכנסין

לארץ לח, + אם מקבלי׳ (מקבלים ד^2) בניך את השבת הם נכנסי׳

(נכנסים ד^2) לארץ ואם לאו אינן נכנסין ד^{21} . ר׳| רבי ד^2 .

ברכיה| ברכי׳ ר^2; + אמ׳ א^{21}, +ואומ׳ ח .

20: ר׳| ח׳ לגו²א²¹ד²¹ח. אעזר| ח׳ לגו²א²¹ד²¹ח. ר׳| ור לו²¹ד²¹,
ח׳ ח. חלבו| ח׳ א²¹ח. בש׳| בשם גד², ח׳ א²¹ח. ר׳| רבי ד²,
ח׳ א²¹ח. אבין| ענן ו², אבון ד²¹, ח׳ א²¹ח. בר יוסי| ח׳ א²¹.
כת׳| כתי׳ א¹ד²¹, כתיב ד². הדבר| בדב׳ ד¹. יהושע| יהוש׳ ו².
אמר| לא¹ד²¹, א׳ גו², אל̃ א², דבר + לגו²ד²¹ח, מה דבר + א².

21: להן| להם לא¹ד²¹ח, (ראה המילה הקודמת א²). יהושע| ח׳ ח; +
ומלן לגו²ד²¹, + ומלם ח. אמ׳| א׳ ו², אמר ד²¹ח, ח׳ גא²¹.
להם| להן ו², לישראל ח, ח׳ גא²¹. מה| ומה ל, וכי מה א¹, ח׳ א².
סבורים| סבורין לגו²א²ד²¹. שאתם נכנסין| (ניכנסין ו²) ו²ד²¹ח,
שתכנסו א²¹. לארץ| + ישראל א¹. ערלים| עריילם ג, בלא מילה א²¹.

22: אמ׳| א׳ גו²א², אמר ח. הקבה| הק׳ גו², הב̃ה א²¹.
לאברהם| ח׳ א²ח; + אבינו ד²¹. אחריך| וגו׳ ו², + וגו׳ לד²¹, +
את ארץ מגוריך ח. על מנת| ע̃מ א².

23: תשמור| תשמר לגד², תש׳ ו², תשמו׳ ד¹; + מלן א¹, + מיד מלן
א². תשמר| תש׳ ו², תשמור א²¹ד²¹ח, תשמו׳ ד¹. ר׳| א̃ר א²¹, ח׳ ח.
הונא| חונא גו², חגא רבה א²¹, ח׳ ח. אמ׳| א׳ לה ו², ח׳ א²¹ד²¹ח.
רב| רבנין ו², ח׳ א²¹ד²¹ח. ור׳| א̃ר א²¹, ח׳ ח. רב| רבנ׳ ו²,
אמ׳ רב א¹, ר הונא ד²¹, ח׳ א². אמ׳| א׳ ג, אומ׳ ד¹, אומר ד²,
אמר ח, ח׳ א²¹. ואתה| ח׳ א²¹. ואתה| ח׳ א²; + אתה מיכן לג,
(בגליון של ל: את בריתי תשמ׳), + אתה מיכאן ו², + את בריתי
תשמור מכאן א¹, + מכאן א²ח, + מיכן ד²¹.

24: למהול| למוהל גו²א²ד²¹. שיהא| שיהיה ו². מוהל| מהול
גו²א²¹ד²¹. ר׳| רא̃ א², ור׳ ד¹, ורבי ד², (חסר מכאן עד "שיהא
מוהל" א¹). יוחנן| יוח׳ ו², ח׳ א². אמ׳| א׳ גו², אמר ד²,
(ראה המילה ר׳ לעיל א²). המל| המול גו²א²ד²¹ח. מיכן| מכאן א²ח.

למהול| למהול לו[2]א[2]ד[21] , ח׳ ג. שיהא| שיהיה ו[2].
מוהל| מהול לגו[2]א[2]ד[21]ח.

:25 תנ׳| תניא א[2]ד[2]. ישרא׳| יש׳ לו[2], ישר׳ ג, ישראל א[21]ד[21].
מוהל| מל א[2]. קל וחומר| קל וחומ׳ לו[2]ד[1], קו א[21].
ונמלתם| ומלתם א[2], ונמלת׳ ד[1]. בשר| בש׳ ו[2], ח׳ לא[2].
בערלתכם| ערלת׳ לבבכם לא[2], ערלתכם גד[2]ח, ערלת׳ ו[2]א[1], ערלתכ׳ ד[1].

:26 כנומי| כנמ׳ גא[2], בנמי ו[2]. הוא| + היא ל. בגוף| בגוי ג.
מעשה| ומעשה לגד[2]ח, ומעש׳ ד[1]. במונבז| במונב א[1]; + המלך ד[21].
ובזויטוס| וזויטוס ל, וביזוטוס גו[2], ובויטוס א[21], ובזוטוס ד[21],
וביזוניוס ח. בניו| בני לגח, בניי ו[2], ח׳ א[1].
שלתלמי| תלמי לגח, של תלמי א[2]ד[21].

בַּסֵּפֶר

1 שהיו קורין בֹּראֹשית כיון שהיגיעו לפסוק זה ונמלתם את בשר ערלתכם

2 הפך זה פניו לכותל והיה בוכה וזה הפך פניו לכותל והיה בוכה הלך זה ומל

3 את עצמו והלך זה ומל את עצמו לאחר ימים היו יושבים וקורין בספר

4 בראשית וכיון שהיגיעו לפסוק זה ונמלתם את בשר ערלתכם אמֹ אחד

5 לחבירו אוי לך אחי אמֹ ליה את אוי לך ולא אוי לי גילו את הדבר זה לזה

6 כיון שהרגישה בהן אימן הלכה ואמרה לאביהן עלת נומי בבשרן

7 שלבניך וגזר הרופא שימולו אם לה וימולו מה פרע לו הקֹבֹה אמֹ רֹ פנחס

8 בשעה שיצא למלחמה עשו לו סיעה פיסטון וירד המלאך והצילו

9 בן שמנת ימים ימול לכם   תני הלוקח עובר בר שפחתו שלגוי רֹ יוחנן

10 אומֹ ימול לשמונה ותני רֹ חמא בר יסא אמֹ ימול לשמונה ותני

11 שמואל כן מה דמר שמואל לבן או לבת לבן מכל מקום לבת מכל

12 מקום המול ימול מילה ופריעה מילה וציצין המול ימול מיכן אֹ

13 למהול שיהא מוהל המול ימול להביא את הנולד מהול תני רֹ שמעון

14 בן לעזר אֹ לא נחלקו דבית שמי ודבית הלל על נולד כשהוא מהול

15 שצריך להטיף ממנו דם ברית מפני שהיא ערלה כבושה על מה

16 נחלקו על גֹ שנתגייר מהול שבית שמי אומֹ אינו צריך להטיף דם

17 ברית ובית הלל אוֹ צריך להטיף ממנו דם ברית   רֹ אלעזר בנו שלרֹ

18 אלעזר הקפר אומֹ לא נחלקו בית שמי ובית הלל על זה ועל זה שצריך

19 להטיף דם ברית ועל שנולד מהול וחל שמיני שלו להיות בשבת

20 שבית שמי אוֹ צריך להטיף ממנו דם ברית ובית הלל אוֹ אינו צריך

21 להטיף מֹ דם בֹר   רֹ יצחק בר נחמן בשֹ רֹ הושעיה הלֹ כד התלמיד

22 וערל זכר אשר לא ימול רֹ חגיי בשֹ רֹ יצחק רֹ ברכיה בשֹ רֹ יצחק

23 וכי יש ערל נקבה אלא ממקום שהוא ניכר אם זכר הוא ואם נקבה

167

24 היא משם מוהלים אותו   את בריתי הפר זה המושך תני המושך
25 צריך למול ר̇ יהודה או̇ לא ימול מפני שהיא ערלה כבושה אם̇ לפני
26 ר̇ יהודה והלא הרבה היו בימי בן כוזבה וכולם היו חוזרים
ומולים

168

1: קורין| יושבין וקורין לגד[21]ח, יושבין וקוראין ו[2], יושבין
קורין א[1]. בספר| בספ׳ ד[1]. בראשית| בראשי׳ ד[1].
שהגיעו| שהגיע ל, שהגיעו גו[2]א[21]ד[21]ח. זה| הזה לו[2]ד[21]ח, ח׳ גא[2].
ונמלתם| ונמלת׳ ד[1]. את| ח׳ ל; + ערלת לבבכם א[2]. בשר| בש׳ ו[2],
ח׳ ל. ערלתכם| ערל׳ ו[2], ערלתכ׳ ד[2], ח׳ ל.

2: והיה| והתחיל לגו[2]ד[21]ח, ח׳ א[21]. בוכה| ובכה א[21]. הפך| הופך
ח, ח׳ לד[1]. לכותל| ח׳ לד[1]. והיה| והתחיל לגו[2]ד[21], ח׳ א[21]ח.
בוכה| ובכה א[21], ובוכה ח. הלך| הלכו ד[21]. זה| שניהם ד[21].
ומל| מל ל, ונימולו ד[21].

3: את| ח׳ ל ד[21]. עצמו| ח׳ ד[21]. והלך| וזה גו[2]א[21], ח׳ לד[21]ח.
זה| וזה לח, הלך גו[2]א[21], ח׳ ד[21]. ומל| מל לח, ח׳ ד[21].
את| ח׳ לד[21]. עצמו| ח׳ ד[21]. יושבין| ח׳ א[21].
וקורין| וקוראין ר[2], קורין ח.

4: בראשית| בראשי׳ ד[2]. וכיון| כיון גד[21], (ראה המילה הבאה א[2])
(א[1] חסר מכאן עד ערלתכם). שהגיעו| שהגיעו לגד[21]ח, שהגיע ו[2],
וכשהגיעו א[2]. זה| הזה ו[2]ד[21], ח׳ ל. את| ח׳ ל. את| וגו׳ ח, ח׳ לא[2].
בשר| ח׳ לא[2]ח. ערלתכם| ערלתם ג, ערל׳ ו[2], ח׳ לא[2]ח.
אמ׳| א׳ גו[2], אל̃ א[1], אמר ח. אחד| א׳ א[21]; + מהן ו[2].

5: לחבירו| לחברו ח. אוי לך| אילך לגו[2]א[21], אי לך ד[21]ח.
אחי| + וחבירי א[1]. אמ׳ ליה| א׳ ליה גו[2], א׳ לה א[1], אל̃ א[2],
אמר לו ח. את| אחי א[1], אתה א[2]. אוי לך| אילך לגו[2]א[21], אי לך
ד[21]; + אחי ל, + אנא ג, + אני ר[2]א[1], + לי ד[21]. ולא| לא גו[2]ד[21],
ח׳ א[21]. אוי לי| לי ל, אילי גו[2], אילך א[1], אוי ד[21], אי לי ח,
ח׳ א[2]. גילו| גלו א[21]ד[21]. הדבר| + הזה א[1].

6: כיון| ח׳ א[21] .   שהרגישה| הרגישה א[21] .   בהן| בהם ח, ח׳ לא[21] .
אימן| אמם לא[21]ח.   ואמרה| ואמ׳ ל, ואמר׳ ד[1].   לאביהן| לאביהם
לגא[21]ח.   עלת| עלתה ח; בניך + לגו[2]א[21]ד[21]ח.
נומי| נמי לגו[2]א[21] .   בבשרן| בבשרם לגא[21] .

7: שלבניך| ח׳ לגו[2]א[21]ד[21]ח.   הרופא| הרופ׳ ד[1].   סימולו| סימול
ו[2].   אמ׳| א׳ גו[2], אמר ד[2]ח.   לה| ח׳ ל.   וימולו| ימולו גא[21]ד[1].
לו| לה א[1].   הקבה| הבה א[21]ד[1].   אמ| א׳ גו[2], אמר ד[2], ח׳ א[21].
ר׳| רבי ד[2], ח׳ א[21].   פנחס| פינחס לד[21], ח׳ א[21].

8: בשעה| ח׳ א[21] .   שיצא| כשיצא א[21] .   עשו| עשה ר[2]א[21] .
פיסטון| פיסמון ג, פוסטון ר[2]א[2], פושטון (?) א[1], של פסטון ד[21].
המלאך| מלאך ח.

9: ובן| בן ר[2].   שמנת| שמונה ר[2]א[2]ד[21].   שמונה א[1].   ימים| ח׳ א[1].
ימול| וג׳ ר[2].   לכם| וגו׳ ל, ח׳ גו[2]; + כל זכר א[2].
תני| תני׳ ד[1], תניא ד[2].   עוברן| בן א[1].   שלגוי| של גוי ד[1]; +
ימול ג.   ר| רבי ד[2].   יוחנן| יוח׳ ר[2].

10: אומ׳| א׳ ג, או׳ ר[2], אמ׳ א[21]ד[21], ח׳ ל.   לשמונה| לח׳ ר[2].
ותני| ותאני ד[21].   חמא| חייה ר[2].   ברן| בן א[2].   יסא| יוסי לגו[2]ד[21]
דוסא א[21].   אמ׳| א׳ ג, או׳ ר[2], ח׳ א[21]ד[21].   לשמונה| לח׳ לו[2].

11: שמואל| שמוא׳ ר[2].   כן| בן לג, ח׳ ר[2].   מה| מן ג, ח׳ ר[2]א[21].
דמרן| דאמ׳ לא[2]ד[1], דא׳ ג, דאמר א[2]ד[2], ח׳ ר[2].   שמואל| ח׳ א[21].
לבן| לכן ד[2].   או| ח׳ ר[2].   לבת| ח׳ ר[2].   לבן| ח׳ ד[21].
מכל מקום| מ̃מ או א[2].   לבת| ח׳ ר[2]ד[21].   מכל מקום| מ̃מ א[21], ח׳
ר[2]ד[21].

:12 המול| המל לא^1. מילה| ומלה ג. המול| המל ל, (א^{21} חסרים
מכאן עד.... מוהל). מיכן| מיכאן ו^2, מכאן ח.

:13 למהול| למוהל לו^{2}ד^{21}, להמול (?) ג. שיהא| שיהיה ו^2.
מוהל| מהול לו^{2}ד^{21}. המול| המל לא^2. את| ח' ח. הנולד| שנולד
לגו^{2}א^{21}ד^{21}. ר' שמעון| ר' שמע' לגו^2, רשׁ א^{21}, רבי שמעון ד^2.

:14 לעזר| אלעזר לגא^{1}ד^{21}, אלע' ו^2, אלעז' א^2. א'| אום' ד^1,
אומר ד^2, ח' גו^{2}א^{21}. דבית שמי| בית שמי ל, בית שמאי ו^{2}ד^{21},
בשׁ א^{21}. ודבית הלל| (הילל ג) ג, ובית הלל לו^{2}ד^{21}, ובהׁ א^{21}.
נולד| שנולד גו^{2}א^{21}ד^{21}. כשהוא| ח' לגו^{2}א^{21}ד^{21}.

:15 שצריך| שהוא צריך גו^{2}א^2 (צרי' ד^1) ד^{21} (א^1 חסר מכאן עד...
כבושה והושלם בגיון ביד אחר). מפני| ח' ל. שהיא ערלה| שהוא
ערלה ג, שהיא עורלה ו^2, שהערלה א^2, ח' ל. כבושה| ח' ל.
על| ועל גו^{2}א^{2}ד^{21}.

:16 על| (ל חסר מכאן עד... ועל שנולד מהול). נ'| מ' ג, גר
רא^{2}ד^{21}. שנתגייר| ח' א^{21}. שבית שמי| שבית שמאי ו^{2}ד^2, דבשׁ
א^{21}, שבי' שמאי ד^1. אום'| או' גו^2, אומרים א^{1}ד^2. אינו| ח'
גו^{2}א^{21}ד^{21}. צריך| שהוא צרי' (צריך ד^2) ד^{21}.
להטיף| + ממנו גא^{21}ד^{21}.

:17 ברית| ח' ד^2. ובית הלל| ובית הילל ג, בית הלל ו^2, ובהׁ א^{21}.
או'| אומרים א^1, אום' א^{2}ד^1, אומרי' ד^2; + אינו גו^{2}א^{21}ד^{21}.
צריך צרי' ד^1. להטיף| ח' גא^{1}ד^{21}. ממנו| ממ' ו^2, ח' גא^{1}ד^{21}.
דם| ח' גא^{1}ד^{21}. ברית| ח' גא^{1}ד^{21}. אלעזר| אליעזר ג, אלע' ו^2,
אלעז' א^2, עזר ד^1. בנו| ח' א^{21}. שלר'| של ר' ד^{21}, ח' א^{21}.

18: אלעזר| אליעזר ר^2, יוסי ד^{21}, ח´ א^{21}. הקפר| הגלילי ד^{21},
ח´ א^{21}. אומ´| א´ גו^2. לא נחלקו| בית שמאי ובית הלל ר^{2}ד$^2_1$,
בש̃ ובה̃ א^1, בי´ שמי ובי´ הלל ד^1. בית שמי ובית הלל| (הילל ג)
ג, בש̃ ובה̃ א^2, נחלקו ר^2, לא נחלקו א^{1}ד^{21}. על| לא + ג.
ועל| ח´ ד^{21}. זה| וזה ד^{21}. שצריך| שהוא צריך גו^2 (צרי´ ד^1)
ד^{21}.

19: להטיף| + ממנו גו^{2}א^{21}ד^{21}. ברית| ובה̃ אומרים אינו א^1.
ועל| על לגו^{2}א^{21}ד^{21}; על (למחר ר^2, ועל א^{2}ד^{21}) מה (ח´ ו^2)
נחלקו + ר^{2}א^{21}ד^{21}, + מי ג, + מה א^2. וחל| שחל גא^1, חל ו^2,
וכשחל ד^{21}. שמיני שלו| ח´ ד^1; יום + ר^{2}ד^{21}; להיות בשבת א^2.
להיות בשבת| (להיות ח´ א^1, להיו´ ד^1) לגו^{2}א^{1}ד^{21}, שמיני שלו א^2.

20: שבית שמי| שבית שמאי ד^2, בש̃ א^{21}, שבי´ שמאי ד^1. או´| א´
א^1, אומ´ א^{1}ד^1, אומרים ד^2. צריך| צרי´ א^1. ברית| ברי´ ד^1.
ובית הלל| בית הלל ר^2, ובה̃ א^{21}, ובי´ הלל ד^1. או´| א´ א^1,
אומ´ א^{2}ד^1, אומרי´ ד^2. אינו| ח´ ו^2.

21: להטיף| ח´ לגא^{21}ד^{21}. ממ´| ממנ´ ר^2, ח´ לגו^{2}א^{21}ד^{21}.
דס| ח´ לגא^{21}ד^{21}. בר´| ברית ר^2, ח´ לגא^{21}ד^{21}. ר´| ור´ א^1,
רבי ד^2. יצחק בר נחמן| יצח´ בן נח´ ו^2. בש´ ר´| בשם ר´ גד^2,
בש̃ א^{21}. הושעיה| הושעיא לגו^{2}א^2, אושעיא א^1; + אמ´ א^1.
הל´| הלכה לגו^{2}א^{21}ד^{21}. כד´| כדב´ ל, כדבר´ גו^{2}א^{21}ד^{21}.
התלמיד| התלמי´ ד^1.

22: זכר| זכ´ ו^2. אשר| אש´ ו^2, ח´ לד^{21}. לא| ח´ לד^{21}.
ימול| ח´ לד^{21}; + את בש´ ער´ ו^2, + את בשר ערלתו ח. ר´| ח´
א^{2}ח. חגיי| חגי גא^{1}ד^{21}, ח´ א^{2}ח. בש´| בשם ג, אומ̃ר א^1, א^{2}ח.
ר´| ח´ א^{21}ד^{21}ח. יצחק| יצח´ ו^2, ח´ א^{21}ד^{21}ח. ר´| ח´ א^{21}ד^{21}ח.
ברכיה| ברכי´ ו^2, ח´ א^{21}ד^{21}ח. בש´| בשם ג, ח´ א^{21}ד^{21}ח.

ר׳ | ח׳ א[21]ד[21] . יצחק| יצ׳ ר , ח׳ א[21]ד[21]; + אום׳ ח.

23: נקבה| נקיבה ו[2]ד . שהוא ניכר| שניכר לא[21] . זכר| הוא א[1]ח.
הוא| ח׳ לא[2]ד[21], זכר א[1]ח. ואם| אם לגא[21]ד[21] .
נקבה| נקיבה גו[2]ד[21], היא א[1].

24: היא| הוא ו[2] , נקבה א[1], ח׳ לגד[21]ח. משם| ח׳ ד[21].
מוהלים| מוהלין גא[21], מולין ר[2]. אותו| אתו ל. הפר| היפר ו[2].
המושך| המשוך לגו[2]א[2]ד[21]ח. תני| תניא א[2]. המושך| המשוך
לגו[2]א[21]ד[21]ח.

25: צריך| צרי׳ ד[1]; אינו + ד[21]. למול| לימול לגו[2]א[21]ד[21]ח.
ר׳| רבי ד[2]. יהודה| יודה ל, יהוד׳ ר[2]ד[1]. או׳| א׳ לו[2], אום׳
א[21]ד[1]ח, אומר ד[2]. לא| ח׳ ד[21]. מפני| ח׳ א[2]. שהיא| שהוא גו[2].
ערלה| ערל׳ ד[1]. אמ׳| אמרו לגו[2]א[21]ח, אמר׳ ד[1], אמר ד[2].

26: ר׳| ח׳ ו[2]. יהודה| יהוד׳ ד[1]. הרבה| כמה ל. היו| היה
גא[21], הוא ו[2]. בימי| ממי גו[2]. בן| ח׳ ח. כוזבה| מזכה ג,
כוזבא א[21], כוזיבא ד[21]. וכולם| לכולם ל, לכולהם ג, לכולהן ו[2],
לכלהן א[1], לכלהון א[2], לכולהון ד[21], והולידו כולם ח; + בנים לגו[2],
+ בני׳ ד[1], + בנין ד[2],+בנים נימולים ח. היו| ח׳ לגו[2]א[21]ד[21]ח.
חוזרים| וחוזרין ג, חוזרין ר[2]א[21]ד[2], חוזרי׳ ד[1], וחוזרים ח.
ומולים| ומוהלים ל, ומלין ר[2]א[2], ומולי׳ ד[1], ומולין ד[2].

1   הדה היא המול ימול אפילו ארבעה וחמשה פעמים את בריתי הפר זה

2   המושך

1 : הדה היא| הֹהֹד לאא[21]ד[21], הדהי ג, הד׳ היא ו[2], היינו דכתיב ח.
המול| ח׳ א[1]. אפילו| אפי׳ א[2]ד[21], ח׳ א[1]. ארבעה| ד׳ לאא[21]ד[21].
וחמשה| וה׳ לא[21], ה׳ ד[21]. פעמים| פעמ׳ ל. הפר| היפר ו[2].

2 : המושך| המשוך לגאא[21]ד[21]ח.

BERESHIT RABBA, CHAPTER 67

SCRIBE C

20 ויחרד יצחק חרדה   סֹז   פרשׁ

21 חרדת אדם יתן מוקשׁ וגֹו חרדה שׁהחרידה רות לבועז [שׁגֹ]

22 ויחרד האישׁ וילפת יתן מוקשׁ בדין היה לקללה אלא ובוטח

23 בֹיֹי ישׁוגב נתן לו וביירכה ויאמר ברוכה את לֹיֹי בתי חרדה

24 שׁהחריד יעקב ליצחק ויחרד יצחק חרדה יתן מוקשׁ בדין

25 והיה לקללו אלא ובוטח בֹיֹי ישׁוגב נתן בלבו וביירכו גם ברוך יהיה

26 ויחרד יצחק חֹר אמֹ רֹ חמא ביֹר חנינה מאד מחרדה שׁ

176

20: פרש׳ | פרשה גד[2], פרשתא ו[2], פרשת א[21], אין כאן פרשה בד[1] וח.
ס׳ ז׳ | ס ה א[1]. חרדה | + וגו׳ ל, + גדולה עד מאד גח, + גדולה
א[1]ד[21].

21: חרדה | כת׳ + לג, כתי׳ + א[21]ד[1]ח, כתיב ד[2]. וגו׳ | ובוטח
(ובוט׳ ו[2]) ביי ישוגב (ישוג׳ ו[2]) לגו[2]א[21]ד[21]ח. שההחרידה | שהחריד
ו[2], שחרדה ד[21]. לבועז | + שנ׳ לגח, + שנא׳ א[21]ד[1], + שנאמר ד[2].

22: האיש | ח׳ ד[1]. וילפת | וילפ׳ ו[2]. היה | הוא ל. אלא | אל׳ ו[2].

23: ישוגב | ישוג׳ ו[2]. לו | בלבו לגו[2]א[21]ד[21]ח. ובירכה | וברכה
גו[2]א[21]ח. ויאמר | ויא׳ ו[2]א[2], ויאמ׳ ד[1], ח׳ לא[1]; שנ׳ + לגח,
שנא׳ + א[21]. ברוכה | וברוכה א[2], ברוכ׳ ד[1]. את | ח׳ ל.
חרדה | ד"א חרדת אדם יתן מוקש + א[2].

24: יעקב | יצח׳ ו[2]. ליצחק | ליעק׳ ו[2], את יצחק א[21]; + שנ׳ גח, + שנ׳ גח, +
אביו א[21], + שנא׳ ד[21]. ויחרד | ח׳ לא[21]. יצחק | ח׳ לא[21].
חרדה | חר׳ ו[2], ח׳ לא[21]; + גדולה עד מאד ד[21], + גדולה ח.
יתן | ח׳ לגא[2]. מוקש | ח׳ לגא[2].

25: והיה | היה לגו[2]א[21]ד[21]ח. ובוטח | ח׳ ל. בײ | ח׳ ל.
ישוגב | ישגב ג, ח׳ ל. נתן | ח׳ ד[21]. בלבו | ח׳ ד[21].
וביר כו | וברכו גו[2]א[1]ח, לברכה א[2], שברכו ד[21]; + שנ׳ לגח, + שנא׳
א[21], + ואמר ד[21].

26: ויחרד | גלו ג, (ח׳ ל מכאן עד... חנינה) ח׳ ח. יצחק | יצחק עד גא[2],
יצח׳ ו[2], ח׳ ח. חר׳ | מאד גא[2], חרדה א[1]ד[21]ח, + גדולה עד מאד א[1]ח,
גדולה וגו׳ (וגומ׳ ד[2]) ד[21]. אמ׳ ר׳ | א׳ ר גו[2]א[2]ד[1], אמר ר׳ ד[2].
חמא | אחא א[21]. ביר | בר גו[2]א[2]ד[21], ח׳ ח. חנינה | חני׳ ו[2],

חנינא א[21], ח´ ח. מאד| עד מאד ל, אחד ו[2], ח´ ח. מחרדה| יותר + ח.

112

1 שחרד על גבי המזבח אמ׳ מי הוא זה שנעשה סרסוֹר׳ בינו לבין

2 הקֹבֹה שיטול יעקב את הברכות כלפי רבקה אמרו אמ׳ ר׳ יוחנן

3 מי שיש לו שני בנים אחד נכנס ואחד יוצא חרד אלא בשעה אתמהא

4 שנכנס עשו נכנסה גהינם עימו רב נתן בשם ר׳ אחא התחילו

5 כותלי הבית מרתיחים היא דהוא אמ׳ מי אפוא מי הוא זה שהוא

6 עתיד ליפֿות כן אני בני אٰ אמ׳ לו הקֹבֹה לא את ולא בנך אלא הוא אٰ

7 הצד ציד הוא צד הצייד אמ׳ ר׳ לעזר ביר׳ שמעון ציידה חיך אٰ

8 צידך פכור הרעייה היך תרעך פכיר ומקלקלהדא היא לא

9 יחרוך רמיה צידו וגו׳ רבנן אמרי לא יארוך ואל יאחר הקבה

10 לרמיי ולצידו דמר ר׳ יהושע בן לוי כל אותו היום היה עשו צד

11 צבאים וכופתן ומלאך בא ומתירן עופות ומסרסן ומלאך בא

12 ומפריחן כל כך למה והון אדם יקר חרוץ כדי שיבא יעקב אٰ

13 ויטול את הברכות שהן עיקרו שלעולם חרוצות לו ר׳ חנונה

14 בר פפא שאליה לר׳ אחא אמ׳ ליה מהוא דכ׳ והון אדם יקר חרוץ

15 אמ׳ ליה חרוצה היא ביד הצדיקים שאינן נוטלים מן יקר

16 שלהם לעתיד לבא בעולם הזה ואוכל מכל ר׳ יהודה ור׳ נחמיה

17 ר׳ יודה אמ׳ מכל מה שנברא בששת ימי בראשית ר׳ נחמיה אוֹ׳

18 מכל טוב שהוא מותקן לצדיקים לעתיד לבא אמ׳ לו עיקרו

19 שלדבר מה האכילך אמ׳ לו איני יודע אלא טועם הייתי טעם

20 פת טעם בשר טעם דגים טעם חגבים טעם כל מעדנים

21 שבעולם אמ׳ ר׳ ברכיה כיוון שהזכיר בשר מיד בכה אמ׳ אני

22 קערה אחת שלעדשים האכילני ונטל את בכורתי אתה

23 שהאכילך בשר על אחת וכמה אמ׳ ר׳ לוי לפי שאבינו

24 יצחק מתפחד ואומר תומר שלא עשיתי כשורה שעשיתי

25 את שאינו בכור בכור וכיון שאמ׳ את בכורתי לקח אמ׳ יאות

26 ברך אמ׳ ר׳ לעזר אין קיום הגט אלא בחותמיו שלא תאמר

1: שחרד| שהחריד א^{21}. על גבי| עג̃ א^{21}. המזבח| המז׳ ר^{2}.
אמ׳| א׳ ר^{2}, אמר א^{1}ח. זה| ח׳ לו^{2}ד^{2}.

2: הקבה| המקום לגא^{21}ד^{1}ח, המקו׳ ר^{2}ד^{2}. שיטול| שנטל ד^{21}.
יעקב| יעק׳ ר^{2}. אמרו| אמו לח, אמנו א^{1}. אמ׳ ר׳| א̃ ד̃ גר^{2}א^{21},
אמר רבי ד^{2}. יוחנן| יוח׳ ר^{2}.

3: שני| ב׳ לו^{2}. אחד| א׳ א^{21}. נכנס| יוצא ד^{21}ח. ואחד| וא׳
א^{21}. יוצא| נכנס ד^{21}ח. חרד| חריד ד^{2}ֹ + אתמהא לגו^{2}ד^{21}.
אלא| אל׳ ר^{2}.

4: עשו| יעֹקֹב א^{2}; + אצל אביו ד^{21}. גהינם| גיהינם ל, גיהנם ג,
עמו ד^{21}. עימו| עמו לו^{2}א^{21}ח, ועמו ג°, גיהנם ד^{21}.
רבן| ח׳ ד^{21}ח. נתן| ח׳ ד^{21}ח. בשם| בש׳ לו^{2}א^{21}, ח׳ ד^{21}ח.
אחא| + אמ׳ א^{1}ד^{1}ח, אמר ד^{2}. התחילו| התחיל ר^{2}, כותלי א^{2}.

5: כותלי| כתלי גד^{21}, הבית א^{2}. הבית| התחילו א^{2}.
מרתיחים| מרתיחין לגו^{2}א^{2}ח, מותחין א^{1}, מרתיחים ד^{21}.
היא דהוא אמ׳| ה̃ ד̃ ל, היאדן אמ׳ ג, היא דהוא א׳ ר^{2}, זהו שאמר
א^{1}, זש̃ א^{2}, ה̃ ה̃ דהוא אמ׳ ד^{1}, הדא הוא דהוא ד^{2}, אמר ח. מי| (ח׳
א^{21} מכאן עד... הוא הצד). אפוא| איפה ג, איפוא ר^{2}ד^{21}ח.
זה| ח׳ ל. שהוא| ח׳ ל.

6: עתיד| שעתיד לו^{2}. ליפות| ליאפות ר°גו^{2}ד^{21}ח, לאיפות ל.
כן| כאן לו^{2}ד^{21}ח. אני| + או ר°גד^{21}ח. בני| יעקב בני ח.
אמ׳| א׳ ר^{2}, אמר ד^{2}. הקבה| הק׳ גו^{2}, הבה̃ ד^{1}, הקו׳ ב"ה ד^{2}.
לא| ח׳ ג. את| אתה ח. ולא| לא ל. בנך| יעקב בנך ח.

7: הוא| ח׳ א^{21}, (ח חסר מכאן עד... לא יחרוך). צד| הצד גו^{2}ד^{21},
ח׳ א^{21}. הצייד| ציד ר^{2}, הציד ד^{21}, ח׳ א^{21}. אמ׳ ר׳| א̃ ד̃ גו^{2}

א[21]ד[21] . לעזר| אלעזר גו[2]א[21]ד[21] . ביר שמעון| בר שמ׳ לגו[2],
ברשׁ א[21], בר שמעון ד[21] . ציידה| ציידא לא[1]ד[21] .
חירן| היר לגו[2]א[21]ד[21] .

8: צי׳ד׳ך| צדוך לו[2]א[2]ד[21] , ציידך ג, צדייך א[1] . פכור| פכיר ל,
סכור (?) ג.   תרעייה| תרעיא גד[21] , תרועיא א[1] , תרועה א[2] .
פכיר| פכור ר[1]א[21]ד[21] . ומקלק| ומקלקל ו[1] , ומקולקל גא[2]ד[21] ,
ומלקלק א[1] . הדה היא| אׁ אׁ ד׳ לא[1]ד[21] , הדהי ג, אׁ אׁ ו[2] , כת׳ ח.

9: יחרורן| יחרך ו[2] . רמייה| רמיה גא[2]ד[21]ח, רמיו א[1] .
וגו׳| ח׳ לגו[2]א[21]ד[21]ח. רבנן| רבנין לגו[2]א[21] . אמרי| אמ׳ ל,
אמרין גא[1] , אמר׳ ו[2] ; + יחיינו (תחיינו א[2]) מיומים ונחיה לא
יחיה הקבה (הבֹה א[2]) לא לרמאי ולא לצידו ר׳ אלעזר בנו שלר׳ יוסי
הגלילי אומר (אומ׳ א[2]) א[21] . יארורן| יארך ו[2] , יאריך א[21]ח,
יאחר ד[21] . ולא| לא ל. יאחרן| יאריך ד[21] .

10: לרמיי| לרמאי לא[21]ד[21]ח; לא + א[1] . ולצידו| ולא לצידו לו[2]
גא[1] ; + ר׳ ליעזר (אליעזר גד[21] , אליע׳ ו[2]) בנו שלר׳ יוסי הגלילי
(הגלי׳ ו[2] , ח׳ ד[21]) (+ או׳ גו[2] , + אומר ומה הוא לא יחרוך ד[21])
לא יארוך (יארך ו[2] , יאריך ד[21]) לא (ולא ג, ח׳ ו[2]ד[21]) יאחר
(ח׳ ו[2]ד[21]) הקבה (הק׳ ו[2]) לרמאי (לרמיי גו[2]) ולצידו (+ ר׳
אליעזר בנו שלר׳ יוסי הגלילי או׳ לא יארוך לא יאחר הקבה לרמאי
ולצידו ג) לגו[2]ד[21] . (וראה לעיל... אמרי). דמרן| דאמ׳ לחד[2] , דא׳
גו[2] , דאמר ד[1] . (ראה המלה הבאה א[21]) . ר׳ יהושע בן לוי| רבי ד[2] ,
ר׳ יהושׁ׳ בן לוי לגו[2] , אריבֹל א[21] . אותו| ח׳ ל. היה| ח׳ ל.
עשו| ח׳ ג.

11: עופות| ועופות ד[21] . ומסרסן| ומסכסן גא[1] , ומסכסכן א[1] ,
וממרטן ח.   ומלאך| ובא לו[2]א[21]ח. בא| מלאך לו[2]א[2]ח.

:12 ומפריחן| ומתירן ומפריהן ג.   כל| וכל גא[21]ד[21]ח.   והון| הון
ל.   שיבא| שיבוא לו[2]גא.   יעקב| + שהוא יקרו שלעולם ד[21].

:13 ויטול| ויקבל ח.   את| ח' ו[2]א[21].   הברכות| ברכותיו א[21].
שהן| שהוא לגו[2]א[21]ח, ח' ד[21].   עיקרו| עקרו ל, יקרו ג, שמעיקר
ד[21].   שלעולם| העולם ד[21].   חרוצות| (ח חסר מכאן עד... ואוכל
מכל).   חננה| חננא לגו[2]ד[21], חנינא א[1], חיננא א[2].

:14 שאליה| שייליה א[21].   שאל ד[21].   לר'| את ר' ד[1], את רבי ד[2].
אמ' ליה| א' ליה ר[2], אל א[21].   מהוא| מהו לגו[2]א[21], מה הוא ד[21].
דכ'| דכת' לגו[2]א[21], דכתיב ד[21].   והון| הון לו[2]ד[21].
אדם יקר חרוץ| אד' יק' ח' ו[2].

:15 אמ' ליה| א"ל גא[21], א' ליה ר[2], אמר ליה ד[21].   היא| ח' א[21].
הצדיקים| הצדיק א[21].   שאינן| שאין א[21], שאינם ד[21].
נוטלין| נוטלים ד[21].   יקר| יקרם ד[21].

:16 שלהם| ח' לגו[2]א[21]ד[21].   לעתיד| שלעתיד לגא[21]ד[21], שלעתי' ו[2].
לבא| לבוא לגו[2]א[21].   בעולם| בעו' ר[2], ח' א[1] (והושלם בין השורות
בעוז וראה המלה הבאה).   הזה| הז' ר[2], ח' א[1].   ר'| רבי ד[2].
נחמיה| נחמי' ר[2], נחמיא א[21]ד[21].

:17 יודה| יהודה לגא[21]ד[21]ח, יהו' ר[2].   אמ'| א' ר[2], אומר א[1]ד[2],
אומ' א[2]ד[1]ח.   מכל| כל לגו[2].   שנברא| + העולם א[1].   בששת| בו' א[2].
בראשית| בראשי' ו[2].   ר| רבי ד[2].   נחמיה| נחמיא א[2].
או'| אמ' לגא[2], א' ר[2], אומר א[1]ד[2], אומ' ד[1]ח.

:18 טוב| מה א[21], ח' ג.   שהוא| ח' א[1].   מותקן| שמתוקן א[1],
מתוקן א[2]ד[21]ח.   לצדיקים| לצדיק' ל, לצדיקי' ר[2]א[21], ח' ד[21].

לעתיד| לעת' ו[2], לעתי' ד[1]. לבא| לבוא לגא[21], לב' ו[2].
אמ' לו| א' לו ו[2], אֹל א[21], אמר לו ד[2]ח.

19: אמ' לו| אֹלו ו[2], אֹל א[21], אמר לו ד[2]ח, ח' ל. אלא| ח' א[2].

20: פת| ח' ל. טעם| טע' ו[2], ח' ל. טעם דגים| טע' דגי' ו[2].
טעם| ט' ו[2], ח' א[2]. חגבים| וחגבים א[21].

21: שבעולם| שבעו' ו[2]. אמ' ר| אֹר גו[2], אר א[21], אמר רבי ד[2].
ברכיה| ברכי' ו[2]. כיוון| כיון לגו[2]א[21]ד[21]ח. שהזכיר| + טעם
לגא[21], + לו ח. מיד| ח' לגא[21]. בכה| ח' ג. אמ'| א' גו[2],
אמר ד[2]ח. אני| אם ח.

22: אחת| ח' לגו[2]א[21]ח. שלעדשים| של עדשים גא[21]ד[2]ח, של עדשי'
ד[1]. את| ח' ח. אתה| עתה ל, עד ו[2], ואתה ח, ח' א[21].

23: שהאכילך| כשהאכילך א[21]. על אחת כמה וכמה| על אחת כמ' וכמ'
ל, על אֹכֹ וֹכֹ ו[2], עאכֹו א[21]ד[21]ח. אמ' ר| אֹר גו[2], אמֹר א[1],
אֹר א[2]ד[21]. לוי| ח' א[21]. שאבינו| שהיה לגו[2]א[21]ד[21]ח; + אבינו
לגו[2]ד[21], + אבי א[2], + יצחק.

24: יצחק| יצח' ו[2], אבינו ח. ואומר| וא' ל. ואו' גו[2], ואומ'
א[2]. תומר| תאמר לגו[2]ד[21]ח, שמא א[2], ח' א[1]. שלא| לא א[2],
שעשיתי ח. עשיתי| שלא ח.

25: בכור| ח' א[1]. וכיון| כיון לגו[2]א[21]ד[21]ח. שאמר| שאמ' לגא[2]
ד[1], שא' ו[2]; + לו ג. אמ'| א' ו[2], אמר ד[2]ח.

26: ברך| ברכתי א[21]ד[21]ח. אמ' ר| אֹר גו[2]א[21], אמר רבי ד[2].
לעזר| אלעזר לגו[2]א[21]ד[21]ח, אלעז' א[2]. הגט| גט לו[2]ח.
בחותמיו| חותמה לו[2], חותמיה ג. תאמר| תאמ' ד[1].

1 אילולי שדימה יעקב אבינו את אביו לא נטל את הברכות תל' לו

2 גם ברוך יהיה אמ' ר' יצחק בא לקללו אמ' לו הקבה הזהר שאם

3 מקללו את נפשך את מקלל שכן אמרתה לו אררוך ארור

4 אמ' ר' לוי ששה דברים מששמים את האדם שלשה ברשותו

5 ושלשה שאינן ברשותו העין והאוזן והחוטם ברשותו חמי מה

6 דלא בעי שמע מה דלא בעי מריח מה דלא בעי הפה והיד והרגל

7 ברשותו הפה אין בעי הוא לעי באוריתא אין בעי הוא אמר לישן

8 ביש אין בעי הוא מחרף אין בעי הוא מגדף היד אין בעי הוא

9 מפלג מצוון אין בעי הוא גנב ואין בעי הוא קטל הרגל אם רוצה הוא

10 הולך לבתי כנסיות ולבתי מדרשות ואם לאו הוא הולך לבתי

11 תיאטריות ולבתי קרקסיות ובשעה שאדם זכה הקבה עושה

12 אותן שהן ברשותו שלא ברשותו הפה וגם ברוך יהיה היד

13 ותיבש ידו וגו' הרגל בני אל תלך בדרך אתם כי רגליהם לרע ירוצו

14 וגו   ⊕   כשמע עשו את דברי אביו וגו' אמ' ר' חנינה כל מי

15 שהוא אומר שהקבה ותרן יתותרון בני מעוי אלא מאריך

16 רוחיה וגבי דידיה צעקה אחת הזעיק יעקב לעשו ואיכן נפרע

17 לו בשושן הבירה ויזעק זעקה גד' ומרה   ⊕   ויאמר בא   א

18 אחיך במרמה וגו' ר' יוחנן אמ' בחכמת תורתו   ⊕   ויאמר הכי

19 קרא שמו יעקב ר' שמעון בן לקיש אמ' התחיל מחכך בגרונו א

20 ויאמר הכי ושתקתי לו והנה עתה לקח ברכתי ויאמר הלא מן

21 הניצולת   ⊕   ויען יצחק ויאמר לעשו אמ' ר' ברכיה הן

22 גביר שמתיו לך בלרכה השביעית ולמה הוא אומרה לו תחילה

23 אלא אמר לו מלך עשיתיהו עליך וברכותיך שלו הן עבדה ומה'

24 דיליה למריה ואת כל אחיו נתתי לו לעבדים וגו' ברם לך פיתה

25 אפייה ר' יוחנן ור' שמעון בן לקיש ר' יוחנן אמ' הרף ממני שפרזניך

26 שפורניתו אפייה לפניו בכל מקום ר' שמעון בן לקיש אמ' הרף

---

‡ הערה: בשוליים לשורה 5; שלא

184

1: אילולי| אלולי ד[21]. שדומה| שרימה לוא[2]א[1]ד[21], שרמה א[2]ח.
יעקב| אבינו לג[2]. אבינו| יעקב לג, יעק' ר[2], ח' א[21]ד[21].
את אביו| באביו ר[2]א[1]ד[21]ח, לאחיו א[2], ח' לג. לא| ולא ל.
תל' לו'| ת' ל' ג, תֹל א[21]ד[21]ח.

2: גם| ח' ל. אמ' ר'| אר גו[2], אר א[21]ד[21], אמר ר' ח.
יצחק| יצח' ר[2]. בא| + יצחק ח. אמ' לו| א' לו ו[2], אל א[21],
אמר לו ד[21]. הקבה| הק' ר[2], הבֹה א[2], הקדוש ברוך הוא ד[2], ח' ג.
הזהר| + בך א[1].

3: מקללו| תקללו ל, את ג, אתה א[21]ח. את| מקללו גא[21]ח, ח' ל.
נפשך| לנפשך לג[2]א[21]ד[21]ח. את| אתה לא[2]ח. שכן| שכך גו[2]א[21],
ח' ד[21]. אמרתה| אמ' ל, אמרת גא[21]ח, א' ר[2], דאמרת ד[21].
לו| ח' ר[2]ד[21]. אררירך| אוררך א[1], אוררירך א[2]ד[21]ח.
ארור| + ומברכיך ברוך לגא[21], + ומבר' בר' ר[2].

4: אמ' ר'| אֹר גו[2]א[2]ד[1], אמר ר' ד[2]. ששה| ו' ר[2].
דברים| דברי' ד[1], ח' א[21]. מסמסים| מסמשין גו[2]א[21]ד[21]ח.
שלשה| ג' לו[2]א[2]ד[1], שלש א[1]; + הן א[2].

5: ושלשה| וג' לו[2]א[21]ד[21]. שאינן| אינן ר'לג[2]ד[21]ח.
שלא| ר', אין ג, אינן א[21], אינם ח, ח' ר. חמי| רואה ח.

6: דלא| שאינו ח. בעי| רוצה ח. שמע| שומע ח. מה| ח' ל.
דלא| שאינו ח, ח' ל. בעי| רוצה ח, ח' ל. מריח| ומריח ל,
ח' גא[2]. מה| ח' א[2]. דלא| שאינו ח, ח' א[2]. בעי| רוצה ח,
ח' א[2]; + וג' הן ברשותו א[1]. והיד| היד ל.

7: ברשותו| ח' א[1]ח. הפה| ח' לג[2]א[21]ד[21]ח. אין| אי ר[2]א[21],
אם ח. בעי| הוא ח. הוא| רוצה ח, ח' לא[21]. לעי| מדבר ח.

באוריתא| באוריתא ר[2], באורית' א[2], בדברי תורה ח. אין| אי ר[2]
א[21]ד[21], ואם ח. בעי| הוא ח. הוא| רוצה ח, ח' לא[21]ד[21].
אמר| אמ' ל גא[21], א' ר[2], מדבר ח, ח' ד[21]. לישן| לישנא ד[21],
בלשון ח.

8: ביש| בישא ד[21], הרע ח. אין| אי ר[2]א[21]| אי ר[2]א[21], אם ד[21], ח' לח.
בעי| ח' לח. הוא| ח' לא[21]ד[21]ח. מחרף| מחרף א[1], ומחרף ח.
אין| ואי ר[2], אי א[21], ח' לד[21]ח. הוא| ח' לא[21]ד[21]ח.
מגדף| ומגדף לד[21]ח, מגדף א[1]. אין| אי א[21]. בעי| הוא ח.
הוא| רוצה ח, ח' לא[1].

9: מפלג| מפליג גא[21], עביד ד[21], עושה ח. מצוון| מצון ג,
מיצון א[21], מצוותא ד[21], מצות ח. אין| אי א[21], אם ח.
בעי| הוא ח. הוא| רוצה ח,חלא[1]. גנב| גניב גא[21]ד[21], הוא ח.
ואן| אין גו[2], אי א[21], ואם ד[21], גנב ח, ח' ל. בעי| הוא ח, ח' ל.
קטל| קטיל ל, קטיל גוא[2]א[21]ד[21], רוצה ח; הוא + גו[2]א[2]ד[21].
הרגל| רגל ל. אין| אי א[21]ד[21]ח. רוצה| בעי לגוא[2]א[21]ד[21], הוא ח
הוא| רוצה ח, ח' ל.

10: הולך| אזיל לגוא[2]א[21]ד[21]; הוא + ח. כנסיות| כנסיות לג,
טרטסיאות ד[21]. מדרשות| קרקסיאות ד[21]. ואם| אם ל, אי א[21],
ואין ד[21]; + בעי הוא אזיל לבתי כנסיות ולבתי מדרשות אי א[1].
לאון| בעי א[21]ד[21], הוא ח. הוא| רוצה ח, ח' ל. הולך| אזיל
א[21]ד[21]; הוא + ח.

11: תיאטריות| תרטיאיות ר[2], טרטיאות א[1], תרטיאות א[2], כנסיות
ד[21], קרקסאות ח. ולבתי| ובתי ד[21], ח' לגא[21].
קרקסיות| קרקסיאו' ר[2], וקרקסיאות א[21], מדרשות ד[21], טרטיאות ח,
ח' לג. שאדם| שהוא ד[21]. זכה| זכיי| זכיי ו°לג, זכאי ו[2]א[2]ח,
זוכה ד[21], זבחי א[1]; + ובשעה שאדם זכאי א[2]. הקבה| הק' ג,
הבֿה א[2]ד[1]. עושה| עוש' ד[1].

186

12: אותן| אותם לא[1]ח. שהן| שהם א[1]ח, ח´ ד[21].
ברשותו| שברשותו ד[21]. הפה| ח´ ד[21]; + נאמ´ ח.
גם ברוך יהיה| ח´ ד[21]. היד| ח´ ר[2].

13: והיבש| ויאמ´ + ח. וגו´| אשר שלח אליו וגו´ ל, אשר שלח
אליו גא[21]ח, אשר שלח אליו ולא יכול להשיבה עוד ר[2], אשר שלח
אותה אליו ד[1], אשר שלח עליו הפה גם ברוך יהיה ד[2]. הרגל| + נאמ´
ח. בני| ח´ ח. אל| לא תלך עמהם ולא תאור את העם כי ברוך הוא
ח (בנגוד לשאר כ"הי מכאן עד... וגו´.) בדרך| בד´ ר[2]. אתם| וגו´
א[2]; + מנע רגלך מנתיב´ ג, + מנע רג´ מנתי´ ר[2]. כי| וגו´ ל,
ח´ א[21]. רגליהם| ח´ לא[21]. לרע| ח´ לא[21]. ירוצו| ח´ לא[21].

14: וגו´| וימה´ לשפ´ דם ר[2], ח´ לא[21]ד[21]. כשמע| כשמ´ ר[2],
כשמוע א[1]ד[21], ויצעק א[2], (ח חסר מכאן עד... הזעיק).
עשו| צעקה א[2]. את| וגו´ ל, גדולה א[2]. דברי| ומרה א[2].
אביו| אב´ ר[2], ח´ א[2]. וגו´| ח´ לו[2]א[21]ד[21]. אמ´ ר´| אֹרֹ גו[2]א[21]ד[1],
אמר ר´ ד[2]. חנינה| חני´ ר[2], חנינא א[21]. מי| האו (?) ג, ח´ ר[2].

15: שהוא| שֹשומֹע ל, ח´ גא[21]. אומר| שֹא´ ל, או´ ר[2], שאומר א[1],
שאומ´ א[2], אומ´ ד[1], ח´ ג. שהקבה| הקבה לגא[1], שהק´ ר[2], הבֹה א[2],
שהקדוש ברוך הוא ד[2]. וותרן| ותרן א[2]; + הוא לו[2]א[21]ד[1].
יתוותרון| יתוותרן ל, יוותרון גא[1], יוותרן א[2]; + ימיו וחייו א[1].
בני| ובני א[1], ח´ לא[2]. מעוי| מעיה גא[1], מעוה´ א[2]ד[21]; + וחייו
א[2]. מאריך| מוריך ל.

16: רוחיה| אפי ד[21]. וגבי| וגביה ג, וגאבי ד[21]. דידיה| דיליה
ד[21]. צעקה| זעקה לגא[21]ד[21], זעק ר[2]. אחת| ח´ ר[2]. הזעיק| ח´ ר[2];
ויצעק צעקה גדולה זעקה זאת + ח. לעשו| + דכתי´ + לעשו| דכתי´ (דכתיב ד[2])
כשמו´ (כשמוע ד[2]) עשו את דברי אביו ויזעק זעקה ד[21].
ואיכן| והיכן גא[21]ד[21].

187

17: הבירה| הבי׳ ו[2], שנ׳ לגח, שנא׳ א[21], שנאמ׳ ד[1], שנאמר ד[2].
ויזעק| ויצע׳ ו[2]. זעקה| צעקה ג, צעק׳ ו[2]. גדו׳| גדולה לגא[21]
ד[21]ח. ומרה| ומר׳ ל, ח׳ א[1]; + וגו׳ ל, עד מאד ד[1].
ויאמר| ויא׳ ו[2], ח׳ א[2]ד[1].

18: במרמה| במ׳ ו[2]. וגו׳| ויקח ברכתך א[1], ח׳ לגו[2]א[2]ד[21]ח.
ר| רבי ד[2]. יוחנן| יוח׳ ו[2]. אמ׳| א׳ ו[2], אמר א[1]ד[2]ח; + בא ד[21].
ויאמר| ויא׳ ו[2], ויאמ׳ ד[1]. הכי| (א[2] חסר מכאן עד... ויאמר
הלא...).

19: קרא| קר׳ ו[2]. יעקב| יעק׳ ו[2]; + וגו׳ לגא[1], + ויעקבני ד[21].
ר׳ שמעון בן לקיש| ריש לק׳ ו[2], ריש לקיש ד[21], (לגח חסרים מכאן
עד... ויאמר הכי, א[1] חסר מכאן עד... ויאמר הלא...) אמ׳| א׳ ו[2],
אמר ד[2]. בגרונו| + כמאן דמחייך וזורק רוק מפיו ד[21].

20: ויאמר הכי| לקח בכורתי ל, את בכורתי לקח גו[2]ח; + ויעקבני את
בכורתי לקח ד[21]. לו| ולא רי (?) לו אלא ח. והנה| ועתה ח.
עתה| הנה ח. לקח| לק׳ ו[2]; + את ח. ברכתי| + ושתקתי לו ד[21].
ויאמר| ויא׳ ו[2], ח׳ ד[21], (ח חסר מכאן עד... ויען יצחק).
הלא| + אצלת (אצל׳ ו[2]) לי ברכה לגו[2]א[21]ד[21]. מן| ח׳ ו[2].

21: הניצולת| הנצולת לג, ח׳ ו[2]. יען| (א[2] חסר מכאן עד... הן
גביר). יצחק| יצח׳ ו[2]. ויאמרן| ויא׳ ו[2], ויאמ׳ ד[1]. לעשו| וגו׳
ל, לעש׳ ו[2]; + הן גביר שמ׳ לך ו[2], + הן גביר ד[21], + הן גביר
שמתיו לך ח. אמ׳ ר׳| אל׳ גו[2]ד[1], אמר רבי ד[2], אמר ר׳ ח, ח׳ א[1].
ברכיה| ח׳ א[1].

22: שמתיו| שמת׳ ג, ח׳ ו[2]ח. לך| ח׳ ו[2]ח. היא| ו[2], ח׳ ולגו[2]
ד[21]ח. השביעית| שביעית א[21]ד[21]ח. ולמה| למה א[21]. הוא| ח׳ לא[21].
אומרה| אומר ל, אום׳ א[1], אלֹ א[2]. לו| (א[2] ראה המלה הקודמת),

ח׳ לגא[1]. תחילה| תחלה א[21]ד[21]ח.

23: אלא| אלי א[1] ו[2], ח׳ א[21]. אמר לו| א׳ לו לו[2], אמ׳ לו גד[1], אֵל
א[21]. עשיתיהו| עשיתהו ל, שמתיו גא[21]ח. עליך| לכל ג.
וברכותיך| וברכתיך א[1]. עבדה| עבדא לג[2]א[21]ד[21]ח. ומה| למה לג,
דיליה א[1], דמאן ד[21], ח׳ א[2]; + נכסי דמאן עבדא כל מה ד[21].

24: דיליה| דליה לו[2], נכסיה ג, למאן א[21]. למריה| למאריה לגד[21],
דמאריה א[2]. ואת| את לו[2], (א[21]ח חסרים מכאן עד... וגו׳)
נתחי| נתן ג, נת׳ ו[2]. לעבדים| לע׳ ו[2]. וגו׳| ודגן ותירוש
סמכ׳ ולך איפה ל, ודגן ותיר׳ סמכתיו ולך איפ׳ ג, וד׳ ות׳ ס׳
ולי איפוא ו[2], ולך איפה א[21]ח, ולך איפוא ד[21].
פיתה| פיתא גא[21]ח, פיתך ד[21].

25: אפייה| איפוא ל, אפיא גא[21]ח, אפויה ד[21]. ר׳| רבי ד[2],
(ל חסר מכאן עד... ר שמעון בן לקיש אמ׳ הרף, ח חסר מכאן עד...
הנה משמני הארץ). יוחנן| יוח׳ ו[2]. ור׳ שמעון בן לקיש| ר׳ שמע׳
בן לקיש ג, וריש לק׳ ו[2], ורשֿבל א[21], וריש לקיש ד[21]. ר׳| רבי
ד[2], (ג חסר מכאן עד... ר׳ שמעון בן לקיש אמ׳ הרף). יוחנן| יוח׳
ו[2]. אמ׳| א׳ ג, אמר ד[21]. הרף| הרף א[1]. ממני| מיני ו[2],
ממנו א[21]ד[21].

26: שפורניתו| שפורניותו ו[2], שפורנייתו א[1] (שפַזַרניתו (?) ו)
אפייה| אפויה א[21]ד[21]. ר שמעון בן לקיש| ר׳ יוחנן לג, ריש לק׳
ו[2], רשֿבל א[21], ריש לקיש ד[21]. אמ׳| אמר א[1], ח׳ ו[2]. הרף| הרף א[1].

113

1 ממני שאף וחימה מסורין לו ר̄ שמלאי ואמרין לה בשם ר̄ "

2 אבהו אמ̇ לו הק̇ב̇ה̇ כך היתה או ולכה אפוא אמ̇ לו יוחן אמ̇ לו

3 רשע הוא בל למד צדק לא כיבד את הוריו אמ̇ לו בארץ נכוחות

4 עתיד הוא לפשט את ידיו בבית המקדש אמ̇ לו אם כן השפע

5 לו שלוה בעולם הזה ובל יראה גאות י̇י̇ לעתיד לבא ⊙ ויען

6 יצחק אביו ויאמר אליו הנה משמני הארץ וג̇ו הנה מש̇ הא̇ יה̇ מו̇

7 זו איטליא מטל השמים מעל זו בית גוברין ד̇א הנה משמני הארץ

8 משמיניה דארעא אנטונינוס שלח לגב רבינו אמ̇ לה בגין דתיסווריה

9 חסירין מה נעביד ונמלייא יתהון נסתייה לשליחה ואעליה

10 לגו פורדיסה שרי עקר פולגין רברבין ושתיל דקיקין תורדין

11 רברבין ושתיל דקיקין חסין רברבין ושתיל דקיקין אמ̇ לה הב לי

12 אנטיגרפ̇ה̇ אמ̇ לה לית את צריך סליק לגביה אמ̇ לה הן היא א

13 אנטיגרפה אמ̇ לה לא יהב לי כלום אמ̇ לה ומה אמ̇ לך אמ̇ לה לא אמ̇

14 לי כלום אמ̇ לה לא עבד קומיך כלום אמ̇ לה נסתי ואעלי לגו פרדיסא

15 שורי עקר פולגין רברבין ושהל דקיקין תורדין רברבין ושהל א

16 דקיקין חסין רב̇ וש̇ דקיקין שורי מפקד:כ̇דין ומעל דוקסין עד

17 זמן דאתמלון תיסוורייה ⊕ ועל חרבך תחיה וג̇ו אמ̇ ר̄ לוי

18 עו̇ל חרבך ואת חיי ואת אחיך תעבד אמ̇ ר̄ חונה אם זכה תעבוד

19 ואם לאו תאבד והיה כאשר תריד אמ̇ לו אתה יש לך ירודים ואני

20 יש לי ירודים והוא יש לו ירודים אתה יש לך נימוסות̇אמ̇ ר̄ יוסי

21 ביר̇ חלפתה אם ראיתה יעקב אחיך פורק עול תורה מעל צוארו

22 גזור עליו שמדים ואת שלט בו הדה היא כי אתה אבינו כי אברהם

23 לא ידענו וג̇ו ויצחק איכן הוא מי שהוא או לו ג̇זור עליו שמדים

24 ואת מתכיפו לאביתם ⊕ וישטם עשו את יעקב וג̇ו אמ̇ ר̄ לעזר

25 ביר̇ יוסי נעשה לו שונא ונוקם ונוטר עד כדון קראיין סנטרוי

26 דרומי ויאמר עשו בלבו הרשעים ברשות לבן אמ̇ נבל בלבו ⊙

הערה: בשוליים לשורה 20; והוא יש לו נימסות

1: ממני| מיני לגו[2], ממנו א[21]ד[21]. וחימה| וחמה ד[21]. לו| לך ל,
בו א[1]. שמלאי| שמליי ר[2]. ואמרין| ואמ' ל, ואמרי א[21]ד[21].
לה| ליה גו[2]. בשם ר'| מש' ר' ל, משו' ר ו[2], בשׄר א[21]

2: אמ' לו| א' לו ו[2], אׄל א[1], כשאׄל א[2], אמר לו ד[2]. הקבה| הק'
לו[2], הבׄה א[1], הקדוש ברוך הוא ד[2], ח' א[2]. כן| כד ג, כה א[1], ח'
א[2]. היתה| היתה ל, הויתה ג, היית ד[21], ח' א[21]. או'| א' ל,
אמ' ג, תאמר א[1], אומ' ד[1], אומר ד[2]; + לו א[1]. ולכה| ולך לג.
אפוא| איפוא לגו[2], איפה א[21]ד[21]. אמ' לו| א' לו ו[2], אׄל א[21],
אמר לו ד[21], יצחק להבׄה א[2]. אמ' לו| א' לו ו[2], אׄל א[21], אמר לו ד[2].

3: הוא| + אמ' לו ל°ג, + א' לו ו[2], + אׄל א[21], + אמר לו ד[21].
בל| ובל ר[2]. אמ' לו| א' לו ו[2], אׄל א[21], אמר לו ד[21]; + הקבה ד[1],
+ הקדוש ברוך הוא ד[2]. בארץ| ארץ ו[2]. נכוחות| נכוחו' א[1]; +
יעול לגא[21]ד[21], + יעות ו[2].

4: הוא| ח' ג. לפשוט| לפשוט גא[21]ד[21]. את| ח' לגו[2]א[21]ד[21].
ידיו| ח' ל. אמ' לו| א' לו ו[2], אׄל א[21]. אם כן| אׄכ א[1], ח' ל.
השפע| השפיע גו[2]ד[21], תשפיע א[21].

5: שלוה| שלווה ד[21]. בעולם| בעו' ר[2]. ובל| בל לגו[2]א[21].
גאות| גיאות ג, בגאות ו[2]. לעתיד| לעת' ר[2]. לבא| לבוא לא[2],
לב' ר[2]. יען| (א[2] חסר מכאן עד... הנה משמני הארץ)

6: אביו| ח' לד[21]. ויאמר| ויא' ר[2], ויאמ' ד[1]. אליו| לעשו לו[2],
ח' ד[21]. הנה משמני הארץ| הנ' משמ' הא' ר[2]. וגו'| יהיה מושביך
גא[21]ד[21], י' מ' ר[2], יהיה מושבך ח. הנה מש' הא' יהי' מו'| ח'
לגו[2]א[21]ד[21]ח.

7: זו| ח׳ לגו[2]. איטליא| איטלייא לו[2], איטאליאה ד[2]ח; + שליון
א[21]. מטל| ומטל גא[21]ד[21]ח. מעל| ח׳ א[2]. גוברין| גברין לגו[2]
א[21]ד[21]ח. ד׳ א| דבר אחר ד[2]. הנה| ח׳ ח. משמני הארץ| מש׳ הא׳ ר[2].

8: משמיניה| מן שמיניה לגו[2], משומיניא א[21], מן שמיניא ד[21],
מן שמניה (?) ח. דאראא| + מן הן מתעבדא ארעא שמניא שמינין מן
סלא ומטל השמי׳ מעל ד[21]. אנטונינוס| אנטובינוס ו[2], (ח חסר מכאן
עד... ועל חרבך תחיה). לגב| אצל א[21], ח׳ לד[21]. רבינו| לרבינו
לד[21]. אמ׳ לה| אמ׳ ליה ל, א׳ ליה ו[2], אֵל א[21], אמר ליה ד[21],
ח׳ ג. בגין| ח׳ ו[2]. דתיסווריה| דתיסבריא גד[1], דתיסוריא (?)
א[1], דתיסווריא א[2], דתיסוורתא ד[2].

9: חסירין| חסרין לגא[21], חסרים ד[21]. נעביד| נעבד ו[2].
ונמליא| ונמלא לד[21], ונמליא ג, ונמלי א[21]. נסתיה| נסותיה ג,
נסתיה ו[2], נסביה א[21]ד[21]. לשליחה| לשליחא לגו[2]א[21]ד[21].
ואעליה| ועייליה א[21]ד[21].

10: לגו| גו גו[2]. פורדיסה| פרדיסה ל, פרדיסא גו[2]א[1], פרדסא
א[2]ד[21]. שרי| שורי ו[2]. ושתיל| ושתל לגו[2]. תורדין| (לא[1]ד[21]
חסרים מכאן עד... אמ׳ לה, א[2] חסר מכאן עד... חסין).

11: ושתיל| ושתל גו[2]. ושתיל| ושתל גו[2]. אמ׳ לה| אמ׳ ליה ל,
אֵל גא[21], א׳ ליה ו[2], אמר ליה ד[21].

12: אנטיגרפֿה| אנטיגרפין ל, אנטיגרפֿ׳ ו[2], אנטיגרפא א[21]ד[21].
אמ׳ לה| אמ׳ ליה לגד[2], א׳ ליה ו[2], אֵל א[21], אמר ליה ד[1].
סליק| סלק לו[2]ד[21]. אמ׳ לה| אמ׳ ליה לגד[1], א׳ ליה ו[2]א[2], אמר
ליה ד[2] (א[1] חסר מכאן עד... אמ׳ ליה לא עבד...). הן| הין לג,
דין ד[21]. היא| הן ד[21], ח׳ א[1].

13: אנטיגרפה| אנטיגרף' לו[2], אנטיגרפא א[2]ד[21]. אמ' לה| אמ' ליה
ד[1], אֵל גא[2], א' ליה ו[2], אמר ליה ד[2]. יהב| נתן ל, יהיב ד[21].
אמ' לה| א' ליה ו[2] אֵל א[2], אמ' ליה ד[1], אמר ליה ד[2], ח' לג.
אמ'| א' ו[2], אמר ד[2]. אמ' לה| אֵל ג, א' ליה ו[2], אֵל א[2], אמ' לו
ד[1], אמר לו ד[2], ח' ל. אמ'| אמר ד[2].

14: לי| ח' ו[2]. אמ' לה| אמ' ליה גד[1], א' ליה ו[2], אֵל א[1], אמר
ליה ד[2], (לא[2] חסרים מכאן עד... אמ' ליה נסתי). לא| ולא גא[1]ד[21].
קומין| קמך גו[1]א[2], קודמך ד[21]. אמ' לה| אלא ל, אֵל גא[21], א' ליה
ו[2], ח' ד[21]. נסתי| נסבני א[21]ד[21]. ואעלי| ומעלי ג, ואעלני א[1],
ואעליני ד[21]. לגו| ח' ל. פרדיסא| פרדוסא ג, פרדסא א[2]ד[21].

15: שורי| שרי לא[21]ד[21]. ושתל| דשתל ו[2], ושתיל א[21]ד[21].
דקיקין| דקיק' ג. תורדין| תרד' ג, תרדין א[2]ד[21]. (ל חסר מכאן
עד... שורי, א[1] חסר מכאן עד... חסין). רברבין| רברביין ג.
ושתל| דשתל ו[2], ושתיל א[2]ד[21].

16: דקיקין| דקיק' ג. חסין| חסינין א[2]°, (א[2] חסר מכאן עד שורי
והושלם בגליון). רב'| רבר' ג, רברבי' ו[2], רברבין א[21]°ד[21].
וש'| ושת' ג, ושתל ו[2], ושתיל א[21]°ד[21]. דקיקין| דקיק' ג, דקיקי'
ד[1]. שורי| שרי לא[21]ד[21]; + מיד הבין ד[21]. מפקד:וכסין| מפק
דוכסין לגא[21]ד[21], מפק דוקסין ו[2]. ומעל| ומעיל לגא[21],
ומעיל ו[2]ד[21], ועייל א[1]. דוקסין| דוכסין לגא[21].

17: דאתמלו.ן| דיתמלון לג, דתמלון ו[2]א[2], דתימלון א[1], דאיתמליין
ד[21]. תיסורייה| תיסורייא ל, תיסוריא ג, תיסוריא א[1],
תסבריא ד[1], תסוורתא ד[2]. וגו'| ח' לגו[2]א[21]ד[21]ח. אמ' ר' לוי| אֹר
לוי גו[2]א[2], ארֹל א[1], ר' לוי אמ' ד[1], רבי לוי אמר ד[2].

18: עול| ר°ל°, על ולא[21] . ואת| את א[21] . תעבד| תעב׳ ר[2],
תעבוד א[21][21]ד[21] . אמ׳ ר׳| אׄׄ גו[2]ד[2], ח׳ א[21]ח. חונה| הונא לד[21],
אחא ג, חונא ר[2], ח׳ א[21]ח. תעבוד| תעבד לגא[1], תיעבד ר[2].

19: תאבד| תעבד א[2], תעביד ח. תריד| + וגו ל, + ופרקת עולו ג,
ופרקת עולו מעל צוארך א[1]ח. אמ׳ לו| א׳ לו ר[2], אמר לו ח, ח׳
א[21]ד[21] . אתה| את לגו[2]א[1]ד[21] . ירודים| ידידים ל, ירידים גא[21]ד[2]ח,
יירדין א[2], יריד׳ ד[1]; + שוקים ד[21].

20: ואני יש לי ירודים| ח׳ לגו[2]א[21]ד[21]ח. ירודים| ידידים ל,
ירידים גא[21]ח, ירידין ר[2], שווקים ד[21]. אתה| את לגו[2]א[1]ד[21].
נימוסות| נימוסיות א[21]; + והוא יש לו נימוסות (נימוס׳ ר[2],
נימוסיות א[21]) ר°לגו[2]א[2]ד[21]ח, ח׳ ר. אמ׳ ר׳| אׄׄ גו א[21]ד[21],
אמר ר׳ ד[2].

21: ביר| בר לגו[2]א[2]ד[21]ח, בן א[1]. חלפתה| חלפתא לגו[2]א[2]ד[21]ח,
חלפת׳ א[1]. ראיתה| לגו[2]א[21]ד[21]ח. אחיר| ח׳ א[1]. עול| עולה
לוא[2]א[21]ד[21], מעל ח. תורה| תורה לגו[2]א[21]ד[21], צוארו ח.
מעל| מעליו ד[21], עולה ח, ח׳ א[2]. צוארו| של תורה ח, ח׳ א[2]ד[21].

22: ואת| ואתה א[2]ד[21]ח. שלט| שליט לו[2], שולט גא[21]ד[21]ח.
הדה היא| הׄ הׄ דׄ לא[21]ד[2], הדהי ג, הׄ הׄ ו[1]ד[2], דכתי׳ ח.
אבינו| אבי׳ ר[2]. אברהם| אב׳ ג.

23: ידענו| ידע׳ לו[2]. וגו׳| ויש׳ לא יכירנו ל, ויש׳ לו יכיר׳
ר[2], וישראל לא יכירנו א[21]ד[2], וישראל לא הכירנו ד[1], ח׳ ח.
ויצחק| ח׳ גח. איכן| היכן לא[21]ד[21], ח׳ גח. הוא| הוא ח׳ גח.
מי שהוא| משהוא א[2]. או׳ לו| אומר גא[1], או׳ ר[2], אומ׳ א[2],
אומר לי ד[1], אומר לו ד[2]ח.

24: ואת| את לגו‎², אתה א‎²¹ח. מתכיפו| מכפיתו א‎².
לאביתֿם| לאבות לגו‎²א‎²¹ד‎²¹ח. וישטם| וישטום לא‎¹ד‎²¹ח.
את| ח‎´ ד‎²¹. יעקב| יע‎´ ר‎², ח‎´ ד‎²¹. וגו‎´| ח‎´ לגו‎²א‎²¹ד‎²¹ח.
אמ‎´ ר‎´| א‎´ ר‎´ ל, אֹר גו‎²א‎²¹, אמר ר‎´ ד‎¹, אמר רבי ד‎².
לעזר| אלעזר גא‎²¹ד‎²¹ח, אלע‎´ ר‎².

25: ביר| בר לגו‎²א‎²¹ד‎²¹א‎²¹, ח‎´ ח. יוסי| יוסף א‎¹, ח‎´ ח.
נעשה| סנטירו ונעשה ד‎²¹, (א‎²¹ חסרים מכאן עד... עד כדון).
ונוקם| נוקם לג, ונוק‎´ ד‎¹. כדון| כאן א‎²¹. קראיין| קראין לגו‎²
א‎²ח, קורין א‎¹, קריין ד‎²¹. סנטרוי| סנטארוי א‎¹, סנתרוי א‎²°.

26: דרומי| ברומי ד‎¹; + שנעשה שונא ונוקם ונוטר א‎²¹.
ויאמר| ויאמ‎´ ר‎²ד‎¹. הרשעים| הרשעי‎´ ר‎²ד‎¹. לבן| לבם לג, ליבן
ר‎²; + שנ‎´ לג, + שנא‎´ א‎²¹. אמ‎´| אמר לגו‎²ד‎²ח, ויאמר א‎¹.
נבל| עשו א‎¹. בלבו| + אין אלים א‎².

1 ויאמר עשו בלבו וַיֹאמֶר הָמָן בְּלִבְּן ויאמר ירבעם בלבו אבל

2 הצדיקים לבן ברשותן והנה היא מדברת על לבה ויאמר דוד

3 אל לבו וישם דניאל על לבו דומים לבוראן ויאמר יֹי אל לבו

4 ⊕ יקרבו ימי אבל אבי רֹ יודה ורֹ נחמיה ורבנן רֹ יודה

5 אֹמֹ בא לו עשו במתונה אֹמ מה אני מכריע את אבא אלא

6 יקרבו ימי אבל וגֹו רֹ נחמיה אֹמֹ הרבה סייחים מיתו ונעשו א

7 עורותיהם שטיחים על גבי אומותיהם רבנן אֹמ אם הורגו אני

8 יש שם ועבר שניהם עֹליו בדין ואֹו לי למה הרגתה את אחיך

9 אלא הרי אני הולך ומתחתן לישמעאל והוא בא ועורר עמו על

10 הבכורה והורגו ואני עומד עליו בגואל הדם והורגו וירש שתי

11 משפחות הדה היא יען אמרך את שני הגוים וגֹו מן אמר דאמר

12 כן אֹמ רֹ יודן הקֹבֹה אמר כן ויֹי שם היה אֹמֹ רֹ ברכיה כפר עשו

13 ואֹם לא אמרית הדה מלתא אֹמֹ לו הקֹבֹה לית את ידע דאנה בדוקהֹוֹן

14 דלבבייה אני יֹי חוקר לב ובוחן כליות ⊕ ויוגד לרבקה

15 את דברי עשו וגֹו מי הגיד לה הֹ חגיי בשם רֹ יצחק האימהות

16 נביאות היו ורבקה היתה מן האמהות רֹ ברכיה בשם רֹ יצחק

17 אפילו הדיוט אינו חורש תלם בתוך תלם ונביאים חורשים

18 תלם בתוך תלם וחֹמר אל תגעו במשיחי ⊕ ותשלח

19 ותקרא ליעקב בנה הקטן כמת הוא תוהא עליך כמת הוא מתנחם

20 עליך וכבר הוא שותה עליך כוס תנחומים ⊕ ועתה בני שמע

21 בקולי וישבת עימו וגֹו אֹמֹ רֹ חנינה בן פזי נא כן אחדים ונאם

22 להלן אחדים מה אחדים שֹנ להלן שבע שנים אף אחדים שֹנ

23 כאן שבע שנים עד אשר תשוב חמת אחיך כצדקתה אמרה אמו

24 עד אשר תשוב חמת והוא לא עשה כן אלא ויטרף לעד אפו

25 רֹ שמעון בן לקיש אֹמ עוברתיה נוחרתה לא זעייה מן פומיה

26 למה אשכל גם שניכם יום אחד ⊕ ותאמר רבקה אל יצחק

1: ויאמר| אמר א[1], ויא' ר[2]. עשו| עש' ג, נבל א[1], ירבעם א[2],
ח' המן ח. בלבו| + אין אלים א[1]. וּיֹאֹמֶֹרֹ| ויאמ' ר[2]ד[1], (א[2] חסר
מכאן עד... לבוראן). הֹמֹןֹ| ירבעם לגו[2]ד[21]ח, עשו א[1]. ויאמר| ח'
לו[2]. ירבעם| המן גא[1]ד[21], עשו ח, ח' לו[2]. בלבו| ח' לו[2].
אבל| ח' ר[2].

2: הצדיקים| הצדי' ר[2]. לבן| לבם לח, ליבן ד[1].
ברשותן| ברשותם לא[1]ח; + שנ' לג,+שנאמ' א[1]. מדברת| מדבר' ר[2].
ויאמר| ודוד ג, ויאמ' ר[2]ד[1], ח' ח. דוד| אמר ג, ח' ח.

3: אל| ח' ח. לבו| ח' ח. על| אל גד[21]. דומים| דומין לגו[2]א[1]
ד[21]; + אל א[1]. לבוראן| אל בוראן א[1], לבוראם ח; + לבורא א[2]; +
שנ' ר[2]ח. ויאמר| ויא' ר[2]. לבו| + וגו' ל, לא אוסיף ח.

4: אבי| + וגו' ל, + ואהר' את יעקב ג, + ואה' אצ יע' אחי ר[2], +
ואהרגה את יעקב אחי ח. ר'| ח' לח. יודה| יהודה גו[2]א[2]ד[1],
נחמיא א[1], יהוד' ד[2], ח' לח. ור'| רבי ד[2], ח' לח.
נחמיה| נחמי' ר[2], יהודה א[1], נחמיא א[2], ח' לח.
ורבנן| ורבנין גו[2]א[2], ח' לד[21]ח; + ר יהודה ור נחמיה ורבנין ג.
ר| רבי ד[2]. יודה| יהודה לגא[21]ד[21]ח, יה' ר[2].

5: אמ'| א' לו[2], אומר א[1]ד[1], אומ' א[2], אמר ד[2].
במתונה| במתינה לגא[21]ד[21]ח. אמ'| א' ר[2], אמר א[1]ד[2].
אני| אנא א[2]ח. מכריע| מכריע/ מעכיר ר[2]א[2], אעורר א[1], מעכר ח.
אבא| אבה ל, אבי ג.

6: אבל| ח' א. וגו'| אבי לגו[2]א[21]ד[21]ח; + וגו' ל, + ואה' את
יעקב ג, + ואהרגה ד[21], + ואהרגה את יעקב אחי ח. ר'| רבי ד[2].
נחמיה| יעקב ל, נחמ' ר[2], נחמיא א[2]. אמ'| א' ר[2], אום' ד[1]ח,
אומר ד[2]; + בת קול אומר' (אומרת ד[2]) ד[21]. סייחים| סיחים גו[2],

סוסין א^1, סוסים א^2. מיתו| מתו לגא^{21}ד^{21}ח.

7: עורותיהם| עורותיהן גו^{2}א^{21}ח, עורתיהם ד^{21}. שטיחים| שטיחין
לגו^{2}ח, שטוחין א^{21}, ח׳ ד^{21}. על גבי| על לג, עڭ א^2.
אומתיהם| אמותיהם ל, אימותיהן ג, אמותיהן ר^{2}ד^{21}ח, אמותם א^1,
אמותן א^2. רבנן| רבנין לגו^2, ורבנין א^{21}. אמ׳| אמרין גא^1,
אמרי א^{2}ד^{21}ח; + אמ׳ ח. הורגו| הורגו אני א^{21}ח. אני| הורגו א^{21}ח.

8: יש| אין ר^2, הרי א^{21}ח,ח׳ ל. שניהם| יושבין לגו^{2}א^{21}ד^{21}ח.
עליו| עלי לגו^{2}א^{21}ד^{21}ח. בדין| לדין א^1. ואו׳| ואומ׳ ג,
ואומרין ר^{2}א^{21}, ואומרים ד^{21}ח, (לֹ חסר מכאן עד... אלא)
לי| לו א^1. הרגתה| הרגת גו^{2}א^{21}ד^{21}ח.

9: הרי אני| אני לח, הריני גא^{21}ד^{21}. ומתחתן| ומחנן אני לפני
ר^2. לישמעאל| ישמעאל ר^2. בא| + עמו א^2. ועורר| ומעורר ח.
עמו| עמ׳ א^{1}ד^1; + על ר^{0}א^{2}ד^{21}ח, + את א^1.

10: לבכורה| בבכורה ג, הבכורה ר^{0}א^{21}ד^{21}ח. עליו| ח׳ ר^{2}ח.
בגואל| כגואל גו^{2}א^{21}ד^{21}ח. והורגו| והורג אני את ישמעאל ר^2.
וירש| ויורש לגו^{2}א^{21}ד^{21}ח; + אני לגו^{2}ד^{21}ח, + אני את א^{21}.
שתי| ב׳ לו^2.

11: משפחות| משפחת ג, המשפחות א^{21}ד^{21}ח. הדה היא| הֹהֹד לא^{21}ד^1,
הדהי ג, הֹ הֹ דכת׳ ו^2, הדא הוא דכתיב ד^2,היינו דכתי׳ ח; + בן
אדם לגו^{2}א^{21}ד^{21}ח. אמרך| אמורך ר^2. את| על לגו^{2}א^{21}.
שתי| שני ר^{2}א^{1}ד^{21}ח. הגוים| גוים ר^{2}א^{21}, הגוי׳ ד^1.
 וגו׳| ואת שתי הארצות (משפחות ד^1) לי תהיינה וירשונה ויי שם היה
ר^{0}ד^{21}, על שני משפחות לי תהיינה וירשתם ויי שם היה ל, ועל שתי
(שני א^1) משפחות לי תהיינה וירשנוה (וירשתים ר^2, וירישתים א^1)
ויי שם היה גו^{2}א^{21}, ואת שני משפחות לי תהיינה וירשנוה ויי שם

היה ח´ . מן| מאן ד[21] (ח חסר מכאן עד אמ´ ר´ ברכיה.) . אמר| אמ´
לגא[21]ד[1] . דאמר| דאמ´ א[21]ד[1], ח´ ל.

12: אמ´ ר´| אֹר גו[2]א[2], אמר ר´ א[1], אמר רבי ד[2] . הקבה| הק´ ו[2],
אמ´ ד[1], אמר ד[2] . אמר| אמ´ גא[1], אמרו ו[2], הקבה ד[1], הבֹה ד[2],
ח´ לא[2] . כן| ח´ לגו[2]א[21]ד[21] . אמ´ ר´| אֹר גו[2]א[21]ד[21] .
ברכיה| ברכי´ ו[2].

13: ואמ´| וא´ ו[2], ואמר א[21]ד[21]ח; + לפני הק´ ו[2] . לא| לה ג.
אמרית| אמרתי א[1] . הדה| הדה לגא[21]ד[21]ח, דא ו[2] . מלתא| מילתא
גו[2]א[21]ד[21]ח, מילת´ א[1] . אמ´ לו| א´ לו ו[2], אֹל א[21], אמר לו ד[21].
הקבה| הק´ ו[2], הבֹה א[2] . את| אנא גא[1] . ידע| יודע א[1].
דאנה| דאנא לגא[21]ד[21]ח, ואנא ו[2]; + הוא לגא[21]ד[21]ח . בדוק| בדוק
הוֹן ו°, בודקיהון לד[21]ח, בודקהון גו[2], טרקנא א[1], בודקנא א[2].

14: דלבבייה| דלבביא ל, דליבביא גו[2], דלבביא א[21]ד[1], דליביא
א[2], דלבביה ח; + שנ´ לגו[2]ח, + שנא´ א[21] . אני| כי + א[1].
ובוחן| וגו´ ל, בוחן ג, ח´ ו[2]ד[21] . כליות| ח´ לו[2]ד[21].
וייגד| וייגד לגו[2]א[1].

15: את| וגו´ ד[21], ח´ ל. דברי| דב´ ו[2], ח´ לד[21] . עשו| לד[21].
וגו´| בנה הגדול גח, ח´ לו[2]א[21]ד[21] . מי| ומי א[2], ח´ ו[2].
הגיד| ח´ ו[2] . לה| ח´ ו[2] . ר´| רבי ד[2], ח´ ח. חגיי| חגיי
לא[21]ד[21], ברכיה א[1], ח´ ח. בשם ר´| בש´ ר´ לו[2], בשׂר א[2], ר´ ח.
יצחק| יצח´ ו[2]; + א´ ו[2], + אמ´ ר´א[2]ד[1], + אמר ח.
האימהות| אימהות ל, אמהות גו[2]א[21]ד[21]ח.

16: היו| היה ל. היתה| היתה ג . האימהות| האמהות לא[21]ד[1]ח,
האמהו´ ד[2] . ר´| ח´ א[2]ד[21], (ח חסר מכאן עד... ותשלח ותקרא)
ברכיה| ברכי´ ו[2], ח´ א[2]ד[21]; + אמ´ ג . בשם| מש´ לו[2], ח´ א[2]ד[21]
ר´| רבי ד[2] . יצחק| יצח´ ו[2]; + אמ´ ר´א[2]ד[1], + אמר א[1]ד[2].

199

17: אפילו| אפי' א[1]; + תלם ד[21]. אינו| אני א[1].
ונביאים| ונביאין א[2]. חורשים| חורשין א[21].

18: תלם| תל' ר[2]. ותֹמר| ואת אמ' לא[2], ואת אמר גד[21], ואת א' ר[2],
ואת אומר א[1]. במשיחי| + וגו' ל, + ובנ' אל תר' ר[2], + ובנביאי
אל תרעו ד[1], + ולנביאי אל תרעו ד[2]. ותשלח| מתנחם א[21].

19: ותקרא| ותק' ר[2], לך א[21]. ליעקב| ליע' ר[2], להרגיך א[1],
להורגך א[2]; + אמרה לו הרשה הזה ד[21]. בנה| וגו' ר[2], ח' א[21]ד[21].
הקטן| וגו' ל, ח' ר[2]א[21]ד[21]; + ותאמ' אֹל הנה עשו אחיך מתנחם לך
להורגך ג. כמת| במה א[21]. הוא| שהוא ר[2]. כמת| במה א[21].

20: הוא| ח' לד[21]. שותה| שתה ד[21]. עליך| ח' א[1] והושלם בין
השורות. תנחומים| תנחומין גא[21]ד[21]ח, תנחומי' ר[2]. ועתה| ח'
א[2]ח. בני| ח' א[2]ח. שמע| ח' א[2]ח.

21: בקולי| בקו' א[1], ח' א[2]ח; + וגו' לג, + וכתיב א[1], + וקום
ברח לך ד[21]. וישבת| וישבתה ל. עימו| עמו לגו[2]א[21]ד[21]ח.
וגו'| ימי' אחד' ר[2], ימים אחדים וכת' (וכתיב א[1], כתי' ד[1], כתיב
ד[2], וכתי' ח) ויעבד (ויעבוד א[1]ד[21]ח) יעקב ברחל שבע שנים ויהיו
(ויהי ג) בעיניו כימים (כימ' ל) אחדים (+ וגו' ל) לגא[1]ד[21]ח,
ימים אחדים וכתי' ויהיו בעיניו כימים אחדים א[2].
אמ' ר'| אֹר גו[2]א[2], אמר ר' א[1], אמר רבי ד[2]. חנינה| חננא לא[2],
חיננא ג, חני' ר[2], חנינא א[1]ד[21]ח. בן| בר לגא[2]ד[21].
נא'| נאמ' לא[1]ד[1], נאמר גא[1]ד[2]ח. כזן| כאן לגו[2]א[21]ד[21]ח.
ונאמ'| ונא' ר[2]א[2], ונאמר א[1]ד[2].

22: אחדים| ויעבד יעק' ברח' שבע שנ' ויה' בע' כי' אח' ר[2].
אחדים| אחדי' ר[2], להלך ד[21]ח. שנ'| הא' ר[2], האמור א[1], שנא' א[2],
ח' ד[21]ח. להלן| כאן א[1], אחדים ד[21], ח' ח. שבע| ז' ר[2]א[2].

אף| אפ־א[1]. אחדים| ח׳ ח. שנ׳| האמור א[1], שנא׳ א[2], שנאמ׳ ד[1],
שנאמר ד[2], ח׳ ח.

23: כאן| להלן א[1]. שבע| ז׳ ו[2]א[2]. אשר| ח׳ ל. תשוב| שוב ל,
תש׳ ג, תשו׳ ו[2]. חמת| חמ׳ ו[2], אף ל. אחר| אחי׳ ו[2].
אמו| אימו א[21]°, ח׳ ו. כצדקתה| אמרה ג, בצדקותה א[1], בצד׳ א[2].
אמרה| בצדקתה ג, אמ׳ א[2].

24: עד אשר| ח׳ ג. תשוב| תשו׳ ו[2], ח׳ ג. חמת| ח׳ ו[2], ח׳ גא[1];
+ אחיך לא[2]ד[21]ח, + אח׳ ו[2]. אלא| ח׳ ל. ויטרף| ויטרוף לגו[2]
א[2]ד[21]ח, ויטרף א[1]. אפו| + ועברתו (ועבר׳ ג, ועב׳ ו[2]) שמרה
(שמ׳ לו[2]) נצח (נצ׳ ו[2]) לגו[2]א[21]ד[21]ח.

25: ר׳ שמעון בן לקיש| ר׳ שמע׳ בן לקיש לג, ריש לק׳ ו[2], רשב־ל
א[21], ריש לקיש ד[21], (ח חסר מכאן עד... ותאמר רבקה).
אמ׳| א׳ ו[2], אמר ד[21]. עוברתיה| עוברתי ו[2], עברותיה א[21].
נוחרתה| נוחרתיה ל, ניחרתיה ג, נוחרתי ו[2], ונחרותיה א[1],
ונוחרותיה א[2], ונחרתיה ד[21]. זעייה| זעיא לגא[1], זיעה א[2],
זיעא ד[21]. מן| ח׳ לא[21]ד[21]. פומיה| מפומיה לא[21]ד[21].

26: למה| ח׳ א[2]. אשכל| אש׳ ג, ח׳ א[2]. גם| ח׳ א[2].
שניכם| שניהם ג, שני׳ ו[2], ח׳ א[2]. יום| וגו׳ ל, ח׳ א[2]ד[21].
אחד| אח׳ ו[2], ח׳ לא[2]ד[21]. יצחק| יצ׳ ו[2].

114

1 קצתי בחיי וגו֗ אמ֗ ר הונה התחילה גורפת מחוטמה ומשלכת

2 אם לוקח יעקב אשה וגו֗ קופח֗ת זו וזו ⊖ ויקרא יצחק

3 אל יעקב וגו֗ אמ֗ ר אבהוא לפי שהיו מפוקפקות בידו איכן נתאששו

4 בידו כן ויקרא יצחק אל יעקב וגו֗ אמ֗ ר לעזר אין קיום הגט אלא

5 בסותמיו שלא תאמר אילולי שדימה אבינו יעקב באביו לא נטל

6 את הבכרות תל֗ לו֗ ויקרא יצחק אל אמ֗ ר ברכיה לבן מלכים

7 שהיה חותר לאביו ליטול ליטרה אחת שלזהב אמ֗ לו למה בטמוננית

8 בא וטול לך בפרהסיא ויקרא יצחק אל יעקב ויברך אתו וגו֗ יעל

9 בנות אשכל וממרא ⊖ וישמע יעקב אל אביו ואל אמו הדה

10 היא דרך אויל ישר בעיניו דרך אויל ישר בעיניו זה שמשון

11 ויאמר שמשון אל אביו אתה קח לי וגו֗ ושומע לעצה חכם זה

12 יעקב וישמע יעקב אל אביו וגו֗ ⊖ וירא עשו כי רעות וילך

13 עשו אל ישמעאל ר֗ יהושע בן לוי אמ֗ נתן דעתו להתגייר מחלת

14 שמחל הקב֗ה על עוונותיו בשמת שנתבסמה דעתו עליו אמ֗ לה

15 ר֗ לעזר אילו הוציא את הראשונות יפה הייתה או֗ אלא על נשיו

16 כיב על כיב תוספת על בית מלי ר֗ יודן בשם ר֗ אייבו בפשע א

17 שפתים מוקש רע ממרד שמירדו עשו וישמעאל בקו֗ בֹ֗ה באת

18 להם תקלה ויצא מצרה צדיק זה יעקב ויצא יעקב ⊖

---

*הערה: בשוליים לשורה 8; הזהירו

1: קצתי| קצ׳ ר². וגו׳| מפני בנ׳ ח׳ ר², וגומ׳ ח, ח׳ גא²¹ד²¹.
אמ׳ ר׳| אׄר גא²¹ד², א׳ רב ר². הונה| הונא לגא¹ד²¹, חונא ר²ח,
אבהו| א². ומשלכת| מושלכת לו²א¹.

2: אם| ח׳ א². לוקח| לקח ר²ד²¹, ח׳ א². יעקב| יעק׳ ר², ח׳ א².
אשה| וגו׳ ל, ח׳ ר²ד²¹. וגו׳| מבנות חת גח, מבנ׳ ח׳ כא׳ ר²,
מבנות חת (כנען בא¹ ותוקן) כאלה אם כאלה א²¹, מבנות חת כאלה
ד²¹. קופחֹת| זו + א²¹. וזו| לזו א¹ד²¹; + וזו בידו ל, + לזו
א², + וזו לזו ד²¹, + וזו ח. ויקרא| ח׳ א².
יצחק| יצח׳ ר², ח׳ א².

3: אל| ח׳ א². יעקב| יעק׳ ר², ח׳ א². וגו׳| ויברך אתו וגו׳ ל,
ויב׳ אתו ר², ויברך אותו א¹ד²¹ח, ח׳ ג. אמ׳ ר׳| אׄר גו²,
ר׳ ד¹, רבי ד², ח׳ א²¹. אבהוא| אבהו לגו²ד²¹ח, ח׳ א²¹; + אמ׳
ד²¹. שהיו| + הברכות ח. איכן| והיכן א¹ד²¹.
נתאששו| נתאוששו ד²¹.

4: כן| כאן ר²א²¹ד²¹ח, ח׳ לג. יצחק| יצח׳ לג. יעקב| יעק׳ ג.
וגו׳| ויברך אתו ל, אׄר אבׄהו לפֿי שהׄיו ויברך אותו ג, ויבר׳ ת׳ (?)
ר², ויברך אותו א²¹ח, ח׳ ד²¹. אמ׳ ר׳| אׄ ר גא²¹, א׳ רבי ר²,
אמר רבי ד². לעזר| אלעזר לגו²א²¹ד²¹ח. הגט| גט לו²ח.

5: בסותמיו| בחתימה ל, בחותמיה ג, בחותמה ר²ח, בחותמיו א²¹ד²¹.
שלא| ח׳ ל. תאמר| תאמ׳ ד¹, ח׳ ל. אילולי| אלולי לא¹ד²¹.
שדימה| שרימה לגו²א¹ד²¹, שרמה א²ח. אבינו| אב׳ ר², ח׳ לגא²¹
ד²¹ח. יעקב| יעק׳ ר². באביו| לעשו א¹, לאחיו א². לא| ח׳ לג.
נטל| ונטל לג, היה נוטל ר².

6: את| ח׳ לגו²ד²¹. הברכות| בדכות גו², הברכה א²¹, ברכותיו
ד²¹. תל׳ לו׳| תל׳ לומ׳ ל, תֹֿל גא²¹ד¹ח, תלמוד לומר ד².

יצחק| יצח' ו'.^{2} אל| + יעקב ויברך אותו (אתו ל) לגא^{21}ד^{21}ח, יע'
ויברך את' ו'.^{2} אמ' ר| אׄר' גו^{2}א^{21}, אמר ר' ד', אמר רבי ד'.^{2}
ברכיה| ברכי' ו'.^{2} לבן| משל + ו'א^2.^{1}

7: ליטול| ח' לגא^{21}ח.   ליטרה| ליטרא לגא^{1}ד^{21}ח, ליטרות א^2.
אחת| ח' א^{21}.   אמ' לו| א' לו ו'^{2}, אֵל' א^{21}, אמר לו ד^{21}ח.
בטמונית| בטמונית ל, במטמונינות ג, במטמונית ו'^{2}, במטמוניות
א^{21}ד^{21}ח.

8: בא| בוא לגו^{2}ח.   לר| ח' א^{21}.   בפרהסיא| + שנ' לג, + כך ו'^{2}ח,
+ שׄנא' א^{21}.   ויקרא יצחק| ויק' יצ' ו'^{2}.   אל| את ג.
יעקב| יעק' ו'^{2}.   ויברך| ויב' ו'^{2}, וגו' ל, ח' א^{21}.   אתו| אותו
גא^{2}ד^{21}ח, את' ו'^{2}, ח' לא^1.   וגו'| ויצוהו ויאמר לו לא תקח ג,
ויצוהו ו'^{2}א^{21}ד^{21}ח, ח' ל.   הזהירו| ו'^{0}, היזהרו ל, ח' ו.

9: בנות| + ענו לגו^{2}א^{21}ד^{21}ח.   אשכל| אשכול ו'^{2}א^{21}ד^{21}ח.
אביו| יעקב ו'^{2}, אחיו א^2.   ואל| וגו' ל, ח' א^2.   אמו| ח' לא^2.
הדה היא| הה"ד ל^0, הדהי ג, ההׄד ו'^{2}א^{1}ד^1, הׄ הׄ דׄכ א^2, הדא הוא
דכתיב ד^2, היינו דכתיב ח (ל חסר מכאן עד... וירא עשו...,
והושלם בגליון).

10: דרך| כל + (בו ונמחק) גו^{2}א^{2}ד^{21}ח.   אויל| ו'^{0}ל^0, איש וגו'^{2}
א^{2}ד^{0}^{21}ח.   בעיניו| ל^0 בעי' ו'^{2}; + ושומע לעיצה חכם ל^0, + ותוכן
לבות יׄי ושמע לעצה חכם ג, + ויש' לעצ' חכ' ו'^{2}, ושומע לעצה חכם
א^2, ותוכן לבות יׄ ושומע לעצה חכם ח.   דרך| ל^0, ח' א^1; כל +
(בו ונמחק) גו^{2}א^{1}ד^{21}ח.   אויל| ו'^{0}ל^0, איש גו^{2}א^{2}ד^{21}ח, ח' א^1.
ישר| ל^0, ח' א^1.   בעיניו| ל^0 בעינ' ג, ח' א^1.
שמעון| + שנ' ל^{0}גו^{2}ח, שנא' א^{21}.

204

11: ויאמר| ויאמ׳ ד[1], ח׳ ל°. שמשון| שמ׳ גו[2], ח׳ ל°.
אל| ח׳ ל°. אביו| אבי׳ ר[2], ח׳ ל°. אתה| אותה ל°גא[21]ד[21]ח.
וגו׳| כי היא ישרה בעיני ל°גא[21]ד[21]ח, כי ה׳ יש׳ בעי׳ ו[2].
ושומע| ושמע ל°ג, ויש׳ ו[2]. לעצה| לעיצה ל°ג, עצה ד[1].
חכם| ח׳ ר[2]. זה| ח׳ א[2].

12: יעקב| יעק׳ ר[2], ח׳ א[1] ; + שנ׳ ל°גח,+שנא א[21]°. יעקב| יע׳
ר[2]. אל אביו| ח׳ ר[2]. וגו׳| ואל אמו ל°א[2]ח, ואל אמו וגו׳ ג,
אל אמו וילך ד[21], ח׳ ר[2]א[1]. וירא| (א[21]°ח חסרים מכאן עד...
וילך). רעות| רע׳ ר[2] ; + בנות כנען וגו׳ לג, + בנות כנען ד[21].

13: אל| ח׳ א[1]. ישמעאל| ישמע׳ ר[2], ח׳ א[1] ; + ויקח את מחלת גח,
+ וי׳ את מח׳ ר[2]. ר׳ יהושע בן לוי| (רבי ד[2]) ר׳ יהוש׳ בן לוי
לו[2], אריב֞ל א[21]. אמ׳| א׳ ר[2], אמר ד[2], ח׳ א[21]. נתן| עשו + א[1].

14: שמחל| + לו לגו[2]א[21]ד[21]ח. הקבֹ֞ה| הק׳ ר[2], הבֹ֞ה א[2], הקדוש
ברוך הוא ד[2]. על| ח׳ ח; + כל א[21]ד[21]. עוונותיו| עונותיו
גא[21]ד[21]ח. שנתבסמה| שנתבסמת ל, שנתבשמה גא[1], שנתבסמת ר[2]א[2],
שניתבסמה ד[1]. אם לה| אם ליה ל, א֞ל גא[21], א֞ ליה ר[2], אמר ד[21],
אמ׳ לו ח.

15: לעזר| אלעזר לגא[1]ד[21]ח, אלע׳ ר[2], אלעז׳ א[2]. הייתה| היית
גח, אתה א[21], היה ד[21]. או׳| א֞ ל, אומ׳ גא[2], אומר א[1]ח, ח׳ ד[21]
על נשיו| ח׳ ח.

16: כיב| כוב ר[2], כאב א[1]ד[21]. כיב| כוב ר[2], כאב א[1]ד[21] ; + ד֞א
כוב על כוב ד[21]. תוספת| תוספה לו[2]ח, תוספא ג, ותוספת א[1],
ותוספה א[2]. בית| כי לגח. מלי| יתמלי לח, יתמלא ג, מלא א[21]ד[21] ;
+ ס֞ א֞ תוספה על בית מלי ל. ר׳| רבי ד[2], ח׳ ח. יודן| ח׳ ח.
בשם ר׳| בש׳ ר׳ לו[2], בש֞ר א[21], בשם רבי ד[2], ר׳ ח.

205

איבו| איבו גא[21]; + אמ' א[21]ד[1], + אמר ד[2], + אומ' ח.
בפשע| בפ' ר[2].

17: רע| + ויצא מצרה צדיק לגו[2]א[21]ח, + ויצא מצרה צדיק בפשע
שפתים מוקש רע ד[21]. ממרד| מימרד ר[2]. שמירדו| שמרדו לגו[2]א[21]
ד[21]ח. וישמעאל| וישמע' ג. בקו̃ בֿהֿ| בהקבה לו[2]א[1]ד[1]ח, בהק' ר[2],
בהבֿה א[2], בהקדוש ברוך הוא ד[2]; + והכעיסו אותו וכן נשיו שהכעיסו
אותו ד[21]. באת| תלה א[1], באתה א[2]ח.

18: להם| להן ר[2]. מצרה צדיק| מצ' צד' ג. יעקב| יעק' ר[2]; +
שני' לג, + שנא' א[1], + שנאמ' א[2]. יעקב| + מבאר (מב' ר[2]) שבע
לגו[2]ד[21]ח, + מבאר שבע וילך חרנה ד[21].

BERESHIT RABBA, CHAPTER 81
SCRIBE D.

25   פרשתא   פֿ אׄ

26   ויאמר אלים אל יעקוב קום עלה בית אל מוקש אדם ילע קודש

25: פרשתא| פרש׳ לו.[2], פרשה גד[21], פרשת א[21], ח׳ ח.

פֿא| עֿט ד[1], ח׳ ח.

26: ויאמר| ויא׳ ר.[2], ויאמ׳ ד[1]. אים| אדים ל, אלהים גא[1],
אהים ר.[2], אליֿם א[2]ד[1], אלה׳ ד.[2], אלקי׳ ח. יעקוב| יעקב לגא[21]
ד[21]ח, יע׳ ר.[2]. קום| ח׳ ל. עלה| ע׳ ר.[2], ח׳ ל. בית אל| בית א׳
ר.[2], וגו׳ ד[21], ח׳ ל; + כת׳ ג, + הֿהֿד א[1], + כתי׳ א.[2].

מוקש| מוק׳ ר.[2], (ח חסר מכאן עד... אמ׳ ר׳ יניי).

קודש| קדש א[21]ד[21].

1 תבא מאירה לאדם שהוא אוכל קדשים בלועו   תני ר חייא

2 תבא מאירה לאדם שהוא נהנה מן הקודש ואן קודש אלא ישׄ

3 שׄ קודש ישראל ליׄיׄ ראשית תבואתו וגׄ ואחר נדרים לבקר

4 אמׄ רׄ יניי איחר אדם את נדרו נתבקרה פינקסו ואחר נדרים

5 לבקר אמׄ רׄ יניי ורׄ חייא בן לוליינו צריך מכות הׄכ דׄ בקרת

6 תהיה לא וגׄ תידע לך שכן יעקב אבינו על ידי שאיחר את נדרו

7 נתבקרה פינקסו ויאמר אלים אל יעקב וגׄ   אם נבלתה
בהתנשא

8 בן עזאי ורׄ עקיבה בן עזאי אוׄ אם ניבלתה עצמך על דברי תורה

9 סופך להתנשא בהם ואם זממתה יד לפה אם נזדמזמו אחריך

10 דברים יד לפה חד ידע תרין לא ידעין ⊕   רׄ עקיבה אמׄ מי

11 גרם לך להתנבל בדברי תורה על ידי שנשאתה בהם רבינו הוה

12 עבר על סימוניה יצאו אנשי סימונייא לקראתו אמרו לו רבי

13 תן לנו אדם אחד שייהא מקרא אותנו ומשנה אותנו ודן את

14 דינינו נתן להם לוי בן סוסי עשוׄ בימה גדולה והושיבו אותו

15 למעלה ממנה ונתעלמו דברי תורה מפניו שאלו אותו שלוש

16 שאילות   אמרו לו גרמת יבמה היאך היא חולצת ולא הושיבן

17 רקה   דם מה הוא ולא הושיבן אמרו דילמא לית הוא בר אולפן
אֹורִיֹתֹ

18 בר אגדה הוא נשאלינֵיה קריי אמרין לה מהוא דׄכ את הרשום

19 בכתב אמת אם אמת למה רשום ואם רשום למה אמת ולא

20 הושיבן וכיוון שראה שרצתו צרה השכים בבוקר והלך   לו
בֵֻך

21 אצל רבינו אמׄ לו מה עבדון אנשי סימונייה אמׄ לו אל תזכיריני

22 צרתי שלוש שאילות שאלו אותי ולא יכולתי להשיבן אמׄ לה

23 ומה הינין אמׄ גדמת במה היא חולצת אמׄ לו ולא היית יודע להשיב

24 אם אפילו בשיניה אפילו בגופה שָׂרָקָה דם מה הוא אמׄ לו ולא היית

25 יודע להשיב אם יהיה בו צחצוחית שלרוק יהיה כשר ואם לאו

26 הרי זה פסול   אבל אגיד לך את הרשום בכתב אמת אם אמת

---

* הערה: בשוליים לשורה 11; עצמך. לשורה 24; יבמה

1: תבא| תהא ג, תבוא ו'א'^{21}ד'^{21}, (ל' חסר מכאן עד... תבא מאירה
לאדם שהוא נהנה); ואחר נדרים (נדרי' א'^{2}) לבקר (לב' ל') + לגא'^{21}
ד'^{2}, אח' נד' לב' מוקש אדם יל' קו' + ו'^{2}. מאירה| מארה א'^{1}.
שהוא| שיהא ג. קדשים| קדשי' ד'^{1}. תנ'| תאנ' א'^{21}. ר'| רבי ד'^{2}.

2: תבא| תבוא לו'א'^{21}ד'^{21}, תהא ג. מאירה| מארה ל. שהוא| ח' ל.
נהנה| שנהנה ל, אוכל קדשים ונהנה א'^{21}. הקודש| הקדש ל, ההקדש
גא'^{21}ד'^{21}. ואן| ואין לגו'א'^{2}ד'^{21}. קודש| קו' ג, קדש א'^{21},
הקדש ד'^{21}. ישר'| יש' לו'^{2}, ישראל א'^{21}ד'^{21}.

3: שנ'| שנא' א'^{21}, שנאמר ד'^{2}, ח' לו'^{2}. קודש| קדש לא'^{21}ד'^{21}.
ישראל| יש' לו'^{2}, ישר' ג. לייי| ליי גו'א'^{21}ד'^{21}, ח' ל.
ראשית תבואתו וגו'| ראש' ת כ א י ר ת א נא יי ו'^{2}, ח' לגא'^{21}ד'^{21}.
ואחר| אחר ו'^{2}. נדרים| נד' ו'^{2}. לבקר| לב' ו'^{2}.

4: אמ' ר'| אר' גו'א'^{21}, אמר ר' ד'^{1}, אמר רבי ד'^{2}. יניי| ינאי
לא'^{21}ד'^{21}ח, דברא א'^{2}. איחר| אחר ד'^{21}. את| ח' ו'^{2}ח.
נתבקרה| להתבקרה ג. פינקסו| פנכסו (?) ג, פינכסו ו'^{2}, פנקסו
א'^{2}ח. ואחר| איחור ו'^{2}; + איחור ג, ח' א'^{2}, (ד'^{21} חסרים מכאן עד...
ויאמר אלהים אל יעקב, ח חסר מכאן עד... שכן יעקב).
נדרים| נדרי' ו'^{2}, ח' א'^{2}.

5: לבקר| לבק' ו'^{2}, ח' א'^{2}. אמ' ר' יניי| ח' לגו'א'^{21}.
ור'| ר' לו'א'^{21}, רבי ג. בן| בר לגו'א'^{21}. לוליינו| לוליאני
לו'א'^{21}, לוליוני ג; + אמ' לגא'^{21} + א' ו'^{2}. מכות| (ב ג נראית
כ"משת"!) הכ דת'| היך דאת אמ' ל, כמדמר ג, היך כ ד א ו'^{2},
כדא̃ א'^{21}. בקרת| בקורת ו'^{2}א'^{1}.

6: לא וגו'| וגו' ל, ח' גו'א'^{21}. תידע| תדע לגו'א'^{21}.
יעקב| אבינו לג, אבי' ו'^{2}. אבינו| יעקב לג, יע' ו'^{2}, אבי' א'^{2},

ח׳ א׳[1]. על ידי| ע̃י א[21]. שאיחר| שאחר א[21]. את| ח׳ א[21]ח.

7: נתבקרה| ניתבקרה לא[1]. פינקסו| פנקס (פנקש?) ג, פינכסו ו[2],
פנקסו א[2]ח; + שנא׳ גא[21]. ויאמר| ויא׳ ר[2], (ח חסר מכאן עד... ר
אבא בר כהנא אמ׳) (הפסוק הזה מופיע בסוף המאמר הזה בכ"י ר[2]לגא[21],
ובהתחלת המאמר הבא בכ"י ר[2]ד[21]). אים| אהים לו[2], י̃י ג, אלהים
א[1]ד[2], אלים א[2]ד[1]. יעקב| יע׳ ר[2]. וגו׳| קום עלה בית א׳ וגו׳ ל,
קום עלה בית אל גא[2]ד[21], קום ע׳ בי׳ ר[2], עלה בית אל א[1].
אם| הה"ד + א[1]. נבלתה| נבלת לגו[2]א[21]ד[21]. בהתנשא| בהתנש׳ ו[2]; +
וגו׳ ל, + ואם זמות (זמו׳ ו[2]) יד לפה ו[2]א[21]ד[2].

8: בן| ר׳ א[2]. עזאי| עזיי לו[2], עקיבא א[2]. ור׳| ובן א[2], ורבי
ד[2]. עקיבה| עקיבא גד[21], עקי׳ ר[1]א[2], עזאי א[2]. עזאי| עזיי לו[2].
או׳| אומ׳ א[21], אומר ד[21]. ניבלתה| ניבלת ל, נבלת גא[21]ד[21].
על| ח׳ לגו[2]א[21]ד[21]. דברי| בדברי גו[2]א[21]ד[21], ח׳ ל.
תורה| בתארה ל, תא׳ ו[2]. בהם| בהן גא[2].

9: זמותה| זמות לגא[21], זמ׳ ו[2]. אם| ואם ג. נזדמזמו| נזדממו ג,
ניזדמזמו ו[2], נזדמנו א[21], ניזדממו ד[21]. אחריך| לך א[21].

10: לא| ולא ג[2]. ר׳| רבי ד[2]. עקיבה| עקיבא גא[2]ד[21], עקי׳ ר[1]א[2].
אמ׳| א׳ לו[2], או׳ ג, אמר ד[21].

11: בדברי תורה| בדב׳ תו׳ ו[2], בד̃ת א[1]. על ידי| ע̃י א[1].
שנשאתה| שנשאת לו[2]א[21]ד[21], שנישאת ג; + עצמך ו[o]לגו[2]א[21], + את
עצמך ד[21]. בהם| מהן ג, בהן ו[2], בהון ד[21]. רבינו| רבנו ל,
ר׳ א[1]. הווה| הוה לגו[2]א[2]ד[21], היה א[1].

12: עבר| עובר א[1]. סימוניה| סימוניא גא[21]ד[21]. יצאו| ויצאו ד[21].
אנש׳| אנשים ל. סימוניא| סימוניה לו[2], סימוניא גא[21]ד[21].
אמרו| אמ׳ ל. רבי| ר׳ לד[1], רבינו ג, ח׳ א[21].

211

13: אחד| א׳ א, א^2, ח׳ לא^1. שייהא| שיהא לו^{2}א^{21}ד^{21}, שהיה ג.
אותנו| ח׳ ל. ומשנה| ושונה ד^{21}. את| ח׳ ל.

14: להם| + את א^1. לוי| ר׳ + א^{1}ד^1, רבי + ד^2. בן| בו ד^{21}.
סוסי| סיסי לגו^{2}א^{21}. עשו| ועשו ד^{21}. לו| ו°, אותו א^2.
והושיבו| והושיבוהו ל. אותו| לו ר^2, ח׳ ל.

15: למעלה| בה ל, עליה א^1. ממנה| ממנו ר^{2}ד^{21}, ח׳ לא^1.
ונתעלמו| + ממנו ל. תורה| תו׳ ר^2. מפניו| ממנו ג, מפיו
א^{2}ד^{21}, ח׳ ל. שאלו| שאלוהו ל. אותו| ממנו ג, ח׳ ל.
שלוש| ג׳ לו^{2}ד^1, שלש גא^1, שלשה ד^2, ח׳ א^2.

16: שאילות| הלכות ל, שאלות א^{1}ד^1, ח׳ א^2. אמרו לו| ח׳ לגו^2
א^{21}. גרמת| גידמת לו^{2}א^1, גירמת ג, יבמה א^2, גדמת ד^{21}.
יבמה| גדמת א^2, ח׳ לגו^{2}א^1. היאך| במה לגו^{2}א^{21}. היא| ח׳ ד^{21}.
ולא| לא ל. הושיבן| ו°, השיבן לוו^{2}א^{21}ד^{21}, השיבה ג.

17: רקה| רקקה א^{21}ד^{21}; + היבמה א^1. דם| + היבמה לגו^2.
מה הוא| מהו לגו^{2}א^{21}ד^{21}. ולא| לא ל. השיבן| + הר׳ תרין א^{21},
+ כלום ד^{21}. אמרו| אמ׳ ל, אמרי א^{21}ד^{21}. דילמא| דיל׳ ג,
דילמ׳ א^1, ח׳ ר^2. הוא| ח׳ לד^{21}. אוריׄתׄ| ו°, אורייא ל,
אוריא ג, אוריתא א^{21}, ח׳ רו^{2}ד^{21}.

18: בר| דילמ׳ + ל, דיל׳ + ג. אגדה| אגדא ל, הגדה גו^{2}א^{21}.
הוא| ח׳ ל. נשאלינה| שאלוהו ל, נישאלינה ג, נשאליה א^{21}ד^{21}.
קריי| קראי לגו^{2}ד^{21}, קרא א^{21}. אמרין| אמרו גא^{21}, אמרון ד^{21},
ח׳ ל. להן| ליה ר^{2}א^{21}ד^{21}. מהוא| מהו לגו^{2}א^{21}ד^{21}; + דין ד^{21}.
דכ׳| ג, דכת׳ לו^2, דכתי׳ א^{21}ד^1, דכתיב ד^2. את| ח׳ ג.
אמת| אמ׳ ר^2.

19: ואם| אם ל. ולא| לא ל, ח׳ א[2].

20: הושיבן| ר°, השיבן לוד[2]א[21]°ד[21], ח׳ א[2]. וכיוון| כיון ל,
וכיון גו[2]א[21]ד[21]. בבוקר| בבקר לגו[2]ד[21], ח׳ א[21].

21: רבינו| רבנו ל, ר׳ א[1]. אמ׳ לו| אמ׳ ליה ל, ליה ו[2], אֵל א[21],
אמר ליה ד[21]. עבדון| עשו א[2]. ברן| לך ד[21]. אנשי| בני ל.
סימונייה| סימוניה לו[2], סימוניא גא[21]ד[21]. אמ׳ לו| א׳ לו ו[2],
אֵל א[2], אמר לו ד[21]. תזכיריני| תזכרני לו[2]א[1], תזכריני ג,
תזכירני א[2]ד[21].

22: צרתי| צרותי א[1]. שלוש| ג׳ לו[2]א[2]ד[1], שלש גא[1], שלשה ד[2].
שאילות| שאלות לגא[21]. שאלו| שאלוני לגו[2]א[21]. אותי| ח׳ לגו[2]
א[21]. להשיבן| לחזירן להושיבן ג. אמ׳ לה| אמ׳ ליה ל, אמ׳ לו
גו[2], אֵל א[21]ד[1], אמר ליה ד[2].

23: ומה| ומאן (?) ג. הינין| אינון לגא[21]ד[21]. אמ׳| אמ׳ ליה
ל, אמ׳ לו ג, א׳ לו ו[2], אֵל א[21]°, אמר ליה ד[21].
גדמת| גידמת לו[2]א[1]ד[21], גירמת ג. חולצת| + ובמה חולצת ל.
אמ׳ לו| א׳ לו ו[2], אֵל א[21], אמר לו ד[21], (ל חסר מכאן עד... אמ׳...
והושלם בין השורות). ולא| לא א[1]. היית| היית ו[1], היית ו[2].
יודע| + מה גו[2]א[21]. להשיבן| להשיב א[1].

24: אמ׳| אמ׳ לו לג, א׳ לו ו[2], אֵל א[1], אמ׳ ליה אין ד[1], (א[2]
חסר מכאן עד... עם יהיה בו). אפילו| ואפילו ג, אפי׳ א[1].
בשיניה| + חולצת א[1]. אפילו| ואפי׳ א[1]. יבמה| ר°, ח׳ וד[21].
שרקה| ר°ו[2], שרקת ל, שקרה (?) ג, שרקקה א[1], רקקה ד[21].
מה הוא| מהו לגו[2]א[1]. אמ׳ לו| א׳ לו ו[2], אֵל א[1], אמר ליה ד[21],
(ל חסר מכאן עד... אם יהיה, והושלם בין השורות). ולא| לא א[1].

213

25: יודע| + מה גו[2]א[1] . להשיב| להשיבן א[1]; + אמ' ל, + אמ' לו
ג, + א' לו ר[2], + אֵל א[1], + אמר ליה ד[21] . יהיה| יש לא[21].
צחצוחית| צחצחות ג. שלרוק| ח' ל. יהיה| הרי הוא גא[21]ד[21],
הרי זה ר[2], ח' ל. ואם| (ל חסר מכאן עד... אמ' לו רשום עד שלו
נגזרה...)

26: הרי| ח' ג. זה| הוא א[21], ח' ג. הרשום| הרש' ו[2].
בכתב| בכת' א[2].

214

144

1 למה רשום ואם רשום למה אמת אמ׳ לו ולא היית יודע להשיב

2 אמ׳ לו רשום עד שלא נגזרה הגזירה אמת משנגזרה הגזירה מה

3 הוא חותמו שלהקב̇ה ר׳ ביבי בשם ר׳ ראובן אמ̇ אמת מה הוא אמת

4 אמ̇ ר׳ שמעון בן לקיש אלף בראשון שלאותות מים באמצעיותיו

5 תיו בסופן על שם אני ראשון ואני אחרון וגו׳ אמ̇ לו ולמה לא

השבתה

6 אותן כשם שהישבתה אותי אמ̇ לו עשו לי בימה גדולה והושיבו

7 אותי למעלה ממנה וטפח רוחי עליי ונתעלמו דברי תורה ממני

8 וקרא עליו אם נבלתה בהתנשא וגו׳ אמ̇ ר׳ בון בר כהנא אם חישבתה

9 ליבך לעשות דבר מצוה ולא עשית נח לך ליתן זמן על פיך ולא

10 לפסוק אמ̇ ר׳ יודן מה ידך סמוכה לפיך כך יהיה נדרך סמוך

11 לפיך רבנן אמ מה מה ידך קודמת לפיך כן יהיה נדרך קודם לפיך תידע

12 לך שכן יעקוב אבינו על ידי שאיחר את נדרו נתבקרה פינקסו

13 ויאמר אלים אל יעקוב קום וגו׳ ר׳ אבא בר כהנא אמ̇

14 בשעת עקתי נדרי בשעת רווחי שזבי אמ̇ ר׳ לוי מהולתך טרשה

15 אקיש עלה קום עלה בית אל שלאל ועשה שם מזבח לאל מה עשו נודו*

16 ואינו מקיים אף את נודר ואן את מקיים ⊙ ויאמר יעקב

17 אל ביתו ר׳ קיריספא בשם ר׳ יוחנן אן אנו בקיים בדיקדוקי עבודה

18 זרה כיעקוב אבינו דתנינן המוצא כלים ועליהם צורת וגו׳ אמ̇ רבי

19 יוחנן כל כסות בכלל עבודה זרה ויתנו אל יעק̇ ר׳ ישמעאל

20 בר יוסי סליק למצלייה בהדה ירושלם עבר בהדה פלאטנוס

21 וחמתיה חד שמריי אמ̇ לה להן את אזל אמ̇ לה מסוק מצלייה

22 בירושלם אמ̇ לה ולא טב לך מצלי בהדן טורה בריכה ולא

23 בביתה קיקילתה אמ̇ לו אומ̇ לכם למה אתם דומין לכלב שהיה

24 להוט אחר הנבלה כך לפי שאתם יודעים שעבודה זרה טמונה

25 תחתיו ויטמון אותה יעקוב וג׳ לפיכך אתם להוטים אחריו אמרין

26 דין בעי מסאבא קם וערק בליליא ⊙ ויסע ויהי וגו׳ אמ̇

---

*הערה: בשוליים לשורה 15; לביתו

215

1: רשום| רשו׳ ו[2]. אמ׳ לו| א׳ לו ו[2], אל א[1∘2], אמר לו ד[2], ח׳
א[1]. היית| היתה א[1]. יודע| + מה גא[21] . להשיב| להשיבן א[1].

2: אמ׳ לו| א׳ לו ו[2], אל א[21], את הרשום בכתב מהו + ל.
רשום| ח׳ א[1]. עד| קודם ל. שלא| ח׳ לו[2]. נגזרה| שנגזרה ו[2],
ח׳ ל. הגזירה| גזירה לגד[21], גזירה א[21], אמת| רשום א[∘1], ח׳ א[1].
משנגזרה| משנגזר׳ ד[21], ח׳ א[2]. הגזירה| גזירה גד[21], הגזירה א[1],
ח׳ א[2]; + אמת א[21] . מה הוא| מהו לג, מה א[1], ומה הוא ד[21], ח׳ ו[2].

3: שלהקבה| שלהק׳ ו[2], של הקבה א[1], של הבה א[2]ד[1], של הקדוש ברוך
הוא ד[2]; + אמת לגא[21]ד[21]. ר׳| רב א[1], רבינו ד[21]. ביבי| אייבו ג,
ח׳ ד[21]. בשם ר׳| מש׳ ר׳ לו[2], בשׂר א[21], בשם רבי ד[2].
ראובן| שמואל ג. אמ׳| א׳ ו[2], אמר ד[2], ח׳ לא[2]. אמת| ח׳ לגא[21].
מה הוא| מהו לגו[2]ד[21].

4: אמ׳ ר׳ שמעון בן לקיש| אמ׳ ר׳ שמע׳ בן לקיש ל, א׳ ר׳ שׁבׁל ג,
א׳ ריש לקיש ו[2], ארׁשׁ בן לקיש א[1], ארשׁבׁל א[2], אמ׳ (אמר ד[2]) ריש
לקיש ד[21]. אלף| אלפ׳ א[1]. בראשון| בראש לג, בראשן ו[2]א[2]ד[21],
בראשם א[1]. שלאותות| האותיות ל, שלאותיות גו[2], של אותיות א[21]
ד[21]. מים| תיו לו[2], היו (?) ג, מס א[21]ד[21].
באמצעיותיו| בסופן לגו[2], באמצעיתן א[21], באמצע ד[21]; +
שלאותיות לגו[2].

5: תיו| מ׳ לג, מס ו[2], תו א[2]. בסופן| באמצען ל, באמצעיתן ג,
באמצע ו[2], בסוף ד[21]; + של אותיות גו[2]. על שם| על שום מנ׳ ו[2],
עׁשׁ א[2]. ראשון| רא׳ ו[2]. אחרון| אחר׳ ו[2]. וגו| וגו[2]
(מבלעדי ג, ומבלעדי א[2]) אין אלהים (אהים לגו[2], אליׄם א[2])
לגו[2]א[21], וכו׳ ד[21]. אמ׳ לו| א׳ לו ו[2], אמר לו ד[2], ח׳ לא[21]
לו| ח׳ ו. הישבתה| השבתם ל, השבת גא[2], השבתה ו[2], השיבות א[1]ד[21].

6: אותן| להם א[21], ח' ל. כשם| כמו א[21]. שהישבתה| שחשבת ל;
שהשבת ל°גא[2], השבתה ר[2], שהשיבות א[1]ד[21]. אותי| לי ל, אותו ג.
אמ' לו| אמ' לי ל, א' לו ר[2], אלֹ א[21]ד[1], אמר ליה ד[2].
והושיבו| והושיבוני ג, ח' ל.

7: אותי| ח' לג; + עליה ד[21]. למעלה| ח' ל. ממנה| הימנה ד[21],
ח' ל. וטפח| וטפח ל, טפה ג, ועפה ר[2], טפח א[1], תפח א[2], וטפה
ד[21]. עליי| עלי לגו[2]א[21]ד[21]. ונתעלמו| ונעלמו ל. דברי| ממני
לד[21]. תורה| דברי לד[21], תו' ר[2]. ממני| תורה לד[21], מפניי גו[2],
מפני א[1], מפי א[2].

8: וקרא| קרא לגא[21]ד[21]. עליו| + המקרא הזה ד[21].
נבלתה| נבלת לו[2]א[21]ד[21], נב' ג. בהתנשא| בהתנ' ג, בהתנש' ו[2].
וגו'| ואם זמות יד לפה גא[21], ח' לו[2]ד[21]. אמ' ר'| ר' גא[21]ד[1], א' רבי
ו[2], אמר רבי ד[1]. בון| אבון לו[2], אבין ג, אבא א[21]ד[2], אב' ד[1].
כהנא| כה' ו[2], כהנ' ד[1]. חישבתה| חישבת לגו[2], חשבת א[21]ד[21].

9: ליבך| בלבך ד[21], ח' לגו[2]א[21]. לעשות| לעש' ו[2], דבר א[21]ד[21].
דבר| מצוה א[21]ד[21], ח' ל. מצוה| לעשות א[21]ד[2], לעשו' ד[1].
עשית| עשיתו לו[2]א[21], עשיתי ג. נח| נוח לגא[21]ד[21], כוח ו[2].
לך| לו ד[21].

10: לפסוק| ליפסוק ו[2]. אמ' ר'| אֹ' גא[2]א[21]ד[1], אמר רבי ד[2].
ידרן| ידיר ד[21]. סמוכה| סמוך ג. לפירן| לפיכך ל. כן| אף א[1],
אף א[2]. יהיה| יהא ל, נדריך א[21]. נדרן| יהיו א[21].
סמורן| סמוכין א[21].

11: רבנן| רבנין לגא[21], רבני' ו[2]. אמ'| אמרין ג, אמרי' ו[2],
אמרי א[21]ד[21]. קודמת| קודמ' א[2], קודם ד[21]. כן| כך גו[2]ד[21],

217

אפֿ א[1] , אף א[2] . יהיה| נדריך א[21] , ח׳ ל. נדרך| יהיו א[21] .
קודם| קודמת ל, קודם סמוך ג, קודמין א[21] . תידע| תדע לגו[2]א[21]ד[21] .

12: שכן| + שהרי ד[21] . יעקוב| יעקב לגא[21] , אבי׳ ר[2], אבינו ד[1] .
אבינו| יע׳ ר[2], אבי׳ א[2], יעקב ד[21] , ח׳ ל. על ידי| עֵי א[21] , ח׳
ל. את| ח׳ לגא[1]ד[21] . נתבקרה| נבקרה א[2] . פינקסו| פינכסו גו[2] ,
פנקסו א[2]ד[21] .

13: שֵׁנֵ׳| (ו°, שנא׳ א[21] , שנאמר ד[2] , (לח חסרים מכאן עד... ר אבא) ,
ח׳ ר. ויאמר| ויא׳ ר[2], ויאמ׳ ד[1] . אליֹם| יֹי ג, אדים ו[2] .
יעקוב| יעקב גו[2]א[21]ד[21] . וגו| עלה ביתאל גא[21]ד[21] , עֵ ביתאֹ ו[2], ח׳
לח; + ושב שם ועשה שם מזבח ד[21] . ר׳| אמ׳ ר׳ לגח, א׳ ר׳ ו[2], אֹֹר
א[1]ד[1] , אמר רבי ד[2] , (א[2] חסר מכאן עד... ועשה שם מזבח) .
בר| ח׳ לגח. כהנא| כהנ׳ ו[2]ד[1] , ח׳ לגח. אמ׳| ח׳ לגו[2]א[1]ד[21]ח.

14: עקתי| עקתא ד[21] . נדרי| נדרא ד[21] . רווחי| רווחי לגו[2] ,
רווחא ד[21] . שזבי| שטפי לגח, טפשי ר[2], שבקי א[1] , שיטפא ד[21] .
אמ׳ ר׳| אֹר גו[2]א[1]ד[1] , אמר רבי ד[2] , (ח חסר מכאן עד... קום עלה...) .
מהולתך| מהילתך ל, מחילתך ג, מחולתך ו[2]ד[21] .
טרשה| טפשה גו[2] , טרשא א[1] , טפשא ד[1] , חרשה ד[2] .

15: עליה| עלה גא[1]ד[1] ; + אֹל הבֹה יעקב שכחת נדרך ד[1] , + אמר ליה
הקדוש ברוך הוא ד[2] . עלה| על׳ ו[2] . בית אל| ביתאל לגו[2]א[1]ד[21]ח; +
קום עלה לא[1]ח, + עלה ג, + קום על׳ ו[2] . לביתו| ו°, ביתו א[1] .
שלאל| של א׳ ג. שם| שֹ׳ ו[2] . מזבח| מ׳ ו[2] . לאל| וגו׳ ל, ח׳ ג;
+ הנר׳ אל׳ בברח׳ מ׳ ע׳ א[2] ו[2] , + הנראה אליך (ח׳ א[2]) בברחך מפני
עשו אחיך א[21]ח, + הנראה אליך ואם אין את עושה כן הרי את כעשו
ד[21] . נודר| ו°, ח׳ ו.

16: אף| אפ̇ א̇[1]. את| אתה לא[21]ח̇. נודר| נדרת ל. ואן| ולא ל,
ואין גו[2], ואינך א[21]ד[21], ואינו ח. את| ח̇ לא[21]ד[21]ח̇.
מקיים| קיימתה ל. ויאמר| ויא̇ ר̇[2], ויאמ̇ ד[21], ח̇ א̇[2] (ח חסר
מכאן עד... ויסע ויהי וגו̇) יעקב| יעק̇ ר̇[2], ח̇ א̇[2].

17: אל| ח̇ א̇[2]. ביתו| + וגו̇ לג, + ואל כל אש̇ ע̇ הס̇ א̇ אה̇ ו̇[2], +
ואל כל אשר עמו הסירו את אלהי הנכר א̇[1], + הסירו את אלהי הנכר
א̇[2]. ר̇| רבי ג; א̇ + ד̇[1], אמר + ד̇[2]. קיריספא| כרוספדי לד[21],
כרוספדיי ג, כרוספדאי ר̇א[21]. בשם ר̇| בש̇ ר̇ לו[2], בש̇ר א̇[1],
אמ̇ ר̇ ד̇, אמר רבי ד̇[2], ח̇ א̇[2]. יוחנן| יוח̇ ר̇[2], ינאי א̇[1],
ח̇ א̇[2]; + אמ̇ גא[21]. אן| אין לגו[2]א[21]ד[21]. אנו| אני ג.
בקיים| בקיין ג, בקיאי̇ א̇[21], בקאים ד̇[1], בקיאים ד̇[2].
בדיקדוקי| בדקדוק א̇[21]ד̇[21]. עבודה זרה| עבו̇ זרה ל, עבו̇ זר̇
ו̇[2], עז̇ א̇[21]ד̇[1], עבדה זרה ד̇[2].

18: כיעקוב| כיעקב לגו[2]א[21]ד̇[21]. אבינו| אבי̇ ר̇א[2], ח̇ ל.
דתנינן| דתנן א[21]ד̇[21]. צורת| כצורת ג. וגו̇| חמה ל, חמה
(החמה גו[2]) צורת (כצורת ג, ח̇ א[21]) לבנה (הלבנה גו[2], ולבנה
א[21]) צורת הדרקון (דרקון גא[21], הדרנקור ו̇[2]) יוליכם לים המלח
ו̇גו[2]א[21]ד̇[21]. אמ̇ רבי| א̇ ר̇ גו[2]א[21]ד̇[21], אמר רבי ד̇[2], (ל חסר
מכאן עד... ויתנו לך).

19: יוחנן| יוח̇ ר̇א[2]א[1]. כסות| כסו̇ ד̇[1]. עבודה זרה| עבו̇ זר̇
ר̇[2], עז̇ א̇[21]ד̇[1]. ויתנו| ויטמון א̇[2]. אל| אותם א̇[2].
יעק̇| יעקב לגא[21]ד̇[21]; + וגו̇ לג, + א̇ כ̇ א̇ ה̇ א̇ ב̇ וג̇ ר̇[2], + תחת
האלה א̇[2]. ר̇ ישמעאל| רש̇ א[21], רבי ישמעאל ד̇[2].

20: בר| + ר̇ ד̇[21]. סליק| סלק לגו[2]א[1]. למצלייה| מצלייה לו[2],
מצליא ג, למצליא א[21], לצלאה ד̇[21]. בהדה| ח̇ לגו[2]א[21]ד̇[21].
ירושלם| בירושלם לגו[2]א[21]ד̇[21]. בהדה| בהדין לגו[2]א[21]ד̇[21].

פלאטנוס| פלטייס ל, פלטאנוס ג, פלטנוס ר^{2}א^{1}ד^{21}, פלטרוס א^2.

21: וחמתיה| וחמא יתיה גא^{21}ד^{21}. שמריי| שמדיי ל, סמריי ג,
סמראי א^1, סמרא א^2, שמראי ד^{21}. אמ' לה| אמ' ליה לגד^1, א' ליה
ר^2, אל א^1, אמר ליה ד^2. להן| לאן לגו^{2}א^{21}, להיכן ד^{21}.
אזל| אזיל גו^{2}א^{21}ד^{21}. אמ' לה| אמ' ליה לגד^1, א' ליה ר^2. אמר
ליה א^{1}ד^2, אל א^1. מסוק| (ניסוק ? ר), למסק ל, למיסק ג, מיסק
ר^2, מסק ד^{21}, ח' א^{21}. מצלייה| מצליא ג, למצליא א^{21}, מצלי ד^{21}.

22: בירושלם| בירוש' ר^2, ירושלם ד^{21}, בהד' + ד^{21}.
אמ' לה| אמ' ליה לא^{1}ד^1, א' ליה גו^2, אל א^2, אמר ליה ד^2.
מצלי| למצליא א^{21}. בהדן| בהדין לגו^{2}א^{21}, בהדי ד^{21}.
תורה| טורא גא^{21}ד^{21}, ח' ר^2. בריכה| בריכא גד^{21}.

23: בביתה| ביית לו^2, בכיתה ג, בביתא א^{21}, בההיא ד^{21}.
קיקילתה| קיקלתה לו^2, קיקילתא ג, קקילתא א^1, קלקלתא א^{2}ד^2,
קלקלת' ד^1. אמ' לו| א' לו ר^2, אמ' להם א^1, אל א^1, אל' ד^1,
אלא ד^2; + לא גו^2. אומ' לכם| אומר לכם לא^{1}ד^2, או' לכם ג,
א' לכם ר^2, אומ' לך א^2. למה| למ' ג. דומין| דומים לא^{2}ד^1,
דומי' ד^1. שהיה| שהוא ר^{2}א^{21}, ח' לג.

24: להוט| שלהוט ל. אחר| אח' ד^1. הנבלה| נבלה לא^{21}, נבילה
ר^2. יודעים| יודעין גו^{2}א^{21}, יודעי' ד^1. שעבודה זרה| שעבו'
זרה ל, שעבו' זר' ר^2, שעז א^{21}ד^{21}.

25: תחתיו| + שנ' ג, + שנא' א^1, + שנאמר א^2, + דכת' ד^1, +
דכתיב ד^2. ויטמון| ויטמן לו^{2}א^{1}ד^{21}, ויתנו ג. אותה| אותם לא^{21}
ד^{21}, אל ג, את' ר^2. יעקוב| יעקב לגא^{21}ד^{21}, יע' ר^2. וג'| את
כל אלהי הנכר ג, הא הא א ע ש ר^2, ח' לא^{21}ד^{21}. לפיכך| ח' א^2.
אתם| אדם ל, ח' ג. להוטים| להוטין גו^{2}א^{21}, להוטי' ד^1.

אחריו| תחתיו ג. אמרין| אמ׳ ל, אמרי׳ א[21].

26: מסאבא| מסאבה לו[2], מיסבא ג, מיסבה א[21], מנסבה ד[21]; + פי׳
מאחר שזה יודע שעֿז טמונה שם ודאי יקחנה ונתייעצו עליו להרגו
ד[21]. קם| וקם לגו[2]א[21]. בליליא| בליליא לגו[2]א[21]ד[21].
ויסע| ויסעו לגו[2]א[21]ד[21], ח׳ ח. ויהי| ויהי| וגו׳ ל. וגו׳| תחת
(ח׳ ו[2]) אלהים (אדים ו[2], אליֿם א[2]ד[1], אלקי׳ ח) גו[2]א[21]ד[21]ח,
ח׳ ל. אמ׳ ר׳| אֿ ר גו[2]ד[1], אֿר א[2], אמר רבי ד[2].

1 ר׳ שמעון בר נחמן שלשה מקומות נכנסו אומות העולם לעשות

2 מלחמה עם בני יעקוב ולא הֹניח להם הֹקבֹה ויסעו ויהי וגו׳ נתרגז
הֹא

3 ויירב היער לאכל בעם וגו׳ אמֹ ר׳ לעזר בקשו לרדוף ולא הניח להם

4 הקבה ואיכן נכנסו במצור הדא היא רק כל הערים העומדות וגו׳

5 ר׳ יודה או במסורה שרפה הֹקבֹה אמֹ למשה ומשה אמר ליהושע

6 ויבא יעקוב לוזה וגו׳ ולמה נקרא שמה לוז אמֹ ר׳ אבא בר
כהנא

7 שכל מי שנכנס לשם וגו׳ דכבת ⁓ קדמייה ותמת דבורה

8 מיניקת רבקה ר׳ נחוניה אמֹ לשון יוונית אלהאֹחֶר שהוא משמר עַד

9 אבלה שלדבורה באת לו בשירתה שלאימו הדא היא וירא אלים אל

10 יעקוב וגו׳ מה ברכה בירכו ר׳ אדא בשם ר׳ אחא בירכת אבלים

11 בירכו

1: שמעון| שמע׳ גר^{2}, שמואל א^{21}ד^{21}ח. בר| בן ר^{2}, ח׳ ד^{21}ח.
נחמן| נח׳ ר^{2}, ח׳ ד^{21}ח. שלשה| בג׳ לר^{2}א^{2}ד^{1}, בשלשה גד^{2}ח.
מקומות| מקומ׳ ר^{2}, מקומו׳ ד^{1}. נכנסו| נתכנסו ר^{2}א^{21}ד^{21}.
אומות| או׳ ל, אומ׳ ר^{2}, אומו׳ ד^{1}. העולם| העו׳ לר^{2}, העול׳ ד^{1}.
לעשות| לעשו׳ ד^{1}.

2: יעקוב| יע׳ ל, יעקב גא^{21}ד^{21}ח, יעק׳ ר^{2}. הניח| הניחן ג,
הניחם א^{21}. להם| ח׳ לגא^{21}. הקבה| הק׳ גר^{2}, הבה֝ א^{2}ד^{1}, הקדוש
ברוך הוא ח; + דכת׳ ד^{1}, + דכתיב ד^{2}. ויסעו| ויס׳ ר^{2}, (ג חסר
מכאן עד... ואיכן). ויהי| וגו׳ ל. וגו׳| חתת (ח׳ ר^{2}) אלהים
(אהים ר^{2}, אלי֝ם א^{2}ד^{1}, אלקי׳ ח); + ההד׳ א^{21}°, + ב׳ בימי יהונתן
שנ׳ ד^{1}, + שנית בימי יהונתן שנאמר ד^{2}, + וגו׳ ח. הא׳| הארץ
לר^{2}א^{21}ד^{21}ח; + וגו׳ ל, + ותהי לחרדת אלהים (אהים ר°ר^{2}, אלי֝ם
א^{2}ד^{1}, אלקים ח) ר°ר^{2}א^{21}ד^{21}ח.

3: ויירבן| וירב לר^{2}א^{21}ד^{21}ח. לאכל| לאכול ל^{2}א^{21}ד^{21}ח.
בעם| וגו׳ לר^{2}ח, ח׳ א^{2}. וגו׳| ח׳ לר^{2}א^{21}ד^{21}ח. אמ׳ ר׳| א׳ ר׳ ר^{2},
א֝ר א^{21}, אמר רבי ד^{1}, אמר ר׳ ח. לעזר| אלעזר לא^{1}ד^{21}ח, אלע׳ ר^{2},
אלעז׳ א^{2}; + ג׳ (שלשה ד^{2}) בימי יהושע (יהוש׳ ד^{1}) ד^{21}.
בקשו| ביקשו ל. לרדוף| לרדוף׳ א^{1}. הניח| הניחם לגר^{1}, הניחן א^{2}.
להם| הבה֝ ד^{1}, הקדוש ברוך הוא ד^{2}, ח׳ לא^{21}.

4: הקבה| הק׳ ר^{2}, הבה֝ א^{2}, להם ד^{21}. ואיכן| והיכן גד^{21}, היכן
א^{21}. נכנסו| נתכנסו לגר^{2}א^{2}ד^{21}ח, נתכנשו א^{1}, + אומות העולם
לרדוף אחרי בני יעקב א^{1}. בחצור| לחצור גד^{21}ח. הדא היא| הה"ד
לא^{21}, הדה׳ ג, הה֝ ר^{2}, דכתי׳ ד^{1}, דכתיב ד^{2}, היינו דכת׳ ח.
רק| ח׳ א^{21}. כל| ח׳ ד^{21}. הערים| העולם (?) ל, הערי׳ ר^{2}.
העומדות| העמ׳ ר^{2}, העומדים א^{1}, העומדו׳ ד^{1}. וגו׳| על תלם לא
שרפם יהושע וגו׳ ל, על תלם (תילם ג) לא שרפם (שרפ׳ג) יהושע
(יהוש׳ ג, ישראל א^{21}ד^{2}) זולתי חצור (את חצור א^{1}ד^{2}) לבדה (+ וגו׳

ג, + שרף יהושע ד^2) גא^{21}ד^{21}, על תלה ו^2, על תלם לא שרפם וגו׳ ח.

5: ר׳| רבי ד^2, (ח חסר מכאן עד ... ויבא יעקוב). יודה| לעזר
לו^2, אלעזר גא^{1}ד^2, אלעז׳ א^{2}ד^1. או׳| אמ׳ לא^{21}ד^1, א׳ ו^2, אמר ד^2.
שרפה| שרפם ל. הקבה| הק׳ גו^2, הבה א^{2}ד^{21}. אמ׳| א גו^2, אמר
א^{1}ד^2. ומשה| משה לגו^2. אמר| אמ לא^{21}ד^1, א גו^2.

6: ויבא| ויבוא א^2. יעקוב| יעקב לגא^{21}ד^1, יעק׳ ו^2, + שלם א^2.
וגו׳| ח׳ גו^{2}א^{21}ד^{21}. ולמה| למה גא^{21}ח (ד^{21} חסרים מכאן עד ...
שכל מי). שמה| שמו ג. אמ׳| ר׳| ר׳ ג, א׳ רבי ו^2, אר א^{21}.
בר| ח| ח. כהנא| כה׳ ו^2, + אמ׳ ג.

7: לשם| שם א^1, לתוכו ד^{21}, ח׳ א^2. וגו דכבת קדמייה| וגו׳ א^2,
הטריף (היטריף ו^2, הטריף א^1, הרטיב ד^{21}, א^2 חסר מכאן עד ...
בלוז) מצות (מצות גא^{1}ד^{21}, תורה ח) ומעש׳ (ומעשים ג^{1}א^{1}ח, ומעשי׳
ו^{2}ד^{21}) טובים (טובי׳ ו^{2}ד^2) בלוז (כלוז גד^{21}, וכו׳ דכתיב בפרשת
פ׳ עד סוף הפרשה א^1, בפרשה פ׳ עד סוף הפרשה א^2°) רבנין (רבני׳
ו^2, א^{2}ד^{21}ח חסרים מכאן עד סוף המאמר) אמ׳ (אמרין ג, אמרי׳ ו^2)
הלוז (מה לוז ג) הזה (זה ג, ח׳ ו^2) אין לו פה כך לא היה אדם יכול
לעמוד על פתחה (פיתחה גו^2) שלעיר (של מערה ג) אמ ר׳ סימון (אר סים
ו^2, ג חסר מכאן עד ... והיה לוז חלול) לוז היה עומד על פתח
(פיתחה ו^2) העיר (שלעירי ו^2) ר׳ לעזר בר מרום בשם (בש׳ ו^2) ר׳ פינחס
(פנח׳ ו^2) בר חמא לוז היה היה עומד על פתח (פיתחה ו^2) המערה (שלמערה
ו^2) והיה לוז חלול והיו נכנסין דרך הלוז למערה ודרך המערה לעיר
ההד (הדהי ג, הה ו^2) ויראו השומרים (השמ׳ ג, הש׳ ו^2) איש יוצא מן
העיר ויאמר (ג חסר מכאן עד ... ר ינאי) לא (לו ו^2) הוא (הרא׳ ו^2)
וגו׳ (את מב׳ הע׳ ועש׳ ע׳ ח׳ וא׳: ויראם את מב׳ הע׳ ו^2) ר׳ ינאי
(יניי גו^2) בש׳ (בשם ג) ר׳ ישמעאל עבד לה אפטרה (הפטרה ג) מה (ח׳
ג) אם זה שלא הלך (הילך גו^2) לא בידיו ולא ברגליו (+ אלא גו^2)
על (על ידי ג) שהראה לו (להם גו^2) באצבעו (באצבע ו^2) ניצול מן
הפורענות ישר׳

(יש׳ ו[2]) שעושין (שהן עושין ו[2]) חסד עם גדוליהם (גדוליהן ו[2])
בידיהם (בידיהן ג) ורגליהם (ובּרגליהן ג, ורגליהן ו[2]) על אח׳
כמ׳ וכמה (על אחת כמה וכמה ג, על א׳ כ׳ וכ׳ ו[2]) לגו[2].
ותמת| ח׳ א[21]. דבורה| ח׳ א[21].

8: מיניקת| וגו׳ ל, מיניקת גח, מינ׳ ו[2], מנקת ד[21], ח׳ א[21].
רבקה| ח׳ לא[21]; + ותקרא את שמה אלון בכות ג, + ותקרא שמו אלון
בכות א[1],+ויקרא שמו אלון בכות א[2], + וגו׳ ויקרא שמו אלון בכות
ד[21], + וגו׳ ח. ר נחוניה| ר׳ שמואל בר נחמן לגא[1]ד[1], רבי
שמוא׳ בן נח׳ ו[2], ר"ש בר נחמן א[2], רבי שמואל בר נחמן ד[2], ר׳
שמואל ח. אמ׳| א׳ ו[2], אמר א[2]. יוונית| יונית לא[1]ח, יוני גא[2]
ד[21]; + הוא לגו[2]א[21]ח, + היא ד[21]. אחר| ו°, בכות ל, אלון אחר
ו[2], ח׳ ר. שהוא| ח׳ ל. משמר| שמשמר ג.

9: שלדבורה| של דברה ג, של זו א[21]. באת| בא׳ א[1], באתה א[2]ח,
באה ד[21]. לו| להם ג, ליה ד[21]. בשירתה| בשורתה ל[2]ח, בשורת ג,
שמועה א[21], בשורתא ד[21]. שלאימו| שלאמו לו[2]א[2]ח, אמו ג, שמתה
אמו ד[21]. הדא היא| הֲהֲ לא[21]ד[1], הדהי ג, ה ה׳ ו[2], הדא הוא
דכתיב ד[2], היינו דכת׳ ח. איֹם| אהים ג, אדים ו[2], אלהים א[1]ד[2],
אליֹם א[2]ד[1], אלקי׳ ח.

10: יעקוב| יעקב לגא[21]ד[21]ח, יעק׳ ו[2]. וגו׳| וגומ׳ ד[2], עוד
גו[2]א[21]ח; + בבואו מפדן ארם ויברך אותו א[21], + ויברך אותו ד[21].
ברכה| ח׳ ל. בידכו| ברכו א[21]ד[21]ח. ר׳| רבי ד[2]. אדא| אחא
לגו[2]א[21]ד[21]ח. בשם ר׳| בש׳ ר׳ ל, בשם רבי ג, בש׳ רבי ו[2], בשֹׁר
א[21], ח׳ ח. אחא| יונתן לגו[2]א[21]ד[21], ח׳ ח; + אמר א[2]ד[1], אמ׳
א[2]ד[1]ח. בירכה| ברכה ו[2]א[21]ד[21]ח. אבלים| אבילים ו[2], אבלי׳ ד[1].

11: בירכו| ברכו ו[2]א[21]ד[21]ח, ח׳ ל.

FACSIMILIES

Scribe A

שולטת ביום ובלילה כד יעקב יש לו חלק בעולם הזה
ובעולם הבא שאר קוטעם דכבת החדש קומי אורי כי
בא אורך· ואת הכוכבים אמ ר אחא למלך שהיה לו
שני אפטרופוס אחד שליט בעיר ואחד שליט במדינה
א'ג המלך הואיל ומיעטו זה עצמו להיות שולט בעיר
גזר אני עליו בשעה שהוא יוצא תהא אבולי ורמוס יוצאה
עמו ובשעה ישהוא נכנס תהא בולי ורימוס נכנסת עמו
כך אג הקבה הואיל והלבנה הוו מיעטה עצמה להיות
שולטת בלילה גזר אני עליה בשעה ישהיא יוצאה יהיו
הכוכבים יוצאים עמה ובשעה ישהיא נכנסת יהיו
הכוכבים נכנסין עמה ודכוותה וישב אחיו יקטן שהיה
מקטין את יעקיו מה זכה זכה להעמיד שלש עשרה
משפחות ומה אם הקטן על ידי ישהיה מיקטין את עסקיו
זכה להעמיד שלש יעשרה משפחות גדול שהוא מקטין
את עסקיו אתמהא ודכויתיה וישלח וישרא· אתימינו וישת
על ראיש אפרים והו א ה הצעיר ואת שמאלו על ראש מנשה
וג' א ר חוניה וכי מן התולדות אין אנו יודעין ישהוא
צעיר אלא שהיה מצער את עסקיו ומה זכה וכד ה
לבכורה ומה אם הצעיר על ידי ישהיה מצער את עסקיו
וכה לבכורה גדול שהוא מצער את עסקיו אתמ הא
על אחת כמה ואחת במה   ··· יהי אית·
אהוב ברי ין הישעיב להאיר יעלה הארי·   אג ב · ··ינן ·
שלשה דבריב נתן מתנד לעולב יאיל הי התיר· ··
והמאירות והדגעעיב התיר מעיי· ייתן אלמשד·
ככל ה·   הצאיר ת מעיי ייתן אתב בריעה השמים

עשה לנו נסים בלילה אנו אומרין לפניך שירה בלילה
עשיתה לנו נסין ביום ואמרנו לפניך שירה ביום הדד
היא ותשר דבורה וברק בן אבינעם וגו' עשית לנו נסין
בלילה ואמרנו לפניך שירה בלילה הדד היא השיר יהיה
לכם כליל התקדש חג וגו'   לך נאה לומר שירה ביום
ולך נאה לומר שירה בלילה למה שאתה הכינות מאור
שמיש ואתה עשית את שני המ אורות הגדוליב ויעש .
איב את שני המאורות הגדלים את המאור הגדול וגו' יורד
בשב ר תנזום ביו' חייה ר פנחס בשב ר סימון מאחור
שהוא אותן גדוליך אתמרא הוא חוזר ופוגג אתמהא
את המאור הגדול לממשלת היום ואת המאיר הקט' . .
לממשלת הלילה ואת הכוכביב   אתמהא אלא על ידי
שנבנס בתחומי שלחבירו אג ר פנחס בכל הר בנית
כת שעיר עיים אחד חטאת ושעיר חטאת אחד ובראש
החדש כת ושעיר עיים אחד לחטאת ליהוה אג הקב"ה
אנו הוא שגרמתי לי להיכנס בתחומו שלחבירו ומה אס
זה שנבנס ברשות כד פגעי הכתוב הנכנס שלא ברשות
אתמיהא יעל אחת כמה יאחת אני ... ד ... לויבשט
ר יוסי בירבי אליננאי דרך הארץ היא ישיא הגדול .
מונה לגדול והקטון מונה לקטון עשו מונה לחמה שהיא
גדולה ויינקב מונה ללבנה שהיא קטנה אג רב נחמן .
והא סימן טב לישראל יעש מונה לחמה שהיא גדולה
מה החמה הזאת שוליטת ביום ואינה שוליטת בלילה
כד יעשו יש לו חלק בעל ב הזה ואין לו חלק לעוב הט
יעקב מונה ללבנה שהיא קטנה מה הלבנה הזאר כ

229

במטמוניות אמר להן כתחילה כראה לי ונתכארה בפנו והפליגה מאד ומיאה
לו פעם שנייה ימ לו מוספת אני על דבריך אמורה הייתי לה נשא ליאחי
אמיה ועלי ידי שנערתי עמי בבית נגאברתי בעניניו וילך ומשא ליאשה
אחרת ואינה נאה כמיתי   מעשה באשה בחמיר אחד שמחה נשיי
לחמירה אחת ולאה העמידו בנים זה מיה אמרו אין אנו מדעילין להקבה
כלום עמדו וגרשו זה את זה הלך זה ומשא ליריטעה אחת ועשת אותו
ריטע וזו נשאת לריטע אחר ועשת אותו צדיק שהכל מן האשה
שאלו אתך יהוטע מפני מה האיש יוצא ופניו למטה והאטה ירנאה
ופניו למעלה ימ להן האיש מביט למיקום טעבא וזו למקום בריייתה
מפני מה האשה צריכה להתבטס והאיש אינו צריך להתבטס ימ להן
אדם נברא מאדמה ואינה מסרחת לעולם וחוה נברא מן עצם מטי
אם תניח אדם בטר שלטה ימס בלא מלח מיד הוא מסריח ומפני מה
האשה קולה הולכת ואין קולו טלאיש הולך ימ להם מטל אם תמילא
קדירה בטר אין קולה הולך וכיון שאת נותן לתוכה עצם מיד אחר מיד
קולה הולך ומפני מה האיש נוח להתפתות והאטה אין נוחה להתפתות
ימ להם אדם נברא מאדמה כיון שאתה נותן לתוכה טיפת מים מיד
היא נישוית וחוה נברא מעצם אפילו אתה שורה עצם כמה ימים
במים אינו נישור מפני מה האיש תובע באטה ואין האטה תובעת
באיש ימ להן לאחד שאיבד אבידה הוא מבקש אבידתו ואבידתו אינו
מבקשתו מפני מה האיש מפקיד זרע באשה ואין האשה מפקדת זרע
באיש ימ להם לאחד שיש בידו פיקדון ומבקש אורם נאמן שיפקידנו
בידו מפני מה האיש יצא וראשו מגלה והאשה יוצא וראטה
מכוסה ימ להם לאחד שעבר טעבירה והוא מתבייט רבני אדם לפיכך
יוצא וראשה מכוסה ומפני מה הן הולכות אצל המית תחילה על ידי
שגרמו מיתה לעולם לפיכך הן מהילכות תחילה איטל המת ואחריו כל
אדם ומפני מה ניתן להם מיצות נידה ימ צ תחילה ימ להן מפני שטפלה

יֹי הוא שמֹי הואשעֹי שקֹדֹיאלֹי אדֹם הראשון חזר וֹהעבֹיֹרֹין לפֹנֹיו
זונֹעֹת זונֹעֹת ימֹ לֹכֹלֹ יֹשׁ בֹו זֹוגֹ לֹיֹ אֹין לֹי בֹן זֹוגֹ וֹלֹאֹדֹם לֹא מֹצֹא עֹזֹר
אֹתֹמֹחֹא וֹלֹמֹה לֹא בֹרֹאֹה לֹו מֹתֹחֹילֹה אֹלֹא צֹפֹה הֹקֹבֹֹי שֹׁהֹוֹא קֹוֹרֹא
עֹלֹיֹה תֹיֹגֹֹרֹ לֹפֹיֹכֹֹ לֹא בֹרֹאֹה לֹו עֹד שֹׁתֹבֹעֹה בֹפֹיֹן כֹיֹוֹן שֹׁתֹבֹעֹה בֹפֹיֹ
מֹיֹר וֹיֹפֹֹל יֹי אֹלֹהֹיֹם תֹרֹדֹמֹה ר יֹהֹוֹשֹׁע דֹֹסֹכֹנֹין בֹעֹר לֹוֹי תֹחֹילֹת מֹפֹוֹלֹת
שֹׁינֹה דֹמֹר לֹה וֹלֹא לֹע דֹמֹֹ לֹה וֹלֹאֹ עֹבֹיֹד עֹבֹיֹדֹֹ דֹמֹ   שֹׁלֹשׁ
תֹרֹדֹמֹוֹת הֹן תֹרֹד מֹת שֹׁינֹה תֹרֹד מֹת נֹבֹוֹאֹ תֹרֹד מֹת מֹוֹר מֹיֹטֹֹרֹ
תֹרֹד מֹת שֹׁינֹה וֹיֹפֹֹל יֹי עֹל הֹאֹדֹס שֹׁינֹה תֹרֹד מֹת נֹבֹוֹאֹ וֹיֹהֹי הֹשֹׁמֹשׁ
לֹבֹוֹא וֹתֹרֹד מֹ נֹפֹ עֹל אֹבֹרֹס דֹוֹרֹמֹיֹטֹֹה אֹין רֹוֹאֹה וֹאֹין יֹוֹדֹ עֹוֹ וֹאֹין מֹזֹֹין
כֹיֹ כֹלֹס יֹשֹׁנֹיֹס כֹיֹ תֹרֹד מֹת יֹֹי רֹבֹנֹן יֹגֹֹ אֹף תֹרֹד מֹת שֹׁלֹטֹוֹת כֹיֹ
נֹסֹֹ יֹי עֹלֹיֹכֹֹם רֹוֹח תֹרֹד מֹֹ וֹ יֹעֹנֹס עֹנֹיֹכֹֹם   ר חֹנֹנֹא בֹרֹיֹצֹחֹק יֹמֹ
שֹׁלֹשׁ נֹכֹֹלֹ תֹהֹן נֹכֹֹלֹ תֹ נֹֹיֹ תֹה שֹׁינֹה נֹפֹֹלֹ תֹ נֹבֹוֹאֹ חֹלֹוֹס נֹכֹֹלֹ תֹ עֹוֹלֹט
הֹבֹֹאֹר אֹבֹיֹן מֹוֹטֹֹיֹ עֹוֹד תֹֹרֹיֹ תֹין נֹכֹֹלֹ תֹ אֹוֹרֹה שֹׁלֹמֹעֹלֹן גֹֹלֹגֹֹלֹ חֹמֹֹה
נֹכֹֹלֹ תֹ חֹנֹמֹֹה שֹׁלֹמֹעֹלֹן תֹוֹרֹה   וֹיֹקֹֹח אֹחֹת מֹיֹ צֹלֹעֹתֹיֹו   רֹ
שֹׁמֹיֹאֹל בֹֹר נֹחֹמֹֹ יֹמֹ מֹסֹטֹֹרֹוֹיֹיֹ הֹיֹד מֹֹ ר דֹֹמֹ וֹ וֹלֹעֹלֹעֹ הֹמֹשֹׁכֹֹן וֹשֹׁמֹיֹאֹל
יֹמֹ עֹלֹעֹ עֹאֹ יֹאֹחֹת מֹבֹין שֹׁתֹֹי יֹנֹלֹעֹת נֹטֹֹל תֹחֹתֹיֹה אֹין כֹֹתֹכֹֹ אֹלֹֹֹא
תֹחֹתֹנֹ יֹמֹ רֹ חֹנֹנֹא בֹרֹיֹה רֹֹי אֹחֹֹא מֹיֹתֹֹא חֹיֹלֹ תֹהֹסֹֹפֹֹר יֹעֹד כֹֹן אֹינֹו כֹֹתֹֹ
סֹמֹֹד כֹֹיֹוֹן שֹׁנֹבֹרֹאֹ תֹ נֹבֹרֹֹא הֹסֹֹטֹֹן עֹיֹמֹֹה וֹאֹס יֹאֹמֹֹר לֹֹ אֹדֹֹס חֹוֹא
הֹטֹוֹבֹֹב אֹתֹכֹֹל אֹיֹֹין הֹזֹֹין אֹמֹיֹֹן לֹו בֹעֹֹ דֹרֹוֹת הֹכֹֹתֹֹוֹב מֹֹדֹבֹֹר יֹמֹֹ רֹ
חֹנֹֹא מֹֹר יֹֹצֹחֹק עֹֹשֹׂה לֹו עֹֹאֹ לֹתֹחֹתֹינֹו כֹֹדֹֹי שֹׁלֹֹאֹ יֹֹהֹֹ אֹ מֹֹ תֹֹ גֹֹבֹֹז
כֹֹפֹֹהֹֹמֹֹה רֹ יֹֹינֹֹיֹ וֹד יֹֹנֹֹיֹ חֹֹד יֹֹמֹֹ עֹֹשֹׂה לֹֹו מֹֹ נֹֹעֹֹיֹֹל וֹאֹיֹֹפֹֹפֹֹוֹרֹין כֹֹבֹֹוֹשׁ
עֹֹלֹֹיֹֹו כֹֹֹרֹֹי שֹׁלֹֹאֹֹ יֹֹחֹֹ אֹֹ צֹֹינֹֹעֹֹער בֹֹטֹֹעֹֹה שֹׁהֹֹוֹאֹ יֹֹוֹשֹׁב וֹֹאֹֹחֹֹרֹֹנֹֹא יֹֹמֹֹ
עֹֹשֹׂה לֹֹו כֹֹסֹֹתֹֹוֹ תֹֹ רֹֹ אֹֹלֹֹי וֹד אֹֹמֹֹי חֹֹד יֹֹמֹֹ עֹֹשֹׂה לֹֹו קֹֹבֹֹוֹרֹֹה וֹֹחֹֹד יֹֹמֹ
עֹֹשֹׂה חֹֹלֹֹ תֹֹ כֹֹדֹֹרֹֹיֹֹכֹֹיֹֹו   מֹֹטֹֹרֹֹונֹֹא שֹׁאֹֹלֹֹה לֹֹר יֹֹסֹֹי לֹֹמֹֹה גֹֹנֹֹבֹֹ יֹֹמֹ
לֹֹח מֹֹשֹׁל אֹֹסֹֹ חֹֹפֹֹקֹֹיֹֹר אֹֹדֹֹם אֹֹינֹֹלֹֹ יֹֹאֹֹנֹֹקֹֹיֹֹאֹֹאֹֹחֹֹת שֹׁלֹֹכֹֹסֹֹף בֹֹחֹֹשֹׁיֹֹי
תֹֹחֹֹזֹֹיֹֹ   לֹֹו לֹֹיֹֹטֹֹרֹֹא שֹׁלֹֹכֹֹסֹֹף כֹֹפֹֹרֹֹהֹֹסֹֹיֹֹא זֹֹוֹ גֹֹנֹֹבֹֹה יֹֹמֹֹ לֹֹח וֹֹלֹֹמֹֹד

מה הוא צדיק רשע אמרו לו צדקה אמ להם איני דן ארן
האדם אלא בשעתו ٥ קומי שאי את הנער ויפקח את
אתעניה ר בנימן בר לוי ר יוחנן בר עירם תרויהון אמ הכל
בחוקת סומים עד שהקבהמאיר את עיניהם מן הכד ה
ויפקח צליס את עיניה ותרא וגו הדה אמרה מחוסרת אמנ
היית ٥ ויהי צליס את הנער ויגדל ר. וישמעאל שאל
את ר עקיבה אמ לו טטימשותה אתנחם איש גד וו עמריס
ושותס שנה אכיס רכס מעוטים איתם גמיס ריבויים חרי
את דב הכה מהוא אמ לו צאמ ויהי צליס נער היה הדבר
קשה אלא את הנער אמ להכי לא דבר רק הוא ואסרקא
הוא מכם שאין אתם ודעעס לידרוט אלא את הנער הוא
וחידו וגמ לי ובנו בתוי וישב במדיבר ויהי ובן קשת רבה
וביקושותו אמרו תורה מתלמד בקשת רבה על כל חמורים
בקשת רבה על כל חמורים בקשת ٥ וישב במדבר א
פארן אמ ר יצחק זרק חוטרא לאוירא ועל עטריה הוא
קאיס כך לפי שבת ולה שפחה מיצ ושמה הגר לפיכך ותקח
לו אמ אשה מארץ מצרים ٥ פרש לב

בריעות יי
ויהי בעת ההיא ויאמר אבימלך
דרכי איש ר יוחנן אמ וו אשתו אויב שלאיש אנשי בתו
מעשה באשה אחת שקבלה על בעלה לשילטון והתיז את
ראשו ויש אומ אפחתיו את ראשה ר שמואל בר נחמן אמ
זה הנחש תעה ר חילפתא בר שאול הנחש הזה להוט אחר
השום אמ ר שמואל בר נחמן מעשה בנחש אחד שירד י.
מההר לבית ומצא קערה שלשום ואכלה והקיא בתוכה ותש
בבית ולא היה יכול לעמוד בו וכיון שיצא לו ירד ומילאה
עפר ר יהושע בן לו אמ זה יצר יע בעריה שבשלס אדם

שלום כת זכרו נפלאותיו אל עע מופתיו משפטיפיהו מופת מרדי
למי שהוא מימא ממרד פיו כל מי שמורה כשני עולמים יקדיאר
זרע כלמי שהוא אינו מורה בשני עולמים אין נקרא לך זרע
וישכם אברהם בבקר ויקח לחם וחמתמים ביט שלאברהם
אבינו ומתרגים היו שנ וישכם אברהם נבק ויק לה שכנו דרך י
שיהא עבדים מים ביאק עס על שכמה ואת הילד בן עשרי ב
ושבע שנה ותמר שם על שכמה אלא מלמד שהכניסד בו עין
רעה ונכנסה בו חמד ועצבות תידע עד שכן דיך ויביל הם יט
שכן דרך החולה להיות שותה בכל שעה ותשלך את הילד
ונ אמר מאיר שכן דרך הרתמים להיות גדולים במדבר צ
ריסא ש שם השיחו עמה מלאכי השרת ○ ותלך ותשב
לה מנג הרחק ונ הכה איתמר ותלך ותשב לה מנג הרח
כמטחוי קשת ולהלך איתמר אך רחוק יהיה ונ האלמדע
עב מעב הרחק מרחוק אמ יעחק שני חוטיט בקשת מיל
א לברכיה כמרכתת דבריים כלפי למעלן אמרה אתמור ל
אמירתא לי הרבה ארבה את זרע עשיו הוא מת בצמא
הדה היא נודי ספרידה אתה לנידודיה פרתה אתה שימה
דמעתי בנאדך באותה בעלת כור הלא בסיפרתך כשב
שכתוב בספר תליים שמעה תפילתי יי אל דמעתה שלהגר
לא החרשתה ועל דמעתי אתמחריש ואן תימר על ידי
שהיתה גיורת היתה חביבה אף אני כי גר אנכי עמך ונ
○ ויקרא מלאך אלה בזכותו שלאברהב באשר הוא
שם בוכות עצמו יפה תפילת החולים לעצמו תר מכל א
באשר הוא שם צ ר יודה ביר סימון קפצו מלאכי השרד
לקטרגו אמרו לפניו ריבוע שלעולם אדם שהוא עתי ד
להמית את בניך בצמא את מעלה לו הבאר צ להב עפשיו

233

מילכה		לב בשרים לבומרפא וגו׳ ד׳ ברמיה בשם ר׳ יצחק
אם את תהא לך ומה טוב חיי בשרים וגו׳ עד שהוא עומד
בהר המוריה נתבשר שנולד ריווגן שלבנו הנה ילדה מלכה
וגו׳ רפאות תהי לשרך וגו׳ ד׳ ברכיה בשם ר׳ יצחק אם רופא
את תהי לך מה טוב רפאות וגו׳ שער שהוא עומד בהר המוריה
נתבשר שנולד ריווגן שלבנו הנה ילדה וגו׳ מים קרים על וגו׳
מה מים׳ על נפש עיפה מה שמועה טובה ברוך הטוב והמטיב
אף מים קרים ברוך הטוב והמטיב כמים קרים על נפש עיפה
כך שמועה טובה מ׳ מר׳ שער שהוא עומד בהר המוריה וגו׳ הנה
ילדה מלכה וגו׳ אחר הדברים האלה היהודי רבריה הי׳ שם
מי הרהר אברהם הרהר אמ׳ לו   מת בהר המוריה לא היה מת
בנים בנים עשיו נעשה אשיאנו מבנות ער׳ אשכל ומר׳ א
הוא שהן צדיקות וכי מה אכפת להן בוחסין אמ׳ לו הקב״ה אין ?
אתה צריך כבר עליד ריווגן שלבנך הנה ילדה מלכה וגו׳ היא גם
היא מה זו בני בני גבירה שמונה ובני פילגשיך ארבעה אתה בני ?
גבירה שמונה ובני פילגשים ארבעה דא עתיראמן היסורים
אמ׳ לו הק״ב״ה אין את צריך כבר עליד מי שייקבלם את ועץ בדו
וגו׳   s   את ועץ בכורו וגו׳ איוב אימתי היה ר׳ שמעון בן לקיש
בשם בר קפרא בימי אברהם היה את ועץ בכורו ואת וגו׳ ובוב
איש היה בארץ עוץ וגו׳ ד׳ אבא בר כהנא אמ׳ בימי יעקב היה דמ׳
ר׳ אבא בר כהנא דינה אשתו שלאיוב היתה ר׳ לוי אמ׳ בימי שב
שבטים דב אשר חכמים יגדרו וגו׳ ומה שבר נטלו עלכך להם
לברם נתנה הארץ וגו׳ ר׳ יוסי בר׳ חלפנה אמ׳ בירידתן למצריים
עליד ובעלייתן מת מוצא עיקר שנו שלאיוב לאהיו אלא
מאתים ועשר שנים ועשו ישראל במצרים מאתים ועשר שנים
ובא שטן לקטרג וגירה אותו באיוב ר׳ חננא בריה דר׳ אחא ור׳

חנעה זّמ לו השבעلו שאין מנסה אותי עוד מעתה למّלך א

שהיה נّשָׂאוי למטרונה ילדה ממנו בן שיני וגّرשה שينّי ۲

וגّرשה שليשי וגّריشה וכיون שيلدה ממנו בן עשירי נّתّמّו

כولם ואמרו לו השבעלנו שאין את מגّרש את אימּינו עّוّד

מעתّה כّך כيון שّنّתّنּסّה אברהם נּסّיّون עשّירّי زّمّ לو השבّע

لי שאין את מנّסّה אותّי עّוד מעّתּה زّمّّد חنّין כي יّעّन זّשّّ

עّשّيּתّ את הّדّבّر הّזّה אلّא זּה נّס האّחّרّון שّהّוّא שّקّל כّنّّد

הّכّל שّזّيّلّوّلّי שّקّّبّل עّليّוّ נّס הّزّה האّחّרּون איّבّד אّתّ כّلّמّה

שّעّשّّ ۰ בّيّבّرّﭓ אّבّרّﭓ وّﭏّ بّرّﭏّה لّزّב בّرّﭏّה لّبّן ﭏّ

רבّوّת לّزّב רّבّوّת لّבّן וّيّرّش זّרّעّ زّتّﭏّשّעّ זّﭏّيّבّيّו ﭜّ ﭏّﭏ זّה תّﭏّﭜّﭏّوّر

זّשّﭜّﭜّﭏّ כّלّ ﭜّ שّﭜّﭏّﭏ רّﭏّﭏّﭜ בّﭜّﭜّﭏّﭏّﭜّﭜ שّﭜ'تّﭜّﭏّﭜّﭜ שّﭜّﭜّﭜ'

שّﭜّﭜّﭜّﭜّﭜّﭜ

Scribe D

ברכיה בשם ר׳ לוי מ׳ מקיים דבר עבדו אן אנו יודעין שעצ׳ת
מלאכין ישלים אלא מלאך אחר נגלה על אבינו יעקב ואמר לו עמד
הוא להעלות עליך בבית אל ולהחליף את שמך ואני עומד שם
הדה היא בית אל ימצאנו ושם ידבר עמנו אין כת׳ כן אלא ושם
ית׳... תגלה עליו הקב״ה בשביי לקיים דבריו שלמלאך ירוש של
שכל הנביאין מתנבאין עליה על אחת כמה וכמה וירא אים את יע
וירא אים א׳ יעקב׳ ר׳ יוסי בן חנינה אמ עוד נבראשונה מד׳ד
הראשונה מה הראשונה יעל ידי מלאך אף אף השמיה על יד
מלאך. אמ׳ ר׳ אבא בר כהנא עוד אינו מיחד שמי על בשריד
אלא לאחד. אמ׳ ר׳ יודן עד פעם אחת אינו נגלה עלן ויברך אתו
מה ברכה ברכתן ל חונה מ׳ ר׳ יונתן ברכת אכלים בירכו
ויאמר לו... אנו אל שדיי ר׳ יודן בשם ר׳ יצחק היורד אוכ
ראובן כבר הוא מבחוץ שמעון כבר הוא מבחוץ ובנימין כבר
יצא מחלציך ועד אין הוא במעי אמו חזרתי ואמרתי צו וזה
בעמין וקהל עמים זה מנשה ואפרים ר ברכיה ר חלבו משם
ר שמואל בר נחמן ועלכים מחלציך יצאו זה ירבעם ויהוא רבנ
אמ אפשר אבגר אדם צדיק זה חולך על מלכית בית דוד אלא
מדרש דרש והגיליך את אויש בושת הזה היא דכ ימלכי בש
מחלציך יצאו זה שאול ואיש בושת מה ראו ליתן ולרחוק גבעת
בגבעת אלא מקרא קראו ידרבו מיהרא קראו ודייהן ממרא ראו
וקרבו גני וקהל גוים קראו ורחקן אפרים ימנשה׳ ר׳ יודן ו׳
אימ׳ אשייר נערי בשם ר יחנן עתיריי בניך לעשות גוי בקה
עמים מה קהל עמים מיחדטם אסור בגיה אם בעד מימי ימב
אסור במ׳ האמ׳ר בר שילה בשם ר׳ יחנן מייתי לד מן הס ך
ויקח אליהן שתים עשרה אבנים שמ... שם חיי
אמרו לו מי ויהל ... יה ממך ר שמלאי

ר׳ שמעון בר נחמן שלטה מקונגיות נכנסו אומרת העולם לעשות
בלחמה יענד בני יעקוב ולא הניח להם הקבה ויסעו ויהי ותרגם הׄ
מירב הׄ עד לאבל בעס ונׄ אמׄ ׄ לעזר בקשו לירדוף ולא הניח להם
הקבה ואיבן נכנסו במעׄ ר הדא היא ריך כל העכיים העמריות ונׄ
ר׳ יודה או במסורת שרפה ה׳ריׄׄבה אמׄ למשה ומשה אמׄ ליהושע
ובא יעקוב לווה ונׄ ולביה ניׄ א שגמה לוׄ אמׄ ר׳ אבא בר חנא
שכל מי שנכנס לשם ונׄ וכבת יׄׄ קדמייך׳ אמׄ   ותמת דבורה
מימיׄ רבקה ׄ׳ נחוניך ׄ׳ לשון יומ׳מת אלׄ עד שהוא משמר
אמלה שלגבורה באת לו בטיירׄה שלאומ׳ הדא היא וירא איׄס אל
יעקובונׄ מה ברכה בירכו ר אראׄ בשׄ ר׳ אחא בירכת אבלים
בירכו

יעקוב׳ עשה עמי אות לטובה׳ עריתע במתצות וניחמׄר יׄ
בברכות׳ שרתבע ויסעו ויהי מתת ונׄ וניחמתע בבריסת וירא
איׄס אלׄ יעׄ יעׄ   ׄ יצחק פתח מזבח אדמה ת׳ עשרה לו
אמׄ מה אס וׄ בׄנה מזבח לשמׄ קׄרי אנכ נגלה עליו ומברכו יעקב
שאיקוׄמן שׄׄ תקזיקה בכסאׄ על אחת כמה וכמׄ הׄ וירא אׄ׳יס אׄ
יעקב ונׄ ׄ לׄה פתח ושׄ ואׄ לשלמים׳ אמׄ מה אס הׄ
שהקריב שור ואׄ ׄ לישׄ׳יה יׄ אני עלה עלׄ ומטרבי יעקוב
שאׄ׳קׄׄנין ונׄ ואחת כמׄ וׄדא איׄס אל עׄ   ברוך אתה בבוׄא
ונׄ נבואו לבׄת חמׄיׄ נטׄׄ ברכות נבׄאו אל בׄת חׄׄ נטׄ׳ יׄ
ברׄ׳מׄׄ ׄ ואׄ שׄ׳ יׄׄ אותך ונׄ ובצאׄ׳ מבׄׄ חׄׄ צׄׄ
ברכׄׄ ׄ   ׄ ׄ אׄ׳ יׄׄ׳ ונׄ   ר׳ ברׄמה פתח ותׄ׳ד אׄׄ
ויקׄ׳ לׄ׳ ותׄעׄ ויקׄ׳ לׄ׳ זה יעׄ׳׳ ועׄ דרׄׄ נׄׄ׳ האור עׄ שׄ׳
דרׄׄ נׄׄ אור נבׄׄ לבׄ׳ חׄׄ נטׄ ברׄׄ ואׄ׳ ונׄׄ׳
מבׄ׳ חׄׄ וירא אׄׄ אׄ יעׄ   מקׄׄ דבׄ עבׄ ׄ

מפקד לחברייה לא תהון יתבין עלמיסטובבייתה דקדרא
בר עלה בסיתוא דחיין עיניך סגן ר אבהוא נחת למיסחי
והוה מסתמר עלתריין עיתיין חדמן ימינה וחד מן שמלה
אתון למשרעא אמרין להר כל הדן חיילה איתבך וארע
עריך לאין אמ להם ואין אנו מעינים לנו כלם ליקנותינו
תדעולך שכן אבינו יעקב עלידי שכתבו היתי ביום אכילנו
חורבו וגו כיון שהזקין באלידי חולי הדה היא ויחי אחר
הדברים האלה ויאמר ליוסף וגו אמר יודיך ביר סימון
אברהם תבעיקנה אמ לפנו רבון העולמים אב ובט נכנסים
למקום ואין אדם יודע למי יכבד ומתוך שאת מעטרו לאב
בויקנה אדם יודע למי יכבד אמ לו הקבה חייך דבר טוב
תבעתה וממך אנו מתחיל מתחילת הספר ועד כאן אין כת
זקנה וכיון שעמד אבינו אברהם נתן לו ויקנה ואברהם
זקן בא בימיך יצחק תבע יסורין אמ לפנו רבון העולמיך
אדם מת בלא יסורין ומידת הדין מתוחזה כנגדו ומתוך
שאת מביא עליו יסורין אן מידת הדין מתוחזה כנגדן
אמ לו הקבה חייך דבר טוב תבעתה וממך הוא מתחי
מתחילת הספר ועד כן אין מ יסורין וכיון שעמד יצחק
נתן לו יסורין ויהי כי זקן יצחק וגו יעקב תבע את החולי
אמ לפנו רב העולמים אדם מת בלא חולי ואינו מישב בן
בנו מתוך שהדא חלה שנים שלשה ימים הוא מישב בן
בנו אמ לן הקבה חייך דבר טוב תבעתה ממך הוא מתחיל
ויאמר ליוסף הנה אביך חולה וגו ר לוי אברהם חידש
זקנה יצחק חידש יסורין יעקב חידש את החולי הא
חזקיהו חולי שני אמ לפנו רבון העולמים העמדת אותו

לפליטה בחיי נעביה ר׳ אבא בר זמינא אמ׳ ר׳ חלבו ור׳ חמא
ביר׳ חנינה חד מיהון אמ׳ אמת שם וגקבר שם שתי צרות
בידו אמת שם ונקבר כאן צרה אחת בידן וחדנה אמ׳ אפילו
צרה אחת אין בידן קבורה שכן מכפרת על מיתה שלהן
רבי בר קוריאיר לעזר הוון יתבין לעיין באוריתא בהדיה
אילסיס דטיבריה ראו ארועת באוב מחוץ לארם אמליה
ר׳ בר קורייא ליר לעזר קורא ז׳ ׳ על אילו חייכם ונחלתי
שמתם לתועבה ובמותיכם ותבאו ותטמאו את ארצי אמ׳
לה לא כיון שהן מגיעם לארץ ישראל הן נוטבין עליהם גש
עפר ומכפר עליהם ומה טען וכפר אדמתו עמו ׃ ס
ושכבתי עם אבתי וגו׳ אמ׳ ר׳ יצחק העבד עשה
מעבדותן ובן חורים עשה כחירותו העבד עשה כעבדות
וישם העבד את ידו וגו׳ ובן חורים עשה בחירותו ויאמר
אנכי אעשה כדבריך ויאמר השבעה לי וגו׳ ר׳ יוחה ביר׳
סימון ר׳ חנן בשם ר׳ שמוא׳ בר רב יצחק כיון שר אה אבינו
יעקב מעשים שרימת לאה באחותה מתן דעתן לגרשה
וכיון שפקדה הקבה בבנים אמ׳ לאמן שלאילי אנ מגרשה
אתמהא ובסוף הוא מודה על הדבר וישתחו ישראל ע׳
ראש המטה מי היה ראש מטתו של יעקב אבנו לאה ר׳ ׳
יצחק אמ׳ שכינה ראה הדה היא ידוך ל׳ כלמעטיך וחסי
יברכו ׃ ס

רוח איש יכלכל וגו׳ מרוח איש שיכל מזלהו ורוח נבאה
מי ישא מי שרוחו נבאה עליו מנערותו ועד זקנתו מי
ישאנה אמ׳ ר׳ ישמעא׳ ביר׳ יוסי אבנם שישבעו עליהם
בנערותינו עשו עמנו מלחמה בזקנותינו ר׳ יוסי הוזה

וימרדו יהו ורבין וג בן שהזמיר לאחיו בן שהזמיר לו
אחיו בן שהזמיר לאדונתו בן שהזמירה לו אדונתו אבל
אינו יודע מי ירבה תלילו ורובו וישטמוהו בעלי חייבין
אילו בעלי מחיצתו שהשליכו עליו דברים קשיים בחץ
חצי גבור שנונם וגו מה ראה למשלן בחצם מבלבל יין
שכל כלי וין מכין ממקומו וזה מכה מרחוק טד הוא לשן
הרע אומ ברומי והורג בסורייה ולא בכל גחלים אלא בגחל
רתמים שכל גחלים כבו מבפנים כבו מבפנים אלא גחלי
רתמים אפעלפ שכבו מבחוץ אלא עדיין בוער הוא מבפנים
כך כל מי שהוא מקבל לשון הרע אפעלפ שאת הולך
ומפיסו והוא עפוס אלא עדין בוער הוא מבפנים מעשה
בדותם אחד שהזמינתו בו את הואיר ועשה דילק שמונה
עשר חודש חורף וקיץ וחורף

קשתו זו אכסלו שהוא ואעשה מול קשת וג ריחזן מיגב
לך להידחות בין האיתנם קישות שנתקשתה עם אדונו
דמר ר שמואל בר נחמן נמתחה הקשת וחזרה הדה הוא
ותשב באיתן קשתו אכ ג יחזק נתפזר זרעו ויצא לו וכן
עיתפרע ידיו ופוו זרועי ידיו רחותא משט ג אבא איקונין
שלאמר ראה וזגו דמו מישם רועה אבן ישר מי עשה מי
אביך ויעירך מ אבך ברבת שמים מעל וו

אסכרות בבעל ברכות תדום תדום ד יבצת תדת זובית שאן
וענג השקי ברכות שדים ורדין ר לוליני בר טיברים בשם
ר יצחק בלוד בהמה בירכו אי ירתה צא יראה איזה דבר
דריה במיקים דחמה ואן את ייצא אלא בהמה ר אבא

Scribe A³

אמר רבניד בלחיתים שבטבריי... נקרא כנרת ילמה הוא
קורא איתה ע̇נ̇צר רבנן א... גענסריב א̇ר̇ יודה ב̇ר̇ סימון
עליב ̇שתלי שרים א... מידבר בשופטתו הדה היא ותשלח
ותקרא י̇ע̇ ומשכתי אליך י̇ג̇ הנותן אמרי שפר זו שירדד
שאמרה ותשר דבורה י̇ג̇ מידבר בבית ̇וינע̇דו̇ר̇ יוסי בריה
ד̇ר̇ יעקבבר אידי בשם ̇ר̇ אחא הנותן אמרי שפר שהן ̇,
משפרים א̇מ̇רים שנתנו בשופר יבתריו־עה אתמיוצ̇א
בשיעה יש̇י̇ע̇ל לריבור את אבני י̇יע̇כ̇ב̇ באו בני חת ליעדר
עמיהם על היתבורה רין נפתלי כאיילה ̇והג̇יא אני ממעדים
יטפר עלידי אחין   ̇פ̇   בן פירת יוסה ̇יג̇ בן שהפר
לאחיו בן שהפירו לי אדין בן שיאזר לאדונתו בן שהפירה
לו אדינתו אג̇ ̇ו̇ ̇אב̇ ̇זב̇ ̇ופ̇רת̇ רביתד יוסה בפרת רביתה
יוסה כילם כתיב ̇הנ̇ג̇שון̇ה̇שפחית ̇יג̇ ותגש גב לאה ̇י̇ג̇ ̇ויביסה
נ̇ת̇ ̇אחר נ̇ג̇ט יוסף̇ ̇י̇ג̇ אתמיהא אלא אני̇סה וירשיע דזה
עגו̇ ̇ו̇מ̇ד היא שלא יולד אתנ̇ענ̇ ̇יביט באימה ̇יעמד
ל̇ ̇ו̇שעיה גבהה קומ̇ט יכ̇יפ̇ת אתה היא דהוא אצלה בן
פירית יוסה י̇ג̇ בפ̇ינ̇ו ̇רבו̇נה̇ יכ̇ה̇ בן פירת עי עו̇ר
ברי̇י בשם ̇ר̇ סימוי עלי לפרו̇ילד את אתה̇ ̇ה̇ען̇ בני̇ה
צ̇י̇י̇ עליש̇י̇ר̇ את מוצא בשיע̇ו̇ שינא יסה ימרי̇ן
̇ש̇ אריני̇ ̇י̇דרים הי בנות מילכים מיצ̇יע̇ה̇ע̇רי דרד
הד̇ה̇נ̇ע̇ הי מישליכות עלי שוירין̇ ̇ו̇דלין̇ ̇נ̇ומי̇ ̇ב̇
̇וטבינ̇ת̇ נ̇די שיתלה עניו יביט בדע אפ̇עלפ̇יב̇ ̇לאהד̇.
גיש̇ט̇ו בדרב אג̇ לו הרב̇בד אתה לא ̇ו̇ליו̇ר את עניך והבטוה
̇ה̇נ̇ חייך ישאע נתו לבני צעורה ̇מ̇ד̇א צעורה ̇ת̇יש̇ה̇

CHARTS

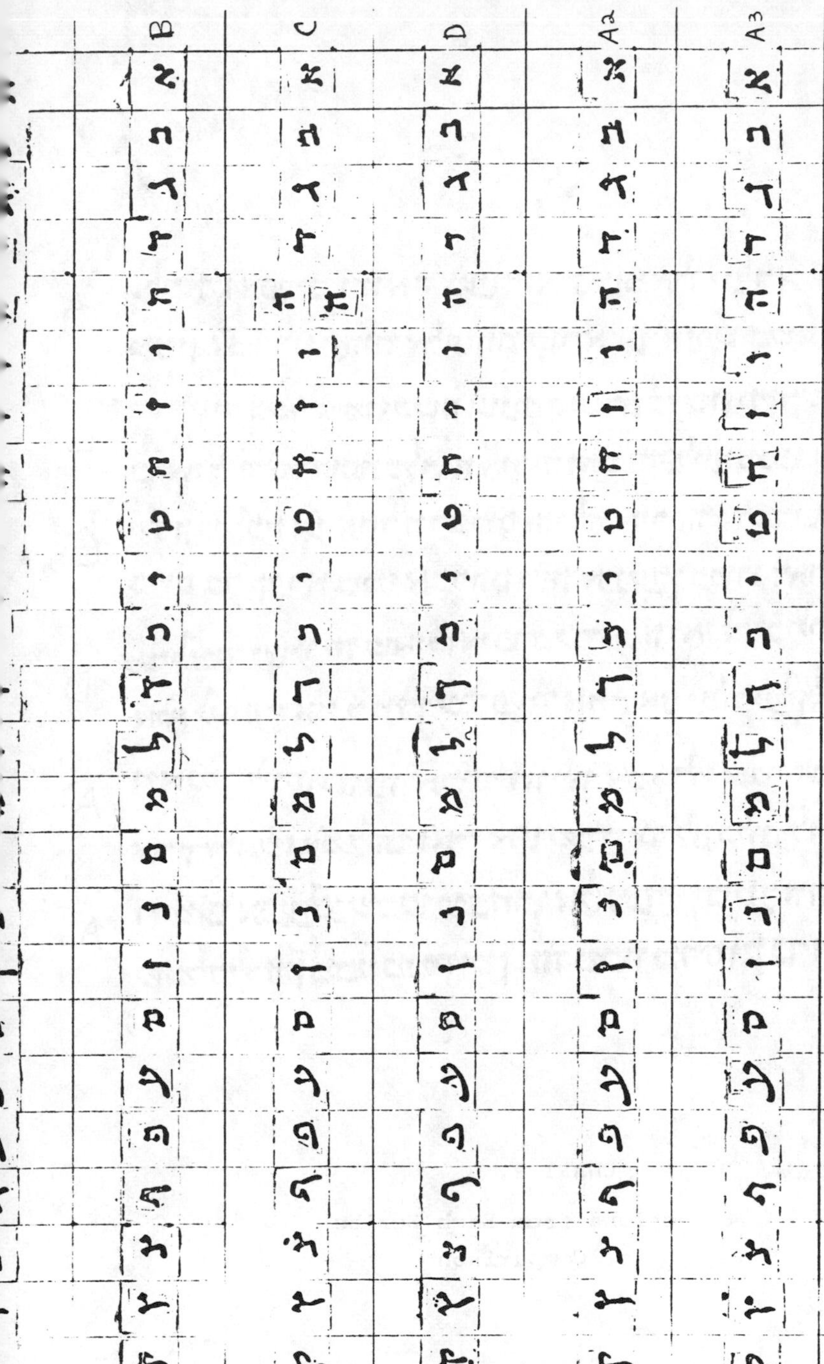

CHART 1.

Typical Alphabet
From Each Scribe

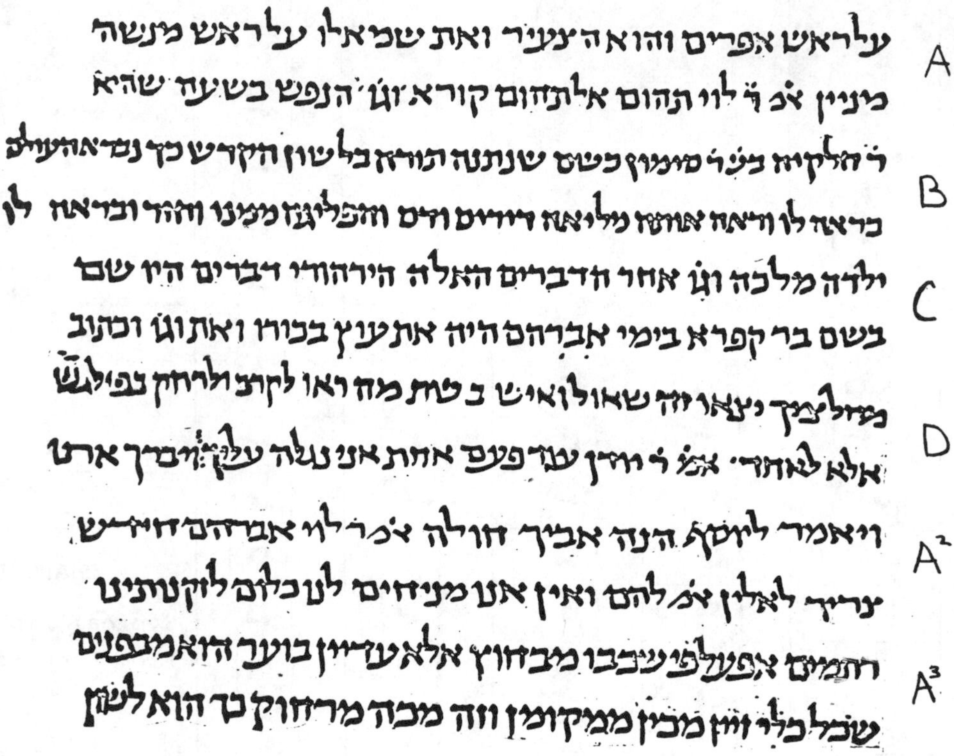

עלראש אפרים והוא ה צעיר ואת שמאלו עלראש מנשה A

מניין אב ד' לוי תהום אלתהום קורא זנ' הנפש בשעד שהיא

ד' הלקיח בער' סימוך בטט שנתנה תורה בלשון הקרש כך נסראהעלא B

כראה לו וראא אותו מליאא רויים ודם והפליגז ממנו וחזר וכראא לו

ילדה מלכה וג' אחר הדברים האלה הירהורי דברים היו שם C

בשם בר קפרא בימי אברהם היה את עץ בכורו ואת וג' ומעב

מזלצמך יצאו זה שאולואיש ב טת מה ראו לקוץ ולריחק נפ וללש

אלא לאחר' אם ר וזין עוד פעם אחת אנו נעלה על פ' ומרך ארט D

ויאמר ליוסא הנה אביך חולה צמ ר לו אברהם דיר ש A²

עריך לאלין צמ להם ואין אנו מניחים לנ כלום ליקמותינו

רחמים אפעלפ עבבו מבחוץ אלא עטריין בוער הזא ממפנעם A³

שבל כלי וזן מבין ממקומן וזה מכה מרחוק ט הוא לשן

CHART 2.

Selections from Each Scribe
for Comparison

246

APPENDIX I

ARAMAIC PASSAGES FROM VAT. 30

SCRIBE A

1.   f. 8v,11-19; T.A., 44,11-45,4.

ר כוהן אחוי דר חייא

ברבה הווה .פרש בימא אם ליה לאחוי צלי עלי אם ליה
מה נצלי עלך הן דאת קטר לולבך קטור ריגלך אין עללת
לכנישתא ושמעתון מצליי דמטרא לא תסמוך על צלותי
ר יהושע בריה דר תנחום בירבי חייה דכפר אגין הווה
באסייה בעה דיפרוש אמרת ליה ⌐ באילין יומיא פרשין
אתמהא אתחזי ליה אבוי בחילמא אם ליה ברי דלא קבורה
לא היתה לו אתמהא ולא שמע לא למילוי דֵדֶן ולא למילוי
גִידְדֶן וכן הוות ליה Θ

---

* הערה: בשוליים לשורה 6; מטרונה

2. f. 9,21-25; T.A., 48,1-3.

דלמה ר שמוא אחוי דר פינחס בר חמא הוה

דמך בציפורין והוון חברייה גביה אתת מִילָה ושרון
דחכין אם לון כמה נפשיה דאחוה דההוא גברה   א
מקצצה ארזין ומקצצה אילנין ואתון יתיבין הכא ולא
ידעין   Θ

SCRIBE B

1. f. 22,16-22; T.A., 247,2-6.

משאדם משיא את בתו ומוציא יציאות הוא או לה לא יהא

ליך מחזרו הכה רבן גמליא אסב ברתיה אם ליה אבא צלי עלי אם לה לא
יהא ליך מחזרו להכה ילדה בן זכר אם ליה אבא צלי עלי אם לה לא שלי
הו ווי מפומיך אם לו אבא שתי שמחות שבאו את מקללני אם לה תרתיהון
צלוון מן גוא דאת הויה לשלם בביתיך לא יהוי לך מחזרו להכא ומן גו
דהוי בריך קיים לא שלי ווי ווי מן פומיך ווי דלא אכל ברי ווי דלא אישתי
ברי ווי דלא אזל ברי לבכנישתא

249

2. f. 31v,11-22; <u>T.A.</u>, 296,5-297,5.

והמים גברו מאד ר יונתן סלק למצלייה

בירושלם עבר בהדין פלטאנוס וחמתיה חד שמריי אם ליה להן

את אזל אם ליה נסוק למצליה בירושלם אם ליה לא טב לך מצלי

בהדין טורא ברוכא ולא בההיא קיקילתא אם ליה ולמה הוא

בריך אם ליה דלא טף מוי דמבולא נתעלמה הלכה מעיני ר יונתן

לשעה אם ליה חמריה ר תרשיני ואני משיבו אם ליה הין אם ליה

אין מן טוריא רמיא הוא הכת ויכסו כל ההרים הגבהים ואין מן

מכיכיא הוא לא אשגח ביה קרא מיד ירד לו ר יונתן מן החמור

והרכיבו שלשה מילין וקרא עליו שלשה פסוקין לא יהיה בך עקר

ועקרה ובבהמתך אפילו בבהמין שלכם כפלח הרמו. רקתך אפילו

ריקים שבכם רצופים תשובות כרמון ה ה כֹפֿלֹחֿ ה כל כלי יוצר עליך

לא יצלח

3. f. 32v,2-6; <u>T.A.</u>, 300,5-301,2.

ר יהושע בן לוי סלק לרומי

חמא חמן עמודיא דמכסיין בטפטין בצינה שלא יקרשו ובחמה שלא

יתבקעו וממהלך בשוקא חמא חד מסכן מכרך בחדא מחצלה ואית

דאם פלגא מרדיעא דחמר על אינון עמודייא קרא צדקתך כהררי א הן

דאת יהב אשפעת על ההוא עניא קרא משפטיך תהום רבה הן דמחיית

גזיית

4. f. 32v,7-20; <u>T.A.</u>, 301,2-303,1.

אלכסנדרון מקדון אזל לגב מלכו קציא לאחורי צלמי הרי חשך

שלחשך נפקין טעין ליה גרזמי דדהב בגו דיסקוס דדהב אם להון א

ולממוניכון אנא צריך אמרון ליה ולא הוה לך מה מיכול בארעך דאתית

לך ליידן אם להון לא איתבעי למידע אלא היך אתון דיינין מן יתיב

גבייהו

אתא חד בר נש קבל על חבריה **אם** הדין גברא זבן לי חדא קיקלא ואשכחית

250

בגוה סימא קיקלא ס̇ זבני סימא לא זבני ההוא דזבין אם קיקלא ומה
דבגבה זבינית אם לחד מנהון אית לך בר דכר אם ליה אין אם לחורן אית
לך ברת אם ליה אין אם ליה איזל אסב דא לדין ויהא ממונא לתריהון
חמניה יתיב תמן אם ליה מה לא דנית טבאות אם ליה אין אם ליה אילו
הוה גביכון היך הויתון דנין אם ליה קטלין דין ודין ומלכותא נסבא
ממונא

דתרתיהון אם ליה גביכון אַיָת מסר נחת אם ליה אין אית גביכון שמשא דנח
אם ליה אין אית גביכון בעיר דקיק אם ליה אין אם ליה חֿ$ תפח רוחיה
דההוא גברא דלא בזכותיכון מיטרנא נחתי עליכון ולא בזכותכון מ̇
שמשא

דנח עליכון אלא בזכותא דבעירא דקיקא דכת אדם ובהמה תושיע ייי
אדם בזכות בהמה תושיע יי

5.   f. 33,11-23; T.A., 304,6-305,5.

ביומי דר תנחומא צרכון יש לתעניתא אתון לגביה
אמרון ליה ר גזור תעניתא גזר תעניתא יום קדמי יום חנין יום
תליתיי ולא
נחת מטרא על ודרש להון אם להן בניי אתמלון רחמים אילו על אילו
והקבה מתמלא עליכם רחמים כשהן מחלקין צדקה לעניהן ראו אדם אחד
שנתן מעות לגרושתו אתו לגביה ואמרון ליה ר מה אנן יתחבין הכא
ועבירתא
הכא אם להם מה ראיתם אם לו ראינו אדם פלו נותן מעות לגרושתו שלח
בתריהון ואייתינון לגו ציבורא אם ליה מה היא לך זו אם לו גרושתי
היא
אם לו מפני מה נתחה לה מעות אם לו ר ראיתי אותה בצרה ונתמלאתי
עליה רחמים באותה שעה הגביה ר תנחומה פניו כלפי למעלן ואם רבון
כל
העולמים מה אם זה שאין לזו עליו מזונות ראה אותה בצרה ונתמלא
עליה
רחמים ואתה שכתו בך חנון ורחום יי ואנו בניך בני ידידיך בני
אברהם

251

יצחק ויעקב על אחת כמה וכמה שתתמלא עלינו רחמים מיד ירדו גשמים
ונתרווח העולם

6. f. 33,23-33v,3; <u>T.A.</u>, 305,5-8.

רבינו הוה יתיב לעי באורייתא קומי כנישתא דבבלאי
בציפורין עבר חד עגל קדמוי אזל למיתחנכסא ושרי געה היך מימור
שיזבי אם ליה מה אני יכול לעשות לך ולכך נוצרתה וחשש את שינו שלש
עשרה שנה אם ר יוסי בר אבין כל אותן שלש עשרה שנה שהיה ר חושש
את שינו לא הפלה עברה בארץ יש ולא נצטערה יולדת בתר יומין עבר חד
שרץ קומי ברתיה ובעת מקטל יתיה אם לה ברתי שבקיניה דכת ורחמיו
על כל מעשיו

7. f. 33v,3-23; <u>T.A.</u>, 305,8-307,6.

רבינו הוה ענוון סגי והוה אם כל מה דאם ליה בר נש אנא
עבד חוץ ממה שעשו דבית בתירא לזקני שירדו מגדולתן והעלו אותו
ואין סליק רב הונא ריש גלותא להכא אנא קאים ליה למה דהוא מן   א
יהודה ואנא מן דבנימן והוא מן דכרי דיהודה ואנא מן נוקבתא אם ליה
ר חייה רבה הרי הוא עומד בחוץ נתכרכמו פניו שלר וכיון שראה   כי
נתכרכמו פניו אם להן ארונו הוא אם ליה פוק חמי מה בעי לך לברא
נפק ולא אשכח בר נש וידע דהוא נזיף ואין נזיפה פחות משלשים אם ר
יוסי בר אבין כל אותו שלשים יום שהיה ר חייה רובה נזיף מרבינו   א
אליף לרב בר אחתיה כל כלליה דאורייתא ואילין הינון כלליה דאוריתא
אילין . . . . . הילכתא דבבלאי לסוף תלתין יומין אתא אליהו זכור
לטוב בדמותיה דר חייה רבה אצל רבינו והב ידיה על ההיא שינתיה
ואסיתה כיון דאתא ר חייה רבה לגב רבינו אם ליה מה עבדת ההיא שינך
אם ליה מן עונתה דיהבת ידך עלה איתנשמת אם ליה לית אנא ידע מה
הוא דן כיון דשמע כן שרי נהוג ביה באיקר וקרב תלמידיה ומעילליה
מלגב אם לו ר ישמעא בר יוסי ולפנים ממני אם ליה חס ושלום לא יעשה
כן ביש רבינו הוה מתני שבחיה דר חייה רבה קומי ר ישמעא בר יוסי
אם ליה אדם גדול אדם קדוש הוא חד זמן חמתיה ביבני ולא איתכנע

252

מיניה אם ליה ההוא תלמידך דהוות משתבח ביה חמתן בי בני ולא
איתכנע מן קדמיי אם ליה למה לא אתכנעת מיניה אם ליה מסתכל
הויתי בתהילים אגדה כיון דשמע כן מסר ליה תרין תלמידין והון עמיה
עלין לאשונא דלא ישהי ותזער נפשיה

8. **f. 38,14-25;** **T.A.,** **327,3-328,2.**

אם ריש לקיש ברית נחלק לאוירות ר שמע בן לקיש הוה
יתיב לעי באורייתא בהדה . . . . . . אוליסיס דטבריה נפקין   א
תרתיין נשין מתמן אמרה חדא לחברתה בריך דאפקן מהדין אוירה
בישה צווח להון ואם להון מן אתון אמרין מן מזגה אם אנא חכם מזגה
ולית בה אלא תרתין עומרן פתח ואם ברוך שנתן חן למקום בעיני יוש
יושביו   תלמיד מן דר   אסי   הוה יתיב קדמוי הוה למסבר ליה
מסבר ליה ולא סבר מסבר ליה ולא סבר אם ליה למה לית את סבר אם
ליה דאנא גלי מן אתריי אם ליה מן הן את   שהבדיין אתר אם אמר
לית מן גיבת שמו אם ליה ומה הינון . . . . .אוירייה דהתם אם ליה כד
מינוקה מתילד אנך גבלין אדמדמני וטיישין מיחייה דלא יכולתה
ותושייה אם ב הם שנתן חן בעיני יושביו אף לעתיד לבוא כן והסירתי
את לב האבן מבשרכם ונתחי לכם לב בשר   לב בוס. . . . . .לַחבירו

9. **f. 38v,6-17;** **T.A.,** **328,8-330,4.**

אליהו זכור לטוב ור יהושע בן לוי   הוון
יתבין תניין .
כחדא מטון שמועה מן דר שמעון בן יוחיי אמרי הא מרה דשמעתא ניעול
ונישאליה על אליהו זכור לטוב לגביה אם ליה מן עמך אם ליה גדול
הדור
הוא ר יהושע בן לוי אם לו נראתה קשת בימיו אם נראתה קשת בימיו   א
לית הוא כדיי למחמי סבר אפיי ר חזקיה בש ר ירמיה כך הוה ר שמעון
בן יוחיי או בקעה בקעה המלאי דינרי זהב ונתמלאת ר חזקיה בשם   ר
ירמיה כך אם ר שמעון בן יוחיי אין בעי אברהם למקרבה מן גביה ועד
גבי אנא מקרב מן גבי ועד מלכא דמשיחא ואין לא בעי יצרף אחיה

253

השילוני עמי ואנן מקרבין מן אברהם ועד מלכא משיחא ר חזקיה בש ר
ירמיה כך אמ ר שמעון בן יוחיי אין העולם חסר משלשים צדיקים
כאברהם

אין תלתין אנא וברי תריין מנהון ואין עׄרין אינון אנא וברי
תריין מנהון

ואין עשרה אינון אנא וברי תריין מנהון ואין חד הוא אנא הוא

10.   ff. 39v,23-40,6; <u>T.A.</u>, 335,1-7.

ישלחו כצאן עויליהם

אמ ר לוי בערביא צווחין למינוקא עוילא וילדיהן ירקדון כהלין
שידייה היך מה דאת אמ ושעירים ירקדו שם כשהיתה אחת מהן
יולדת ביום היתה אומׄ לבנה צא הבא לי צור לחתוך טיבורך בלילה
היתה אומ לבנה צא והדלק לי את הנר לחתוך טיבורך עובדא הוה
בחדא איתא דיילדת בליליא ואמ לבנה צא והדלק לי את הנר
דנקטע טיבורך נפק ופגע ביה שידה שמרון אמ ליה אויל גליג   א
לאמך דקרא תרנגולא דאילו מני דקרא תרנגולא הוינא מחייתך
וקטל לך אמ ליה אוילׄ את גליג לאימך דלא קטעת אימא שורי
אילו קטעת אימא שורי הוינא מחייתך וקטליתך

11.   ff. 45,12-45v,6; <u>T.A.</u>, 361,6-364,4.

וימת הרן על פני תרח אביו ר חייה בריה דר אבא דרש תרח עובד
פסילים הוה חד זמן נפק לאתר   הושיב אברהם הוה אתי בר נש
בעי דיזבון מנהון והוה אמ ליה בר כמה שנין את והוה אמ ליה בר
חמשין

בר שתין והוה אמ ליה וויי ליה לההוא גברא דהוא בר שתין ובעי
לסגוד

לבר יומיה והוה מתבייש והולך לו חד זימנא אחת חדא איתא טעינה לה
חד פינך דסולת אמרה הא לך קרב קומיהון קם נסב מקלתה ותברון
ויהב ההוא מקלתה בידה דב̇בה מנהון כיון דאתא אבוה אמ לה מן   א
עבד לון הכריז אמ ליה מהיימנך אתת חד איתא טעינה חד פינך דסלת

ואמרת לי הא לך קרב קדמיהון קמית למקרב קדמיהון דן הוה

אמר אנא אכול קדמיי ודן הוה אם אנא אכול קדמיי קם הדין רבה

דביניהון ונסב מקלתא ותברון אם ליה למה את מפלה בי וידעין אינון

אם ליה ולא ישמעו אזניך מה שפיך אום נסתיה ומסריה לנמרוד אם

ליה נסגוד לנורא אם ליה נסגוד למיא דמטיפן לנוֹלֹ לנורא אם ליה

ונסגוד למיא אם ליה ונסגוד לעננא אם ליה ונסגוד לרוחא דמבדר

עננא אם ליה ונסגוד לרוחא אם ליה נסגוד לבר נשה דטבל רוחא אם ליה

את מילין •• משתעי אני איני משתחווה אלא לאור הרי אני משלים

לתוכו ויבוא ויבוא איה שאתה משתחוה לו ויציל אותך ממנו הוה תמן הרן

קאים

פליג אם מה נפשך אנא בהדי מן דנצח אין נצח אברהם אנא בהדיה ואין

נצח נמרוד אנא בהדיה כיון שירד אבינו אברהם לתוך כבשן האש וניצול

אמרון ליה מן דמן את אם מן דאברהם נטלוהו והשליכוהו לאש

ונחמרו

בני מעיו ויצא ומת על פני אביו הד הי וימת הרן על פני תרח אביו

12.   f. 51v,4-11;   T.A., 393,6-10.

אם השמאול ואימינה ואם

הימין ואשמאילה אין את לשמאלא אנא לדרומא אין אנא לדרומא

אך לשמאלא מן כל אתר לדרומא אנא אמ ר יוחנן לשני בני אדם

שהיו להם שני כריים אחד שלחיטים ואחד שלשעורים אם ליה אין

חיטיא דידי שערייא דידך ואין שעריר דידך וחיטיא דידי מן

כל אתר חיטיא דידי כך אם השמאל ואימינה ואם הימין ואשמאילה

אם ר חננא בר יצחק ואשמאל אין כת כן אלא ואשמאילה מן כל אתר

אנא משמאל לההוא גברא

255

13. f. 62v,8-14; <u>T.A.</u>, 451,8-452,4.

ר ברכיה בש ר אבא בר כהנא יבעי דיני א

גבך לשני בני אדם שהיו חבושים בבית האיסורין נמצא המלך עובר
אם חד מנהון א מ למלך אדני תבע דיקי דידי אם המלך אפקוה אם ליה
חבריה יבעי דיני גבך אילו אמרת יבעי מלכא דיקי דידן כמה דאפקוך
כן אפיקו יתי וכדו דאמרת תבע דיקי דידי לך אפיק לי לא אפיק כך
אמרה שרה אילו אמרת אנו הולכים עירירים כמה דיהב לך כך יהב לי
כדו דאמרת אנכי הולך עירירי לך יהב לי לא יהב

SCRIBE C

1. ff. 94v,20-95,10; <u>T.A.</u>, 648,4-650,4.

חמרתיה דר פינחס בן יאיר ....תה לסטאי

עבדת גבהון תלתה יומין ולא טעמת כלום אמרין סופה מייתה
ומסרייה מה דהכה עלינ¹ ועלת בביתיה דמרה וכיון דעלת
נהקת וחכם קלה אם פיתחו לאותה עניה ויהבו לה דתיכול דאית
לה תלתה יומין לא טעמת כלום יהבין לה סעריך ולא טעמתון
אם לה ר יהבנן לה סעריך ולא טעמתון אם להון תקינתון אם לה
אן אם לון אפקתון דמיי אם ולא כן אלפן רבי הלוקח זרע לבהמה
קמח לעורות שמן לנר לסוך בו את הכלים פטור מן הדמיי
אם להון מה נעבד לה והיא מחמרה על גרמה ר ירמיה שלח
לר זעירה חד קרטל דתאנין ר ירמיה אם איפשר דר זעירה
אכילהון דלא מתקנן ר זעורה אם איפשר דר ירמיה משלח
להון דלא מתקנן בן דן לדן אתאכלן תאנייה בטבולין מחר קם
ר ירמיה עם ר זעורה אם לה תקנת איליך תאינייה אם לה לא
ר אבא בר זמינא בשם ר זעורה אן הוון קדמאי מלאכין אנן
בנינש ואין הוון בנינש אנן חמרין אם ר מנא אפילו חמרין א
.לית אנן חמרתה דר פינחס בן יאיר יהבין לה סעריך סבולין
ולא טעמתון ואנן אכלין תאנייה בטובלן ⊙

⁎ הערה: בשוליים לשורה 3; שלחו יתה

בשוליים לשורה 14; אם

256

דוקליטיינוס מלכא הוה

רעי חזירין בהדה טיברייה וכיון דהוה מטי סדריה דרבי
הוון מיינוקיה נפקין ומחיין לה בתר יומין אתעבד מלך נחת
ויתב לה בהדה פנייס ושלח כתבין לטיברייה בפתי רמשה
דערובתה אמר אנה קיליוון דיהוון רברבני   דיהודאי קיומין
קודמיי בצפרא בחבשונה פקדיה לשליחא ואמר לה לא
תתן יתהון להון אלא עם מטמעיה דיומה דערובתה נחת ר
שמואל בר נחמן למיסחי חמתיה לרבי קאים סדרה רבה
פניו חוליניות אם לו למה פניך חוליניות אם לה כן וכן אשתדרלן
כתבין מן מלכותה אם לה אתה סחי דבריין עבד ניסים
עלון למיסחי ואתה הדן ארגינט מגחך ומרקד קודמיהון
בעה ר דיזעוף בה אמלה שמואל שובקיה דזמנין על ניסין
הוא מיתחמי אמרין מריך בעקה ואת קאים גחק ומרקד אם להון
אזלין ואכלין ושתין ועבדין שובה טבה ואנה מקים לכון קודמוי
בצפרה דחבשובה בפקי שובתם בתר סדרא נסתון ואקימתון
קודם פילי דפנייס עלון ואמרין לה הא קימין קודם פילי אם   א
סוגרון פילי נסתון ואסיקהון עד טיכסה דמדינתה עלין ואמרין
לה אנה קיליוון תיזון בני תלתה יומין ויעלון ויסחון וייתון
לגבי אזלין ואזון בני תלתה יומין ועל ארגינטי קודמיהון ועלין
וסחון ואתון לגביה אם להון בגין דאתון ידעין דאלהכון עבד
לכון ניסים אתון מקלין למלכה אמרין לה לדליק טיינא רעי
חזירין אקילנן ברם לדוקליטינוס מלכא אנן משעבדין אם
אפילו כן לא תבסרו לא ברומי זעור ולא בגולייר זעור

הערה: בשוליים לשורה 8; קומי
בשוליים לשורה 19; ומזגא

257

3. ff. 105v,11-106,1; T.A., 710,4-712,5.

ⵀ　בימי ר יהושע בן

חנניה גזרה מלכות שיבנה בית המקדש הושיבן פפוס ולולינוס
טרפיזין מעכו ועד אנטוכיה והיו מספיקין לעולה גולה אזלין
אלין כותאי ואמרין לה ידיע להוא למלכא די הן קרייתא דך וגו
מנדה זו מידת הארץ בלו זו פרובוגידון והלך לאנגרוטיקה
אם להון מה נעבד וגזרית אמרין לה שלח אמרין לה שלא
אם להון ישתנה מן אתרה לוסֿפון עלוי חמש אמין או יבצרון
מניה חמש אמין ומן גרמון הינון חזרין כהון והוון קהלה
מצמתין בהדה בקעת רמון כיון דאתון כתבייה שורון בכו
בעיי ממרֿד על מלכותא אמרין יעול חד ברנש חכם ישדל
ציבורא אמרין יעול ר יהושע בן חנניה דהוא איסכוליסטיקה
דאוריתא על ודרש ארי טרף טרף ועמד עצם בגרונו אמר
כל דאתי מפיק לה אנה יהב לה אגרה אתא הדן קורא מצרייה
דמוקדה אריך ויהב מקורה ואפקיה אם לה הב לי אגרי אם
לה אזל תהווי מגלג ואמר דעלית לפימיה דארייה בשלם
ונפקית בשלם כך דיינו שנכנסו לאומה הזו בשלום
ייצאנו בשלום　ⵀ

4. f. 108v,10-18; T.A., 728,4-729,3.

אשר אתה

בבית וכמה נשים היה לו ותמר אֵשֶׁה בבית אלא דהוה ידע מה
עובדיהון אמ ר אבא בר כהנא עובדא הוה בחדה סיעה　א
דפאריטון ... בהדה .כפר חיטיה והוון אכלין בכנישתה
כל אפתי רמש בשובה מן דהון אכלין הוון גרמייא מקלקין על
ספרה חד מינהון מן דמיך אמרין לה למן את מפקד על בניך אם
להון לספרה כמה מה רחמין הוו..לה והווה אם לספרה אלא דהוה
ידע מה עובדיהון כך כמה נשים היה לו ותמר אשר איתה בבית
אלא דהוה ידע מה עובדיהון　ⵀ

הערה: בשוליים לשורה 5; נסבין

258

5. f. 113,7-17; T.A., 761,2-762,3.

ד א הנה משמני הארץ

משמיניה דארעא אנטונינוס שלח לגב רבינו אם לה בגין דתיסווריה

חסירין מה נעביד ונמליא יתהון נסתייה לשליחה ואעליה

לגו פורדיסה שרי עקר פוגלין רברבין ושתיל דקיקין תורדין

רברבין שותיל דקיקין חסין רברבין ושתיל דקיקין אם לה הב לי

אנטיגרפﬞה אם לה לית את צריך סליק לגביה אם לה הן היא

אנטיגרפה אם לה לא יהב לי כלום אם לה ומה אם לך אם לה לא אם

לי כלום אם לה לא עבד קומיך כלום אם לה נסתי ואעלי לגו פרדיסא

שורי עקר פוגלין רברבין ושתל דקיקין תורדין רברבין ושתל   א

דקיקין חסין רבﬞ ושﬞ דקיקין שורי מפקדוﬔכסין ומעל דוקסין עד

זמן דאתמלון תיסוורייה   ⊕

6. f. 116v,11-19; T.A., 784,6-785,5.

⊕   ויחלם אם ר אבהוא דברי

חלום לא מעלים ולא מורידים חד ברנש אזל לגביה דר יוסי

ביר חלפתא אם לה אתאמר לה להההוא גובראˊאזל סב פעליה

דאבוך מן קפאדוקיה אם לה ואזל אבוך לקפדוקייא מן יומוי אם

לה לא אם אזל מני עשרין כשורין ברכסה דביתך ואת משכח

לה אם לית ליה לית בה עשרין אם ליה ואין לית ביה עשרין מני מן א

ראשיהון לסופיהון ומסופהון לרישהון דאת משכח עשרין את   והן

....

משכח לה אזל עבד ואשכח ומניליף לה ר יוסה בר חלפתה   מן

דקפדוקיה   ⁚⁚

─────────────────

הערה: בשוליים לשורה 3; בחילמא

259

7. f. 122v,10-25; T.A., 817,5-819,3.

ויאסף לבן את כל אנשי המקום ויעש   ⊖

א   מש כינס את כל אנשי מקומו אם להן יודעים אתם שהיינו
מדוחקים למים וכיון שבא הצדיק הזה לכאן נתברכנו במים
אמרין לה ומה הני לך אם להון אין בעיי אתון אנה מרמי בה ויהב
לה הדה   לאה ההוא רחם להדה רחל סגין והוא עבד גבן
עוד שבע שנים אחרניין אם לה עבד מה דהני לך אם להון יהבון
לי משכונין דלית חד מינכון מפריש יהבון לה מישכונין ואזל
איותי עליהון חמר משח וקפד הוי . למה נקרא שמו לבן הארמי
שרימה אפילו באנשי מקומו כל ההוא יומא הוו . מכללין בה וכיון
דעל לביתיה ברמשא אם להון מהו כדן אתגמלת חסד בזכותך
הוון מקלסין קודמוי ואמרין הילייה הילייה היא לאה היא לאה
ברמשא אתון מעלתה וטפון בוצינייה אם להון מהוא כדן אמרין
מה את סכי דאנן דביזזיון דכוותכון כל ההוא לילייה צווח לה
רחל והיא ענייה לה בצפרא והנה היא לאה אם לה מה רמיתה
ברת רמאי אמרה ואית ספר דלית לה תלמידין ולא כן הווה צווח
אביך צווח לך עשו ואת עני לה

הערה: בשוליים לשורה 4; עביד
בשוליים לשורה 10; אם ליה

8. f. 132v,6-11; T.A., 883,1-4.

ויצו אותם לאמר רבינו אם   ⊖

לר אפס כתוב חדה איגרה מן שמי למרן מלכא אנטונינוס
קם וכתב מן יהודה נשיא למרן מלכא אנטונינוס נסביה
וקריה וקרעיה אם לה כתוב מן יהודה עבדך למרן מלכא
אנטונינוס אם ליה ר מה את מבזה על כבודך אם לה מה אנא
טב מן סבי לא כך אם כה אמר עבדך יעקב

260

9. ff. 134,23-134v,4; <u>T.A.</u>, 905,5-906,5.

ואמרת לעבדך   ויצו את הראשון לאמר וגו   Θ   א

ליעקב ר ור יוסי ביר יודה היו מהלכין בדרך ראו גוי אחד בא
לקראתן אמרין תלת מילין הוא שאיל לן מה אתון ומה אומנותכון
ולהן אתון אזלין מה אתון יהודיין ומה אומנותכון פרגמטוטין
ולהן אתון אזלין למזבון חיטין מן אוצרה דיווני עמד לו רבי
והטמין עצמו ר יוסי ביר יהודה אם אין אמר מילה אנה אם אחרי
לן אם אם לה ומן הן אית לך הדה אם לה מאבינו יעקב והנה גם הוא
אחרינו   Θ

10. ff. 137,18-137v,2; <u>T.A.</u>, 924,4-925,5.

וישא יעקב את   Θ

עיניו וירא אם ר לוי ארי כועס על בהמה ועל החיה אמרין מן
אזיל מפייס יתיה אם להון הדן תעלה אתון לכון דאנה ידע תלת
מאה מיתלין ואנה מפייס יתיה אמרין אגו מן הלך ציבחר וקם
ליה אמרין לה מה אמר להון אנשיית מאת אם לה אית   במאתיך
ברכן הליך ציבחר וקם ליה אמרין לה מהא אנשיית אוף מאה
אמרין לה אית במאה ברכן וכיון דמטא תמן א אנשיית כולהון
אלא כל חד וחד יפייס על נפשיה כך יעקב ר יודה ביר סימון
אם יש בי כח לסדור תפילה ר לוי אם יש בי כח לערוך מלחמה
וכיון דמטה ויחץ את הילדים על לאה אמר כל אנש ואנש
זכותיה תקום ליה   Θ

11.   f. 138,1-8; T.A., 929,3-930,3.

Θ   ויאמר מי לך וגו כל אותו הלילה נעשו

מלאכי השרת כתים כתים וחבורות חבורות והוון מגעין באלין
דעשו והוון אמרין להון מן דמן אתון והוון אם מן דעשו והוון
אמרין יהבון להון מן דבריה דיצחק והוון אם יהבון להון מן דבר
בריה דאבר והוון אמרין וכיון דהוון אמרין מן אחוי דיעקב   א
אנן הוון אמרין שובקותון דמן דידן הינון לצפרה ואם לה
מי לך כל המחנה הזה אם לה אמרין לך כלום אם לה מכתת
אנה גבהון ויאמר למצא חן בעיני אדני   Θ

_____

הערה: בשוליים לשורה 5; יהבון להון

12.   ff. 138,17-138v,8; T.A., 931,6-933,2.

ויפצר בו ויקח

מתחמי מחזר וידיה פשיטה יהודה ברבי אם מתרפס ברצי
כסף מתיר את הפז מתרצה בכסף ר שמעון בן לקיש סליק   א
למשאול בשלמה דרבינו אם לה צלי עלי דהדה מלכותה בישה
סיגין אם לה לא תיסב מן ברנש כלום ולית את יהב לה כלום
מן יתיב גביה אתת הדה איתה טעינה לה חד דיסקירין
וחדה סכין בגוה קם נסב סכינה וחזר לה דייסקרה אתה חד
בלדר מן דמלכותה וחמתה וחמדה ונסבה בפתי רמשה
סלק ר שמעון בן לקיש למשאול וחמתיה יתיב שחיק אם לה
למה את שחיק אם לה ההיא סכינה דחמית אתה חד בלדר
מן דמלכותה חמתה וחמדה ונסבה אם ליה ולא כן אמרית לך
לא תיסב מן ברנש כלום ולית את יהיב לה כלום חד עם דארע
אם ליה לר הושעיה אין אמרית לך חדה מילה טבה את אם לה
מן שמי בציבורה אם ליה מה היא אם ליה כל אותן הדוריות
שנתן יעקב אבינו לעשו עתידין אומות העולם למחזירן
למלך המשיח לעתיד לבא מה טע מלכי תרשיש ואיים
מנחה יביאו אין כת אלא מנחה ישיבו אם ליה חייך מילא
טבה אמרת מה שמך אנה אם לה

262

13.　ff. 138v,26-139,3; <u>T.A.</u>, 935,3-5.

ויאמר עשו אציגה נא ביקש ללוותו ולא קיבל עליו רבינו

כד סלק למלכותא הוה משתכל בהדה פרשתא ולא נסב עמיה

רומאיין חד זמן לא אשתכל בה ונסב עמיה רומאיין ולא

הגיע לעכו עד שמכר פינס שלו　　　　Θ

SPECIAL SCRIBE ON CORRECTED PAGE

ff.　140,17-140v,5; <u>T.A.</u>, 946,3-948,3.

דילמא ר חייא רבה ור

שמעון בירבי ור שמעון בן חלפותא　　שכחון

מילין מן הדן תרגומה ואתון להדה דערבייה

למלפנון מן תמן שמע קליה אם לחבריה תלי

הדן טעונה עלי תלי הדין יהביה עליי השלך על

יי וג מה את בסי בי מה את מעסי בי ועשותם

רשעים וג אתייה אתון סהייה גלמודה אנה ואני

שכולה וג אתייה אנתון מעוררה למתיך אתייה

אתון מעוררה ללגוייתיך העתידים עורר לויתן

אשאיל ליך מביניך אשאיל ליך מטאטיך וט

וטאטאתיה במטאטי השמד אשאל לי מרגליתיך אשאל

ליך כסיריתיך אפק הדה אמרתה למרעייה אפיק הדה

כסירתה למרעייה אם ר אבא בר כהנא במאה אנקות במאה

טלאים במאה סלעים אם ר סימון קוף קמילייה סט

סיטריון סמך סלעים יוד הא מה עבדיו הכה　　0

──────────────────────

הערה: בשוליים לשורה 3; אגדה

263

פרשתה פ ⊙

ותצא דינה בת לאה וגו ⊙

הנה כל המושל וגו יוסי מעונייה תרגם בכנישתהון

דמעונאי שמעו זאת הכהנים וגו אם עתיד הוא

הקבה ליטול את הכהנים ולהעמידן בדין ואמר

אם להם למה לא יגעתם בתורה לא הייתם נהנים

מבניי עשרים וארבע מתנות והינון אמרין

לה לא הוון יהבין לן   כלום והקשיבו ביח ישראל

למה לא הייתם נותנין לכהנים עשרים וארבע

מתנון שהכתבתי לכם בתורה והינון אמרין

לה על אילין דבית נסייא הוון נסבין כולה   ובית המלך האזינו כי
לכם

המשפט שלכם היה וזה יהיה משפט הכהנים וגו לפיכך לכם ועליכם

עליכם מדת הדין נהפכת שמע רבי וכעס בפתי רמשה על ריש לקיש

למשאול בשלמה ומפייסה יתיה עלוי אם לו רבי צריכין אנו להחזיק

טובה לאומות העולם שהן מכניסין מימסין לבתי תיטריות

ולבתי קרקסיות שלהם ומשחקים בהם כדי שלא יהיו יושבים

ומסיחין אילו באילו ויוסה מעונייה אמר מילא דאוריא   ואקפדת

עלוי אם לה וידע הוא אם לה אן ואולפן קבל אם לה אן ואין שאילנא

לה היא מגיב לי אם לה אן אם לה יסוק וסלק לגביה אם לה מה הוא דכת

הנה כל המושל עליך ימשול וגו אם לו כבית מן האומה כדור כן ‏ל

הנשיא כמזבח כן כהניו כן כהנא אם לפס גנתא גננא אם לה ר שמעון בן

לקיש עד כדון לא חסלות מן מפייס על הדה ואת מיתי לן חורי עיקרו

שלדבר הנה כל המושל מה הוא אם לה לית תורה עגישה עד דברתה

בעוטה לית איתה זני עד דברתה זני אמרו לו אם כן אימינו לאה

זונה הייתה אם להם ותצא לאה לקראתו מלמד שיצאת מקושטת

כזונה לפיכך כת ותצא דינה בת לאה

1. ff. 164,14-164v,3; T.A., 1095,1-1096,3.

ונספר לו ויפתר לנו את וגו

ויהי כאשר פתר לנו כן היה וגו חדה איתה אזלת

לגב ר ליעזר אמרת לה חמת ההיא איתתה בחלמא

תניתה דביתה פקעה אם לה ההיא אתתה מעברה וילדה

בר דכר אזלת וכן הוה לה חזרת וחמת זמן תניין אזלת

.. לגבי ר ליעזר ואמרת ליה ההיא אתתא חמת בחלמה

וגו אם ליה ההיא אתתא מעברא וילדה בר דכר אזלת

וכן הווה לה חמת זמן תליתיי אתת לגביה ולא אשכחתיה

אם לתלמידוי הן הוא רבכון אם לה מה את בעיא מיניה

אמרה נימר להון דלמָא דהינון חכימין דכוות רבהון

חכים אמרה להון ההיא אתתא חמת בחלמה תניתה

דביתה פקעה אמרין לה ההיא אתתא קברה בעלה

אזלת וכן הוה לה וכן דאתא ר אֹיעזר שמע קלה מצווחה

אם להון מהוא כדן תנון לה עובדה אם להון אבדתון גברה

ולכן כת ויהי כאשר פתר לנו

2. f. 167,10-19; T.A., 1128,1-5.

ויאמרו

שנים עשר וגו אם לון והן הוא אם ליה אם זבינן יתיה אם לון

בכמה אם ליה בחמש סלעים אם לון ואן אם לכון ברנש

יהבון לי חמש סלעין ואנא יהיב יתיה לכון עבדין אתון

אם לה אן ואן אם לכון ברנש יהבון לי בכפילה ואנא

יהיב יתיה לכון עבדין אתון אם ליה אין ואן אם לכון   א

ברנש אפילו דאתון יהבין לי כמן לית אנה יהב יתיה לכון

מה אתון עבדין אמרין ליה על מנת כן נחתנן או למקטול

או למקטלה אם להון הוא אשר דברתי אליכם לאמר

מרגלים   Θ

265

3. f. 168v,18-21; <u>T.A.</u>, 1137,5-1138,1.

ר חמא   חד סגי נוהר. הוה יתיב
לעי באוריתיה אמ ליה שלם לך בר חירייה אמ לה ומה את
שמיע דהוא גברא בר עבדין אמ ליה לא אלא שאת בר
חירין לעולם הבא

4. f. 170,5-18; <u>T.A.</u>, 1144,1-1145,3.

⊙   ויצו את אשר

על ביתו וגו   ואת גביעי גביע הכסף וגו הבקר אור וגו אמ
ר לוי עובדא הוה בדרומא דהוה תמן חד פונדקיי והוה
קאים לביש זגוי בליליא ואמר למן דהוה תמן קומו פוקו
לכון דלויתה אני עבדה והוון נפקין ולסטאי מקדמין
להון ומקפחין להון ועלין ופלגין עימיה חד זמן .... ר
מאיר ואתקבל תמן ‸ולבש זגוי ואמ לה קום פוק לך דלויתה
אני עברה אמ לה אית לי חד אחה ואנה יתיב מסכי לה
אמ לה והן הוא אמ לה בכנישתה אמ לה מה שמיה ואנה
אזל קרי לה אמ ליה כי טוב כל ההוא לילייה הווה ההוא
פונדקייה הווה אזל וצווח על תרעה דכנישתה כי טוב
כי טוב ולא הוה ברנש עני לה בצפרא קם ר מאיר ושוי
חמרה דייזל לה אמ לה פונדקייה הן הוא ההוא אחוך
דאמרת אמ לה היידילה וירא אים את האור   ⊙

_____

הערה: בשוליים לשורה 7; קם

5. f. 172v,5-8; <u>T.A.</u>, 1158,1-3.

רמז למנשה ורפש חד רפיש וזעת
כל פלטין אמ ווי דהדן רפשה ‸מן בית אבא כיון דחמה
דמיליייא כן שרי משתעי מלין רכיכין אדני שאל וגו ונאמר
אל אדני יש לנו וגו

_____

הערה: בשוליים לשורה 2; דמי

266

6.   f. 174,9-17;   T.A., 1178,3-1179,3.

א   ואלה שמות בני ישרא ובני   Θ

ישׁכר תולע ופוה וגו   ר מאיר חמה חד שמריי אמ לה

מן דמן אמ ליה מדישׁכר אמ לה מן הן אמ ליה דכ ובני

ישׁכר תולע אלין שמראי אזל לגב איפיטרכה דידהון ופוה ויוב ושמרן

אמ לה אמ לי רבהון דיהודאי חדה מילא והוא חמׄיה

אמ לה מהיא אמ ליה אמ לי מן דמן אתון ואמרית לה מן דיוסף

אמ לי לא ואמרית לה אלא מן דמן אמ לי מן דיישׁכר

ואמרית לה מן הן ואמ לי דכ ובני ישׁכר תולע וגו אלין

שמראי אמ חייך מן יוסף אפקך וליישׁכר לא אעלתך

Θ

הערה: בשוליים לשורה 2 ; מן דמן אתון אמ ליה מן דיוסף אמ ליה

לא אמ ליה אלא מן

בשוליים לשורה 5 ; נ א חמיה

7.   ff. 175,14-175v,7;   T.A., 1183 variant to line 2.

ויען יואב ויאמר

חלילה חלילה לי אלא שבע בן בכרי שמרד בדוד

המלך תנו אותו לי ואני הולך לי מיד ותבוא האשה אל

כל העם מה היתה חכמתה שלשרח בת אשר אלא אמרה

להון מה אתון בעיין מובדה מדינתכון להדה איפרכיה

אזל דוד ולא כבשה או להיידה זאווי אזל יואב ולא

כבשה או להיידן קרב אזלון ולא נצחון הוא בעה

גבהון תרתין מאוון דבנינש לא טב לכון יהבין לה תרתין

מאוון דבנינש ולא מחרבה מדינתכון אמרין לה ויסב

אמרה להון אנה סלקה תובן לאיגרה ופייסה לה

דלמא דהוא שבק מינהון עבדת גרמה סלקה לאיגרה

הערה: בשוליים לשורה 4 ; בחכמתה

267

ונחתה אמרה להון לה בעה אלא מאה אמרין לה
יסב וסלקת תובן ונחתת ואמרת להון לא בעי אא חמשין
וכן תובן לא בעה אלא עשרין וכן תובן לא בעה אלא
עשרה וכן תובן לא בעה אלא חד אמרין לה אן הוה
טב קרתה אנן יהבין יתיה אמרה להון חד הוא ואכסני
הוא אמרין לה ומן הוא אמרה להון שבע בן בכרי   א
שהעיז פנים במלך דויד מיד הנה ראשו מושלך וגו מיד
ויתקע יואב בשופר   Θ

8. **ff. 180v,25-181,5;** <u>T.A.</u>, **1241,8-11.**

ר יוסי הווה

מפקד לחברייה לא תהוון יתבין על מיסטוביתה דסדרא
בר עולה בסיתווא דהינין צנינן סגין ר אבהוא נחת למיסחי
והווה מסתמך על תרין גונתיין חד מן ימינא וחד מן שמליה
אתון למשרוע אמרין לה ר כל הדן חיילה אית בך ואת
צריך לאלין

הערה: בשוליים לשורה 5; וזקפון

SCRIBE B

לפוס גמלא שיחנא . . . . **f. 13,12, T.A., 170,3**

הא גנבא גנבא דגנב דעתא דבריה . . . . . **f. 14v,1, T.A., 177,5**

בשעה חדותה חדותה בשעת אבלה אבלה . . . . **f. 24v,5, T.A., 259,3**

הון זרעין לה חיטין והווה עבדא זונין איליַן זיניַא דבה
מן דרא דמבולא הינון . . . . **ff. 25v,26-26,1, T.A., 266,9**

אמרין ליה למה כדון אם לון כן אם מריה דעלמא דהוא מייחי
מבולא על עלמא אמרון ליה אין אתא ....מבולא לא אתא אלא
על ביתיה דאבוה דההוא גברא . **ff. 28v,17-19, T.A., 272,5-273,1**

בשוק סמייה צוחין לעוירא בר רב אורה 275,12 **ff. 29,23-24, T.A.,**

SCRIBE C

אית תחומין במעייה . . . . **f. 85,4-5, T.A., 590,2-3**

קופרה טבה לפמה וכסה טבה לפימיה (קרא: קופדה)
f. 102v,10-11, T.A., 694,1

לא דמי ההוא דחמי סיליתיה מליַא ושבע לההוא דחמי
סגליליה פנייא יכפן (קרא: וכפן) . . . **f. 108,4-5, T.A., 725,2**

עבדא בישא לא זבינית כספא דאבא את

f. 150v,20-21, <u>T.A.</u>, 1013,6

עבדה זבין ובר אמתה מזבן ובר חורייה עבד לתרויהון

f. 158,14, <u>T.A.</u>, 1055,7

אן לממלא אנה ואין למשמשה אנה ואן למפצעה קים אנה

f. 172,6-7, <u>T.A.</u>, 1155,1

SCRIBE A3

גיסה אתה למגיסא יתהון והינון מגיסין גיסא

f. 190,15-16, <u>T.A.</u>, 1266,9-10

אחברכון תדייה דהכדן אייניקו ומעייה דהכדן אפיקו

f. 191v,3-4, <u>T.A.</u>, 1270,12

מרה דעלמה ניסב הדן חרבא ונתנינה בגו מעיה

f. 193,4-5, <u>T.A.</u>, 1275,3-4

APPENDIX II

REPEATED PASSAGES FROM VAT. 30 AND
A PASSAGE FROM VAT. 60 *

*Passages are transcribed as they appear in the manuscript.
Line numbers are given for the first appearance of the
passage only, to facilitate comparison with the repetitions.
Where a passage appears more than once within Scribe B, the
first appearance is called B^1, the second B^2, etc. After
each passage, the variations between the scribes copying
that passage are presented.

271

Scribe A: ff. 4v-5; <u>T.A.</u>, 32,1-11.

1   ויאמר אים יקוו המים ר ברכיה

ר אבא בר זמינה יעשה מידה למים הכמה דתמר וקו

ינטה על ירושלם ר אבא בר כהנא בשם ר לוי יקבו לי המים

מה שאני עתיד לעשות בהם למלך שבנה פלטין והושיב

5   בתוכה דיורים אילמים והיו משכימין ושאלין בשלומו

שלמלך ברמיזה ובאצבע ובמנוולים אם המלך מה אם

              א   אילו שהן אילמים הרי הן משכימין ושאלין בשלומי

ברמיזה ובאצבע ובמנוולים אילו היו פקחים אתמהא על

אחת כמה וכמה אתמהא הושיב בתוכה המלך דיורים

10 פקחים עמדו והחזיקו בפלטין אמרו אין פלטין זו שלמלך

שלנו היא פלטין אם המלך תחזור פלאטין למה שהיית כך

מתחילת ברייתו שלעולם לא היה קילוסו שלהקבה עולה

אלא מן המים הדה היא מקולות מים רבים ומה היו אומרין

אדיר במרום יי אם הקבה מה אם אילו שאן להן לא פה

15 ולא אמירה ולא דיבור הרי הן מקלסין אותי לכשנבראו בני

אדם אתמהא על אחת כמה וכמה עמד דור אנוש ומרד בו

              א   דור המבול ומרד בו דור הפלגה ומרד בו אם הקבה יפנו

אלו ויבאו אותן הדה היא ויהי הגשם על הארץ ארבעים

         Θ   יום וגו

הערה: בשוליים לשורה 18; ויעמדו

Scribe B: f. 24v; <u>T.A.</u>, 260,2-12.

ויאמר יי אמחה את האדם ר ברכיה

בש ר ביבי בר יומא   היך מה דא אם וקו ינטה על ירושל ר אבא

בר כהנא

בש ר לוי יקוו המים מה שאני עתיד לעשות בם למלך שבנה פלטין

והושיב

בה דיורין אילמין והיו משכימין ושואלין בשלומו שלמלך ברמיזה

ובאמצע ובמנוולים אילו היו פקחין על אחת כמה וכמה הושיב המלך
בתוכה דיורין פקחין עמדו והחזיקו בפלטין אם שלנו היא פלטין אם
המלך תחזור היא פלטין לכמו שהיית כך כתחילה לא היה קילוסו
שלהקבה עולה אלא מן המים הד הי מקולות מים רבים אדי מש ים אם
הקבה מה אם אילו שאין להן אמירה ולא דיבור הרי הן מקלסין אותי
לכשאברא בני אדם על אחת כמה וכמה עמד דור אנוש ומרד דור
המבול ומרד דור המבול ומרד בו אם הקבה יפנו אילו ויבואו אילו
הדה

הי אמחה את האדם

Scribe B		Scribe A	
בש ר ביב בר יומא		ר אבא בר זמינה	2)
ח׳		יעשה מידה למים	
היך מה דא אם		הכמה דתמר	
ירושל		ירושלם	3)
בש		בשם	
יקוו		יקבו	
בס		בהם	4)
בה		בתוכה	5)
דיורין אילמין		דיורים אילמים	
		אם המלך מה אם אילו שהן אילמים	6)
		הרי הן משכימין ושואלין בשלומי	
ח׳		ברמיזה ובאצבע ובמנוולים	
פקחין		פקחים	8)
ח׳		אתמהא	

273

9) אתמהא   ח'
הושיב בתוכה המלך   הנשיב המלך בתוכה

9-10) דיורים פקחים   דיורין פקחין
אמרו   אמ
אין פלטין זו שלמלך   ח'

11) פלאטין   היא פלטין
למה   לכמו

12) מתחילת ברייתו שלעולם   כתחילה

13) הדה היא   הד הי
מקולות מים רבים   מקולות מים רבים אדי' מש' ים
ומה היו אומרין אדיר במרום יי   ח'

14) שאן   שאין
לא פה   ח'

15) ולא אמירה   אמירה
לכשנברא [לכשנבראו]   לכשאברא

16) אתמהא   ח'
ומרד בו   ומרד

17) ומרד בו   ומרד

18) אלו   אילו

19) ויבאו אותן   ויבואו אילו
הדה היא   הדה הי
ויהי הגשם על הארץ ארבעים יום וגו אמחה את האדם

274

Scribe B: ff. 12v-13; _T.A._, 168,5-169,1.

1   ולא יתבששו   והנחש היה ערום   לא היה צריך למימר

קרייה אלא ויעש יי לאדם ולאשתו כתנות עור וילבש   אמ ר יהושע בן

קרחה להודיער מאי זו חיטיא קפץ עליהם אותו הרשע מתוך שראה אותן

מתעסקין בדרך ארץ ונתאוה להן אמ ר יעקב דכפר חנן שלא להפסיק בפרישתו שלנחש

Scribe A2: f. 154; _T.A._, 1031,6-1032,3.

ודכוותה ולא יתבוששו ⟨והנחש היה ערום⟩ לא היה צריך קרייא
אלא למימר ויעש

יי אהים לאדם ולאשתו כתנות עור וג ר יהושע בן קרחה

אם להודיער מאיזו חטייה קפץ עליהם אותו הרשע א

מתוך שראה אותן מתעסקין בדרך הארץ נתאוה לה

אם ר יעקב דכפר חנן שלא להפסיק בפרשתו שלנחש

Scribe A2	Scribe B	
ולא יתבששו	ולא יתבששו	1)
קרייא למימר	למימר קרייה	
ויעש יי אהים לאדם ולאשתו	ויעש יי לאדם ולאשתו	2)
כתנות עור	כתנות עור	
וג׳	וילבש׳	
ר יהושע בן קרחה אמ׳	אמ׳ ר יהושע בן קרחה	
מאיזו	מאי זו	3)
חטייה	חיטיא	

בדרך הארץ	בדרך ארץ	(4
נתאוה לה	ונתאוה להן	

בפרישתו	בפרשתו	(5

SAMPLE 3

Scribe B: f. 13; <u>T.A.</u>, 171,4-7.

ויאמר אל האשה אף   1

כי אמר אים אמ ר חנינא בן סנסן ארבעה פתחו באף ואבדו באף
ואילו הן

נחש ושר האופים ועדת קרח והמן   נחש ויאמר אל האשה אף כי אמר

שר האפים אף אני בחלמי   עדת קרח אף לא אל ארץ זבת חל ו ד   המן

אף לא הביאה אסתר   5

Scribe A2: f. 162v; <u>T.A.</u>, 1084,1-4.

Θ   וירא שר האפים ר חננה בר

באף   סיﬞﬞמון ארבעה הן שפתחו באף ואבדוﬞואילו הן הנחש

ושר האפים ועדת קרח והמן הנחש ויאמר הנחש אל

האשה אף וגו   שר האפים אף אני בחלמי עדת קרח

אף לא אל ארץ זבת חלב ודבש וגו המן אף לא הביאה

אסתר המלכה וגו

Scribe A2		Scribe B	
וירא שר האפים	ויאמר אל האשה אף כי אמר אים	1–2)
ר חננה בר סיﬞמון	אמﬞ ר חנינא בן סנסן	2)
ארבעה הן שפתחו	ארבעה פתחו	
חﬞ (והושלם בגליון)	באף (פעם שניה)	

276

Scribe A2	Scribe B	
הנחש (שתי פעמים)	נחש (שתי פעמים)	3)
ושר האפים	ושר האופים	
ויאמר הנחש אל האשה אף וגו	ויאמר אל האשה אף כי אמר	
אף לא אל ארץ זבת חלב ודבש וגו	אף לא אל ארץ זבת חל׳ וד׳	4)
אף לא הביאה אסתר המלכה וגו	אף לא הביאה אסתר	5)

SAMPLE 4

Scribe B: f. 13v; <u>T.A.</u>, 174,1-4.

1   ותרא האשה כי טוב ר אלעזר בש

ר יוסי בן זימרא שלשה דברים נאמרו בנא   טוב למאכל ויפה לעינים

ומוסיף חכמה ושלשתן נאמרו בפסוק אחד ותרא האשה כי טוב העץ

מכן שהוא טוב למאכל כי תאוה הוא מכן שהוא יפה לעינים ונחמד

5   העץ למ להשכיל מכן שמוסיף חכמה היך מה דא אם משכיל להימן

Scribes C and D: ff. 107v-108; <u>T.A.</u>, 724,6-725,2.

         ⦵   ועשה לי מטעמים ר אלעזר

בשם ר יוסי בר זמרה שלשה דברים נאמרו בנא' טוב למאכל

ויפה לעינים ומוסיף חכמה ושלשתן נאמרו בפסוק הזה

ותרא האשה כי טוב העץ וג   מיכאן שהוא טוב למאכל   כי

תאוה הוא לעינים מיכן יפה לעינים ונחמד העץ להשכיל

מיכן שהוא מוסיף חכמה הכ דת משכיל לאיתן האזרחי |שכן

יצחק או ועשה לי מטעמים וגו לשעבר היית נהנה מן הראיה

עכשיו איני נהנה אלא מן הטעם וכן שלמה או ברבות הטובה

לא דמי ההוא דחמי סיגליתיה מלייא ושבע לההוא דחמי

סגליתיה פנייא וכפן   ⦵

Scribes C & D	Scribe B
ועשה לי מטעמים בש‎ם	ותרא האשה כי טוב בש׳	1)

	Scribes C & D		Scribe B	

<table>
</table>

Scribes C & D	Scribe B	
ועשה לי מטעמים בש‎ם	ותרא האשה כי טוב בש׳	(1
בר זימרה בנאֹי	בן זימרא בנא	(2
זה ותרא האשה כי טוב העץ וגו	אחד ותרא האשה כי טוב העץ	(3
מיכאן כי תאוה הוא לעינים מיכן ח׳	מכן כי תאוה הוא מכן שהוא	(4
מיכן שהוא מוסיף הכ׳ דת׳ משכיל לאיתן האזרחי	מכן שמוסיף היך מה דא׳ אמ׳ משכיל להימן	(5

SAMPLE 5

Scribe B[1]: f. 16v; T.A., 188,2-7.

ואל האשה אמר   1

א   ארבה ר יודן בר סימון ר יוחנן בש ר אלעזר בר סימון
מעולם לא

נזקק הקבה להשיח עם אשה אלא עם אותה הצדקת אף הוא על ידי עילה

ר אבא בר כהנא בש ר ביריי   כמה כירכורין כירכר בשביל להשיח

עמה ויאמר לא כי צחקת והכת ותקרא שם יי הדבר אליה ר יהושע בר   5

נחמיה בש ר אידי על ידי מלאך והכת ויאמר יי לה בש ר חמא בר
חנינא

אם על ידי מלאך ר לעזר בש ר יוסי בן זימרה אם על ידי שם

278

Scribe B[2]: f. 63v; <u>T.A.</u>, 457,3-7.

ותקרא שם יי הדובר אל   ר יהודה בר סימון ר יוחנן

בש ר אלעזר בר שמעון מעולם לא נזקק הקבה לשוח עם אשה

אלא עם אותה הצדקת אף הוא על ידי עילא ר אבא בר כהנא

בש ר כירים כמה כירכורים כירכר לשוח עמה ויאמר לא

כי צחקת והא כת ותקרא שם יי הדובר אל   ר יהושע בר נחמיה

בש ר אחי על ידי מלאך והכת ויאמר יי לה ר לוי בש ר חנינה

בר חמא אם על ידי מלאך ר אלעזר בש ר יוסי בן זימרה על

ידי שם

Scribe B[3]: f. 70; <u>T.A.</u>, 495,6-496,3.

ותכחש שרה לאמ ל צ ר יודן בר

סימון ור יוחנן בש ר אלעזר בר שמעון מעולם לא נזקק הקבה להשיח

עם אשה אלא עם אותה הצדקת אף הוא על ידי עילא ר אבא בר כהנא

בש ר כירי כמה כירכורים כירכר הקבה בשביל להשיח עימה ויאמר

לא כי צחקת והכת ותקרא שם יי הדבר אליה   ר יהושע בר נחמיה בש

ר אחי על ידי מלאך והכת ויאמר לה הנך הרה ר לוי בש ר חמה בר חנינה

על ידי מלאך ר לעזר בש ר יוסי בן זימרא אמ על ידי שם

Scribe C: f. 101; <u>T.A.</u>, 684,3-8.

ויאמר יי לה ר יודה ביר סימון ר יוחנן בשם ר לעזר ביר

שמעון מעולם לא נזקק הקבה להשיח עם אשה אלא עם

אותה צדקת אף היא על ידי עולא   ר אבא בר כהנא בשם

ר כיריי כמה כירכורים כירכר להשיח עימה ויאמר לא כי צח

והכ ותקרא שם יי הדובר אליה ר יהושע ביר נחמיה בשם

ר אידי על ידי מלאך והכ ויאמר יי לה ר לוי בשם ר חמא

ביר חנינה אם על ידי מלאך ר לעזר בשם ר יוסי בן זימרה

אמ על ידי שם

	Scribe B²	Scribe B¹
(1	ותקרא שם יי הדובר אל	ואל האשה אמר ארבה
(2	ר׳ יהודה בר סימון ר יוחנן בש׳ ר׳ אלעזר בר שמעון	ר׳ יודן בר סימון ר יוחנן בש׳ ר אלעזר בר סימון
(3	לשוח הצדקת אף הוא עילא	להשיח הצדקת אף הוא עילה
(4	בש׳ ר׳ כירים כירכורים ח׳ לשוח	בש׳ ר׳ בירריי כירכורין בשביל להשיח
(5	עמה צחקת והא כת׳ הדובר אל׳ בר	עמה צחקת והכת׳ הדבר אליה בר
(6	בש׳ ר אחי והכת׳ ויאמר יי לה ר׳ לוי בש׳ ר חנינה בר חמא	בש׳ ר אידי והכת׳ ויאמר יי לה בש׳ ר חמא בר חנינא

Scribe C	Scribe B³
ויאמר יי לה	ותכחש שרה לאמ' ל' צ'
ר' יודה ביר סימון	ר' יודן בר סימון
ר' יוחנן	ור' יוחנן
בשם ר' לעזר ביר שמעון	בש' ר' אלעזר בר שמעון
להשיח	להשיח
צדקת	הצדקת
אף היא	אף הוא
עולא	עילא
בשם	בש'
ר' כיריי	ר' כירי
כירכורים	כירכורים
ח'	הקבה בשביל
להשיח	להשיח
עימה	עימה
צח'	צחקת
והכ'	והכת'
הדובר	הדבר
אליה	אליה
ביר	בר
בשם ר' אידי	בשם ר' אחי
והכ'	והכת'
ויאמר יי לה	ויאמר לה הנך הרה
ר' לוי בשם	ר' לוי בש'
ר' חמא ביר חנינה	ר' חמה בר חנינה

Scribe C	Scribe B³	Scribe B²	Scribe B¹	
ואמ,	וה,	ואמ	ואמ,	(7
ר לעזל	ר לעזר	ר אלעזר	ר לעזר	
פטמ	פט,	פט,	פט.	
וינברי	וינמרי	וינבוו	וינבוו	
ואמ,	ואמ,	וה	ואמ,	

SAMPLE 6

Scribe B: f. 17-17v; _T.A._, 192,6-193,2.

1 בעצבון תאכ אמ ר אסי קשה היא פרוסה כפלים בלידה בלידה

כת בעצב תלדי בני בפרוסה כת בעצבון תאכ ר אלעזר ור שמואל בן נחמן

ר אלעזר אמ היקיש גאולה לפרנסה ופרנסה לגאולה מה גאולה פלאים אף

פרנסה פלאים מה פרנסה בכל יום אף גאולה בכל יום ר שמוא בן א

5 נחמן אמ וגדולה מן הגאולה שהגאולה על ידי מלאך ופרנסה על

ידי הקבה גאולה על ידי מלאך דכת המלאך הגואל אתי פרנסה

על ידי הקבה פותח את ידך ומשביע ר יהושע בן לוי אמ כריעת

ים סוף לגוזר ים סוף נותן לחם לכל בשר

Scribe A2:   f. 182v-183; _T.A._, 1245,8-15.

המלאך הגואל אותי מכל רע וגו אמ

ר יסא קשה הפרנסה כיפליים בלידה כתוב בעצב תל

בנים בפרנסה כת בעצבון תאכל ר לעזר ור שמוא בר נחמן

ר לעזר אמ הקיש גאולה לפרנסה ופרנסה לגאולה מה

גאולה פלאים אף פרנסה פלאים פרנסה בכל   יום אף

גאולה בכל יום ר שמואל בר נחמן אמ וגדולה מן הגאולה

שהגאולה על ידי מלאך המלאך הגואל אותי וגו ופרנסה

על ידי הקבה פותח את ידיך וגו ר יהושע בן לוי אמ כריעת

ים סוף לגוזר ים סוף לגזרים וגו נותן לחם לכל בשר וגו

הערה: בשוליים לשורה 2; בלידה

Scribe A2	Scribe B
המלאך הגואל אותי מכל רע וגו	1) בעצבון תאכ׳
ר׳ יסא	ר׳ אסי
[הוא]	היא
הפרנסה	פרוסה
כיפליים	כפלים
כתוב (בלידה הושלם בגליון)	בלידה כת׳
בעצב תל׳ בנים	2) בעצב תלדי׳ בני׳
בפרנסה	בפרוסה
בעיצבון תאכל	בעצבון תאכ׳
ר׳ לעזר	ר׳ אלעזר
ור׳ שמוא׳ בר נחמן	ור׳ שמואל בן נחמן
ר׳ לעזר	3) ר׳ אלעזר
הקיש	היקיש
[מה]	4) מה
ר שמואל בר נחמן	ר׳ שמוא בן נחמן
על ידי מלאך המלאך הגואל אותי וגו	5) על ידי מלאך
על ידי הקבה פותח את ידיך וגו	5-6) על ידי הקבה
	6-7) גאולה על ידי מלאך דכת׳
	המלאך הגואל אתי פרנסה
	על ידי הקבה פותח את ידיך
	ומשביע ח׳
לגוזר ים סוף לגזרים וגו	8) לגוזר ים סוף
נותן לחם לכל בשר וגו	נותן לחם לכל בשר

284

Scribe B[1]: f. 21; <u>T.A.</u>, 241,3-243,4.

מן האדמה אשר ארר ה יי עשרה ריעבון באו   1

לעול אחד בימי אדם הראש ארורה האד בע אחד בימי למך מן האדמה

אש ארר ה יי   אחד בימי אברהם ויהי רעב בארץ וירד אברם   אחד

בימי יצחק ויהי רעב בארץ מלבד הרע הראש אשר היה בימי אבר   אחד

בימי יעקב כי זה שנתים הרעב   אחד בימי שפוט השפטים ויהי רעב   5

אחד

בימי דוד ויהי רעב בימי דוד שלש שנים   אחד בימי אליהו חי יי

אשר

עמדתי לפניו אם יהיה השנים האל טל ומטר   אחד בימי אלישע ויהי

רעב

גדול בשמרון   ואחד שהוא מתגלגל ובא לעולם ואחד לעתיד לבוא לא

רעב ללחם ולא צמא למים   ר חונא ור ירמיה בש ר שמואל בר רב יצחק

עיקר אווטינטיא שלו לא היה אלא בימי דוד ולא היה ראוי לבוא   10

אלא בימי שאול

אלא שהיה שאול גרופית שלשיקמה גילגלו הקבה והביאו דוד שילה

חטי ויוחנא משלמה אתמהא אמ ר חייה רבה לזגג שהיתה בידו קופה

מליאה כוסות ודיטרוטין   בשעה שהיה מבקש לתלות את קופתו היה

מביא יתד ותוקעה ונתלה בה ואחר כך הוא תולה את קופתו לא באו

כולן

בימי בני אדם שפופים אלא בימי בני אדם גיבורים שהן יכולין   15

לעמוד

בהן ר ברכיה הוה קרי עליהון נותן ליעף כח ר ברכיה בש ר חלבו

שנים

באו בימי אברהם ר חנא בש ר אחא אחד בימי למך ואחד בימי אברהם

רעב שבא בימי אליהו רעב שלבצורת היה רעב שנה עבדה שנה לא עבדה

רעב שבא בימי אלישע רעב שלמהומה היה עד היות ראש חמור

בשמונים כסף רעב שבא בימי שפוט השופטים ר חונא בש ר דוסא   20

ארבעים ושתים סאים היו ונעשו ארבעים ואחת והתני לא יצא אדם

לחוצה לארץ אלא אם כן היה סאתים שלחטים הולכות בסלע אמ ר

שמעון אמתי בזמן שאינו מוצא ליקח אבל אם היה מוצא ליקח אפילו

סאה בסלע לא יצא חוץ לארץ

Scribe B²: f. 49; **T.A.**, 382,10–383,12.

עשרה ריעבון באו לעולם אחד בימי אַבְרְהָֹם אדם הראשון

כוליה

עניינא עד ואחד לעתיד לבוא לא רעב ללחם ולא צמא למים כי אם לשמ

את דב יי ר הונא ור ירמיה בש ר שמואל בר רב יצחק עיקר אותנטיאה

שלו

לא היה אלא בימי דוד ולא היה ראוי לבוא אלא בימי שאול אלא על שהיה

שאול גרופית שלשקמה גילגלו הקבה והביאו בימי דויד שילה חטא ויוחנה

משתלמה אתמה אם ר חייה רבה לזגג שהיה לו קופה מליאה כוסות

ודיוטרוטין ובשעה שהיה מבקש לתלות את קופתו היה מביא יתד

ותוקעה ונתלה בה ואחרכך תולה את קופתו לפיכך לא באו כלום בימי בני

אדם שפופין אלא בימי בני אדם גיבורים שהן יכולין לעמוד בהן ר

ברכיה

קרי עליהון נותן ליעף כח ר ברכיה בש ר חלבו שנים באו בימי

אברהם ר

חונא בש ר אחא אחד בימי למך ואחד בימי אברהם רעב שבא בימי אליהו

רעב שלבצורת היה שנה עבדה שנה לא עבדה רעב שבא בימי אלישע רעב

שלמהומה היה עד היות ראש חמור בשמונים כסף   רעב שבא בימי

שפוט השופטים ר הונא בש ר דוסא ארבעים ושתים סאים היו ונעשו

ארבעים ואחת ותני לא יצא אדם לחוץ לארץ אלא אם כן היו סאתיים

שלחטים הולכות בסלע אמר֗ שמעון אמתי בזמן   שאינו מוצא

ליקח אֵלָֹא סֹאָֹה אבל אם היה מוצא ליקח אפילו סאה בסלע לא יצא

חוצה לארץ

286

Θ   עשרה

רעבון באו לעולם אחד בימי אדם הראשון ארורה האדמה
בעבו ואחד בימי למך מן האדמה אשר אררה יי ואחד
בימי אברהם ויהי רעב בארץ ואחד בימי יצחק ויהי רעב
בארץ מלבד ואחד בימי יעקב כי זה שנתים הרעב וגו ואחד
בימי שפט השפטים ויהי בימ שפ השפ ויהי רעב בארץ וגו
ואחד בימי דויד ויהי רעב בימי דויד וגו ואחד בימי אליהו
חי יי אי ישרא אשר עמדתי לפניו ואחד בימי אלישע ויהי
רעב גדול בשמרון וגו ואחד שהוא מתגלגל ובא לעולם
ואחד לעתיד לבא לא רעב ללחם וגו ר חונה ר ירמיה בשם ר
שמואל בר רב יצחק עיקר אוותינטייה שלו לא היה בימי דוד
לא היה ראוי לבא אלא בימי שאול אלא על ידי שהיה שאול
גרופית שלשיקמה גילגלו הקבה והביאו בימי דוד שלא חטיא
ויוחנה משתלמה אמ ר חייה רבה לזגג שהיה בידו קופה מלאה
כוסות ודייטרוטין ובשעה שהיה מבקש לתלות את קופתו
היה מביא יתד ותוקעה וניתלה בה ואחרכך היה תולה את
קופתו לפיכך כולם לא באו בימי בנˈ אדם שפופים אלא בימי
בני אדם גיבורים שהן יכולין לעמוד בהם ר ברכיה הוה קרי
עליהון נותן ליעף כח   ר ברכיה בשם ר חלבו שנים באו בימי
אברהם הראשון היה בימי אברהם ר חונה בשם ר אחא א
אחד בימי למך ואחד בימי אברהם רעב שבא בימי אליהו
רעב שלבצורת היה בימי שנה עבדה ושנה לא עבדה רעב שבא
בימי אלישע רעב שלמהומה היה עד היות ראש חמור וגו
רעב שבא בימי שפט השפטים ר חונה בשם ר אחא ארבעים
ושתים סאים היו ~~בימי שפט השפטים ר חונה בשם ר אחא~~
~~ארבעים ושתים סאים היו~~ ונעשו ארבעים ואחת תני והא תני לא
יצא אדם לחוץ לארץ אלא אם כן היו סאתים שלחטים הולכות
בסלע אמ ר שמעון אמתי בזמן שאינו מוצא ליקח אבל אם
היה מוצא ליקח אפילו סאה בסלע לא יצא לחוץ לארץ Θ

287

Scribe B¹   Scribe B²   Scribe C

Scribe B¹	Scribe B²	Scribe C
פסוק		פסוק
ויאמר	ויאמר	ויאמר
כי זה שלשים ויהיו ידיו	כי זה שלשים ויהיו ידיו	כי זה שלשים ויהיו ידיו

(5)

| | | פסוק |
| | | ויאמר |

(4)

| ויאמר | | ויאמר |
| ויהי כאשר ויהי מקץ כן, | ויהי כאשר ויהי מקץ | ויהי כאשר ויהי מקץ |

(3)

| ויאמר, | ויאמר | ויאמר |
| ויהי כאשר ויהי ויהי אמרה | | ויהי כאשר ויהי |

(2)

ליעקב,	ליעקב	ליעקב
אלם ויאמר,	אלם ויאמר ען,	אלם ויאמר
אלרבי ויאמר, כי,	אלרבי ההמרה ען,	אלרבי ההמרה
ויאמר	ותרד ני אייר פל	ותרד ני אייר פל

(1)

| ריהווב | ריהוול | ריהוול |
| כם '' ויהי אמר אלרבי רם | 'ה | 'ה |

Scribe C	Scribe B²	Scribe B¹
ויהי בימי שפ׳ השפ׳ ויהי רעב בארץ וגו		ויהי רעב
ואחד		אחד
דויד		דוד (6
ויהי רעב בימי דויד וגו		ויהי רעב בימי דוד שלש שנים
ואחד		אחד
חי יי אי׳ ישרא אשר עמדתי לפניו	חי יי אשר עמדתי לפניו	(7-6
	אם יהיה השנים האל טל ומטר	
ואחד		אחד (7
ויהי רעב גדול בשמרון וגו		ויהי רעב גדול בשמרון
לבא	לבוא	לבוא (8
לא רעב ללחם וגו	לא רעב ללחם ולא	לא רעב ללחם ולא (9-8
	צמא למים כי אם לשמ׳	צמא למים
	את דב׳ יי	
ר׳ חונה	ר׳ הונא	ר׳ חונא
ר׳ ירמיה	ור׳ ירמיה	ור׳ ירמיה
בשם	בש׳	בש׳

Scribe B¹	Scribe B²	Scribe C
(10) אותותינו	אותותינו	אותותינו
אלא	אלא	י
כלו	לכו	כלו
כליא	כליא	כליה
(11) [כי לא]	לא	אל כי ר
נביא	ריר	ריר
[ועוד]	ריר	ריר
פלפליכם	פלפליכם	פלפליכם
(12) עמי	עמא	עמיי
ריתתה	ריתתה	ריתתת
אותותם	אותותם,	י,
פולח	פולח	ריר
ריר	ריר	אותותם
בליעל	בליעל	בליעא
(13) בליעל	בליעלו	בליעלו
יריכותיכל	יריכותיכל	יריכותיכל
השליכל		

Scribe B¹	Scribe B²	Scribe C
(14) ונהלה	ונהלה	ונהיל
אתר קל	ואתרל	ואתרל
הוא	',	יויל
[להלו]	לכיל	לכיל
לכו ואתו חלכי	אל ואר חלכ	ואל אר חלכ
(15) מספיקים	מספיקל	מספיקים
(16) חלה	חלל	חלה
חלה	ר,	חלל
חפ,	חפ,	חפם
ר חוא	ר, חוחא	ר, חוחא
(17) חיספ אחלחם	חיספ אחלחם	חיספ אחלחם ובראלל חיר חיספ אחלחם
חפ,	חפ,	חפם
ר חוא	ר, חוחא	חלל
(18) חרוה לא גורוי	חרוה לא גורוי	ואוחל לא גורוי
ויהלה	ויהלה	ויהלה
(19) חיקי	ח,	חיקי

Scribe B[1]	Scribe B[2]	Scribe C
(20) לכל מקדשיכם	לכל מקדשיכם	זוז
המקדשים וטמאו	המקדשים וטמא	המקדשים וטמאם
אלהם נודו	אלהם נודו	ספת ,י חורו
רע,	רע,	ספת
אלהם ,ר	אלהם ,ר	אחא
(21) חורו ,ר	חורו ,ר	חורו ,ר
חורי		נהו אח ,יב
(22) לחורי הצאן	לחורי צאן	לחורי צאן
רעה	רעה	רעה
מאהי,ם	מאהי,ם	מאהי,ם
אמר,	אלהם ,ר	אלהם ,ר
לחול לבני אלהם	לחול בני אלהם	לחול לבני אלהם

Scribe B[1]:   f. 30v; <u>T.A.</u>, 290,1–8.

1   יי צדיק יבחן   ורש ואוהב חמס שנא נפש אמ ר יונתן היוצר הזה
אינו בודק

קנקנים מרוערעים שאינו מספיק להקיש עליו עד שהוא שוברו כך אין
הקבה מנסה את הרשעים אלא את הצדיקין יי צדיק יבחן אמ ר יוסי
בר

בן חנינה הפשתני הזה כל זמן שהוא יודע שהפשתן שלו יפה וכל

5   שהוא כותשה היא משבחת וכל זמן שהוא מקיש עליה היא משתמנת
ובשעה שהיא יודע שהפשתן שלו רעה אינו מספיק להקיש עליה אחת
עד שהיא פוקעת מניחה כך אין הקבה מנסה את הרשעים אלא את
הצדיקין יי צדיק יבחן אמ ר יצחק אלעזר לבעל הבית שהיו לו שתי
פרות אחת כוחה יפה ואחת כוחה רע על איזו הוא נותן את העול לא

10 על אותה שכוחה יפה כך הקבה מנסה את הצדיקין יי צדיק יבחן דב
אח יי צדיק יבחן זה נח ויאמר יי לנח בוא את וכ בית א הת כי
או רא

צדיק לפני

Scribe B[2]:   f. 35; <u>T.A.</u>, 314,5–11.

יי צדיק יבחן ורשע ואוהב חמס שנא נפ אמ ר יוחנן א
היוצר הזה אינו בודק קנקנים מרוערעים שאינו מספיק להקיש עליו אחת
עד שהיא פוקעת ומהוא בודק קנקנים בריאים וברורים שאפילו מקיש
הוא עליהם כמה אינן נש   כך אין הקבה מנסה אלא את הצדיקים
יי צדיק יבחן אמ ר יוסי בן   .נינה הפשתני הזה בשעה שהוא יודע
שהפשתן

שלו יפה כל שהוא כותשה היא משבחת וכל שהוא מקיש עליה היא
משתמנת ובשעה שהוא יודע שהפשתן שלו רעה אינו מספיק להקיש א
עליה אחת עד שהיא פוקעת אינו כותשה ואינו מקיש עליה כך אין הקבה
מנסה אלא את הצדיקים אמ ר אלעזר לבעל הבית שהיו לו שתי פרות
אחת כוחה יפה ואחת כוחה רע על איזו הוא נותן את העול לא על אותה

293

שכוחה יפה כך אין הקבה מנסה אלא את הצדיקין יי צדיק יבח‎ דב אח

יי צדיק יבחן זה נח צא מן התבה

Scribe C: f. 84; <u>T.A.</u>, 585,8-586,7.

יי צדיק

יבחן אמ ר יוחנן היוצר הזה אינו בודק אם קינקינים מרוערעים

שאינו מספיק להקיש עליו אחת עד שהוא שוברן והקנקנים

ברורים אפילו מקיש עליו כמה אינו שובר כך אין הקבה מנסה

אלא את הצדיקים יי צדיק יבחן אמ ר יוסי בן חנינה הפישתני

הזה בשעה שהוא יודע שהפישתני שלו יפה כל שהוא כובשה

היא משבחת וכל שהוא מקיש עליה היא משתמנת כך אין‎ א

הקבה מנסה אלא את הצדיקין‎ יי צדיק יבחן אמ ר לעזר לבעל

הבית שהיה לו שתי פרות אחת כוחה יפה ואחת כוחה רע על

מי נותן את העול לא על אותה שכוחה יפה כך אין הקבה מנסה

אלא את הצדיקים יי צדיק יבחן זה אברהם ויהי אח הדברי

האלה והאים‎ ⊖

Scribe B¹ Scribe B² Scribe C

295

Scribe B¹ Scribe B² Scribe C

(5) כתבתי   כתבתי   כתבתי
    דבר   ה,   ה,

(6) ונפקד מושבך אשר אבי כיל מספרו   ונפקד מושבך אשר אבי כיל מספרו   ונפקד מושבך אשר אבי כיל מספרו
    אך לחם אכל שם   אך לחם אכל שם
    כי אליך פלטה   כי אליך פלטה
    גד אבני פרעה   גד אבני פרעה
    נתהלך   נתהלך מעלה אדני קמד בלדו   ה,

(7) את נבאלים   ה,   ה,

(8) ונפקדתי   ונפקדתי   נתהלך
    כי מרד חנך   כי מרד חנך   כי מרד, חנך
    ר, ישראל פנחס   ר, אליעזר   ר, בלהי
    שובי   שובי   שובי, חנך

(9) כי את נבח   כי את נבח   כי אם,
    נותר   ה,   ה,

296

Scribe C	Scribe B²	Scribe B¹
(10 החזקה מכום את החזקים ל	החזקה מכום את אלא החזקים ל	אל החזקה מכום את אלא החזקים
החזקי מכ '' ''	'' מכום המי ''	המי מכ '' ''
אל את ז לו לכאל ''	המחה אל לז את ''	'' ח
לו ח	ח ח	''
(11 לוהב '' מכום	לוהב '' מכום ''	לוהב '' מכום
אנ, רב ‹11-10	אנ, רב	‹ ‹
'' פ ‹ ‹	'' פ	''

297

VAT. 60 TO SAMPLE 8

Ch. 31; T.A., 290,1-8.

Ch. 33; T.A., 314,5-11.

Ch. 55; T.A., 585,8-586,7.

Ch. 31--Cont'd.

משבחת והולכת כך אין הקבה
מנסה את הרשע שאינם
יכולים לעמוד דכת והרשעי
כים נגרש ואת מי הוא מנסה
את הצדיקים יי צדיק יבחן
א ר אלעזר לבעל הבית שהיה
לו שתי פרות אחת כוהה יפה
ואחת כוהה רע על איזו מהן
הוא מטריח לא על זו שכוחה
יפה כך אין הק מנסה את הרש
אלא את הצדיקי יי צדיק
יבחן ד א יי צדיק יבחן זה נח
ויא יי לנח בא אתה וכל ביתך
וגו כי אותך ראיתי צדי לפני
בדור הזה

Ch. 55--Cont'd.

והרשעים כים נגרש ואת
מי הוא מנסה את הצדיקי
דכת יי צדיק יבחן ויהי אח
הדבר הא ותשא אש אדנ
את עי למי על יוסף ויהי אח
הדבר האל והאדים נס א אב
א ר יונתן היוצר הזה כשהוא
בודק את כבשני אינן בודק בקנקנים
מרוערעין למה שכיון שהוא
מקיש עליהן הן נשברים
ובמי הוא בודק בקנקנים
יפים שאף על פי שהוא
מקיש עליהן כמה פעמ אינן
נשברין כך אין הקב מנסה
את הרשעי למה שאין
יכולין לעמוד וגו הך דקדמייה
ד א יי צדיק יבחן זה אברה
ויהי אחרי הדבר האל והאים
נסה את אבר

Scribe B: f. 47; <u>T.A.</u>, 372,6–373,1.

ר יוסי ור הונא   1

משם ר

אליעזר בנו שלר יוסי הגלילי משהקבה מתהי ומתלה .... בעיניהם

שלצדיקים אחר כך הוא מגלה להם טעמו שלדבר כך אל הארץ אשר

אראך על אחד ההרים אש אמר אליך וקרא אליה את הקריאה אשר אני

5   דובר אליך   קום צא אל הבקעה ושם אדבר אותך

Scribe C: f. 85; <u>T.A.</u>, 592,5–8.

על אחד ההרים אשר אום אליך

דמד ר חונה בשם ר ליעזר בנו שלר יוסה הגלילי מי שהקבה

מתהא ומתלה בעיניהם שלצדיקים ואחרכך הוא מגלה להם

טעמו שלדבר אל הארץ אש אמאך על אחד ההרים   וקרא אליה

את הקריאה   קום צא אל הבקעה וגו   ☉

Scribe B

(5) קום אל אלהם ועשה ספר דברה אלהן
ולבד דברה אלבד

(4) אל אמר יהוה אל, אמר אלי
ודבר אליהם את יהוה אלהיך
וקדש את יהוה אלהיך

(3) אחר כל
אל ויאמר אלה שאל אראל
כל

(2) ל, אליעזר
סוס ויעיד
מממתה
בתתה

(1) ל, סוס ל, יהוה
ספס

Scribe C

(5) וזה ועשה אל הספת וזה
הדברים את יהוקחה
אל יהוה הדברים

(4) אל אמר יהוה
ם סדום הדברים
ל, ויאמרו אל אראל
ה,
ראמרו

(3) ראמרו
ם שממה
ממתה
ל, סיכלי

(2) ל, סוס מלהמלי
ל, לעיר

(1) ספס
ל, חחת
אל ליאל ביא אלה אמר יהוה חחת ביום אל
ולר ליאל ריא ספר

301

Scribe B: f. 52; <u>T.A.</u>, 395,9-397,2.

1   ושמתי את זרעך כעפר האר מה עפר

הארץ מסוף העולם ועד סופו כך בניך מסוף העולם ועד סופו ומה

עפר הארץ אינו מהברך אלא במים כך בניך אין מתברכין אלא

בזכות התורה שנמשלה במים ומה עפר הארץ מבלה את כל כלי

5   מתכות והוא קיים לעולם כך יש אומות העול בטלין והם קיימים

ומה עפר הארץ עשוי דייש כך בניך עשוים דייש למלכיות הדה הי

ושמתיה ביד מוגייך מהוא מוגייך אילין דממגיין אפילו כך   א

לטובתך משקשקין ליך מן חוביך היך מה דאת אם ברביבים תמו

חמוגגינה   אשר אמרו לנפשך שחי ונעבורה מה היו עושין להם

10 מרביצים אותם בפלטיות ומעבירים רירם עליהם ר עזריה משם ר

אחא הא סימן טב מה פלטיה זו מבלה את העוברים ואת השבים

והיא קיימת לעולם כך בניך מבלים את כל אומות העול והם קיימין

לעולם

Scribe C: f. 118; <u>T.A.</u>, 794,3-795,2.

          והיה זרעך כעפר הארץ מה עפר הארץ   ⊕

אינו מתברך אלא במים כך בניך אינן מתברכין אלא בזכות

התורה שנמשלה במים מה עפר הארץ מבלה את כל כלי מתכות

והוא קיים לעולם כך בניך מבלים את כל אומות העולם והן   א

קיימין לעולם מה עפר הארץ עשוי דייש כך בניך עשויים

דייש למלכיות הדה היא ושמתיה ביד מוגיך   מהו מוגייך

אילין דמגגין מחתך אפילו כך לטבתיך משקשקין ליך מן חובתיך

הך דת ברביבים תמוגגנה צמח תברך אשר אמרו לנפ שחי

ונעבו מה היו עושים להן היו מרבצים אותם ביפלטריות

ומעבירים לידים עליהם ר עזריה בשם ר אחא הא סימן טוב

מה פלטיאה מבלה   את העוברים ואת השבים והיא קיימת

לעולם כך בניך מבלים את אומות העולם והן קיימין לעולם

Scribe B

(1 ‏ואמרי את דוד עבדי מלך האלי

(2-1 ‏מה עשה ראש האדץ חסוף הילים דוד יסב
‏וזה
‏זסוף הילים דוד יסב הסום זפי

(3 ‏א יל

(4 ‏ותה

(5 ‏ולח ‏ולביל, הגלמ ,אנזנו ,פ,
‏ותה

(6 ‏ותן
‏סזבליס

‏חה יד
‏חה יד

(7 ‏ויזוזם
‏חאא

‏חתה

Scribe C

‏וזזה דולך הסכל האדץ

‏ה,

‏חה

‏ולן ‏אלא

‏חה

‏ולזזה וגללס כל את הזוזח הללים
‏ולז
‏ולז

‏חה
‏סזבליס
‏ולזכ ‏אלזזה

(‏ןלאמנר חזם הסכם ‏חה) ‏הללזזה

‏חתה

303

Scribe B

וזה

(12) כי על אנשיא הגלו

(11) כן

מאם
ליה

(10) מכליאם
מכליאה

(9) ותכתבה ותכתבון
אשר אמרו לגבר שמי ודגדהון
ביני לעם

Scribe C

ותכתבון ליני

וזה

אנבתותה את הקטברי עלדים

כין
אבי

מאם
ליליה
ותכליאה

[מכליאם]
ביי מכליאם

ותכתבה ותכתבון הקטברי אשר
אשר אמרו לבב, שמי ודגל,
ביני לה

(8) לאובתן
ותכה
ותחתה
לני, יה,

304

Scribe B: f. 65; <u>T.A.</u>, 465,1-7.

1   ולא יקרא עוד שמך אברם והיה שמך אברהם בר קפרא אמ כל
מי שהוא קורא לאברהם אברם עובר בעשה   אמ ר לוי בעשה ולא תעשה
שנ ולא יקרא בלא תעשה והיה שמך אברהם בעשה והרי אנשי כנסת
הגדולה קראו אותו אברם שנ אתה הוא האים אשר בחרת באברם שנייה

5 היא שעד שהוא אברם בחרת בו דכוותה הקורא לשרה שרי עובר
בעשה אלא הוא שנצטוה עליה דכוותה הקורא ליש יעקב עובר בעשה
תני לא שעיקר שם יעקב אלא אם יש יהיה שמך יש עיקר ויעקב טפילה
ר זבדיה בש ר אחא מכל מקום יעקב שמך אלא כי אם ישרא יהיה שמך א
יעקב עיקר וישרא מוסיף עליו

Scribe C: f. 136v; <u>T.A.</u>, 920,2-8.

ויאמר   ⊖

אליו מה שמך   ויאמר אליו לא יעקב וגו בר קפרה אם כל שהוא
קורא לאברהם אברם עובר בעשה ר לוי אמ בעשה ולא תעשה
ולא יקרא עוד שמך אברם בלא תעשה והיה שמך אברהם
בעשה והרי כנסת הגדולה קראו שמו אברם אתה הוא יי האים
אשר וגו שנייה היא שעד שהוא אברם בחרתה בו ודכוותיה
הקורא לשרה שרי עובר בעשה הוא נצטוה עליה ודכוותיה
הקורא לישרא יעקב עובר בעשה תני לא שיעקר שם יעקב   א
ממנו אלא כי אם ישרא ישרא עיקר ויעקב טפילה   ⊖
ר זבדיה בשם ר אחא מכל מקום יעקב שמך כי אם
ישרא   יעקב עיקר וישרא מוסף עליו

(1) אבל ירקי קרא צוד דוד עמר אביא החרה יעקב אמל
    החחחח
    ה קבאל
(2-1) צוד ל כ כ אלוא
(2) אלי י ר ליו
(3) אלי י
(4) אלוא
    אלי י
    אלא י חררה אלי ס אפל חררה המאלס
(5) החחח
    חחווחח

א ל אליר יאמרי עמל בת בן עמל ל ויאמר אליר ויאמרי
יעקב רני
קבל ה
בל אלוא
אלא ל רכ
י יאמרי
חררה עמצא אלי רבר
אלא ל רב עמל אלכל אלי חררה המאלס
אפל
אלא י י אלי ס אפל רני
ה, י
חחחחחחח

306

Scribe B

(9) מוסרו

ני אם ידעת, נירו מסן

רם,

(8) רם,
סם יעדו
ני אם ידעת, נירו מסן

(7) מיידו
סם יעדו
סם יעדו, נירו מסן
ני,

(6) לי,
רנונדו
אלא נוד מדבסון

Scribe C

מוסרו

ני אם ידעא
ני,
רסם

ידעא,
ני אם ידעא,
סם יעדו מסטון
מיידו

ליסעא,
רנונודינ
נוד ראמונון

307

Scribe B: f. 70v; T.A., 500,12-501,5.

1
ר אחא בש ר אלכסנדרי

ר שמוא בר נחמן בש ר יונתן אפילו הלכות עירובי חצרות היה

אברהם יודע ר פנחס ר חלקיה ר פנחס בש ר שמואל אפילו שם

חדש שהקבה עתיד לקרות בירושלם ביום ההוא יקראו לירושלם כסא

5
יי   היה יודע אברהם ר ברכיה ור חייה אבוי רבנין דתמן אמרין

בש

ר יהודה אין כל יום ויום שאין הקבה מחדש הלכה בבית דין שלמעלן

מה טעם שמעו שמוע ברוגז קולו והגא מפיו יצא ואין הגא אלא תורה

שנ והגית בו יומם ולילה אפילו אותה הלכה היה אברהם יודע

Scribe C: f. 104v; T.A., 703,3-704,4.

ר אחא בש ר אלכסנדרי משום ר שמואל בר

נחמן מש ר יוחנן אפילו הלכות עירובי חצרות היה אברהם

יודע ר פינחס ר חלקיה בשם ר סימון אפילו שם חדש שהקבה

עתיד לקראת לירושלם ביום ההוא יקראו לירושלם וגו

היה אברהם יודע ר ברכיה ר חייא אבוי רבנן דתמן בשם ר

יודה אומ אין כל יום ויום שאין הקבה מחדש הלכה בבית דין

שלמעלן מה טע שמעו שמוע ברוגז קולי וגו ואין הגא אלא

דברי תורה הכ דת והגית בו יומם ולילה   ⊕

Scribe B

(7) בזה מלא

אברן אומא חזרה דמיל

ויטא מפני אואא

ויאטי

(6-5) אבני מפ, ר, וירו

הירד

(5) ייר ייא אבווא

הירד

(4) הטיטו חזרה יביאו יויטפנ האמ ר

ברחן וברינדה

(3) ר, טיטו

חטסם מפ, ר אבריו

ואבחרה

(2) ר אבריו ריי וירו

טפ, ר, יירו

וטיטו

Scribe C

בני חזרה

אבני מפא חזרה דמיל זיל קרי דמיל

חז טפ,

חזו ר, יירו חז טפ,

טפ, ר, יירו אוא,

הירד

הירד ר, אבווא יירו

הטיטו חזרה יביאו יויטפנ זיל

ברחן וברינדה

ר, חזם וסום

טפ, ר, וסים

ואבחרה

חטן ר, יירי, זיל

טפ, ר, אבא

הטיטו חז יביאואבריו ר

חזוט ה אבריו ר חטסם ר

ואבחרה

309

Scribe C	Scribe B

Scribe C   Scribe B

הכ׳ דת׳   שנ׳ (8

אפילו אותה הלכה היה

ח׳   אברהם יודע

SAMPLE 13

Scribe B: f. 71v; <u>T.A.</u>, 506,1-5.

1   ויגש אברהם ויאמר ר יהודה ור נחמיה

ורבנין ר יהודה אם הגשה למלחמה הדה היא ויגש יואב והעם אשר

עמו למלחמה ר נחמיה או הגשה לפייס ויגשו בני יהֻודָה על יהושע

לפייס רבנין אמרין הגשה לתפילה היך דאת אם ויהי כעלית המנחה

5   ויגש אליהו הנביא ואני עבדך ובדברך עשיתי ר אלעזר פשט לה

אם למלחמה אני בא אם לפייס אני בא ואם לתפילה אני בא

Scribe A2: ff. 171v-172; <u>T.A.</u>, 1154,4-8.

Ø   ויגש אליו יהודה ר יודה ור

נחמיה ורבנן ר יודה אם הגשה למלחמה הכ דת ויגש א

יואב והעם וגו ר נחמיה אם הגשה לפייס הכ דת ויגשו

בני יהודה אל יהושע וגו לפייסו רבנן אמרין הגשה א

לתפילה הכ דת ויהי בעלות המנחה ויגש אליהו וגו ר לעזר

פשט להן אם למלחמה אני בא אם לפייס אני בא אם

לתפילה אני בא

Scribe B

Scribe B

(1) ויאמר אלהם ויאמר

(2-1) ר׳ י...יו ׳ר...׳ר
ר ...יה
ר ...יה
ואף ...דל
ויאמר ...ויאמר, ...
ר ...יה

(3) או׳ אך

ויאמ ...יה על ...יל
...ההיה
לפניו

(4) לפניס
רריר׳
הי׳ל אתו אף

(5-4) ריאה ...הההה ר...יה לפ...יה
ריאה ...הההה ר...ש א...יו וההיא

(5) ר ׳ אלויו ...ממ כו

(6) לפניס

ואמ

Scribe A2

Scribe A2

(1) ...ירה ...אל שר׳׳

(2-1) ר ׳ ...יה ׳ר ...ירה
...יח ...ממ ...יר ...אל ...יר
...יר ...ירה
...ירה יר
ליר׳ ...

(3) אא׳

ריר׳ ...יר ל... אל ...רירה ...רר
ליר׳ו רר, יר,
לי׳, רר,

(4) ...ית, ...יר,
ליר׳
לפ׳׳ס

(5-4) ריר׳ ...ימ ...ימ ר... א...יו ...יר
ר ...ירה ...ממ ...ר... ...ירה ...ר ...

(5) ר ׳ ...יר ...ממ כו
לפ׳׳ס
אא

311

Scribe B: **f. 73v;** <u>T.A.</u>, **518,4-6.**

סדמה תני משם ר נחמיה כל דבר שצריך למד בתחילתו נתן לו הא
בסופו סדמה שעירה מצרימה חרנה אתיבון והא כת ישובו רשעים
לשאולה ר אבא בר זבידא אם לדייטי התחתונה שבשאול

Scribe C: **f. 115;** <u>T.A.</u>, **777,1-2.**

חרנה תני בשם ר נחמיה כל דבר שיצרך למד מתחילתו ניתך
לו הא בסופו סדומה שעירה מצרימה חרנה התיבון והא כת
ישובו רשעים לשאולה ר אבא בר זבדא אם לדייטי התחתונה
שבשאול   Θ

_____

הערה: לשורה 3 למילה לדייטי, במקור לבטי ונראית מתוקנת לדייטי.

Scribe A2:   **f. 157v;** <u>T.A.</u>, **1053,3-6.**

מצרימה]תני בשם ר נחמיה **כל** דבר שצריך למד בתחלתו ניתך לו הא
בסופו שעירה סדומה מצרימה חרנה[חרנה התיבון והא כת ישובו רשעים
לשאולה ר אבא בר זבדא אם לבטי התחתונה שבשאול

Scribe B Scribe C Scribe A2

(3) ונאו ליניאי. (לפני מגיבני ליני
   אוייני ונאו אויא

(2) ונאו ינאני ינ?ני
   נוניו ונוו נוניו
   אביני אלבני ונוו אלבני אלבני אוני אלבני אלבני וניו

(1) ונ ונו ינו
   נוניליו ונוניו ונליוינו
   אביני אביל אביני
   נאו נאו נאו
   נוטני נווו אביניו

313

Scribe B: ff. 77-77v; T.A., 544,5-547,2.

1   ויבא אים אל אבימל בחלם הליל מה בין נביאי יש לבין
נביאי אומות

העולם ר חמא בר חנינה ור ישׂשכר דכפר מנדי ר חמא בר חננה אין א
הקבה ניגלה על נביאי אומות העול אלא בחצי דיבור היך דאת אמר
ויקרא אים אל בלעם אמ ר ישׂשכר דכפר מנדי אין הלשון הזה ויקרא
5   אלא לשון טומאה היך מה דאת אם כי יהיה בך איש אש לא יה טה מקר
ליל אלא ר נביאי יש בלשון שלם בלשון חיבה בלשון קדושה בלשון
שמלאכי הסרת מקלסין בו וקרא זה אל זה ואמ ק ק ק יי צבא   אמ ר
יוסי בן כינה אין הקבה ניגלה על אומות העול אלא בשעה שדרך בני
אדם
באין לפרוש אילו מאילו הדה היא בסעיפים מחזיונות לילה בנפל
תרדמ
10   על אנש   ואלי דבר יגנב ותקח אזני שמץ מנהו אמ ר אלעזר בן מנחם
א
רחוק מרשעים יי אילו נביאי אומות העול ותפילת צדיקים נשמעה
אילו
נביאי יש ואין הקבה ניגלה אל אומות העולם אלא באדם שהוא בא
מרחוק
היך מה דאת אם מארץ רחקה באו אלי מבבל אבל נביאי ישׂרא מיד וירא
ויקרא מה בין נביאי יש לנביאי אומות העול ר חננא בר פפא
ורבנן ר חננא
15   בר פפא אם למלך שהיה בחדר ואוהבו בטרקלין והוא תולה את
הוילון ומד
ומדבר עמו רבנין אמר למלך שהיה לו אשה ופילגש וכשרוצה לדבר עם
אשתו מדבר הוא עמה בפרהסיא וכשרוצה לדבר עם פילגשו הוא מדבר
עמה במטמונית כך אין הקבה ניגלה על נביאי אומות העול אלא
בלילה ויבא
אים אל בלעם לילה   ויבא אים אל לבן הארמי בחלם הליל ויבא אים
אל אבימל
20   בחל הל

314

ⓧ   ויבא אים אל לבן

הארמי בחלום הלילה וגו מה בין נביאי ישר לבין נביאי   א
אומות העולם אלא בחצי הדיבור הכ דת ויקר אים אל בלעם
אמ ר יששכר דכפר מנדי כֹן יֹהֹיֹהֹ בֹשֹׂכֹרֹן אין הלשון
הזה ויקר אלא לשון טומאה דכ דת כי יהיה בך איש אשר לֹא יהיה טהור ....

אבל נביאי ישראל בדיבור שלם בלשון חיבה בלשון קדושה
שמלאכי שרת מקלסין אותו וקרא זה אל זה ואמ וגו ר יוסי בן
חנינה אמ אין הקבה נגלה לנביאי אומות העולם אלא בשעה
שדרך בני אדם לפרוש אילו מאילו הדא היא בסעפים מחזיונות
לילה וגו ואלי דבר יגונב וגו אמ ר לעזר בר מנחם רחוק יי   א
מרשעים וגו אילו נביאי אומות העולם ותפילת צדיקים ישמע
אילו נביאי ישראל מה בין נביאי ישראל לבין נביאי אומות
העולם ר חננא בר פפא ור סימון ר חננא בר פפא אמ למלך   א
ואוהבו שהיו נתונים בטרקלין כל שעה שהוא מבקש לדבר
הוא מדבר עם אוהבו ר סימון אמ למלך שהיה לו אשה ופילגש
בשעה שהוא בא אצל אשתו הוא בא אצלה בפרהסיא ובשעה
שהוא בא אצל פילגשו הוא בא במטמונית כך אין הקבה נגלה
על נביאי אומות העולם אלא בלילה ויבא אים אל בלעם לילה
ויבא אים אל אבימלך בחלום הלילה ויבא אים אל לבן וגו

הערה: בשוליים לשורה 2; אומות העולם ר המא בר חנינא ור יששכר
דכפר מנדי ר חמא בר חנינא אמ אין הקבה
ניגלה על נביאי
בשוליים לשורה 7; בֹלֹשֹוֹן

Scribe B   Scribe C

ויחל יוסיה למלך בן שמנה עשרה שנה במלכו ושלשים ואחת שנה מלך בירושלם ושם אמו ידידה בת עדיה

(1) ויעש הישר בעיני יהוה וילך בכל דרך דוד אביו ולא סר ימין ושמאל

(2) ויהי בשמנה עשרה שנה למלך יאשיהו

(3) שלח המלך

(4) בבא שפן הספר אל בית יהוה לאמר

(5) עלה חלקיהו הכהן הגדול

316

	Scribe B	Scribe C
6)	אלא	אבל
	יש׳	ישראל
	בלשון שלם	בדיבור שלם
7)	השרת	שרת
	בו	אותו
	וקרא זה אל זה ואמ ק ק ק יי צבא׳	וקרא זה אל זה ואמ׳ וגו
8–7)	אמ׳ ר יוסי בן כינה	ר יוסי בן חנינה אמ׳
	על	לנביאי
	העול׳	העולם
9)	באין	ה׳
	בסעיפים מחזיונות לילה בנפל	בסעפים מחזיונות לילה וגו
	תרדמ׳ על אנש׳	
10)	ואלי דבר יגנב ותקח אזני שמץ מנהו	ואלי דבר יגונב וגו
	ר׳ אלעזר בן מנחם	ר׳ לעזר בר מנחם
11)	רחוק מרשעים יי	רחוק יי מרשעים וגו
	העול	העולם
	ותפלת צדיקים נשמעה	ותפילת צדיקים ישמע

Scribe B   Scribe C

(12) ‏שי׳   ‏לאשי׳

(12-14) ‏ואל יהיה הקפה יהיה אל אוראות הגלים
‏אם אלאו את הנקפה את הלוס אווים דם ההגן הוד האם
‏דוד רביל אל׳ ואל ויד ם אלהי הודד הלד
‏את רודם ואל אורא דהי, ם׳ דבד ואדם אלואי

(14) ‏שי׳   ‏ה,

                                            ‏,אלואי
                                            ‏לדיל ווהד,
                                            ‏הדלד
                                            ‏הוהו
                                            ‏דד, ם,הוד

(15) ‏לדדל פודה הודד ואדהוד דודד דם   ‏לדדל ואדוהד פודד הוהדם הדלד,ד
‏דוהא הודה הודד ואדהוד דודד דם   ‏הד פדה פודד הודם לדדד הוד דם אודוד
                                            ‏נד פדה פודד המדפ לדדד הוד דם אודוד
(16) ‏דדד, אפד,   ‏ד ם,הדד אד,

(16-17) ‏ודפדדאד לדדד דם אפדד
‏הפדה פודד אד אאדל אפדד,א
‏דוד דם אאדהד הגלדם,א

                              318

Scribe B

       Scribe B

(17) ונשמעו כדבר כל פקדני ורעשו אור פקישם חזה
    מזה בלע הכמקודינ״ח

(18) ריביאל
    ונשמע

(19) ונבא כדבר ריביאל אל הכמקודי, מקה, הלך
    רישר אל הכמקודי אל כדבר ריבאל אל הלי הפמל רליי

Scribe C

       Scribe C

ונשמעו אנוח אם הכמקודינ״ח
חזה אם אצל פקישם

רנאל
ם רישעו
חח

ונבא כדבר ריכאל אל הכמקודי אל כדבר אל הכמקודי
רנר הלך רנ אל הלי כל אל הפמל רליי
הליכה הכמקודי חמסכ רל פקישע אל אלצ פקישם

SAMPLE PASSAGES REPEATED ONLY IN B

SAMPLE 1

Scribe B[1]: f. 10v; <u>T.A.</u>, 156,9–157,2.

1   ר יהושע דסכנין בש ר לוי תחילת מפולת

שינה דמך ליה ולא לעי דמך ליה ולא עביד עיבידה ר אם שלש

תרדמות הן תרדמת שינה תרדמת נבואה תרדמת מורמיטה

תרדמת שינה ויפל יי על האדם שינה תרדמת נבואה ויהי השמש

5 לבוא ותרדמ נפ על אברם דורמיטה אין רואה ואין יודע ואין מקיץ

כי כלם ישינים כי תרדמת יי רבנן אם אף תרדמת שלשטות כי

נסך יי עליכם רוח תרדמ ויעצם עיניכם   ר חננא בר יצחק אם   א

שלש נכלות הן נכלת מיתה שינה נכלת נבואה חלום נכלת עולם

הבא ר אבון מוסיף עוד תרתין נכלת אורה שלמעלן גלגל חמה

10 נכלת חכמה שלמעלן תורה

Scribe B[2]: ff. 60–60v; <u>T.A.</u>, 438,8–439,6.

ויהי השמש לבוא ותר נפ ע א   אמ ר יהושע דסכנין בש   ר לוי א

תחילת מפולת שינה דמך ליה ולא לעי באורייחא דמך ליה ולא עבד

עבירה   רב אם שלש תרדמות הן תרדמת שינה תרדמת נבואה

ותרדמת מורטיטא תרדמת שינה ויפל יי אים תרדמה ע **ה וישן**

תרדמת נבואה ויהי השמש לבוא ותר נפ ע אבר   תרדמת מורטיטא

אין רואה ואין יודע ואין מקיץ כי כלם ישנים כי תרדמת יי נפלה

עליהם

רבנין אמרין אף תרדמת שלשטות   כי נסך יי עליהם רוח תרדמ ויעצם

את עיניהם   ר חננא שלש ניבלות הן ניבלת מיתה שינה ניבלת נבואה

חלום ניבלת העולם הבא שבת   ר אבין מוסיף תריין ניבלת   אורה

שלמעלן גלגל חמה ניבלת חכמה שלמעלה תורה

Scribe B¹

7) ... ויאמר יהוה אל מֹשה

ר ויתן לו ביאר את

6) ... הֹ וישם אֹהים ה וידבר י

וֹדֹ אֹה,

5) ויֹדבֹם

4-5) ויֹה וֹ על ואשֹם פֹיה

ה,

3) ויֹדבֹם

2) הֹ

ויֹ אֹהיֹ

ר, אֹ,

ר, ויֹדֹם ויֹדֹנֹי

Scribe B²

ר ויֹדֹ

אֹיֹם ויֹה וידֹב ויֹאֹם אֹ ויֹ

ויֹדֹל אֹבֹ

... הֹ וישֹם הֹ וידֹבֹם וֹ ויֹדֹם

וֹדֹ ואֹם הֹ וֹדֹ אֹ ויֹדֹ

ויֹדֹם וֹדֹביאֹם

ר וֹ ויֹאֹם ואֹם ויֹ הֹ וֹ

ויֹדֹ הֹויֹדֹם

ויֹל אֹם ויֹדֹם אֹ הֹ ויֹ

ויֹדֹיאֹם

הֹ אֹ,

ויֹ אֹם,

אֹיֹיֹ הֹ

אֹיֹיֹאֹם

ויֹ ויֹאֹם ויֹ וֹ, גֹ, אֹ, אֹ,

321

Scribe B¹

(8)   ובלוה

(ד' בצם) ובלוה

אבר הזח אלם

(9)   ד' אבר ד

טרד התחת ד'

טלוה

ד'

(10)   ובלוה

ויללבפ

Scribe B²

וובלוה

(ד' בצם) ובלוה

אבר הזח והלוה

ד' אבר ד

התרוד

ובלוה

וובלוה

ויללבפ

ויללבפ

SAMPLE 2

Scribe B[1]:   f. 18,2-6; _T.A._, 195,4-196,3.

1   דאמ ר סימון כל

מאה ושלשים שנה שפירשה חוה מן אדם רוחות הזכרים מתחממין

בה והיא יולדת^מהן רוחות הנקבות מתחממות מן האדם ויולדות

ממנו הד ה אשר בהעוותו והוכח בשבט אנש ובנגעי בני אדם בנויי

5   דאדם קדמאה מן דאמר רוחוהן   דביתה טבין דרבין   א

עימיה מן דאם דהינון בישין דחכמין יצריה

Scribe B[2]:   f. 20,6-11; _T.A._, 236,1-5.

דאמ ר סימון כל מאה ושלשים

שנה שפירשה חוה מאדם היו רוחות הזכרים מתחממין ממנה והיא

יולדת מהן רוחות הנקבות מתחכמות מאדם ויולדות ממנו הד הי

אשר בהעוותו והוכחתיו בשבט אנשים ובנגעי בני אדם בנויי א

דאדם קדמאה מן דאמ רוחויי דחקלא טבא טבין דלא רבון עמיה

ומן דאם דהינון בישין דחמון דחמון יצריה

323

Scribe B²	Scribe B¹
מאדם	2) מן אדם
היו רוחות	רוחות
ממנה	3) בה
מאדם	מן האדם
הד הי	4) הד ה
... והוכחתיו בשבט אנשים	... והוכח׳ בשבט אנש׳ ...
דאמ	5) דאמר
רוחויי	רוחוהן
דחקלא	דביתה
טבא טבין	טבין
דלא רבון עמיה	דרבין
עמיה	6) עימיה
ומן	מן
דחמון	דחכמין

Scribe B[1]: f. 50v; <u>T.A.</u>, 389,2-390,3.

1 והכל אום על דבר שרי אשת אברם אמ ר ברכיה

א

על דטולמיסך למקרב למסנא דמטרונא וכל אותה הלילה היתה שרה

שטוחה על פניה ואומרת רבון העולמים אברהם יצא בהבטחה ואני יצאתי

באמונה אברהם חוץ לסירה ואני בתוך הסירה אתמה אם לה הקבה וכל

5 מה שאני עושה בשבילך אני עושה והכל אום על דבר שרי אשת אברם

אמ ר ברכיה על דטולמיסן למיקרב למיסנא דמטרונא אמ ר לוי כל או**תו**

הלילה היה המלאך עומד ומגלב בידוי אין אמרת לי מחי מחי אין אמרח

לי שבוק שביק וכל כך למה שהיתה אומרת לו אשת איש אני ולא היה

פורש ר אליעזר דתני לה בש ר אליעזר בן יעקב או שמענו בפרעה שלקה

10 בצרעת ובאבימלך בעיצור מן ליתן את האמור^שלזה בזה ואת האמור ש**לזה**

בזה תל לו על דבר על דבר **ג**זירה שוה

Scribe B[2]: ff. 78v-79; <u>T.A.</u>, 553,6-554,6.

והכל אום על דבר שרי אש אברם אמ ר ברכיה על דטן דטולמיסו א

למיעקרא למסנא דמטרונה כל אותו הלילה היתה שטוחה על פניה

ואום רבון העול אברהם יצא בהבטחה ואני יצאתי באמנה אברהם חוץ

לסירה ואני בתוך הסירה אם לה הקבה כל אשר אני עושה בשבילך

אני עושה והכל אום על דבר שרי אש אברם אמ ר לוי כל אותו

הלילה היה המלאך עומד ומגלב בידו אין אמרת ליה מחי מחי ואין

אמרת ליה שבוק שביק כל זה למה שהיתה אומרת לו אשת איש אני

ולא היה פורש ר אלעזר תני לה בש ר אליעזר בן יעקב שמענו בפרעה

שלקה בצרעת ואבימלך שלקה בעיצור ומנין ליתן את האמור כן

להלן ואת האמור ^בכ^אן להלן תל לו על דבר על דבר גזירה שוה

Scribe B²	Scribe B¹
אש׳ אברם	1) ... אשת אברם
דטן דטולמיסו	2) דטולמיסן
למיעקרא	למקרב
דמטרונה	דמטרונא
כל	וכל
אותו הלילה	אותה הלילה
שטוחה	2-3) שרה שטוחה
ואומ׳	ואומרת
רבון העול	רבון העולמים
באמנה	4) באמונה
ח׳	אתמה׳
כל אשר אני עושה	4-3) וכל מה שאני עושה
אש	אשת
ח׳	6) אמ ר׳ ברכיה על דטולמיסן למיקרב
	למיסנא דמטרונא
בידו	7) בידוי
ליה	לי
ואין	אין
ליה	לי
כל זה למה	8) וכל כך למה

Scribe B²	Scribe B¹
ר׳ אלעזר	9) ר׳ אליעזר
תני	דתני
ח׳	או׳
ואבימלך	10) ובאבימלך
שלקה בעיצור	בעיצור
ומנין ליתן	מנ׳ ליתן
כן להלן ... כן להלן	שלזה בזה .... שלזה בזה

APPENDIX III

GENIZA FRAGMENTS

Transcription of Geniza Fragments in <u>Palestinian Syriac</u>
<u>Texts</u>, ed. Agnes Smith Lewis and Margret Dunlop Gibson,
(London, 1900) Plate II, Fragment II and Plate III, Fragment III.*

*Three dots at the beginning or end of a line indicate
damage in the text. Within the lines, dots signify the
approximate number of letters which cannot be read. Dots
under letters indicate that the reading is probable.

PLATE II, FRAGMENT II

COLUMN I
(lines 1-3 illegible)

מר   לה   מתנה   ...

5   א   מיעיר ... יהי אור זה אברהם ...

א   ויקרא אים לאור יום זה יעקב ולחשך ...

עשו ויהי ערב .. עשו ויהי בקר זה יעקב ...

. נתן לו .... יום אחד אי זה זה ...

לקיש ... קריה במלכיות ובארץ ...

10   א   ארץ והנה תוהו וב׳ ....! ...

יוון שהחשיכה עיניהם שלישראל ...

כיתבו על קרן שור שאין להם חלק ...

הרישעה מה תהום הזה ... לו חקר ...

א   אי זה זכות אם ממשמשת ובאה ...

15   תשובה שנמשלה במים שפכי כמים לבך: ...

מים אפילו בשעת שרב רוחה שייפה ...

עומד ותוה׳ עבר ר׳ יהושע ושאל ...

השיבו בשלישית השיבו בבהילות א׳ לו ...

תודיעני מאיין הרגליים א׳ לו משתכל הייתי ...

20   בין מים העליונים לתחתונים כשתי וכשלוש ...

א   כׄת כן אלא מרחפת כעוף הזה שהוא ...

אינן נוגות ... ר׳ יהושע ואמר לתלמידין ...

קלים ובן זומה בעולם ⊙ ר׳ א . ..וא ור׳ חייה ...

ברייתו שלעולום צפה הק בה מעשיהן שלצדקין ...

25   א   היתה תו׳ ובו׳ אילו מעשיהן שלרשעים ...

א   מעשיהן ש .... אבל איני יודע ...

א   ממה צכ׳ וירא ... ...

א א   ין שלצדיקין ....

מת ..... שלעולום צפה ... ...

30   בנוי בראשית ברא אים הרי בנוי ...

ארץ היתה תו׳ ובו׳ הרי חרב הכ׳ דתמר ...

330

1 ראיתי את הארץ וגו׳ ויאמר ...

... וגו׳ ... .

ויאמר אים יהי אור ....

האורה נבראת תחילה למלך שביקש ...

5 מה עשה הדליק נירות ופנסין לידע היאך ...

נברא תחילה ור׳ נחמיה א׳ העולם נברא ...

בנירות .. כאן דרש ר׳ יודן אתא ר׳ פ..... ...

שמואל בר רב יצחק פתח דבריך יאיר ...

יבי אור 0 ר׳ ברכיה בש׳ ר׳ יודה ביר סימון ...

10 ר׳ ברכיה בש׳ ר׳ יודה ביר סימון לא בעמל ולא ...

בדבר יי וגו׳ • שַׁמַּיִם נעשו אוף הכה ויאמר

ויהי אור כבר היה ר׳ שמעון בן יוחי פתח שמחה ...

זה הקָוֹבֹה לֹֹ איש מלחמה במענה פיו ויאמר ...

מה טוב וירא אים את האור כי טוב 0 ר׳ שמ...

15 את ר׳ שמואל בר נחמן א׳ לה בשביל ששמעת ...

גרשה דקומי אורי כוליה 0 א׳ ר׳ סימון ומש... ...

חמשה ספרי תורה ויאמר אים יהי אור ...

נתעסק הקָוֹבֹה ובָרא את עולמו ויהי אור ...

יצאו ישראל מאפילה לאורה וירא אים את ...

20 מלא הלכות הרבה ויבדל אים בין האור כנגד...

יוצאי מצרים לבאי הארץ ויקרא אים ...

שהוא מלא הלכות .... מתיבין חברייא ...

תורה שהוא מלא הלכות הרבה א׳ להם אף ...

לאור יום לא הוא אור לא הוא יום אתמהא ...

25 ימי בראשית להאיר ביום אינה יכולה ...

אינה יכולה שלא ..... להאיר אלא ב ...

מותקנת לצדיקים ..... לבוא שנ׳ והיה ...

לא שלושה הן אתמהא לא ..ביעי נבראו ...

331

דאמר כן וכן אנה מפקד לשבעתי יום.. ...
30 שבעת ימי אבלו שלמתושלח הצדיק ...
וירא אים את האור וגו׳ ר׳ זעירה ...

PLATE III, FRAGMENT III

יצחק בני לאחד שישוור את אגוס והשביר את בנו עימו ד׳ א׳ מה צורך
לשבועה הזאת ר׳ לוי בש׳ ר׳ חמא ביר חנינה א׳ לו השבע לו שאן מנסה
אותי עוד מעתה למלך שהיה נשאוי למטרונה ילדה ממנו בן שיני וגרשה
שיני וגרשה שלישי וגרשה וכיוון שילדה ממנו בן עשירי נתכסו כולם
ואמרו לו השבע לנו שאן את מגרש את אימינו עוד מעתה כך כיוון א׳
שנתנסה אברהם ניסיון עשירי א׳ לו השבע לי שאן את מנסה אותי עוד
מעתה א׳ ר׳ חנין כי יען אשר עשית את הדבר הזה ניסיון עשירי הוא א׳
ותמר כי יען אשר עשית את הדבר הזה אלא נס האחרון שהוא שקול
כנגד הכל שאילולי שקיבל עליו נס הזה האחרון איבד את כל מה שעשה O
כי ברך אברכך וגו ברכה לאב ברכה לבן רבות לאב רבות לבן וירש זרעך
את שער איביו רבי א׳ זה תדמור אשריו כל מי שהוא רואה במפלתה א׳
שלתדמור שהיתה שותפה בשני חורבנות ר׳ יודן ור׳ חונא חד מינהון א׳ א׳
חורבן ראשון העמידה שמנים אלף כשטים ובחורבן השני העמידה
שמונת אלף כשטים וחרנה א׳ בחורבן הראשון העמידה ארבעים אלף
כשטים ובחורבן השני העמידה ארבעת אלפים כשטים O וישב אברהם
אל נעריו יצחק איכן הוא ר׳ ברכיה בש׳ רבנן דתמן שילחו אצל שם ללמד
ממנו תורהו לאשה שהעשירה מפילחה אמרה הואיל ומן השלח הזה א׳
העשרתי עוד אינו זז מתחת ידי לעולם ר׳ יוסה בן חנינה א׳ שילחו א׳
בלילה מפני העין שמשעה שעלו חנניה מיש׳ ועזר׳ מכבשן עוד לא

VARIANTS TO PLATE III, FRAGMENT III FROM VAT. 30

1) לאחר, אגום, עמו

2) בשם, אמ׳, שאין

4) וכיון

5) שאין, כיון

6) אמ׳, שאין

7) אמ׳

8-9) ח׳ בו:ניסיון עשירי הוא ותמר כי יען אשר עשית את הדבר הזה

11) ר׳

12) אמ׳

13) חרבן, בשטים

16) בשם

17) תורה

18) יוסי, אמ׳

19) מישאל

20) לאיכן, אמ׳, בעין

21) אמ׳

22) ח׳ בו: נא

23) בשם, מישאל ועזריה

25) בשם

26) המוריה

27) בשם

335

BIBLIOGRAPHICAL NOTE

A Partial List of Works Cited by
Theodor and Albeck

Theodor utilized all extant published medieval commentators.
On the unpublished commentaries see J. Theodor, "מאמר על פירוש
בראשית רבא," Festschrift zu Israel Lewy's siebzigsten
Geburtstag (Breslau, 1911), Hebrew section, pp. 132-154.
Reference is made to the Apocrypha, Pseudepigrapha, Philo,
Josephus and the Church Fathers Hieronymus, Ephrem, and
Origen. For later aggadic development: manuscripts of
Midrash Haggadol; Midrash Aggadah, ed. Solomon Buber (Wilna,
1894); Lekach-Tob, ed. Solomon Buber (Wilna, 1884); Sechel
Tob, ed. Solomon Buber (Berlin, 1900); Raymudi Martini,
Pugio fidei adversus Mauros et Judaeos (Leipzig, 1687).
Dictionaries: Aruch Completum, ed. Alexander Kohut (Vienna,
1878); Jacob Levy, Neuhebräisches un Chaldäisches Wörterbuch
uber die Talmudim und Midraschim (Leipzig, 1876); J. Levy,
Chaldäisches Wörterbuch uber die Targumim (Leipzig, 1867);
Gustaf H. Dalman, Aramäisch-Neuhebräisches Handwörterbuch
(Frankfurt a. M., 1901); Samuel Krauss, Griechische und
Lateinische Lehnwörter (Berlin 1895), with notes by Immanuel
Löw. Modern works on Rabbinic exegesis and the aggadah:
Wilhelm Bacher, Die Älteste Terminologie der Jüdischen
Schriftauslegung Leipzig, 1899); and by the same author,
Die Agada der babylonischen Amoräer (Strassburg, 1878): Die
Agada der Tannaiten, (Strassburg, 1890), Die Agada der Pal-
astinensischein Amoräer (Strassburg, 1892); Louis Ginzberg,
Die Haggada bei den Kirchenvätern (Amsterdam, 1899); Israel
Shapiro, Die haggadischen Elemente im erzählenden Teil des
Korans (Leipzig, 1907). Some other works: Adolphe Neubauer,

336

La Géographie du Talmud (Paris, 1869); J. Freudenthal, Hellenistische Studien (Breslau, 1874); M. Joël, Blicke in die Religionsgeschichte (Breslau, 1880); Michael Sachs, Beitraege zur Sprach-und Alterthumsforschung (Berlin, 1852); Leopold Löw, Graphische Requisiten und Erzeugnisse bei den Juden (Leipzig, 1870), as well as many other complete works and articles.

References to parallels from the Palestinian and Babylonian Talmuds, the other early collections of midrashim and the Yalkut Shimoni are found in Theodor's Mesoret Hamidrash; the complete text of the parallels are often quoted in the Minhat Yehudah.

BIBLIOGRAPHY

Albeck, Chanoch. _Einleitung und Register zum Bereschit Rabba._ Berlin, 1931-1936.

Albeck, Chanoch. _Untersuchungen uber die hal. Midraschim._ Berlin, 1927.

Assemanus, Stephanus Evodius, and Assemanus, Joseph Simonius. _Bibliothecae Apostolicae Vaticanae._ Partis Primae, Tomus Primus, Codices Ebraicos et Samaritanos. Rome, 1756. Reprinted Paris, 1926.

Babylonian Talmud. (Standard edition) Wilno, 1928.

Bacher, Wilhelm. Untitled review of the first fascicle of _Midrash Bereshit Rabba_, ed. J. Theodor. _REJ_, XLVI (1903), 301-310.

Ben David, Abba. _Biblical Hebrew and Mishnaic Hebrew._ Tel Aviv, 1967.

Ben Jacob, I. A. _Ozar Ha Sepharim._ Wilna, 1880.

Buber, S. (editor). _Midrash Tanhuma._ Wilno, 1885.

Cassuto, Humbertus. _Bybliothecae Apostolicae Vaticanae._ Vatican, 1956.

Epstein, J. N. _Introduction to Amoraitic Literature._ Jerusalem, 1962.

Epstein, J. N. _Mavo L'nusah Ha-mishna._ Jerusalem, 1965.

Epstein, J. N. and Melamed, E. Z. (editors). _Mekhilta D'Rabbi Sim'on b. Jochai._ Jerusalem, 1955.

Finkelstein, Louis (editor). _Sifre or Torat Kohanim._ New York, 1956.

Frankel, Z. _Introductio in Talmud Hierosolymitanum._ Breslau, 1870.

Freedman, H. _Midrash Rabba._ 10 vols. London, 1939.

Friedman, M. (editor). _Sifre._ Vienna, 1864.

Ginzberg, H. L. "Zu den Dialecten des Talmudisch-Hebräischen,'
MGWJ, LXXVII (1933), 413-429.

Ginzberg, Louis. A Commentary on the Palestinian Talmud.
4 Vols. New York, 1941-1961.

Ginzberg, Louis. The Legends of the Jews. 7 vols.
Philadelphia, 1909-38.

Ginzberg, Louis (editor). Yerushalmi Fragments. New York,
1909.
Goitein, S. D. A Mediterranean Society. Berkeley and
Los Angeles, 1967.

Goldman, Edward A. Parallel Texts in the Palestinian Talmud
to Genesis Rabba. (Unpublished rabbinic thesis,
Hebrew Union College.) Cincinnati, 1969.

Heller, Bernhard. "Der Abschluss von Theodor-Albecks
Bereschit Rabba," MGWJ, LXXVIII (1934), 609-615.

Heller, Bernhard. "Theodor-Albecks Bereschit Rabba," MGWJ,
LXXI (1927), 466-472.

Horovitz, H. S. and Rabin, I. A. (editors). Mechilta
D'Rabbi Ismael. Jerusalem, 1960.

Jastrow, Marcus. A Dictionary. (reprint) New York, 1950.

Kohut, Alexander (editor). Aruch Completum. 8 vols.
Vienna, 1878.

Kutscher, Yehezkel. "Articulation of the Vowels u, i in
Galilean Aramaic and Mishnaic Hebrew Transcriptions
of Biblical Hebrew," Benjamin De Vries Memorial
Volume, ed. E. Z. Melamed. Jerusalem, 1968. 218-251.

Kutscher, Ezekiel. "Lešon Hazal," Henoch Yalon Jubilee
Volume, ed. Saul Lieberman. Jerusalem, 1963.
246-280.

Kutscher, Ezekiel. "Studies in Galilean Aramaic," Tarbiz,
XXI (1949-50), 192-205; XXII (1950-51), 53-63,
185-192; XXIII (1952), 35-60. [offprint, Jerusalem,
1952]

Lauterbach, Jacob Z. (editor). Mekilta. 3 vols. Philadelphia, 1949.

Lerner, M. Anlage und Quellen des Bereschit Rabba. Berlin,
1882.

Levine, Ephraim. "A Geniza Fragment of Genesis Rabba," JQR, XX (1908), 777-783.

Levinger, D. S. "New Fragments from the Palestinian Talmud, Tractate Pesachim," Alexander Marx Jubilee Volume. New York, 1950. Hebrew Section, pp. 237-286.

Lewis, Agnes Smith and Gibson, Margret Dunlop, (editors). Palestinian Syriac Texts. London, 1900.

Levy, Jacob. Neuhebräisches und Caldäisches Wörterbuch. 4 Vols. Leipzig, 1889.

Liddel, Henry George and Scott. A Greek-English Lexicon. Oxford, 1968.

Lieberman, Saul. Ha-y'rusalmi Ki-fshuto. Jerusalem, 1935.

Lieberman, Saul (editor). The Tosephta. 3 vols. New York, 1955-1967.

Maas, Paul. Textual Criticism. Oxford, 1958.

Margulies, Mordecai (editor). Midrash Haggadol on the Pentateuch: Genesis. Jerusalem, 1947.

Margulies, Mordecai (editor). Midrash Wayyikra Rabba. 5 vols. Jerusalem, 1953-1960.

Martin, Malachi, S. J., The Scribal Character of the Dead Sea Schrolls. Louvain, 1958.

Midrash Rabba on the Pentateuch and Five Megillot. Warsaw, 1924 (offset: New York, 1952).

Mihaly, Eugene. "A Rabbinic Defense of the Election of Israel," HUCA, XXXV (1964), 103-143.

Palestinian Talmud (Yerushalmi). Venice, 1523; Krotoshin, 1866.

Rosenthal, A. S. "Lešonot Soferim," Yuval Shay, A Jubilee Volume dedicated to S. Y. Agnon, ed. B. Kurzweil. Ramat Gan, 1959. 293-325.

Rosenthal, Franz (editor). An Aramaic Handbook. 2 vols. Wiesbaden, 1967.

Rosenthal, Franz. The Techniques and Approaches of Muslim Scholarship. Rome, 1947.

Rosenberg, H. "Un Fragment de Mishna au British Museum," REJ, LIII (1907), 212-219.

Segel, M. H. A Grammar of Mishnaic Hebrew. Oxford, 1927.

Smith, J. Payne. A Compendious Syriac Dictionary. Oxford, 1903.

Sokoloff, Michael. "The Hebrew of Bereshit Rabba According to Ms. Vat. Ebr. 30," Lešonenu, XXXIII, No. 1 (October, 1968) 25-42; Nos. 2-3 (January-April, 1969) 135-149.

Sperber, Alexander (editor). The Bible in Aramaic. 4 vols. Leiden, 1959-1968.

Steinschneider, M. Catalogues Librorum Hebraeorum in Bibliotheca Bodleiana. Berlin, 1931.

Strack, Herman L. Introduction to the Talmud and Midrash. New York, 1959.

Taylor, Charles (editor). Cairo Geniza Palimpsests. Cambridge, 1900.

Theodor, Judah. "Drei unbekannte Paraschas aus Bereschit Rabba," Festschrift zum siebzigsten Geburtstage Jakob Guttmanns. Leipzig, 1915. pp. 148-171.

Theodor, Judah. "Der Midrasch Bereschit Rabba," MGWJ, XXXVII (1893), 169-173, 206-213, 452-458; XXXVIII (1894), 9-26, 436-440; XXXIX (1895), 106-110, 241-247, 289-295, 337-343, 385-390, 433-441, 481-491.

Theodor, Judah and Albeck, Chanoch (editors). Midrasch Bereschit Rabba. Berlin, 1903-1929. Second printing Midrash Bereshit Rabba. 3 Vols., with Introduction and Registers by Chanoch Albeck. Jerusalem, 1965.

Tobia ben Elieser. Lekach-Tob, ed. Solomon Buber. Wilna, 1884.

Wacholder, Ben Zion. "The Date of the Mekilta De-Rabbi Ishmael," HUCA, XXXIX (1968), 117-144.

Weiss, I. H. Dor Dor we-Dorshaw. 5th ed. 5 vols. New York and Berlin, 1924.

Yalon, Hanoch. Introduction to the Vocalization of the Mishna. Jerusalem, 1964.

Yelon, Henoch, "Nachtrag zur palastinischen Aussprache des
    Schluss – m wie n," MGWJ, LXXVII (1933), 429-431.

Zunz, Leopold. Die gottesdienstlichen Vorträge der Juden.
    Berlin, 1832. Translated into Hebrew by Chanoch
    Albeck. Hadrashot B'yisrael. Jerusalem, 1947.